Wellness Tourism

As core values of society, health and wellbeing impact today on all aspects of our lives, and have also increasingly influenced patterns of tourism consumption and production. In this context wellness has developed into a significant dimension of tourism in a number of new and long-established destinations. However, although it is consistently referred to as one of the most rapidly growing forms of tourism worldwide there still remains a dearth of academic literature on this topic.

This book fills the gap by uniquely focusing on the supply-side of wellness tourism from a destination perspective in terms of the generation and delivery of products and services for tourists who seek to maintain and improve their health. This approach provides a better understanding of how wellness tourism destinations develop; and explores the specific drivers of that growth in a destination context and how destinations successfully compete against each other in a globalised marketplace. A range of wellness destination development and management issues are examined including the importance of authenticity, uniqueness, delivery of high-quality goods and services, participation of a broad range of stakeholders and the development of networks and clusters as well as collaborative strategies essential for a successful development and management of a wellness tourism destination. International case studies and examples from established and new wellness tourism destinations are integrated throughout.

This timely volume written by leaders in this sector will be of interest to tourism and hospitality students and academics internationally.

Cornelia Voigt has worked as a researcher and lecturer at different universities. Her research on wellness tourism won several awards and she has published in leading international tourism journals.

Christof Pforr is Course Coordinator for Tourism and Hospitality and Group Leader of the Research Focus Area 'Sustainable and Health Tourism' with the School of Marketing, Curtin University, Australia.

Routledge advances in tourism
Edited by Stephen Page
School for Tourism, Bournemouth University

Wellness Tourism

A destination perspective

Edited by Cornelia Voigt and Christof Pforr

Routledge
Taylor & Francis Group

LONDON AND NEW YORK

First published 2014
by Routledge
2 Park Square, Milton Park, Abingdon, Oxon OX14 4RN

and by Routledge
711 Third Avenue, New York, NY 10017

Routledge is an imprint of the Taylor & Francis Group, an informa business

British Library Cataloguing in Publication Data
A catalogue record for this book is available from the British Library

Library of Congress Cataloging in Publication Data
Wellness tourism: a destination perspective / edited by Cornelia Voigt and
Christof Pforr.
    pages cm – (Routledge advances in tourism; 33)
    Includes bibliographical references and index.
    1. Medical tourism. 2. Travel–Health aspects. I. Voigt, Cornelia.
    RA793.5.W46 2013
    613.6'8–dc23
                                                            2013017246

ISBN: 978-0-415-64467-9 (hbk)
ISBN: 978-0-203-07936-2 (ebk)

Typeset in Times New Roman
by Wearset Ltd, Boldon, Tyne and Wear

Contents

Figures

Tables

Contributors

Coeditors

Cornelia Voigt has worked as a researcher and lecturer at different universities. Her PhD thesis, titled 'Understanding Wellness Tourism: An Analysis of Benefits Sought, Health-Promoting Behaviours and Positive Psychological Well-Being' was awarded with the 'Sustainable Tourism CRC Sir Frank Moore Award for Excellence in PhD Research', an annual, national award acknowledging the best tourism thesis written in each year. Her research won several additional awards and she has published in leading international tourism journals. Dr Voigt's expertise in wellness tourism has led to the acquisition of competitive research grants and a number of invited speeches at international conferences.

Christof Pforr (PhD) is Course Coordinator for Tourism and Hospitality and Group Leader of the Research Focus Area 'Sustainable and Health Tourism' with the School of Marketing, Curtin Business School. He holds a PhD in political science from the Northern Territory University and a *Staatsexamen* in geography and political science from the University of Tübingen (Germany). His academic background is reflected in his main research interests, which include tourism policy and planning, sustainable (tourism) development, health tourism, coastal tourism and geotourism as well as destination governance with a specific focus on network management and network analysis, all fields he has frequently published in. He has contributed to more than 100 publications and numerous international research collaborations. Dr Pforr has authored, co-authored or coedited five books. He is also on the editorial board of the *International Journal of Safety and Security in Tourism/Hospitality* and book review editor of the *International Journal of Tourism Policy*.

Contributors

Monika Bachinger is working as a managing director at the regional development agency of the Ingolstadt region. She has been working in the field of regional marketing, economic development and cluster building at public and private organisations for several years. Her special interest is focused on the formation of regional cooperation networks. She recently received a PhD from the Catholic University Eichstätt-Ingolstadt, where she worked as a research fellow at the Chair of Tourism and the Center for Entrepreneurship.

Tom Baum is Professor of International Tourism and Hospitality Management in the Department of Human Resource Management, University of Strathclyde, Scotland. He specialises in the area of tourism and work and has researched and consulted in themes relating to workforce planning and development for the tourism sector in over 40 countries worldwide. He is widely published in the area and has supervised over 30 PhD candidates to completion in topics relating to the complex and, sometimes, contradictory environment of tourism, employment and their social context. He teaches a specialist module in Wellness Tourism and HRM on the MA in Wellness and Spa Service Design and Management for the University of Tartu, Pärnu College in Estonia.

Delphine Berbigier holds a Bachelor in English and Spanish, and a Master in communication from the University of Lille, France. After a few years working in the tourism industry in Puerto Rico, she completed an MBA at James Cook University, Australia, in 2012, and worked as research assistant with Dr Bruce Prideaux in 2011.

Melanie Dawkins successfully completed a Bachelor of Commerce degree in tourism management at Curtin University (Perth, Western Australia) and also completed a one-year Honours program. Her Honours project was based on the emerging wellness tourism market in Western Australia.

Margaret Deery is Adjunct Professor at Curtin Business School, Curtin University of Technology. Previously, she was the Director and Professor of the Centre for Hospitality and Tourism Research at Victoria University in Melbourne and Professorial Research Fellow with the Australian government-funded Sustainable Tourism Co-operative Research Centre (STCRC). She has over 100 peer-reviewed publications and has written for academic and industry audiences. She is the Coeditor-in-Chief of the *Journal of Hospitality and Tourism Management* and the Regional Editor for the *International Journal of Event and Festival Management*. She is on the editorial board of a number of other international journals. Margaret has been the recipient of a large number of funding grants including ARC and industry funded grants. She has also led the Travel and Wellbeing research group at Victoria University.

Patricia Erfurt-Cooper lectures in Tourism Resource Management, Health and Wellness Tourism and Community Development. She has published a number of books, book chapters and articles in the fields of tourism and environmental planning. Her main research interests are geotourism in volcanic and geothermal environments with a special focus on risk management and sustainability.

Sebastian Filep is a lecturer at the Department of Tourism, School of Business, University of Otago in New Zealand. Until recently, Dr Filep was a Research Fellow at the Centre for Tourism and Services Research at Victoria University, Melbourne, Australia. He is the co-author of *Tourists, Tourism and the Good Life*, an introductory book on positive psychology and tourism, published by Routledge. He has published internationally on the topics of psychological wellbeing and happiness, tourist satisfaction and positive psychology. In 2009, he received his PhD in tourism at James Cook University, Australia. He is a Member of the International Positive Psychology Association, a Member of the Australian Centre on Quality of Life and a Pacific Asia Travel Association Young Tourism Professional.

Warwick Frost is a senior lecturer in Tourism and Events and Coordinator of the Events programs at La Trobe University in Melbourne, Australia. His research interests include heritage, events, regional development, nature-based attractions and the interaction between media, popular culture and tourism. He has published in journals such as *Annals of Tourism Research*, *Tourism Management* and the *International Journal of Heritage Research*. He has edited two books: *Zoos and Tourism* (Channel View, 2011) and *Tourism and National Parks* (with C.M. Hall, Routledge, 2009). He is one of the founding convenors of the biennial International Tourism and Media Conferences, the fourth of which was held in Italy in 2010.

Emma Gaunt successfully completed a double-major degree of tourism management and public relations at Curtin University and completed a one-year Honours program in tourism management at Curtin. Her Honours project was based on the emerging niche market wellness tourism in Western Australia.

Michael Hughes is a lecturer and researcher in the Tourism and Hospitality program at Curtin University. He has more than ten years of research experience in the field of nature-based tourism and recreation. This includes research on how people cognitively and affectively respond to different natural area experiences and the relationship between access to nature and health.

Judith Jochmann, Dipl.-Geogr., is Head of Department for City Marketing and Culture at the municipality of Herzogenaurach (Germany, Bavaria). Up to 2011 she was a research assistant at the Chair of Tourism/Center for Entrepreneurship (Prof. Dr Harald Pechlaner) at Catholic University of Eichstätt-Ingolstadt, Germany.

Jennifer Laing is a senior lecturer in Events at La Trobe University, Melbourne, Australia. She has a law and marketing background, and her research interests include travel narratives; the role of myth in tourism; extraordinary tourist experiences; and the role of events in society, heritage tourism and wellness tourism. She has published in leading international tourism journals and is a member of the editorial boards for *Tourism Review International* and *Journal of Travel Research*. She is a coeditor of the Routledge Advances in Events Research series.

Cornelia Locher is Associate Professor in Medicinal Chemistry in the School of Medicine and Pharmacology at the University of Western Australia. She is a member of the Australasian University Pharmacy Complementary Medicines Education (AUPCME) Group. Next to her expertise in natural product chemistry, she has developed a keen interest in alternative and complementary medicines, particularly phytomedicines, and their contribution to health and wellbeing.

Leonie Lockstone-Binney is Senior Lecturer, specialising in event studies at Victoria University's School of International Business. Her main areas of research interest relate to volunteering, commemorative events and event management education. Leonie has published work in top-tier journals including *Leisure Sciences*, *Tourism Analysis*, *International Journal of Hospitality Management* and *International Journal of Tourism Research*. She continues to collaborate on projects with leading researchers from Australia, the UK and New Zealand.

Harald Pechlaner holds a chair in Tourism at the Catholic University Eichstätt-Ingolstadt, Germany, and is Scientific Director of the Institute for Regional Development and Location Management at the European Academy of Bozen-Bolzano (EURAC research), Italy. He earned a Doctorate in Social and Economic Sciences at the University of Innsbruck. He is a board member of the Association Internationale d'Experts Scientifiques du Tourisme (AIEST) and was President of the German Association of Tourism Research (DGT) from 2003 to 2012.

Bruce Prideaux is Professor of Marketing and Tourism Management, James Cook University, Australia, and has published extensively in a range of issues including destination development, natural area tourism, disaster management, tourism transport issues and climate change.

László Puczkó is a managing director and head of tourism section at Xellum management consulting company and an international speaker. He is president of the Association of Tourism Consultants (Hungary), Guest Professor at Parnu Kolledz (University of Tartu, Estonia), HAAGA-HELIA University of Applied Sciences (Helsinki-Porvoo, Finland) and was a Member of the Travel and Tourism Research Association Europe Chapter Board. His main areas of expertise are laid in tourism research, strategy preparation, planning and management in the following areas: health/wellness/medical/spa tourism, heritage and cultural tourism, national/regional/local planning, and product and project development. In recent years he has been involved in many development projects aiming at thermal bath developments, at regional, local and site level. His work included conceptualisation, financial and market feasibility and marketing planning. He is a co-author of professional books on health and wellness tourism, the impacts of tourism, visitor management and tourism management in historic cities.

Christopher Reuter is a research associate at the Chair of Tourism and a scholarship holder of the sustainability graduate school of the Catholic University Eichstätt-Ingolstadt, Germany. His research involves topics from destination as well as regional development, while his PhD research focuses on sustainable adaptation strategies towards climate change in the tourism sector.

Melanie Smith is an associate professor and researcher in Tourism at the Budapest College of Communication and Business in Hungary and has been a tourism academic for more than 15 years, specialising in wellness and medical tourism. She is founder of the ATLAS Spa and Wellness Special Interest Group and Visiting Lecturer for Pärnu College (University of Tartu) Estonia for the MA in Wellness and Spa Service Design and Management. She is also co-author of the book *Health and Wellness Tourism* (Butterworth-Heinemann, 2009), as well as several journal articles, book chapters and research reports on this theme.

Michelle Thompson is a PhD student at James Cook University, Australia, and is investigating the development of agri-tourism in regional areas of Australia. Employed as a research assistant at JCU, she has conducted research on tourists' reef and rainforest experiences and co-authored several papers on these issues.

Betty Weiler is a professor in the School of Tourism and Hospitality Management at Southern Cross University, Australia. She has been teaching, researching and writing about tourism planning, management and marketing for 20 years and has published over 100 journal articles and book chapters. Professor Weiler is on the editorial board of six international peer-reviewed tourism journals including *Tourism Management* and *Journal of Sustainable Tourism*. She has managed or co-managed 25 major funded research projects and nine international and national consultancy projects related to ecotourism, heritage and nature interpretation/communication. She has served as principal investigator on many nationally competitive grant-funded projects and is best known for her applied research focus and close work with industry.

Meredith Wray is a senior lecturer in the School of Tourism and Hospitality Management at Southern Cross University, Australia. Her studies and research work focus primarily on tourism policy, planning, sustainable destination management, marketing and development. She led a major Sustainable Tourism Co-operative Research Centre (STCRC) research project that examined best practice principles for destination development, marketing and management involving 21 regional tourism destinations across Australia. She was also a member of an STCRC research team that investigated medical and wellness tourism in Australia. In addition, she has recently completed a ten-year strategic tourism plan for Daylesford, Byron Bay, Broken Hill and Eurobodalla Shire Council. She is currently working with Destination New South Wales developing a Regional Development Plan for Inland NSW Tourism.

Preface

Organised by the Curtin Business School Tourism Research Cluster, on 13 February 2012 *The Business of Health Tourism* symposium was held in Perth, Western Australia. It provided a forum for delegates from academia, government, industry and the community to discuss various dimensions of health and wellbeing as they relate to tourism. *Wellness Tourism: A Destination Perspective* is an edited research text which emanated from the presentations of international and national experts in the field and many very stimulating discussions during the symposium.

As core values of society, health and wellbeing impact today on all aspects of our lives, and have also increasingly influenced patterns of tourism consumption and production. In this context wellness tourism has developed into a significant dimension of tourism in a number of new and long-established destinations. But although it is consistently referred to as one of the most rapidly growing forms of tourism worldwide, there is still a lack of scholarly discourse on this topic.

In this book we adopt a destination perspective on wellness tourism. Such a destination perspective is a novel contribution to the still limited scholarly activity on the supply-side of wellness tourism. The book contributes to a better understanding of the way in which wellness tourism destinations develop, and explores the specific drivers of that growth in a destination context. This perspective is also crucial since destinations increasingly compete against each other in a globalised marketplace. Uniqueness and authenticity thus become important constituents of destination competitiveness as does the ability to deliver high quality as well as sustainable goods and services. Furthermore, a destination's resources and competencies as well as the active participation of a broad range of stakeholders and their effective coordination are also considered to be important to remain competitive. Thus, the development of networks and clusters as well as collaborative strategies are crucial prerequisites for a successful development and management of a wellness tourism destination.

This research text, which is organised into five parts, is global in scope and focuses on both theory and practice. The introductory part defines, describes and characterises wellness tourism. This part is followed by 14 chapters which address a range of development and management issues of wellness tourism destinations in differing settings. The final chapter of the book provides a synthesis of the themes and findings of the various contributions. The text has been compiled for a broad audience and aims to generate further interest, debate and research on this rapidly emerging field of study. We hope you enjoy the book *Wellness Tourism: A Destination Perspective* and will use it to further progress wellness tourism in theory and/or in practice.

Acknowledgements

No book is written in isolation; in fact, most require the efforts of a wide range of people. This text is no exception and we therefore wish to thank a number of people for their personal and/or professional support throughout the process.

First, a big 'thank you' to the 21 authors from all parts of the globe for contributing fascinating aspects of wellness tourism to this book – it was a pleasure to work with you and to read your contributions! We also wish to acknowledge the support of the publisher Routledge and its staff, who have been extremely helpful throughout the process.

Christof Pforr would like to thank a number of people for their assistance and encouragement for this project. First of all, I would like to thank my coeditor Cornelia Voigt. This book is our first joint project and I think we have worked extremely well together across a number of time zones between Perth and Vienna. I have thoroughly enjoyed working with her on this volume and I am looking forward to many more joint projects in the years ahead! I would also like to acknowledge Curtin Business School and in particular express my thanks to my colleagues from the Tourism Research Cluster, Kirsten Holmes, Michael Hughes, Paull Weber, Jack Carlsen, Marg Deery and Roy Jones. Finally, I would like to thank my family, my partner Connie and our three beautiful girls Anda, Mona and Leah for their continued understanding of the, at times 'unhealthy', lifestyle of an academic.

Foremost, Cornelia Voigt would also like to extend her gratitude to her coeditor Christof Pforr. When I started my research on wellness tourism in 2005 it seemed that few tourism academics had even heard this term. Since then the situation has dramatically changed and I am extremely grateful for having met someone who is as enthusiastic to explore and advance this field as I am. In particular I am thankful for Christof's trust, patience and unfailing optimism especially towards the end of this project when my little son Nicolas was born who made me reschedule my priorities and who taught me an entirely new meaning to 'wellness'. Thanks also go to Curtin Business School for still giving me a home in academia as well as in Australia and the Tourism Research Cluster for welcoming me so warmly in their midst. My final appreciation goes to my husband Christian and our son Nico for filling my life with so much joy and laughter in a way that all tasks become more easily tackled and managed.

Christof Pforr (Perth) and Cornelia Voigt (Vienna), March 2013
The Coeditors

Part I
Introduction

1 Wellness tourism from a destination perspective

Why now?

Cornelia Voigt and Christof Pforr

The growth of wellness tourism

As core values of societies throughout the world, health and wellbeing have steadily become essential factors shaping all areas of people's lives and have also increasingly influenced patterns of consumption and production. Wellness tourism constitutes one part of an explosively growing, largely private market of health goods and services, frequently referred to as the *wellness industry* (Kickbusch and Payne 2003; Pilzer 2007). Trend researchers consistently predict health and wellness to be crucial, if not the most important, drivers for successful business growth and major innovations in the future. For instance, Nefiodow (2006) argues that holistic health will be the new megamarket of the twenty-first century. Similarly, Pilzer (2007), speaking of a wellness revolution, estimates that the wellness industry has grown to sales of over $500 billion in the United States alone, but still suggests the industry is just in its infancy. He specifically contrasts the wellness industry with traditional health care, which he thinks should be more appropriately called sickness care or sickness industry. Yeoman (2008: 91) refers to the World Health Organization's (WHO) prediction that health will be the world's biggest industry by 2022 and posits that health *and* tourism will constitute the largest sectors globally, together building 'an unbeatable consumer force'.

These forecasts set the scene for the current popularity of wellness tourism and explain why it is repeatedly cited as one of the fastest growing tourism niche markets. Thereby it is important to emphasise that we concur with those scholars who have differentiated wellness and medical tourism as fundamentally different segments of health tourism (e.g. Connell 2011; Müller and Lanz Kaufmann 2001; Puczkó and Bachvarov 2006). These differences arise because medical tourism is firmly grounded in the biomedical paradigm of health, where the emphasis lies on the treatment or cure of diseases, whereas wellness tourism is guided by an alternative approach to health, where the focus is on the promotion of health and wellbeing and where a balance and holistic integration of multiple health dimensions (e.g. body/mind/spirit, environmental, social), active self-responsibility, healthy lifestyles, subjectivity and actualisation of human potential play major roles. Moreover, wellness and medical tourism cater to contrasting needs of tourists and thus different tourist markets, they offer essentially different types of services, they are typically set in locations with very different characteristics and they employ staff from very different source pools (see Chapter 2, this volume for a more detailed explanation and definition of wellness tourism). Nevertheless, both wellness and medical tourism are spreading to all corners of the globe and scholars have noted a constant diversification in supply, some forms of hybridisation, as well as a significant specialisation of target markets (Gustavo 2010; Voigt and Laing 2013; Yeoman 2008).

Due to a lack of consistency in health or wellness tourism definitions as well as a general lack of available data, it is impossible to report reliable figures on global size, scope or economic significance of wellness tourism. However, there are other indicators that reflect and substantiate the growth of wellness tourism. Recently an increased professionalisation of the wellness tourism industry has been noticeable in form of a mounting number of industry associations and in form of university and college subjects or even entire degrees dealing with wellness and spa tourism management. For instance, the online directory *Spa Opportunities* lists over 800 institutions worldwide which offer educational courses in this area and the Global Spa and Wellness Summit (2012) specifically refers to more than 60 universities, universities of applied sciences and polytechnic colleges where wellness and/or spa tourism is being taught. Another indicator is the continuous creation of relevant consumer magazines such as *Spa Secrets*, *Healing Lifestyles and Spas*, *Organic Spa Magazine* or *Spa Asia*, where thus far the spa sector clearly dominates, as well as the emergence of more and more print and online directories such as *Spa Finder*, *RELAX Guide*, *Retreat Finder*, *Find The Divine*, *Healing Hotels of the World* and *New Life Hotels*, with each directory specialising on specific wellness tourist markets. Another sign of wellness tourism's growth is that an increasing number of tourism destinations are developing or reinventing themselves as wellness tourism destinations. Before discussing wellness tourism destinations and the related purpose of this book, the next section provides a brief overview of megatrends that have contributed to the recent growth of wellness tourism.

Megatrends contributing to wellness tourism growth

Megatrends constitute epochal processes of transformation. Their defining characteristics include that they have a half-life of at least 50 years, that they are apparent in all areas of life (e.g. everyday life, economy, politics, consumption) and, although they do not have to be equally developed all over the world, that they represent a truly global phenomenon (Horx 2010). In the following, six megatrends are listed that have driven the rise of wellness tourism supply and demand.

1   Holistic health and increased health consciousness
     Since the 1960s consumers are largely responsible for the foray into a new, more holistic and positive understanding of health, a consumer movement

which is often referred to as holistic health or wellness movement. Nowadays infectious diseases have been replaced as major causes of death by chronic and lifestyle-related illnesses such as cancer, cardiovascular diseases and diabetes, but conventional health care has proven to be largely ineffective in managing or preventing these. Mounting scepticism towards the effectiveness of orthodox health-care services has motivated an ever-increasing amount of people in the West to turn to complementary and alternative medicine (CAM), not necessarily as a substitute, but as an augmentation (Eisenberg *et al.* 1998; Yeoman 2008). From the beginning the holistic health movement drew heavily on non-Western healing systems and globalisation and large-scale migration have facilitated their dissemination and acceptance. At the same time individuals are no longer passive recipients of health care, they have become more informed and educated about their own health and the availability of contrasting health-care options. Thus, at least for those who can afford it, health care has become pluralistic and more consumer-directed. They have become more health conscious and accepting in taking responsibility for their wellbeing by living healthier lives. It already has been alluded to that wellness tourism is firmly linked to an alternative, holistic paradigm of health and it has been suggested that healthy lifestyle choices are the fundamental basis for wellness tourism demand (Hall and Brown 2006).

2   Pace of life acceleration

Ever since the industrial revolution, when clock time rather than natural time started to dictate daily schedules and new technologies produced profound changes in how work was organised, the pace of life has increasingly accelerated. Nowadays, life is often compared to a rat race, where individuals have little choice than to hurry from one appointment and activity to the next with one eye always on the clock. Additionally, employees all over the world report increased workloads and greater day-to-day pressures which result in a notable rise of stress-related disorders such as emotional strain (e.g. tension, fatigue, aggression) or psychological diseases (e.g. depression, burnout, anxiety). Wellness tourism has been suggested as an ideal outlet to escape from daily stressors and a profound means to relax and recuperate (Pollock and Williams 2000) and motivational items such relaxation, stress release, escape and reward for working hard have been found to rank highly in Western and Eastern groups of wellness tourists (Mak *et al.* 2009; Voigt *et al.* 2010).

3   Inconspicuous consumption

One could argue that the more people's lives have become more fast-paced, more materialistic, rationalised and technical, the more consumer movements have emerged which represent a counterbalance and a broad shift in consumer values. These movements could all be gathered under the inconspicuous consumption banner. Wellness tourism has been linked to such movements where people decide voluntarily to move out the fast lane by simplifying their lives and by trading high incomes for more time and increased quality of life. Labels that have been given to those movements range from voluntary simplicity, simple living, and downshifting to Slow Movement (Honoré 2004; Smith and Puczkó 2009). Concurrently, Yeoman (2008) argues that tourists increasingly reinterpret the concept of luxury as one of having time to have experiences of personal fulfilment instead of engaging in conspicuous consumption and showing off materialistic status symbols. In other words, ostentatious decadence is out, modesty and simplicity are in. Another consumer movement that has been linked to wellness tourists is the Lifestyles of Health and Sustainability (LOHAS) movement, a term which was only invented in 1999. LOHAS is a new form of lifestyle in which people not only take into consideration their own personal health, but the health of the environment, the community and social justice when making consumption-related decisions. The eco-social added value of products and services is becoming important and people are increasingly prepared to invest in fair, green, organic and sustainable goods. Consumer research in Western and Eastern countries shows that LOHAS values are progressively becoming mainstream, rather than fringe.

4   Individualisation

In the West, the idea of individualism has become ever-more pervasive. In regard to consumptive practices this means that people increasingly seek out products that express their individuality, they eschew mass consumption and homogenisation and demand personalised and customised goods and services instead. While it has been argued that tourism has generally turned away from mass tourism in favour of independent travel and niche tourism, wellness tourism in particular has been linked to a focus on the self. It has been noted that holistic wellness tourists seek to find their true selves and that the self or the quest to be become more important than external tourism attractions and activities (Smith and Kelly 2006a). Similarly, in a study of actual benefits sought by wellness tourists it was found that transformation of the self was the central, unifying leitmotif (Voigt *et al.* 2010). The German trend researcher Matthias Horx (2005) refers to selfness as the next big megatrend after wellness. Selfness is described as a technique of self-development, a discovery of one's true self and a continuous process of developing one's own potential. Importantly, here, selfness is not equated with selfishness. Horx relates selfness to the concept of soft individualism where values such as experience, tolerance, gratefulness, dedication and spiritualty have replaced values such as materialism, me as number one, and performance that were predominant in the ego era which reigned from the late 1970s until the 1990s (Horx 2005: 40–4). Others, however, have also linked wellness tourism to an obsession with the outer self, a sometimes unhealthy preoccupation with one's appearance, self-image and aspiration to look like supermodels or celebrities (Smith and Puczkó 2009; Yeoman 2008).

5   Quest for spirituality

According to the American trend researcher Patricia Aburdene (2007), the quest for spirituality is the greatest megatrend in the twenty-first century.

Although there has been a decrease in religion, the yearning for spirituality and meaning in life has not diminished. The longing for spirituality has led to the popularity of Eastern spiritual practices such as yoga and meditation, self-help books and pop psychology as well as the New Age movement which is often directly linked to wellness and holistic health (Aburdene 2007; Smith and Puczkó 2009; Miller 2005). In this book we propose that spiritual retreats (often taking place at mediation or yoga centres, ashrams, monasteries or temples) are an integral, but often neglected, part of wellness tourism (see Chapter 2). Furthermore, Aburdene argues that the impact of spirituality on personal lives is currently spreading into institutions. Specifically from a business point of view she foresees the rise of a so-called conscious capitalism where there will be a shift away from greed and profit-making at all costs toward a new economy founded on spiritual awareness, ethics and morals, including environmental values and corporate responsibility. She emphasises that this transformation will not be a sign of altruism, but one of enlightened self-interest, because consciously capitalist companies will outperform their competition in the long run.

6   Ageing populations

Due the combination of longer life expectancies and falling birth rates below the replacement level of 2.1 children per couple, the world's population is ageing. The group that currently drives population ageing is called Baby Boomer generation and consists of individuals born between 1944 and 1965. In comparison with seniors of previous generations, Baby Boomers are generally more affluent, healthier and fitter and also more concerned to stay in good health. Although studies have shown that Baby Boomers do not always constitute the majority of all wellness tourists in all sub-segments or in all countries, and that some markets are considerably younger (Mak *et al.* 2009; Voigt *et al.* 2010), Baby Boomers are frequently cited as one factor responsible for the increased demand of wellness and medical tourism products (Pollock and Williams 2000; Smith and Kelly 2006b; Yeoman 2008).

Focus of this book: a destination perspective on wellness tourism

The aim of this book is to present an overview and discussion of key trends and critical issues pertaining to the development and management of wellness tourism destinations from a variety of different perspectives. From a theoretical standpoint the general question can be posed whether the growth of wellness tourism has also resulted in a growing body of academic literature dealing with this phenomenon. While Hall (2011: 4) suggests that health tourism has 'emerged as one of the fastest growing areas of academic research interest in both tourism and health studies', a close look at the existing literature reveals that health tourism tends to be equated with medical tourism and even though medical tourism is largely driven by private, conventional health care providers rather than the tourism industry, it is actually medical tourism which has received the biggest share of academic interest among scholars. In contrast, the tourism industry is much more involved in the provision of wellness tourism. Despite this and the coupled increasing popularity and demand for wellness tourism experiences it is still treated as a Cinderella subject and there remains a dearth of academic literature on this topic. Moreover, if wellness tourism is discussed as part of health tourism or even if it is specifically highlighted as the main focus, it is often reduced to spa or thermal tourism. For instance, the special issue on healing holidays in the journal *Anthropology & Medicine* (2011, vol. 18, issue 1) includes five papers on spa providers or destinations and three papers on specific medical tourism issues. The focus of the book by Cohen and Bodeker (2008) exclusively deals with spas as one form of wellness tourism and Erfurt-Cooper and Cooper's book (2009) focuses on wellness tourism based on natural water resources (i.e. mineral or geothermal waters). While spas arguably constitute the best-known building block of wellness tourism, other more holistic or alternate business models play an increasingly important role and there are many wellness tourism destinations without water as a central defining element. There are only a few notable exceptions of collated literature published in the English language where wellness tourism has been understood as a more integrative phenomenon beyond just spas: The book *Wellness and Tourism: Mind, Body, Spirit, Place*, edited by Bushell and Sheldon (2009), the monograph *Health and Wellness Tourism* by Smith and Puczkó (2009), as well as the special issues dedicated to wellness tourism in the journals *Tourism Recreation Research* (2006, vol. 31, issue 1) and *Journal of Hospitality and Tourism Management* (2010, vol. 17, issue 1). To the best of our knowledge, a book on a destination perspective of wellness tourism does not exist and we therefore think that this book makes a novel contribution, especially in light of the still limited scholarly activity examining the supply-side of wellness tourism. We hope that this text will contribute to a better understanding of the ways in which wellness tourism destinations develop and are managed.

The focus of this book is also crucial from a practical point of view since tourism destinations increasingly compete against each other in a globalised marketplace. As a result of the growing demand for wellness tourism, increasing examples exist of destinations that are deliberately branding themselves as health tourism or wellness tourism destinations to enhance awareness, appeal and thus profitability. Competition for international and domestic wellness visitors steadily increases and in some mature wellness tourism destinations market saturation has already been reached. In tourism, competition has shifted from the enterprise level to competition between destinations (Ritchie and Crouch 2003).

Although there are many definitions of what constitutes a destination, at the most basic level a destination can be understood as a geographical place that is chosen by tourists as target of their travel and which satisfies their needs. The geographical boundaries of such destinations are not always clear and are sometimes only defined based on administrative structures. These structures are important as in many destinations destination management organisations (DMOs) have been established which are responsible for a strategic, integrated and collaborative management approach to ensure innovation and long-term survival of the tourism destination. It has been argued that wellness destinations with DMOs or other public–private partnerships that are planning and managing the wellness tourism product are most successful (Smith and Puczkó 2009), although there also seem to be a number of successful holistic and alternative organically developed (i.e. uncontrolled) wellness destinations such as Goa in India or Byron Bay in Australia where more regulation may destroy the atmosphere of the place, or where providers would not accept it (ibid.). Moreover, in some destinations where public authorities are not involved in the development of wellness tourism, industry associations may drive place-branding initiatives (e.g. spa associations), or there can be a combination involving several organisations and authorities who either collaborate, or work independently from each other.

Wellness tourism destinations differ extensively in their historic nature of development and in their scale. Some destinations (e.g. Germany, Czech Republic, Japan) have developed employing specific natural resources that have attracted visitors for hundreds or even thousands of years, whereas other destinations (e.g. most Asian-Pacific countries) are relatively new players in the wellness tourism game. In regard to scale, wellness destinations can range from multinational or multiregional developments, entire countries, regions, islands, cities or communities to single, self-contained resort complexes, often referred to in the literature as destination spas (see Table 1.1 for examples).

The structure of the book

This text is organised in five parts and contains 18 chapters. The first part, the *Introduction* (Chapters 1–3), lays the foundation for a better understanding of wellness tourism in a destination context. Such a destination perspective is a novel contribution to the still limited scholarly activity on the supply-side of wellness tourism. In this part we offer an overarching theoretical framework for the book by providing a definitional approach to wellness tourism and by exploring factors of competitive and comparative advantages which play a crucial role in the competitiveness of wellness tourism destinations. In the second part ('The role of stakeholders in wellness tourism destinations', Chapters 4–8) the role different stakeholders play in wellness tourism destinations as well as their levels of interaction are discussed in a variety of contexts. The development of networks and clusters, as well as collaborative strategies, are crucial prerequisites for a successful development and management of a wellness tourism destination. This perspective reflects the current view of destinations as 'loosely bounded networks of organisations that deliver the tourism experience' (Cooper 2012: 32). Chapters 9 to 12 in Part III ('Relationships between nature, wellbeing and destinations') specifically focuses on the position nature and the environment take as part of developing wellness tourism destinations as well as destinations where natural resources help people to achieve higher levels of wellbeing. Whilst the chapters in Parts I to III already draw on international cases and research, Part IV of the text ('Drivers of wellness tourism

Table 1.1 Examples of wellness destinations at multinational, national, regional, local and resort levels

Management level	Destination	Focus of destination promotion and product
Multinational/ multiregional level across borders	'Alpine Wellness'	Alpine Wellness is a transnational marketing collaboration of Alpine regions from Austria, Germany, Italy and Switzerland with a focus product development (i.e. strong, unique Alpine wellness core resources such as hay bathing and specific climate and health-promoting altitude) and a certification process to ensure quality.
	'Nordic Well-Being'	This is a research-driven project exploring the possibility of developing a specific coherent 'Nordic well-being' brand across five Nordic countries (e.g. Norway, Finland, Iceland, Denmark and Sweden) as well developing/strengthening wellness tourism in 'laboratory areas' within each of these countries such as the Icelandic Myvatn region and Southern Denmark.
National level	Germany	The product line 'health and wellness' is a key product line for the German National Tourism Board and has been promoted with an extensive marketing campaign called 'Wellness-Country Germany' with the English tagline 'Germany. Welcome to well-being'. Wellness tourism communication material emphasises the long history and tradition of health and spa offerings in Germany, the strict quality criteria and the different kinds of state-approved health resorts (e.g. mineral spas, seaside resorts, climatic resorts, Kneipp resorts). Additionally, several spa and wellness associations (e.g. the German Wellness Association) drive or support wellness tourism.
	India	The Indian Ministry of Health and Family Welfare and the Ministry of Tourism collaborate to promote India as a health tourism hub. A specific website for medical tourism was developed (indiameditourism.com) which also refers to 'wellness'. Additionally, one part of the 'Incredible India' tourism campaign focuses on wellness tourism with the tagline 'Body Mind and Soul', highlighting the following Indian wellness elements that all have an ancient history: Ayurveda, Pancha Karma, meditation, aromatherapy, Tibetan Medicine, Siddha and yoga.

	Jordan	The Jordan Tourism Board focuses on 'Leisure & Wellness' as one of the key experiences visitors can have. In their promotional material they specifically emphasise unique health benefits of various natural resources, specifically the water and muds from the the Dead Sea and the mineral-rich waters of the Ma'in Hot Springs. To a lesser extent the spiritual significance of the Dead Sea is highlighted as well as the specific cultural tradition of hammam bathing.
State/regional level	Madeira (Portugal)	With the slogan 'Body. Mind. Madeira!' the Madeira Promotion Bureau advertises the Madeira island archipelago as 'mystical' place where tourists may find a balance between their body and mind. A particular emphasis is given to the 13 luxurious four- or five-star spa resorts located on the islands as well as the surrounding nature and its resources (e.g. spring-like climate throughout the year, therapeutic sands) which are presumed to be mainly responsible for the deep relaxation people experience when engaging in wellness tourism on Madeira or the neighbour island Porto Santo.
	Victoria (Australia)	Since 2004, Tourism Victoria has developed a specific spa and wellness tourist strategy, culminating in a recently updated action plan to develop and promote Victoria as key Australian spa destination. Victoria is unique in the Australian context as it possesses both mineral springs and geothermal waters that have been employed for establishing spa-type wellness tourism providers. Tourism Victoria sees potential in the still largely untapped utilisation of these water resources and encourages future tourism development. Furthermore, cross-promotion of the spa product in combination with organic food and wine and nature-based tourism is emphasised.
City/community/local level	Auroville (India)	Auroville is an experimental, international community in Southern India which aims to realise human unity and peace with an emphasis on spirituality and sustainability, founded in 1968. The town plan is based on a spiral galaxy model with the 'Matrimandir', a golden sphere building for meditation and contemplation at its centre. Auroville does not promote 'indiscriminate tourism', but welcomes guests in a number of guesthouses and retreats who are seriously interested in the Auroville lifestyle. Visitors are encouraged to participate in special introduction tours and invited to stay at least ten day to genuinely become familiar with the idea of Auroville. Guests can participate in a range of workshops, seminars and alternative healing practices.

continued

Table 1.1 Continued

Management level	Destination	Focus of destination promotion and product
	Karlovy Vary (Czech Republic)	Karlovy Vary or Carlsbad is marketed as the largest and most famous spa town of the 'Bohemian Spa Triangle' which also includes the cities of Mariánské Lázne and Frantiskovy Lázne. Promotional material highlights the long history of this health resort as exclusive centre for the nobility and the famous (e.g. Casanova, Mozart, Goethe), the medicinal effectiveness of bathing in or drinking the waters of its 12 mineral or thermal springs, and the elegant classicist spa architecture.
Resort level	Chiva-Som (Thailand)	Chiva-Som International Health Resort is a secluded luxurious beachfront resort with three-night minimum programs that can be personalised to the needs of each individual guest, but which typically focus on holistic lifestyle transformation, weight management, anti-ageing, detoxing and de-stressing. Privacy, tranquillity and exclusiveness are emphasised in the communication materials as well as the blend of holistic Eastern therapies with Western diagnostic skills.
	Rancho La Puerta (Mexico)	Rancho La Puerta Fitness Resort and Spa is possibly one of the oldest 'destination spas', as it was established in 1940. Today, it is a 3,000 acre property and focuses on programs that enable a 'healing lifestyle', mind/body/spirit integration which typically last a week. During the day guests can select from five or six activities every hour, ranging from different forms of exercises and mind/body activities and a specific emphasis is also given to creative arts such as photography workshops, dancing, jazz piano or special presenters, including authors and philosophers. Rancho La Puerta is also involved in many eco-activities and community programs and food for its spa cuisine is produced organically on its own farm.

destination development: international experiences') has a particular international focus and discusses how major driving factors (e.g. economic, psychographic, demographic) have led to different developments and different kinds of wellness tourism destinations worldwide. Part V is the concluding part of the text, which synthesises the various contributions and outlines opportunities and priorities for researching wellness tourism destinations. In the following, the structure of the book is mapped out in greater detail.

In Chapter 2 ('Towards a conceptualisation of wellness tourism'), Cornelia Voigt highlights that there is still considerable controversy in the literature about how to define wellness tourism. Consequently, the aims of this chapter are to explore the underlying reasons for these inconsistencies, to identify the different meanings of the wellness tourism phenomenon and to propose a definition of the concept. The chapter starts with an overview about conceptualising wellness as a specific paradigm of health and a brief historical account of health-related travel. It continues with reviewing and analysing existing conceptualisations of wellness tourism before proposing a definition and classification. The final part of the chapter briefly reflects on what kind of conclusions can be drawn from the preceding discussion on the development, marketing and management of wellness tourism destinations.

Bruce Prideaux, Delphinine Berbigier and Michelle Thompson argue in Chapter 3 ('Wellness tourism and destination competitiveness') that one of the key strategies to ensure the long-term success of a tourism destination is to build and maintain a high level of competitiveness in the markets that best match the resources the destination is able to offer. To understand how destinations may enhance competitiveness, the authors investigate the factors that confer competitive and comparative advantages to destinations, specifically in a wellness tourism context. The chapter commences with a brief review of the factors that collectively define a destination and how it operates, followed by a discussion that draws on three models to illustrate how competitiveness can be maintained in the long term. The chapter concludes with a discussion on how competitiveness can be applied to a wellness perspective.

In Chapter 4 ('An examination of the extent of collaboration between major wellness tourism stakeholders in Australia') Cornelia Voigt and Jennifer Laing highlight the importance of stakeholder collaboration in attaining or maintaining a destination. The chapter examines stakeholders that play a crucial role in the supply of the actual wellness tourism product and the extent to which they collaborate. Australia is the geographic focus of this chapter and the analysis is based on qualitative and quantitative data from a nationwide scoping study of Australian wellness and medical tourism. The chapter commences with an overview of tourism stakeholder collaboration and focuses particularly on previous research of wellness tourism development where collaboration was directly or indirectly examined. It continues by discussing major Australian stakeholders of wellness tourism supply, wellness tourism providers, federal and state destination management organisations, wellness industry and accreditation associations, the media and the educational sector as well as the mainstream health care sector.

The aim of Chapter 5 ('Wellness tourism: the factors and processes that drive sustainable regional destinations') is to identify the resources, factors and processes that may be used to develop and enhance wellness tourism as a tool for competitive advantage and for the sustainability of regional tourism destinations. This chapter, written by Meredith Wray and Betty Weiler, begins by briefly examining the potential of wellness tourism as a strategy to distinguish and position some regions within the highly competitive tourism environment. The chapter presents case studies of two significant and distinctive regional wellness destinations in Australia, Daylesford and Hepburn Springs (located in central Victoria) and Byron Shire (located on the far north coast of New South Wales). Both destinations are endowed with natural resources and other ingredients thought to be important to both wellness tourists and destinations.

With Chapter 6 ('Health regions: building tourism destinations through networked regional core competencies'), Christof Pforr, Harald Pechlaner, Cornelia Locher and Judith Jochmann highlight the growing importance of health as a regional development strategy by specifically discussing the development of *health regions* and outlining the role tourism can play in their establishment. Not much research has yet been carried out on these newly established health regions to capture their operations and effectiveness. With the case example of the Health Region Kneippland Unterallgäu in Bavaria, Germany the authors present the issues surrounding the development of one particular health region which is founded on medical and wellness tourism.

In Chapter 7 ('Identification and development of core competencies as a basis for regional development with special focus on health tourism') Harald Pechlaner, Christopher Reuter and Monika Bachinger discuss regional development as a tool to establish networks among different stakeholders on the basis of pre-defined goals in order to activate health-relevant resources of a region. The overall goal is the enhancement of the attractiveness of the entire region; providing a differentiation factor in inter-regional competition. The authors identify several paths that can lead to such a development in the health care sector on a regional level. They concentrate on two case-study regions within the European Metropolitan Region of Munich (EMM), namely Ingolstadt and Garmisch-Patenkirchen. Core competency development through network interaction and the formation of cooperative core competencies especially are explored in greater detail to provide models to analyse the empirical data collated from the two case studies.

The focus of Chapter 8 ('Fit for purpose: delivering wellness tourism through people') by Tom Baum and Leonie Lockstone-Binney is on human resource management as part of managing wellness tourism businesses and destinations. Wellness tourism, in common with other sectors of the industry, depends heavily on human intervention and mediation in the delivery of its services. The people who work in wellness tourism are, arguably, at least as vital to the success of the industry as their counterparts within the wider sector. Yet, their role is largely under-researched in terms of both theoretical analysis and practical management application. The chapter identifies themes and issues that merit both conceptual and empirical analysis and develops a research agenda that will prepare the ground for more academic and practitioner consideration of this area.

The concept for Chapter 9 ('Researching the links between parklands and health') by Michael Hughes was derived from research into the development and subsequent expansion of a program in Australia and New Zealand, known as Healthy Parks, Healthy People. This program is based on the notion that access to parkland is an important means of improving the health of individuals and communities and includes promoting the benefits of outdoor activities as well as the benefits of interactions with nature. The chapter presents a review of published research on the relationship between parklands and health and the subsequent types of knowledge created. Based on this review some potential research directions are suggested that could contribute to a better understanding of the key factors in the relationship between accessing parklands and health.

Chapter 10 ('Exploring visitor wellbeing in parks and nature reserves') reports on a study that examines individual wellbeing of visitors to parks and nature reserves and examines hedonic and eudaimonic psychological benefits of their park experiences. Using the Psychological Benefits of Green Space Questionnaire, Personal Wellbeing Index and Warwick-Edinburgh Mental Well-being scales, the findings show that visitors display slightly lower levels of individual wellbeing compared with national averages, but that they find park experiences psychologically beneficial. In this chapter Margaret Deery, Sebastian Filep and Michael Hughes identify four factors to explain individual wellbeing derived from park experiences. Overall, the findings suggest that there is an association between participants' overall individual wellbeing and the park experience factors identified. Implications for marketing and further studies are noted.

Chapter 11 ('Nature-base wellness tourism: the case of the Margaret River region in Western Australia') aims to contribute to a better understanding of the nature and scope of the wellness tourism sector in Western Australia. The case study explores the Margaret River region in the south-west of Western Australia as one of the state's leading wellness destinations. It is in particular the spectacular natural resources of the region that form the basis of its tourism product offerings, including wellness tourism. With this in mind Christof Pforr, Michael Hughes, Melanie Dawkins and Emma Gaunt investigate the relationship between the natural environment and wellness experiences.

In Chapter 12 ('The Kneipp philosophy: a 'healthy' approach to destination development') Cornelia Locher, Cornelia Voigt and Christof Pforr introduce the German priest and naturopath Sebastian Kneipp, who advocated a holistic approach to health and wellbeing. The authors report that his teachings have strongly influenced medical wellness offerings in many certified spas and health resorts based on traditional water treatments known as *Kneipp Kur* (Kneipp cure). It is argued that Kneipp's philosophy and the way it has influenced complementary therapies to date need to be seen in the context of its time and also Kneipp's personal circumstances. This information therefore forms the requisite background to discuss the development of Kneipp spas and health resorts. In the final part of the chapter the authors explore how Kneipp's philosophy can also be translated into a broader destination context. The Unterallgäu region in Bavaria (Germany) is used as a case example to illustrate how Kneipp's five central tenets have been used as guiding principles to promote regional development.

In Chapter 13 ('Regional trends and predictions for global health tourism'), the future of health tourism is first set in the context of a brief discussion of the meaning of health and wellness in different geographical and cultural contexts, followed by a short analysis of historical traditions. However, the main focus of the chapter by Melanie Smith and László Puczkó is the assessment of contemporary trends in health and wellness destination development around the world and to identify some of the most significant initiatives or products. In doing so, this chapter provides an overview of some of the latest developments in health tourism from around the world.

In Chapter 14 ('Fantasy, authenticity and the spa tourism experience') Jennifer Laing, Cornelia Voigt and Warwick Frost point to the growing popularity of wellness tourism worldwide which has led to the need to better understand these experiences, including the nature of their appeal and how they are marketed to tourists. They particularly focus on spa tourism which can be considered as a major subset of wellness tourism. One of its hallmarks appears to be the blend of authentic and fantasy elements. This chapter explores the nexus between fantasy and heritage in spa tourism through a comparative case study of three international beauty spas – the Gellért Baths in Budapest, Hungary, the Thermae Spa in Bath, United Kingdom and the Polynesian Spa in Rotorua, New Zealand.

Chapter 15 ('Wellness tourism: a perspective from Japan'), written by Patricia Erfurt-Cooper, explores wellness tourism in Japan. Natural hot spring spas and resorts, also known as *Onsen*, belong to Japan's most important destinations for health and wellness. The case studies presented in this chapter include some representative locations to illustrate the major traditions of health and wellness travel in Japan. The chapter further outlines the patterns of wellness tourism in the country by revealing the historical and cultural background of *Onsen* use and by clarifying the role of natural hot and mineral springs for the treatment of various health conditions. The chapter highlights how central natural hot springs are to wellness tourism in Japan, which has annual visitor numbers reaching on average 150 million people.

Christof Pforr and Cornelia Locher, the authors of 'Health tourism in the context of demographic and psychographic change: a German perspective' (Chapter 16), outline the shift from Germany's public health insurance system to a modern health economy that has taken place over the past 30 years. They discuss the impacts this has had on the country's health tourism sector, in particular the wellness industry, which has experienced a boom in recent years, driven mainly by strong demand in the senior market segment.

Taking an Australian perspective, Chapter 17 ('Australia's approach to health care and its implications for health tourism') explores if the specific health-care system adopted in Australia has had an influence on recent trends in health tourism in the country. To some extent, the chapter can be seen as a juxtaposition of the previous chapter. It outlines that historical developments and a different health care system have led to a very different landscape of health tourism in Australia compared to that in Germany (Chapter 16). Cornelia Locher, Christof Pforr and Cornelia Voigt illustrate that although Australia is recognised as a wellness destination, it is outbound medical tourism which appears to be a direct consequence of Australia's health policy.

Lastly, in the final chapter, 'Concluding discussion: Implications for destination development and management' (Chapter 18), the editors synthesise the main themes emerging from this volume. Reviewing the book's many case studies from wellness tourism destinations around the world, Cornelia Voigt and Christof Pforr bring together an array of theoretical and practical insights into the development and management of wellness tourism destinations. In doing so, they highlight the book's contribution to a better understanding of one of the most rapidly growing forms of tourism worldwide and also provide directions for future research.

We believe that the text presented here provides new insights and perspectives into how wellness tourism is supplied at tourism destinations. Nevertheless we do not claim that the sum of the contents presented in these chapters is comprehensive or should be understood as an end result. Rather, we hope that this text is seen as 'work in progress' and a meaningful fundament based on which wellness tourism research will be developed further and wellness tourism destinations will be managed more successfully.

References

Aburdene, P. (2007) *Megatrends 2010: The Rise of Conscious Capitalism*, Charlottesville, VA: Hampton Roads Publishing Company.

Bushell, R. and Sheldon, P.J. (2009) *Wellness and Tourism: Mind, Body, Spirit, Place*, New York: Cognizant Communication Corporation.

Cohen, M. and Bodeker, G. (2008) *Understanding the Global Spa Industry: Spa Management*, Oxford: Butterworth-Heinemann.

Connell, J. (2011) *Medical Tourism*, Wallingford: CABI.

Cooper, C. (2012) *Essentials of Tourism*, Harlow: Prentice Hall – Pearson Education.

Eisenberg, D.M., Davis, R.B., Ettner, S.L., Appel, S., Wilkey, S., Van Rompay, M. and Kessler, R.C. (1998) 'Trends in alternative medicine use in the United States, 1990–1997: results of a follow-up national survey', *The Journal of the American Medical Association*, 280: 1569–75.

Erfurt-Cooper, P. and Cooper, M. (2009) *Health and Wellness Tourism: Spas and Hot Springs*, Bristol: Channel View Publications.

Global Spa and Wellness Summit (2010) 'Spa and wellness education', online, available at: www.globalspaandwellnesssummit.org/index.php/spa-industry-resource/education (accessed 7 November 2012).

Gustavo, N.S. (2010) 'A 21st-century approach to health tourism spas: the case of Portugal', *Journal of Hospitality and Tourism Management*, 17: 127–35.

Hall, C.M. (2011) 'Health and medical tourism: a kill or cure for public health?' *Tourism Review*, 66: 4–15.

Hall, D.R. and Brown, F. (2006) *Tourism and Welfare: Ethics, Responsibility, and Sustained Well-being*, Cambridge, MA: CABI.

Honoré, C. (2004) *In Praise of Slow: How a Worldwide Movement is Challenging the Cult of Speed*, London: Orion.

Horx, M. (2005) *Der Selfness Trend: Was kommt nach Wellness?* Kelkheim: Zukunftsinstitut.

Horx, M. (2010) 'Trend-Definitionen', online, available at: www.horx.com/ zukunftsforschung/Docs/02-M-03-Trend-Definitionen.pdf (accessed 10 November 2012).

Kickbusch, I. and Payne, L. (2003) 'Twenty-first century health promotion: the public health revolution meets the wellness revolution', *Health Promotion International*, 18: 275–8.

Mak, A.H.N., Wong, K.K.F. and Chang, R.C.Y. (2009) 'Health or self-indulgence? The motivations and characteristics of spa-goers', *International Journal of Tourism Research*, 11: 185–99.

Miller, J.W. (2005) 'Wellness: the history and development of a concept', *Spektrum Freizeit*, 27: 84–106.

Müller, H. and Lanz Kaufmann, E. (2001) 'Wellness tourism: market analysis of a special health tourist segment and implications for the hotel industry', *Journal of Vacation Marketing*, 7: 5–17.

Nefiodow, L.A. (2006) *Der sechste Kondratieff: Wege zur Produktivität und Vollbeschäftigung im Zeitalter der Information*, 6th edition, Bonn: Rhein-Sieg-Verlag.

Pilzer, P.Z. (2007) *The New Wellness Revolution: How to Make a Fortune in the Next Trillion Dollar Industry*, New York: John Wiley and Sons.

Pollock, A. and Williams, P. (2000) 'Health tourism trends: closing the gap between health care and tourism', in D.W. Lime and W.C. Gartner (eds) *Trends in Outdoor Recreation, Leisure and Tourism*, New York: CABI.

Puczkó, L. and Bachvarov, M. (2006) 'Spa, bath, thermae: what's behind the labels', *Tourism Recreation Research*, 31: 83–91.

Ritchie, J.R.B. and Crouch, G.I. (2003) *The Competitive Destination: A Sustainable Tourism Perspective*, Wallingford: CABI.

Smith, M. and Kelly, C. (2006a) 'Holistic tourism: journeys of the self?', *Tourism Recreation Research*, 31: 15–24.

Smith, M. and Kelly, C. (2006b) 'Wellness tourism', *Tourism Recreation Research*, 31: 1–4.

Smith, M. and Puczkó, L. (2009) *Health and Wellness Tourism*, Oxford: Butterworth-Heinemann.

Voigt, C. and Laing, J. (2013) 'A way through the maze: exploring differences and overlaps between wellness and medical tourism providers', in D. Botterill, G. Pennings and T. Mainil (eds) *Medical Tourism and Transnational Health Care*, Basingstoke: Palgrave Macmillan.

Voigt, C., Howat, G. and Brown, G. (2010) 'Hedonic and eudaimonic experiences among wellness tourists: an explanatory enquiry', *Annals of Leisure Research*, 13: 541–62.

Yeoman, I. (2008) *Tomorrow's Tourist*, London: Butterworth-Heinemann.

2 Towards a conceptualisation of wellness tourism

Cornelia Voigt

Introduction

There is still considerable controversy in the literature about how to define well-ness tourism. Consequently, the aims of this chapter are to explore the under-lying reasons for these inconsistencies, to identify the different meanings of this phenomenon and to propose a definition of this concept. A confusing array of terms, including wellness tourism (e.g. Smith and Kelly 2006a), health tourism (e.g. Hall 2003), health-care tourism (e.g. Henderson 2004), medical tourism (e.g. Connell 2011), thermal tourism (e.g. Erfurt-Cooper and Cooper 2009), spa tourism (e.g. Puczkó and Bachvarov 2006), holistic tourism (e.g. Smith and Kelly 2006b) and wellbeing tourism (Konu and Laukkanen 2010) are sometimes used interchangeably, but often describe very different concepts. Explanations for the inconsistent use of these terms can be found in the culturally and philo-sophically different meanings attached to the terms *wellness* and *health* as well as diverging historical developments of health-related travel which led to differ-ent service and product offerings all over the world. This chapter starts with an overview about conceptualising wellness as a specific paradigm of health and a brief historical account of health-related travel. It continues with reviewing and analysing existing conceptualisations of wellness tourism before proposing a definition and supply-side based classification. The final part of the chapter briefly reflects on what kind of conclusions can be drawn from the preceding discussion on the development, marketing and management of wellness tourism destinations.

Defining *wellness* broadly as an alternative health paradigm

The concept of *wellness* is notoriously difficult to define. Some tourism scholars have suggested that *wellness* represents a recent artificial combination of the words *well*being and fit*ness* (Konu *et al.* 2010; Nahrstedt 2004; Sheldon and Bushell 2009) or *well*being and whole*ness* (Puczkó and Bachvarov 2006). Although it is accurate that the term wellness was not widely used in the English language until recently, according to *The Oxford English Dictionary*, the first written record of the word stems from 1654 (Simpson and Weiner 1989). After the Second World War the word wellness reappeared as part of the English contemporary vernacular, with Halbert Dunn (1959a, 1959b) generally being attributed as the first scholar to start the modern discourse on wellness. Since then the concept of wellness has been defined as a lifestyle (e.g. Hattie *et al.* 2004), a process (e.g. Travis and Ryan 1988), and a positive psychological state (e.g. Ryan and Deci 2001). In its broadest understanding, however, wellness can be conceptualised as an alternative, holistic and positive paradigm of health that stands in contrast to the orthodox biomedical health paradigm. Table 2.1 depicts a comparison of the biomedical and wellness health paradigms in relation to their relative perspectives on the role of health, disease, the patient and the focus and characteristics of health care.

In the biomedical health paradigm health is defined as the absence of disease, assuming that there is a dichotomy between health and illness. Its primary principle is the body–mind dualism where the body and mind are seen as separate entities that function independently of each other (Engel 1977). The biomedical model of health is reductionist as illness is exclusively seen as deviation from biological and physiological processes due to environmental, social or psychological causes. This paradigm is also described as mechanistic and the body is often compared to a machine consisting of separate components where single parts can be independently cured or replaced (Nettleton 2006). The focus of biomedical health care is on diagnosing as well as alleviating and curing disease symptoms. Anything that the health professional cannot objectively identify during examination tends to be ignored or devalued. Once a diagnosis is established, the prescribed treatment is generally standardised for all patients with the same condition. The mechanistic view of the body often leads to an overreliance on technology and intervention usually involves pharmaceutical drugs, surgery and other invasive procedures. The health professional–patient relationship is often described as emotionally detached, impersonal and objectified (Davis-Floyd 2001; Engel 1977). Whereas the health professional has the authority and control of information, the patient remains largely a passive recipient, his or her input and subjective experiences tend to be minimal.

The World Health Organization's (WHO) definition of health described as 'a state of complete physical, mental and social wellbeing and not merely the absence of disease or infirmity' (WHO 1948) is perhaps the best-known example of a paradigm shift of perspective in health conceptualisations. This definition has been described as 'revolutionary' (Pender *et al.* 2006: 17) because it conceives health as a positive state of wellbeing. It is also groundbreaking as it abandons the exclusive emphasis on physical health and concentrates holistically on multiple dimensions. According to the wellness health paradigm, health is seen as a composition of many elements and high-level health requires a systemic balance among these elements. Disease can be understood as an imbalance in the harmonious interaction of body/mind/spirit and the broader, external environment. Dunn (1959b: 447) emphasises that there is no optimum level of wellness. Instead, each individual strives toward an 'ever-higher potential of functioning' of what they are capable of. Health is not static or something one

Table 2.1 A comparison of the biomedical and the wellness health paradigms

	Biomedical health paradigm	Wellness health paradigm
Definition of health	Absence of disease Separation of mind and body ('body as machine' metaphor)	Positive functioning; a balance between internal and external forces Oneness of body/mind/spirit (body as part of an integrated, multidimensional system) interlinked with external system
Definition of disease	A biological process where pathogens damage the 'body machine'	A systemic imbalance, mostly not reducible to a single biologic cause
Relationship between health and disease	Health and disease are dichotomous opposites Health and disease are objective, observable phenomena	Health and disease are two separate dimensions Health and disease are subjective and perceptual phenomena
Focus of health care	Short-term focus on curing or alleviating disease symptoms	Long-term focus on health promotion
Characteristics of health care and intervention process	Standardised care High tech/low touch Intervention focuses on invasive procedures, pharmaceutical drugs and high-tech diagnostics Consultation is paternalistic	Individualised care Low tech/high touch Intervention emphasises non-invasive procedures, lifestyle-based interventions, 'self-healing' and herbal medicines Consultation is participatory, empowering and empathic
Role of patient	Patient remains largely passive, authority is inherent in the health professional	Patient must assume self-responsibility and needs to become an active participant

can suddenly achieve at a specific time, all actions individuals take potentially affect their wellbeing which is why the role of self-responsibility and self-care are of central importance to the discourse on wellness. Consequently, a broad understanding of wellness as holistic, positive health paradigm subsumes the idea of wellness as a process and as a lifestyle. Very importantly, wellness is a subjective, relative and perceptual concept and health and illness can be seen as two separate dimensions. Individuals without physical and psychological illness symptoms can still feel unwell and conversely, people with serious or even terminal disease are able to strive towards higher levels of wellness. In the wellness paradigm of health, the focus is not so much on the treatment of symptoms, but long-term health promotion. Proponents of the wellness health paradigm also believe in the innate self-healing capabilities of human organisms (Goldstein 1999; O'Connor 2000). Consequently, the role of the wellness health professional is to mobilise self-healing and self-care capabilities of the individual. Feelings, attitudes, subjective experiences and interpretations of patients are an essential part in the intervention process and therapeutic encounters are characterised as open, collaborative and empathic and tailored to the need of the individual, not the condition.

While the biomedical health paradigm still dominates health care particularly in Western countries, it has been increasingly challenged by the *wellness movement*, emerging from both academic and popular sources. The wellness movement is most pronounced in the emergence and resurgence of complementary and alternative medicine (CAM) in the West. Despite diverse cultures and beliefs on which entire non-Western (e.g. Ayurveda, traditional Māori healing) or Western CAM systems (e.g. homeopathy, naturopathy) and CAM modalities (e.g. massage, meditation) are based, they all share a conceptual core based on the wellness paradigm of health as described above. The growth of CAM and its associated dissemination of the wellness health paradigm has been largely driven by consumer demand. Biomedicine has not been able to ignore consumer dissatisfaction and the growing uptake of CAM. Nowadays, the combination of CAM and orthodox medicine, also referred to as *integrative medicine* (IM), is an increasingly popular and accepted phenomenon. Critics have argued that rather than a paradigm shift a co-optation of CAM by biomedicine has taken place mainly for the reasons of utilising CAM for profit-making and a larger market share (Baer and Coulter 2009; Hollenberg 2007). What is definitely the case is that CAM – like wellness tourism – has become commodities sold in a vastly growing private market of health goods and services, often referred to as the *wellness industry* (e.g. Kickbusch and Payne 2003).

While the term wellness in the English language is tied to the contexts of health promotion and the holistic health movement, it also has been assimilated in many European languages where marketers and the media are especially fond of using anglicisms to emphasise stylish, modern and fashionable products and services. The tourism industry in particular has embraced the word and a myriad of wellness hotels have materialised throughout continental Europe. However, as the term has been overutilised to advertise products ranging from cold meat to socks and cat food, it has become a superficial marketing label and the original idea of wellness as particular approach to health was somewhat lost (Ritter 2005). Nevertheless it is likely that the inflationary European use of wellness has contributed to the acceptance of the term *wellness tourism* which can be rarely found in the English academic literature prior to 2005.

Not only wellness, but also terms such as *wellness tourism* or *health tourism* have different cultural and linguistic meanings attached to it (Smith and Puczkó 2009; see also Chapter 13 in this volume). As wellness tourism and how it is understood is inextricably linked to the cultural context in which it occurs the following section provides a very brief overview of the historical development of wellness tourism.

Culturally different meanings of health-related tourism

Several authors have pointed to the long history of health-related travel, manifested as journeys to sacred temples, geothermal and mineral springs, and better climatic conditions (Kevan 1993; Smith and Puczkó 2009). Archaeological evidence and written historical accounts of Syrian, Mesopotamian, Egyptian, Chinese and Greek cultures document bathing and healing complexes, often erected around hot or cold springs, which were regarded as possessing therapeutic and spiritual qualities. Water gods and goddesses, ceremonial and healing water rituals have been and still are central components of spiritual and religious beliefs all over the world (Erfurt-Cooper and Cooper 2009; Strang 2004).

Health-related tourism went through several stages and eras of growth and decline over the centuries. Weisz (2011) suggests that throughout history there has been an ever-changing interplay of two main functions: either the pleasure dimension has dominated or the therapeutic principle was emphasised. To these two functions one can add the third dimension of spirituality. From a Western perspective, one can distinguish four major eras of health-related tourism. Roman *balneums* (community bathhouses) and the larger, more extravagant *thermae* represent the first major era. Romans perceived baths, particularly those fed by mineral or thermal springs, as medical centres where they sought cures for a wide range of diseases (Jackson 1990). However, some *thermae* were famous and luxurious complexes predominantly visited by Roman emperors and the very wealthy who demanded entertainment in addition to therapy. Those facilities became the forerunner of modern pleasure resorts and provided imposing architecture, sport halls, libraries, restaurants, sun terraces, lush residential areas and theatres in addition to immersion baths, pools and steam rooms (Aaland 1997; Jackson 1990). Additionally, many bathing complexes exhibited a religious/spiritual function as temples, shrines or votive altars dedicated to Roman, Germanic or Celtic deities were essential parts of the facility and gifts were offered to the gods either to invoke healing or to express gratitude for receiving a cure (Jackson 1990). With the rise of the Christian church, which generally disapproved of bathing, the use of bathing facilities for therapeutic, social and spiritual purposes declined. Nevertheless, there are numerous places where springs or wells became Catholic pilgrimage sites where the waters were considered to have supernatural healing powers. Pagan holy wells were Christianised and rededicated to saints or the Virgin Mary. Some of these destinations such as St Winifred's Well in Wales or Lourdes in France are still well-known pilgrimage sites to this day.

A second major wave of health-related travel commenced in the Renaissance in Italy where physicians (re-)discovered the value of water as a therapeutic modality in antique texts and started to promote balneology (i.e. the scientific study of the therapeutic use of water in form of bathing and drinking) (Palmer 1990). Although they did achieve a revival of bathing establishments which were well visited, the facilities did fall short in comparison to their Roman forerunners as they were rather primitive and rustic (ibid.). To accommodate growing expectations by aristocratic and wealthy classes who had the time and resources for travel and entertainment as never before, private and public investors in many destinations – particularly in England, Germany and the Habsburg Empire – started to build glamorous spa and seaside resorts. While those places were still perceived as healing centres, they increasingly catered to people interested in recreation rather than recuperation. Accordingly, some spa resorts became exclusive social and cultural centres with an array of amusement facilities such as promenades, ballrooms, theatres, gardens, lavish boutiques and casinos. They were places where business and political deals were conducted, where people found marriage partners and there was also a darker undercurrent of sexual indiscretions and gambling (Corak and Ateljevic 2007; Steward 2002). Case studies by Lempa (2008) and Jakobsson (2004) show that in other spa resorts the therapeutic dimension was at least equally important to the pleasure aspect. They outline that in some spa resorts visitors were subjected to a mandatory daily schedule which consisted of bathing and drinking therapies, balanced meals eaten at set meal times, periods of rest and physical exercise (mostly walking), as well as periods for socialising and leisure.

By the late nineteenth century, Europe saw a massive expansion of spa and seaside resorts, which heralded in the third era of health-related tourism. With the exception of Great Britain, where spa development declined (Bacon 1997), entire townships and hospitality industries sprang up around European springs and along sea coastlines to accommodate steadily growing visitor numbers. There, spa products and services became increasingly medicalised, scientifically analysed and research in the medical branches of balneology, thalassotherapy (i.e. study of the therapeutic use of seawater) and fangotherapy (i.e. study of the therapeutic use of muds and seaweed) increased markedly. Whereas in some countries like France and Portugal biomedicine completely regulated spa tourism (Weisz 2001, 2011), in other countries like Germany spa therapy was regarded as alternative medicine but nevertheless tolerated by mainstream health authorities (Maretzki 1989; see also Chapter 12 in this volume). In most European countries water cures became institutionalised and reimbursable by public health insurance systems. Consequently, even in those destinations where *taking the waters* was originally a luxury only available to a few, it became a democratised, industrialised and secularised commodity claimable by all. This was not the case in Great Britain and in the New World, to which European settlers had brought the idea of taking the waters. There, spa resorts became marginalised; they were neither covered by public health insurances nor accepted by biomedical health professionals (Bacon 1997; Weisz 2011). The different historical developments in Britain and the English-speaking countries of the New World on the one hand and continental Europe on the other led to distinctly different meanings for terms such as *spa* and *wellness tourism*. Whereas the term *spa* in English has a distinct tourism and leisure connotation, spas in Europe imply cure and are linked to medicine (Puczkó and Bachvarov 2006).

Due to a range of sociocultural, economic and demographic changes (see Chapter 1 in this volume) for the last two decades a fourth golden era of health-related tourism has begun reaching most regions in the world and in its wake wellness tourism, its products and its meanings, have become even more diversified. Before the attempt of structuring and classifying modern understandings of wellness tourism, the following section will explore existing definitions and typologies of wellness and health tourism and disentangle different facets as a basis of a new definition.

Exploring existing definitions and conceptualisations

Apart from the apparent agreement that wellness tourism is a form of special interest tourism (SIT) (e.g. Hall 2003; Letho *et al.* 2006), existing definitions vary considerably. As the previous discussion has shown, wellness tourism is a socially constructed phenomenon that varies across times and places. Existing definitions differ in regard to:

- whether medical and wellness segments are considered as separate or whether they are mixed together;
- the extent to which they are informed by the biomedical or wellness understanding of health;
- the emphasis of specific benefits sought by wellness tourists and how they pursue wellbeing;
- the emphasis of specific attributes of the destination, the facilities and/or services; and
- the extent to which elements of general tourism definitions are included.

It is thus perhaps unlikely that a single universally accepted definition can ever be agreed upon. Nevertheless, on the basis of existing definitions and typologies certain components will be drawn out which build the backbone of the conceptual framework that is offered here.

Medical and wellness tourism as separate categories of health tourism

One area of disagreement between tourism scholars is whether wellness tourism subsumes medical tourism (e.g. Sheldon and Bushell 2009), or vice-versa (e.g.

Bookman and Bookman 2007) or alternatively whether wellness and medical tourism are two essentially separate tourism categories (Henderson 2004; Müller and Lanz Kaufmann 2001; Nahrstedt 2004; Puczkó and Bachvarov 2006). Kelly (2010) considers an interchangeable use of medical and wellness tourism as inappropriate and cautions against too broad conceptualisations and generalisations. Based on the theoretical difference between *illness* and *wellness* concepts and their relation to the two underlying health paradigms, the view of those is supported here who differentiate wellness and medical tourism.

How health is viewed by medical and wellness tourism providers has consequences in regard to the products and services they offer and the kind of workforce that is employed. Medical tourism providers are illness-orientated and emphasise a curative approach. The majority of services offered by medical tourism providers are biomedical procedures, including invasive and high-tech diagnostic services. Employees treating medical tourists are typically orthodox health professionals, such as doctors and nurses. In contrast, wellness tourism providers are wellness-orientated with an emphasis on health promotion and disease prevention. Services offered by wellness tourism providers generally fall outside the realm of biomedicine. They encompass a range of service, including CAM therapies, non-invasive beauty treatments, spiritual and lifestyle-based interventions. Employees caring for wellness tourists are normally not mainstream health professionals and consist of CAM practitioners, beauticians, nutritionists and lifestyle coaches, or even religious personnel like nuns and monks. Adopting these perspectives, health tourism then, is a comprehensive umbrella term that is composed of medical and wellness tourism.

Are wellness tourists healthy whereas medical tourists are not?

Some authors have suggested that, in contrast to medical tourists, wellness tourists are generally healthy (Joppe 2010; Müller and Lanz Kaufmann 2001). From a wellness paradigm point of view this argument is perhaps less relevant as there, health is seen as a subjective concept, not necessarily determinable by a catalogue of biomedical illness symptoms. According to biomedical standards, a medical tourist who travels to obtain a cheaper tummy tuck might be considered as healthy, whereas a wellness tourist with a chronic disease would be considered as unhealthy which would not necessarily be the case when employing the wellness paradigm. Furthermore, a recent study with Australian wellness tourists revealed that some of them did grapple with major negative life events which led to health problems such as sleep disorders or burnout syndrome, and some were even being confronted with a life-threatening illness diagnosis (Voigt 2010). What is more relevant here is the outlook of the person who travels. By employing holistic methods and lifestyle-based interventions, a wellness tourist actively assumes personal responsibility for making certain lifestyle choices with the aim of reaching higher levels of wellness, whereas medical tourists turn towards orthodox health professionals and biomedical solutions to let themselves be fixed in a more passive manner. Nevertheless, it also should be acknowledged that research into health status or lifestyle choices of wellness and medical tourists is largely missing and needs to be explored further.

Different benefits sought by wellness and medical tourists

Several wellness definitions stress the importance of specific tourist motivations that are required to classify an experience as wellness tourism. For instance, Müller and Lanz Kaufmann (2001: 7) argue that wellness travel is undertaken by 'people whose main motive is to preserve or promote their health' and The Tourism Observatory for Health, Wellness and Spa (TOHWS 2012: 20) states that wellness tourism activities are proactively pursued by people who want to 'maintain or enhance their personal health and wellbeing'. The centre of attention in these definitions is clearly on health promotion in accordance with the wellness paradigm of health. Wellness tourists and medical tourists have two elementary different underlying needs. While wellness tourists go on vacation in order to maintain or improve their health and wellbeing, medical tourists primarily travel in order to cure or treat a certain illness or medical condition.

Rather than emphasising a broad health promotion motive, Sheldon and Bushell (2009: 11) specify wellness tourist motivations further and argue that wellness tourists are on a 'quest for physical health, beauty, or longevity, and/ or a heightening of consciousness or spiritual awareness, and a connection with community, nature, or the divine mystery'. However, in a study examining actual benefits sought by wellness tourists, longevity and connection with community did not play a role (Voigt *et al.* 2011). There, six benefit factors emerged which were labelled transcendence; physical health and appearance; escape and relaxation; important others and novelty; re-establish self-esteem; and indulgence. While underlying motivations of wellness tourists could be analysed further in additional studies, particularly in the form of cross-cultural comparisons, it is clear that when health is understood as a holistic, multidimensional concept it can be pursued in a myriad of different ways and in form of very different tourism activities. Hence, pure demand-orientated wellness tourism definitions such as 'any kind of travel to make yourself or a member of your family healthier' (Tabacchi 2003, in Erfurt-Cooper and Cooper 2009: 6) are potentially problematic and some additional definitional elements are needed.

Typical wellness tourism facilities and services

Some definitions emphasise the significance of the supply-side. For instance, Goodrich and Goodrich (1987: 217) define health-care tourism as: 'the attempt on the part of a tourist facility (e.g. a hotel) or destination (e.g. Baden, Switzerland) to attract tourists by deliberately promoting its health-care services and facilities, in addition to its regular tourist amenities'. They continue to give examples of these services and facilities and list medical examinations by qualified doctors and nurses at the resort or hotel, Transvital® injections and special medical treatments for various diseases. Clearly, their definition is informed by a biomedical understanding of health care. In contrast, Müller and Lanz Kaufmann (2001: 6) describe a comprehensive service package for individual care which is more consistent with the wellness paradigm of health and focuses on lifestyle-based interventions in the areas of 'physical fitness/ beauty care, healthy nutrition/diet, relaxation/meditation and mental activity/ education'. As alluded to before, wellness tourism services often include an assortment of CAM therapies.

While acknowledging that wellness tourism services and facilities are constantly changing and evolving, a closer look at wellness tourism provider offerings all over the world suggests the following list of modules wellness tourism products can be composed of:

- *Body and facial beauty treatments*
  e.g. facials, body wraps, body scrubs, exfoliation, manicure, pedicure, hair removal
- *Water-based and sweat-bathing treatments and facilities*
  e.g. thalassotherapy, hydrotherapy, floating tanks, Vichy showers, ice grottos, sauna, hammam, caldarium
- *Manual-pressure based and manipulative body-based therapies*
  e.g. massages, acupressure, reflexology, cupping, chiropractic, osteopathy
- *Herbal medicine and natural remedies*
  e.g. homeopathic medicines, Bach flowers, vitamins and other dietary supplements, aromatherapy, natural cosmetics, sulphur therapy, fangotherapy
- *Healthy nutrition and diet*
  e.g. cooking demonstrations, detoxing, fasting, weight management seminars, specific diets (vegan, organic, vegetarian, no additives...)
- *Exercise and fitness*
  e.g. group classes, private classes with personal trainer or self-guided activities, indoor activities such as aerobics, spinning and circuit training, outdoor activities such as jungle boot camp, kayaking, archery, hiking, Nordic walking, facilities such as lap pools, tennis courts, golf course, gymnasium, walking trails
- *Mind/body interventions*
  e.g. yoga, Tai Chi, Qi Gong, Pilates, Feldenkrais method, Body–Mind Centring, Rolfing
- *Meditation and relaxation techniques*
  e.g. transcendental meditation, Vipassana, prayer, chanting, progressive muscle relaxation, autogenic training, hypnotherapy, guided imagery
- *Expressive therapies and creative arts*
  e.g. dance therapy, drumming, poetry, pottery, photography, journalling
- *Energy therapies and New Age*
  e.g. Reiki, healing touch, magnet therapy, rebirthing, astrology, tarot card readings, channelling, crystals

- *Educational activities (counselling, workshops and seminars, religious teachings)*
  e.g. stress management, relationship management, emotional health, work–life balance, seminars on specific health issues such as menopause, burnout, insomnia or pregnancy, dharma or bible classes

Most of the activities provided by wellness tourism providers are designed for individuals. However, a few wellness providers additionally offer corporate wellness programs. Here the idea is to bring employees together to interact and learn about healthier choices outside the familiar work context. This fosters team-building and a better corporate culture, and produces healthier employees which ultimately has a positive impact on the company's bottom line.

As previously discussed, from a Western point of view the historical development of health-related travel is closely linked to the central element of water and the development of spas. This is why wellness tourism often tends to be exclusively associated with the spa sector. Academics and practitioners from continental Europe still perceive water to be the central defining element of spas, if not even of wellness tourism. However, looking at destinations and wellness tourism business models worldwide, it soon becomes obvious that many wellness tourism providers do not offer any water-based treatments and if they do, they are often not connected to mineral or geothermal sources. In contrast, while the spiritual function of wellness tourism had decreased in importance for a long time, it recently went through a time of revival. The importance of the spiritual dimension has been emphasised by several recent conceptualisations of wellness tourism (Smith and Kelly 2006b; Pernecky and Johnston 2006). Many of the above listed wellness tourism services can be seen as *holistic* as they address body, mind and spirit.

Wellness tourism between mindless hedonism and meaningful self-realisation

In contrast to medical tourism, wellness tourism is portrayed to be more hedonistic and based on enjoyment (Schobersberger *et al.* 2004). Similarly, Henderson (2004: 113) describes wellness tourism as consisting of 'hedonistic indulgences of spas and alternative therapies'. In several writings this connection to hedonism has a negative connotation and the entire wellness tourism phenomenon, or at least the spa sector, is often depicted as attracting overindulgent individuals who seek meaningless enjoyment rather than true wellbeing. For instance, Ritter (2005: 80) describes that wellness can be perceived as 'the lazy sister of fitness' and the 'tender loving care of ... [the] sluggish self'. Hall (2003: 273) suggests that the 'popular image' of spa tourists is that of 'overweight or unhealthy people being pampered at some sort of "health farm"' and Dann and Nordstrand (2009: 127) think that spa visitation primarily appeals to 'hedonistic sybarites'. In contrast, those wellness tourists interested in more holistic and spiritual sectors of wellness tourism are portrayed as pursuing more meaningful and more worthy experiences of self-realisation and personal growth. Therefore, Steiner and Reisinger (2006) have proposed that only those wellness tourists who focus on transcendence and spirituality should be regarded as true wellness tourists but that this focus is rarely found in most of the current wellness tourism products on offer:

> [W]hat is marketed as wellness tourism, with its narrow focus on promoting physical or mental health, on indulgent and expensive pampering, or on self-centred inner explorations through psychic tricks and scams may not even touch the transcendent possibilities of being well, focusing instead on the superficial quest for merely feeling well.
>
> (Steiner and Reisinger 2006: 12)

The field of positive psychology may help to obtain a more differentiated understanding of psychological wellbeing which has been based on two broad philosophical traditions: hedonic wellbeing (as indicated by positive affect/pleasure, subjective happiness, satisfaction with life) and eudaimonic wellbeing (as indicated by realisation of one's true potential, a meaningful and fulfilling life). While some contend that hedonism in its extreme forms may have a well-earned negative reputation, hedonic wellbeing should not be regarded as meaningless or even destructive (King *et al.* 2006). Moreover, positive psychologists regard hedonic and eudaimonic wellbeing as equally important to achieve a state of optimal psychological wellbeing (Keyes 2002; King *et al.* 2006; Ryan and Deci 2001). For the context of wellness tourism this means that experiences affording mainly pleasure and relaxation are not necessarily less worthy than those that lead to increased self-realisation and self-actualisation, as both types of experiences may equally lead to a balanced state of psychological health.

The role of the environment, natural and cultural resources

Several wellness tourism conceptualisations highlight the role of natural resources and the significance of the surrounding environment. The historical overview has shown that many wellness tourism destinations have developed around mineral and geothermal waters and later sea water (i.e. thalassotherapy), but other natural resources such as the climate, healing muds, clays, plants as well as vapours increasingly play a role. Additionally, there seems to be the perception that not only specific natural ingredients but also nature itself has healing powers. A common theme is to perceive isolated, natural landscapes as inherently therapeutic in contrast to the harmful, polluted and stressful urban life. Additionally, research from environmental psychology confirms that being in or looking at nature contributes to individual health and wellbeing (e.g. Hartig *et al.* 2003; Herzog *et al.* 2003; see also Chapter 10 in this volume). Many wellness tourism properties are located in rural areas and marketing material frequently praises the beautiful scenery, breathtaking views and quiet, pristine and unspoilt surroundings and/or specific natural resources that are supposed to increase tourists' wellbeing. While generally not discussed in the wellness tourism literature, health geographers have also recognised place as determinant potentially influencing people's wellbeing by introducing the concept of *therapeutic landscapes*. Initially, the concept was primarily linked to natural features, but recently it has been applied to built environments and wellness tourism providers such as spas, yoga retreats and ashrams as well as entire yoga destinations, which have all been discussed as examples of therapeutic landscapes (Frost 2004; Gesler 2003; Hoyez 2007).

Clearly, holistic healing practices are closely related to the cultural, spiritual and indigenous traditions of a place, many of which are thousands of years old. Especially in international tourists, practices with such a rich historic background may evoke the mystic impression of ancient secrets of lifelong health, longevity and happiness, all values that are appealing across cultures. Consequently, Sheldon and Park (2009) and Pechlaner and Fischer (2006) argue that natural, cultural and indigenous wellness resources represent the core competitive advantage of wellness tourism destinations which need to be identified and implemented in the destination's brand. Similarly, TOHWS (2012: iv) proposes that most wellness tourism destinations have a number of unique wellness resources that need to be developed to create distinctive brands with unique selling propositions. They even go a step further and suggest in their definition of wellness tourism that it involves people 'who are seeking unique, authentic or location-based experiences/therapies not available at home'. Such a definition may exclude the proportion of domestic wellness tourists who might prefer the experiential opportunity to explore imported healing traditions unrelated to their home environment. These contrasting notions show the value of exploring different understandings of *authenticity*, or juxtaposing fantastical, mystical or magical, and original or genuine elements; a discussion which has started to penetrate the context of wellness tourism (Cook 2010; O'Dell 2005; Steiner and Reisinger 2006; Chapter 14 in this volume).

Wellness tourism: beyond an individualistic understanding of wellness toward sustainability?

There is no question that wellness tourism is primarily concerned with the wellbeing of individuals. Similarly, the wellness paradigm of health that has been discussed here has so far been largely implemented as a form of private health care option, thereby only focusing on individualistic solutions for those who can afford it, rather than truly reforming public health care available to all. Nevertheless there is a debate in the literature whether wellness tourism is or could potentially be linked to a broader understanding of wellness which includes societal and environmental dimensions.

On the one hand, from a consumer perspective, wellness tourism has long been accused of *conspicuous* consumption. On the other hand, some scholars propose that wellness tourists are actually involved in *conscious* consumption by seeking out products and services that promote general wellbeing as well as sustainability. Accordingly, wellness tourists are said to belong to the LOHAS market, an acronym for Lifestyles of Health and Sustainability (Cohen 2008).

LOHAS consumers broaden the concept of self-responsibility for their wellbeing to include environmental and social dimensions and they prefer products and services like organic food, alternative modes of transport and energy, CAM, or recycled material. In contrast, Hall and Brown (2006) argue that wellness tourists' concentration on the self either in form of body image or spiritual enlightenment is essentially egoistic and at odds with sustainable ideals. Additionally, wellness tourism is often equated with luxury products and five-star services, only available to a pampered minority of wealthy tourists. While it is certainly true that many wellness providers are clustered at the high end of the market, a number of providers, especially at the more holistic, spiritual end, operate as non-profit organisations or even on a donation basis and some groups of wellness tourists actually possess relatively low household incomes (Voigt *et al.* 2010a). Moreover, some foresee the trend of *democratisation* of wellness tourism where specific business models such as budget spas or basic retreats will make wellness affordable to a broader range of tourists (TOHWS 2012).

Similar disputes can be detected in regard to the supply-side of wellness tourism. First, there is the question whether wellness tourist managers and their staff are actually familiar with the theoretical concept of wellness and its broader connection to sustainability. Smith and Puczkó (2009: 58) think that 'the tourism sector does not always have the holistic know-how or the desire' to offer a holistic, sustainable wellness product. Second, there is the danger that some wellness tourism providers perceive wellness just as a handy marketing tool to gain higher profits. Lee and King (2006: 194), for instance, state that many providers 'are focusing exclusively on maximizing short-term profits. They appear to ignore the effects of their actions on local communities and the environment, and their responsibility to the customers'. Clearly, some wellness tourism resorts are located in areas where the contrast between the tourists' pursuit of wellbeing in a walled-off property and the actual poor health status of the surrounding host community could not be starker. Moreover, the utilisation of natural, cultural and indigenous resources for wellness products is often unregulated and there is a genuine risk of overexploitation. However, several wellness tourism providers make extensive efforts to incorporate sustainable business practices and to emphasise their green, organic, zero waste, carbon neutral or fair trade products and services as well as their corporate social responsibility and environment-friendly programs. Whether they do this out conviction or just to satisfy the needs of LOHAS consumers is another matter. However, a recent study has shown that at least some wellness tourism providers are driven by the personal desire to help customers to increase their wellness and not by maximising profits or business growth; however not all of them necessarily integrated sustainable business practices (Kelly 2010).

Reference to general tourism definitions

While tourism, like wellness and wellness tourism, lacks a common definition, there are some definitional factors that are consistently recurring. If one adopts the spatial dimension, to be considered a tourist an individual must travel away from and eventually return home. The World Tourism Organization (WTO) posits that this travel must occur beyond the person's 'usual environment'. Accordingly, Pollock and Williams (2000: 265) define health tourism as 'activities removed from the distractions of work and home'. It appears that the term 'usual environment' is highly subjective particularly in regard to domestic tourism. A review of existing statistics from different countries and regions on demand characteristics in wellness destinations revealed that wellness tourism is generally largely dominated by domestic tourists (cf. Voigt *et al.* 2010b: 44), whereas medical tourism seems to involve mainly international tourists.

A temporal dimension is another factor that determines whether someone can be regarded as a tourist. The WTO suggests a year to be the maximum threshold before one ceases to be a tourist. As the minimum threshold scholars have argued for the experience of at least one overnight stay (Leiper 1981). Commonly, the term excursionist is used if a trip does not incorporate an overnight stay. Referring to both a spatial and temporal dimension in his definition of health tourism, Hall (2003: 74) posits that health tourists are persons 'travelling overnight away from the normal home environment'. Although it is acknowledged that some wellness providers specifically in the spa sector receive proportions of excursionists and even locals, from a destination development point of view tourists who actually stay in the destination may be more relevant.

A new definition and classification of wellness tourism

Resulting from the preceding discussion on relevant definitional wellness tourism aspects the following definition is proposed: Wellness tourism is the sum of all phenomena resulting from a journey by individuals whose motive in whole or in part is to maintain or promote their health and wellbeing, and who stay at least one night at a facility that is specifically designed to holistically enable and enhance people's physical, psychological, spiritual and/or social wellbeing, and that ideally also takes into account environmental and community wellness in a sustainable manner (adapted from Voigt 2010).

In the preceding discussion it was argued that wellness and medical tourism providers can be understood as two contrasting forms of health tourism providers based on the opposing philosophical understandings of health and illness which results in differences in the services they offer and in the kinds of staff they employ. Additionally, while wellness tourism providers cater to tourists who primarily travel to maintain or improve their health and wellbeing, medical tourism providers concentrate on tourists who primarily travel in order to cure or treat a certain disease or medical condition. Still, wellness tourism providers do not represent a homogenous group. Voigt and Laing (2010) have suggested three distinct core providers of wellness tourism (Figure 2.1):

1   Beauty spa hotels/resorts
    The major focus of beauty spa hotels/resorts (generally referred to as *wellness hotels* in the European context) is on the body and non-invasive beauty

treatments as well as a range of water-based and/or sweat-bathing facilities which sometimes utilise mineral or geothermal waters. Customers are usually passive recipients of the treatments provided to them. Although there are exceptions, many beauty spa hotels/resorts occupy the high end of wellness tourism supply and customers of five-star properties nowadays expect the offer of a spa on the premise. Beauty spas are also often combined with other luxury tourism products, such as spa and golf, spa and ski, or spa and wine. Day spas are very similar to beauty spa hotels/resorts, however they do not include or are not attached to accommodation facilities.

2   Lifestyle resorts

Lifestyle resorts are what North Americans tend to call 'destination spas' and their main purpose is to 'set guests on a healthier path for life' (McNeil and Ragins 2004: 32). They always cover a range of health-promoting domains such as nutrition, exercise and stress management. Lifestyle resort visitors commit to the active participation in a very comprehensive program that is usually tailored to their particular needs at the start of their stay. They frequently sign some form of contract where they commit to health-promoting behaviour and pledge to refrain from engaging in health risks such as smoking, or drinking alcohol. The extensive schedule of activities, classes and workshops is usually interspersed with relatively few free periods for leisure and with set meal times which are typically based on a very healthy diet. Amenities normally found at conventional resorts such as internet access, televisions or telephones are often not available, so that guests are not getting distracted in their journey towards a healthier life. Many lifestyle resorts incorporate a beauty spa where treatments can be booked at an additional cost, but the focus on beauty is not as pronounced as in the beauty spa category. Lifestyle resorts come in different sizes and levels of comfort, some are very luxurious and opulent, whereas others have a more rustic barefoot luxury-feel to it, or could even be compared to a boot camp. Lifestyle resorts generally require a high level of investment as a vast range of facilities, staff and general space is needed.

3   Spiritual retreats

The focus of spiritual retreats is on spiritual development. They can be religious or non-religious but always include meditation in various forms. Many are based on some specific teachings or philosophy and/or focus on the study of a specific mind/body technique such as yoga or T'ai Chi, or particular forms of meditation (e.g. Transcendental Meditation, Vipassana). One can distinguish between silent and non-silent spiritual retreats. In silent spiritual retreats, visitors must refrain from talking the entire time; they are supposed to focus entirely on their personal spirituality. Usually, spiritual retreat visitors are governed by a strict routine and time schedule and, in cases of religious accommodation providers (e.g. ashrams, temples, monasteries), this schedule incorporates or is built around the rituals and daily structure of the religious community that lives there permanently. Compared to the two other categories of wellness tourism providers, spiritual retreats tend to be more basic and visitors often have to share austere rooms and/or bathroom facilities. Guests are also sometimes expected to participate in housekeeping activities, such as washing the dishes after meals.

Importantly, the boundaries between the three types of pure wellness tourism providers are not rigidly set. They should be seen as distributed along a continuum where there is a gradual distinction between those types. For example, the emphasis of some lifestyle resorts is more heavily on beauty treatment and massages, whereas others accentuate meditation and mind/body interventions or New Age services. Similarly, spiritual retreats can lean more towards lifestyle resorts by providing some seminars on lifestyle issues, or by combining meditation with creative arts activities.

Overlap between wellness and medial tourism providers

Gustavo (2011: 129) observes an increasing diversification and specialisation in regard to health tourism offerings and that there have been 'unique and sometimes paradoxical fusions and interchanges such as those of the natural and the technological, the scientific and the profane, the western and the eastern'. Similarly, Voigt and Laing (2013) discuss an increased hybridisation between wellness and medical tourism providers which is sometimes referred to as *medical wellness* in the literature. It is not clear where or when the term medical wellness originated and based on the preceding discussion of the contrast between the biomedical and wellness health paradigms, the term appears to make little conceptual sense. However, the term symbolises a new coalescence between orthodox and CAM health professionals and a stronger focus on wellness principles in biomedicine. In the United States, medical wellness is clearly linked to an integrative medicine approach to health care, whereas in Europe it is more

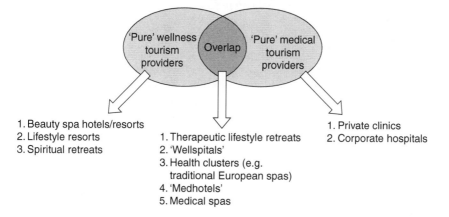

Figure 2.1 The health provider continuum.

directly linked to the tourism industry. While acknowledging that the classification categories are neither permanent nor discrete, Voigt and Laing (2013) suggest five different types of medical wellness tourism business models, depicted in Figure 2.1 and described as follows:

1   Therapeutic lifestyle retreats
    Therapeutic lifestyle retreats are very similar to the wellness tourism provider category of lifestyle resorts. The major difference is that the former have been developed for people who are affected by serious and/or chronic illnesses. Therapeutic lifestyle retreats are firmly based on the wellness paradigm of health and concentrate on empowering individuals to actively work towards a healthy lifestyle and higher levels of wellbeing rather than on treating the disease.

2   Wellspitals
    Similarly to therapeutic lifestyle retreats, 'wellspitals' primarily focus on people with serious or chronic diseases or on people with psychiatric disorders and addictions. The difference is that here biomedical treatment modalities (e.g. psychotherapy, drug therapy, pain management, diagnostics) are combined with CAM, lifestyle-based interventions, mind/body techniques or creative art therapies. This integrative approach is often spearheaded by conventional biomedical institutions with the dual goals of illness treatment and health promotion. Rehabilitation generally meshes very well with the wellness principles of self-responsibility, health promotion, patient empowerment and body/mind/spirit integration and the inability of biomedicine alone to handle chronic diseases has fostered integrative medicine approaches.

3   Health clusters
    The best example of a health cluster is the traditional European spa destination where rigid separation between biomedicine and CAM cannot be made as balneology or spa medicine has been incorporated into biomedicine. To compensate dwindling governmental reimbursement for spa therapies, many traditional European spa destinations have developed a stronger orientation towards wellness in order to attract self-paying guests. Here, biomedicine and alternative approaches, services and staff types are usually mixed, often at the same facility. In traditional European spa destinations one can usually find a range of providers (e.g. clinics, wellness hotels, therapeutic health centres, bathing complexes) that can usually be used by those who want to cure a disease as well as those who want to maintain or promote their health and wellbeing. Health-care cities and health care malls are other examples of health clusters attracting wellness and medical tourists; however, here biomedical and CAM/wellness services seem to just coexist and there is little evidence of an integrated, cooperative approach.

4   Medhotels
    Compared to wellspitals, the involvement of the hospitality industry is much more pronounced in this category of medical wellness providers. In other words, 'medhotels' represent a collaboration between a private, biomedical

clinic and a hotel to attract wellness and medical tourists. Typically, med-hotels do not target people with chronic illnesses as much, but on those with impermanent health problems (e.g. burnout, back pain, sport injuries). Unlike in lifestyle resorts, guests are not enrolled in a comprehensive lifestyle program and while beauty, fitness and spa services may be offered, the focus tends to be on biomedical and high-tech diagnostic services provided by conventional health care professionals.

5   Medical spas
    The main focus of medical spas is on beauty and anti-ageing. However, rather than offering more natural treatments like beauty spas, medical spas concentrate on more invasive treatments which pose greater health risks such as botox filler injections, microdermabrasion, aggressive chemical peels or laser treatments. To ensure quality and safety for the clients, medical spas are supposed to be supervised by a physician.

Many medical wellness providers target medical and wellness tourists at the same time. Even a number of therapeutic lifestyle retreats and wellspitals offer programs for the 'worried well' as a side business. Some of these programs are also utilised by relatives and friends who accompany an ill patient. Little research has been undertaken to examine these hybrid business models, for instance in regard to the extent and success of collaboration between orthodox or alternative health professionals and hospitality managers, or how well it works to mix sick and healthy customer markets. An exception is a case study about a traditional Czech health spa where it was established that doctors resisted the loss of their authority and complained that opening up medical spa therapy to mere tourists has resulted in a detrimental demedicalisation and commodification of balneology (Speier 2011). Furthermore, the doctors feared that when tourists are able to choose their treatments, rather than the doctors, spa therapy may lose its effectiveness or may even harmful to the customers' health. These observations are in line with Weisz (2011: 138) who argues that throughout history the relationship between tourism and medical health professionals has always oscillated between 'permanent symbiosis or tension'.

Concluding discussion: implications for destination development and management

Although wellness tourism is grounded in a history of thousands of years, its renewed explosive growth and diversification reflects a relatively new philosophical approach to health and how health care is managed and delivered – at least from a Western perspective. It is hoped that the discussion and analysis on the development of health-related travel and existing conceptualisations of wellness tourism has demonstrated that it is a very complex and multilayered phenomenon where the literature comprises different, often contradictory and sometimes stereotypical views of what wellness tourism is, how it should be delivered, and what kind of experiences it produces.

Some of these conflicting views can be explained through the different cultural and linguistic meanings attached to terms such as wellness, spa and health tourism. These differences have direct consequences on how destinations and providers need to deliver and promote their services, particularly when international tourists are targeted. There is a definite lack of market transparency which confuses wellness tourists who might expect different things under the same labels and are exposed to contrasting wellness tourism rituals. A Western wellness tourist visiting a Chinese spa might be surprised when treatment referred to as body scrub actually entails the rather painful (but perhaps more healthful) traditional Chinese *Gua Sha* treatment where the skin in firmly scraped with a spoon-like instrument, leaving fiery red marks for days, rather than consisting of a gentle exfoliation of the skin. In contrast, a Chinese wellness tourist might be uncomfortable in German saunas where it is common to be entirely naked and where sexes are not segregated. Therefore, single wellness tourism providers, but also destinations must educate visitors and staff alike and clearly explain what they offer and how they offer it, also taking into account potential language barriers.

From a supply-side perspective it has been shown that health tourism supply is fragmented and highly diverse. This chapter concurs with those who have viewed medical and wellness tourism as two essentially different forms of health tourism. It has mentioned two forms of pure medical tourism providers (i.e. private clinics, corporate hospitals) and it has introduced a continuum of three types of pure wellness tourism providers (i.e. beauty spa hotels/resorts, lifestyle resorts, spiritual retreats). However, the chapter has also acknowledged five types of hybrid business models (i.e. therapeutic lifestyle retreats, wellspitals, health clusters, medhotels, medical spas), where biomedicine and more alternative approaches are brought together in different innovative manners. Using a term coined by Ritchie and Crouch (2003: 21, 69), all those different types of supply then can build the health tourism 'superstructure' at a destination. Unlike normal tourism superstructure tourists select to sleep and eat in order to visit specific kinds of attractions, health tourism superstructure usually builds the focal point of the entire trip and in regard to many of those types, tourists never or rarely leave the property they stay in, especially when they are enrolled in specific programs or regimens. In other words, a health or wellness tourism destination cannot be developed without the presence of any of the here-discussed health tourism provider types. For a destination there are different possibilities to develop and market these superstructures. They can either focus very broadly on health tourism and quite large target markets, or they can advertise themselves as either a wellness or medical tourism destination, thereby breaking down the large market into more specific segments, or they can focus entirely on a specific wellness tourism niche, tailoring their products and services to very particular needs of an audience. For instance, the Indian Ministry of Health and Family Welfare and the Ministry of Tourism promote India as global health tourism destination by emphasising both affordable, high-quality biomedicine available at private hospitals in major Indian cities (e.g. Delhi or Mumbai) as well as India's unique heritage of traditional therapeutic systems and modalities (e.g. Ayurveda, Unani, Yoga). On a more regional level, different Indian destinations focus on specific wellness tourism aspects; for instance the state of Kerala is promoted as the Land of Ayurveda, the Himalayan town of Rishikesh as birthplace and world capital of yoga, and the town Mysore as international centre for Ashtanga yoga which has already attracted celebrities like Madonna and Sting.

While destination managers are able to exert a significant amount of influence and control in regard to development and promotion of health tourism super-structure, a destination's availability of natural resources which can be utilised in wellness tourism, its geographic features defining aesthetic appeal and climate, as well as its cultural, spiritual and indigenous healing traditions are a given. However, the preceding discussion has indicated that natural and cultural resources are key comparative advantages between wellness tourism destinations and it is the task of destination managers to creatively tie them into the destination's development and branding strategies. In contrast, medical tourism providers are rarely located in natural areas with beautiful scenery and modern, cutting-edge technology plays a much bigger role than ancient traditions, which is why natural and cultural resources are less important for medical tourism destination managers.

Over the past 50 years the wellness paradigm of health has spread out as part of a consumer movement, a critique on orthodox biomedical health care and the growing desire of people for more control over their health choices. Through globalisation and an increased privatisation of health care vast private industries have sprung up that capitalise on people's desire for more preventive health-care options, also by increasingly taking into account wellness principles. Wellness tourism providers are one sector of this industry and, whether accepted by bio-medical standards or not, they are informally involved in the provision of health care. Thus, they also must assume certain responsibilities. As the health and wellbeing of tourists are at stake, providers as well as destinations have the responsibility to ensure the quality of treatments and the staff who administers them, to avoid claims of miracle cures, and to steer clear of offering so-called gimmick treatments that have no therapeutic value or are actually harmful to tourists. Recently, calls for more evidence-based wellness tourism have grown increasingly louder and initiatives such as the internet portal *SPAevidence* have been launched where scientific studies are collected to demonstrate the efficacy and safety of CAM treatments and lifestyle-based interventions commonly used in wellness tourism offerings.

Despite the fact that the protection of individual health is paramount in wellness tourism, it also needs to be acknowledged that this form of health care is only available for those who can afford it. This is arguably true for most forms of tourism, but when a public good, namely health, is additionally at stake, this shortcoming seems to become exacerbated. Moreover, a picture of wellness tourism tends to be painted where egoistic individuals mindlessly indulge in conspicuous consumption without truly being interested in increasing their health.

40   *C. Voigt*

This chapter has attempted to demonstrate that this view is grossly one-sided and fails to acknowledge the diversity of the wellness tourism phenomenon. Not all wellness tourism offerings are luxurious and pricey, hedonism can be a legitimate avenue to increased psychological wellbeing, and wellness tourists may be concerned about environmental and social wellness, not only their personal wellbeing.

Nevertheless, there is no question that there are strong issues of equity and equality involved in wellness tourism. This becomes even clearer when the individualistic view on wellness is holistically integrated in the broader idea of sustainability which also takes into account environmental and community wellness. Ritchie and Crouch (2003) have argued that in order to stay competitive, any tourism destination needs to embrace sustainability. A destination that presumes to sell wellness should assume environmental and social responsibilities by definition, especially because wellness tourism is so much connected to the exploitation of natural and cultural resources. Through educational workshops or by establishing and monitoring certification and benchmarking systems, wellness destination management organisations can encourage the implementation of environmentally friendly practices such as water and energy conservation, recycling, waste reduction and the avoidance of hazardous substances. Similarly, they can endorse social responsibility by employing as many local staff as possible, preferring local suppliers and locally sourced products rather than imported products, honouring intellectual property rights that indigenous populations may hold in regard to healing traditions, and attending to wellbeing needs of the staff employed in the wellness sector. In fact, ideally a wellness tourism destination may promote its approach to health and wellbeing not only to attract tourists, but also to attract residents and generally improve quality of life of all humans residing at the destination either temporarily or permanently. Unfortunately, the reconciliation between an economically focused business philosophy and a holistic, sustainable wellness approach to health still remains one of the greatest challenges of the wellness tourism industry. While there is a strong push towards converging wellness and sustainability, there is still a long way to go for actual providers and destinations.

References

Aaland, M. (1997) *Mass Bathing: The Roman Balnea and Thermae*, online, available at: www.cyberbohemia.com/Pages/massbathing.htm (accessed 16 October 2012).
Bacon, W. (1997) 'The rise of the German and the demise of the English spa industry: a critical analysis of Business success and failure', *Leisure Studies*, 16: 173–87.
Baer, H.A. and Coulter, I. (2009) 'Introduction – taking stock of integrative medicine: broadening biomedicine or co-option of complementary and alternative medicine?' *Health Sociology Review*, 17: 331–41.
Bookman, M.Z. and Bookman, K.R. (2007) *Medical Tourism in Developing Countries*, New York: Palgrave Macmillan.
Cohen, M. (2008) 'Spas, wellness and human evolution', in M. Cohen and G. Bodeker (eds) *Understanding the Global Spa Industry: Spa Management*, Oxford: Butterworth-Heinemann.

Connell, J. (2011) *Medical Tourism*, Wallingford: CABI.

Cook, P.S. (2010) 'Constructions and experiences of authenticity in medical tourism: the performances of places, spaces, practices, objects and bodies', *Tourist Studies*, 10: 135–53.

Corak, S. and Ateljevic, I. (2007) 'Colonisation and "taking the waters" in the 19th century: the patronage of royalty in health resorts of Opatija, Habsburg Empire and Rotorua, New Zealand', in P. Long and N.J. Palmer (eds) *Royal Tourism: Excursions Around Monarchy*, Clevedon: Channel View Publications.

Dann, G.M.S. and Nordstrand, K.B. (2009) 'Promoting wellbeing via multisensory tourism', in R. Bushell and P.J. Sheldon (eds) *Wellness and Tourism: Mind, Body, Spirit, Place*, New York: Cognizant Communication Corporation.

Davis-Floyd, R. (2001) 'The technocratic, humanistic, and holistic paradigms of childbirth', *International Journal of Gynaecology & Obstetrics*, 75: S5–S23.

Dunn, H.L. (1959a) 'High-level wellness for man and society', *American Journal of Public Health*, 49: 786–92.

Dunn, H.L. (1959b) 'What high-level wellness means', *Canadian Journal of Public Health*, 50: 447–57.

Engel, G.L. (1977) 'The need for a new medical model: a challenge for biomedicine', *Science*, 196: 129–36.

Erfurt-Cooper, P. and Cooper, M. (2009) *Health and Wellness Tourism: Spas and Hot Springs*, Bristol: Channel View Publications.

Frost, G.J. (2004) 'The spa as a model of an optimal healing environment', *The Journal of Alternative and Complementary Medicine*, 10: 85–92.

Gesler, W.M. (2003) *Healing Places*, Lanham, MD: Rowman & Littlefield Publishers.

Goldstein, M.S. (1999) *Alternative health care: medicine, miracle, or mirage?*, Philadelphia, PA: Temple University Press.

Goodrich, J.N. and Goodrich, G.E. (1987) 'Health-care tourism – an exploratory study', *Tourism Management*, 8: 217–22.

Gustavo, N.S. (2011) 'A 21st-century approach to health tourism spas: the case of Portugal', *Journal of Hospitality and Tourism Management*, 17: 127–35.

Hall, C.M. (2003) 'Spa and health tourism', in S. Hudson (ed.) *Sport and Adventure Tourism*, New York: Haworth Hospitality Press.

Hall, D.R. and Brown, F. (2006) *Tourism and Welfare: Ethics, Responsibility, and Sustained Well-being*. Cambridge, MA: CABI.

Hartig, T., Evans, G.W., Jamner, L.D., Davis, D.S. and Garling, T. (2003) 'Tracking restoration in natural and urban field settings', *Journal of Environmental Psychology*, 23: 109–23.

Hattie, J.A., Myers, J.E. and Sweeney, T.J. (2004) 'A factor structure of wellness: theory, assessment, analysis and practice', *Journal of Counselling & Development*, 82: 354–64.

Henderson, J.C. (2004) 'Healthcare tourism in Southeast Asia', *Tourism Review International*, 7: 111–21.

Herzog, T., Maguire, P. and Nebel, M. (2003) 'Assessing the restorative components of environments', *Journal of Environmental Psychology*, 23: 159–70.

Hollenberg, D. (2007) 'How do private CAM therapies affect integrative health care settings in a publicly funded health care system?' *Journal of Complementary and Integrative Medicine*, 4: 1–16.

Hoyez, A.-C. (2007) 'The "world of yoga": the production and reproduction of therapeutic landscapes', *Social Science & Medicine*, 65: 112–24.

Jackson, R. (1990) 'Waters and spas in the classical world', *Medical History*, 10: 1–13.

Jakobsson, A. (2004) 'Ruled by routine and ritual: spatial organization of the spa environment at Ronneby, south-east Sweden', *Garden History*, 32: 213–28.

Joppe, M. (2010) 'One country's transformation to spa destination: the case of Canada', *Journal of Hospitality and Tourism Management*, 17: 117–26.

Kelly, C. (2010) 'Analysing wellness tourism provision: a retreat operators' study', *Journal of Hospitality and Tourism Management*, 17: 108–16.

Kevan, S.K. (1993) 'Quests for cures: a history of tourism for climate and health', *International Journal of Biometeorology*, 37: 113–24.

Keyes, C.L.M. (2002) 'The mental health continuum: from languishing to flourishing in life', *Journal of Health and Social Behavior*, 43: 207–22.

Kickbusch, I. and Payne, L. (2003) 'Twenty-first century health promotion: the public health revolution meets the wellness revolution', *Health Promotion International*, 18: 275–8.

King, L.A., Hicks, J.A., Krull, J.L. and Del Gaiso, A.K. (2006) 'Positive affect and the experience of meaning in life', *Journal of Personality and Social Psychology*, 90: 179–96.

Konu, H. and Laukkanen, T. (2010) 'Predictors of tourists' wellbeing holiday intentions in Finland', *Journal of Hospitality and Tourism Management*, 17: 144–9.

Konu, H., Tuohino, A. and Komppula, R. (2010) 'Lake Wellness: a practical example of a new service development (NSD) concept in tourism industries', *Journal of Vacation Marketing*, 16: 125–39.

Lee, C.-F. and King, B. (2006) 'Assessing destination competitiveness: an application to the hot springs tourism sector', *Tourism and Hospitality Planning & Development*, 3: 179–97.

Leiper, N. (1981) 'Towards a cohesive curriculum in tourism: the case for a distinct discipline', *Annals of Tourism Research*, 8: 69–84.

Lempa, H. (2008) 'The spa: emotional economy and social classes in nineteenth-century Pyrmont', *Central European History*, 35: 37–73.

Letho, X.Y., Brown, S., Chen, Y. and Morrison, A.M. (2006) 'Yoga tourism as a niche within the wellness tourism market', *Tourism Recreation Research*, 31: 25–35.

Maretzki, T.W. (1989) 'Cultural variation in biomedicine: the Kur in West Germany', *Medical Anthropology Quarterly*, 3: 22–35.

McNeil, K. and Ragins, E.J. (2004) 'Staying in the spa marketing game: trends, challenges, strategies and techniques', *Journal of Vacation Marketing*, 11: 31–9.

Müller, H. and Lanz Kaufmann, E. (2001) 'Wellness tourism: market analysis of a special health tourist segment and implications for the hotel industry', *Journal of Vacation Marketing*, 7: 5–17.

Nahrstedt, W. (2004) 'Wellness: a new perspective for leisure centers, health tourism and spas in Europe on the global health market', in K. Weiermair and C. Mathies (eds) *The Tourism and Leisure Industry: Shaping the Future*, New York: Haworth Hospitality Press.

Nettleton, S. (2006) *The Sociology of Health and Illness*, 2nd edition, Cambridge: Polity Press.

O'Connor, B. (2000) 'Conception of the body in complementary and alternative medicine', in M. Kelner, B. Wellman, B. Pescosolido and M. Saks (eds) *Complementary and Alternative Medicine: Challenge and Change*, London: Routledge.

O'Dell, T. (2005) 'Meditation, magic and spiritual regeneration: spas and the mass production of serenity', in O. Löfgren and R. Willim (eds) *Magic, Culture and the New Economy*, Oxford: Berg.

Palmer, R. (1990) ' "In this our lightye and learned tyme": Italian baths in the era of the Renaissance', *Medical History*: 10: 14–22.

Pechlaner, H. and Fischer, E. (2006) 'Alpine Wellness: a resource-based view', *Tourism Recreation Research*, 31: 67–77.

Pender, N.J., Murdaugh, C.L. and Parsons, M.A. (2006) *Health Promotion in Nursing Practice*, 4th edition, Upper Saddle River, NJ: Pearson Education.

Pernecky, T. and Johnston, C. (2006) 'Voyage through numinous space: applying the specialization concept to New Age tourism', *Tourism Recreation Research*, 31: 37–46.

Pollock, A. and Williams, P. (2000) 'Health tourism trends: closing the gap between health care and tourism', in D.W. Lime and W.C. Gartner (eds) *Trends in Outdoor Recreation, Leisure and Tourism*, New York: CABI.

Puczkó, L. and Bachvarov, M. (2006) 'Spa, bath, thermae: what's behind the labels', *Tourism Recreation Research*, 31: 83–91.

Ritchie, J.R.B. and Crouch, G.I. (2003) *The Competitive Destination: A Sustainable Tourism Perspective*, Wallingford: CABI.

Ritter, S. (2005) 'Trends and skills needed in the tourism sector: "tourism for wellness" ', in O. Strietska-Ilina and M. Tessaring (eds) *Trends and Skill Needs in Tourism*, Luxembourg: Office for Official Publications of the European Communities.

Ryan, R.M. and Deci, E.L. (2001) 'On happiness and human potentials: a review of research on hedonic and eudaimonic well-being', *Annual Review of Psychology*, 52: 141–66.

Schobersberger, W., Greie, S. and Humpeler, E. (2004) 'Alpine health tourism: future prospects from a medical perspective', in K. Weiermair and C. Mathies (eds) *The Tourism and Leisure Industry: Shaping the Future*, New York: Haworth Hospitality Press.

Sheldon, P.J. and Bushell, R. (2009) 'Introduction to wellness and tourism', in R. Bushell and P.J. Sheldon (eds) *Wellness and Tourism: Mind, Body, Spirit, Place*, New York: Cognizant Communication Corporation.

Sheldon, P.J. and Park S.-Y. (2009) 'Development of a sustainable wellness destination', in R. Bushell and P.J. Sheldon (eds) *Wellness and Tourism: Mind, Body, Spirit, Place*, New York: Cognizant Communication Corporation.

Simpson, J.A. and Weiner, E.S.C. (1989) 'Wellness', in J.A. Simpson and E.S.C. Weiner (eds) *The Oxford English Dictionary*, 2nd edition, Vol. 11, Oxford: Clarendon Press.

Smith, M. and Kelly, C. (2006a) 'Wellness tourism', *Tourism Recreation Research*, 31: 1–4.

Smith, M. and Kelly, C. (2006b) 'Holistic tourism: journeys of the self?', *Tourism Recreation Research*, 31: 15–24.

Smith, M. and Puczkó, L. (2009) *Health and Wellness Tourism*, Oxford: Butterworth-Heinemann.

Speier, A.R. (2011) 'Health tourism in a Czech health spa', *Anthropology & Medicine*, 18: 55–66.

Steiner, C.J. and Reisinger, Y. (2006) 'Ringing the fourfold: a philosophical framework for thinking about wellness tourism', *Tourism Recreation Research*, 31: 5–14.

Steward, J. (2002) 'The culture of water cure in nineteenth-century Austria, 1800–1914', in S. Anderson and B. Tabbs (eds) *Water, Leisure and Culture: European Historical Perspectives*, Oxford: Berg.

Strang, V. (2004) *The Meaning of Water*, Oxford: Berg.

TOHWS (The Tourism Observatory for Health, Wellness and Spa) (2012) *4WR: Wellness for Whom, Where and What? Wellness Tourism 2020*, Budapest: Xellum Ltd/Hungarian National Tourism plc.

Travis, J.W. and Ryan, R.S. (1988) *The Wellness Workbook*, 2nd edition, Berkeley, CA: Ten Speed Press.

Voigt, C. (2010) 'Understanding wellness tourism: an analysis of benefits sought, health-promoting behaviours and positive psychological well-being', unpublished thesis, University of South Australia.

Voigt, C. and Laing, J. (2010) 'The structure of Australian wellness tourism providers: definition, typology and current status', paper presented at the *Travel and Tourism Research Association (TTRA) European Chapter Conference*, Budapest, Hungary, 1–3 September.

Voigt, C. and Laing, J. (2013) 'A way through the maze: exploring differences and overlaps between wellness and medical tourism providers', in D. Botterill, G. Pennings and T. Mainil (eds) *Medical Tourism and Transnational Health Care*, Basingstoke: Palgrave Macmillan.

Voigt, C., Brown, G. and Howat, G. (2011) 'Wellness tourists: in search for transformation', *Tourism Review*, 66: 16–30.

Voigt, C., Howat, G. and Brown, G. (2010a) 'Hedonic and eudaimonic experiences among wellness tourists: an exploratory enquiry', *Annals of Leisure Research*, 13: 541–62.

Voigt, C., Laing, J., Wray, M., Brown, G., Howat, G., Weiler, B. and Trembath, R. (eds) (2010b) *Wellness and Medical Tourism in Australia: Supply, Demand and Opportunities*, Gold Coast: CRC for Sustainable Tourism.

Weisz, G. (2001) 'Spas, mineral waters, and hydrological science in twentieth-century France', *Isis*, 92: 451–83.

Weisz, G. (2011) 'Historical reflections on medical travel', *Anthropology & Medicine*, 18: 137–44.

WHO (1948) *Preamble to the Constitution of the World Health Organization as adopted by the International Health Conference*, New York: WHO.

3 Wellness tourism and destination competitiveness

Bruce Prideaux, Delphine Berbigier and Michelle Thompson

Introduction

Destinations are a key building block for the tourism experience and may be described in a number of ways. Scott *et al.* (2008), for example, describe destinations as comprising a network of loosely clustered organisations. From a supply-side perspective this description highlights the organisations that operate within a destination and which, through a process of collaboration and competition, build and market a range of experiences that are offered for sale or consumption by tourists. The system through which this process occurs may be termed the *destination system*. From a demand-side perspective this view of a destination highlights the role of experiences that are sought by tourists. Ultimately the destination system must provide a channel that allows for the creation of products, their promotion, sale and their consumption through a process that brings the buyer (the tourist) and the seller (the organisations that provide tourism goods and services) together in a destination marketplace. Destination success is judged on the ability of this process to meet or exceed tourist expectations. Tourism demand is dynamic, creating new consumer markets and changing others. This process also creates a regular churn in product and experience offerings as new products emerge and others decline. From a destination perspective, a key objective should be to establish mechanisms that allow for early identification of change in demand for new products and experiences, a process described in the Evolved Strategic Window of Opportunity Model (see Figure 3.3). These forces can also be seen in the growing demand for wellness-related products. As Voigt (see Chapter 2 in this volume) reminds us, health-related tourism, of which wellness is a core element, has a long history of growth and decline. The recent re-emergence of demand for wellness experiences has presented destinations with a new opportunity to develop innovative products in this area. The discussion in the remainder of this chapter explores key issues related to developing competitiveness in wellness destinations.

One of the key strategies to ensure the long-term success of a tourism destination is to build and maintain a high level of competitiveness (Richie and Crouch 2003) in the markets that best match the resources the destination is able to offer. To understand how destinations may enhance competitiveness, in this case in the wellness sector, the chapter will investigate the factors that enable destinations to utilise competitive and comparative advantages in product development, sale and consumption. The chapter commences with a brief review of the factors that collectively define a destination and how it operates, followed by a discussion that draws on a framework (Figure 3.1) of three linked models to illustrate how competitiveness can be maintained in the long term. The chapter then examines aspects of destination competitiveness in the wellness sector using two case studies.

The concept of competitiveness

To enable a destination perspective wellness in this chapter is described more broadly than suggested by Voigt (see Chapter 2 in this volume). Here, wellness tourism is understood as the sum of all the experiences located within the destination that promote health and wellbeing, including holistic enhancement of tourists' physical, psychological, spiritual and/or social wellbeing. At a destination level wellness tourism has two distinct elements; the supply-side, which includes physical resources such as mineralised waters, facilities that offer wellness experiences, general tourism-related facilities including airports, hotels, retail and entertainment, specialist staff who deliver wellness services and organisations that promote the destination; and, the demand-side consisting of the visitors who pay to use these facilities and the services they offer.

Competitiveness is a key element in destination success (Dwyer *et al.* 2000) and from a destination perspective can be described in a number of ways based on metrics such as profitability, visitor numbers, growth in bed nights, investment and yield or in terms of its comparative and completive advantages. Dwyer and Kim (2003: 373) note that while an extensive literature has developed on this topic a clear definition and model has yet to emerge and commented 'it is a complex concept because a whole range of factors account for it. Competitiveness is both a *relative* concept (i.e. compared to what?) and is *multi-dimensional* (i.e. what are the salient attributes or qualities of competitiveness)'(original emphasis).

Hassan (2000: 239) defined competitiveness as 'the destination's ability to create and integrate value-added products that sustain its resources while maintaining market position relative to competitors'. Ritchie and Crouch (2000: 5) added the need for sustainability stating that 'competitiveness is illusory without sustainability'. From a destination perspective competitiveness in its most basic form can be described as the ability of a destination to identify its key selling propositions, identify markets that are likely to purchase these propositions, create a market space where these products are able to be purchased and to maintain this process over a long period of time and in a manner that is sustainable. Given the evolving nature of markets driven by continually changing consumer demand and innovations, destinations must embrace a process of continual evaluation of existing markets, ongoing external scanning for new markets and frequent re-evaluation of every aspect of their products if a competitive position is to be retained. Continuing competitiveness relies on a destination, as a collective entity, being able to recognise and respond to changes of this nature. Should opportunities of this nature not be recognised the destination may face a long period of decline as its largest markets look for alternative destinations able to supply them with the experiences they seek. Wellness tourism provides an example of the many new opportunities that have emerged in recent decades (Messerli and Oyama 2004). Twenty years ago wellness was not a term commonly found in the lexicon of the tourism sector. Today wellness has evolved into a range of products and experiences, ranging from those offered by medical tourism providers to wellness providers that include beauty spa resorts, lifestyle resort and spiritual retreats.

In the general economic literature considerable emphasis has been placed on *competitive* advantage which can be described as value-adding activities by firms. In this case firms collectively produce experiences in a destination setting while less emphasis has been placed on comparative advantage. According to Dwyer and Kim (2003: 373) the debate in the literature is characterised by 'de-emphasising *comparative* advantage as a source of international competitiveness' (original emphasis). From a tourism perspective, however, comparative advantage is a fundamental concept that relates to a range of resources available at the destination including scenery, wildlife, protected areas, heritage, infrastructure, organisations that promote the destination, events and festivals, workforce skills and government policy. In a tourism setting 'comparative advantage' describes the resources the destination has to offer while 'competitive advantage' describes how resources are used in the production of products and experiences to create a destination experience perceived by consumers to be better than its competitors and able to meet customer expectations. Specific resources that may affect a destination's comparative advantage in the wellness sector may include mineralised waters, thermal waters, specific firms that offer wellness products and the trained staff who are employed by these firms. Thus, a destination with a comparative advantage in one area of its product offerings may not be competitive because it has failed to achieve a competitive advantage. In a wellness context, a destination that has access to mineralised waters but has failed to develop wellness products has a latent comparative advantage but no competitive advantage. In contrast, a destination may lack a comparative advantage based on organic resources but can create a competitive advantage by 'buying in' resources and value-adding to them.

Before further exploring the idea of competitiveness it is first necessary to understand the factors that together create a destination and govern how it operates. Prideaux (2009: 8) observed that destinations 'are complicated structures, built from a fusion of natural resources, the intellectual capacity of its residents, investors, the workforce, political structures, governance arrangements, residents and the visitors it receives'. Thus, destinations utilise a range of physical, intellectual and financial resources within the applicable political system to create a tourism product that is sold to consumers via a distribution system.

Based on the physical and operational structures that emerge from the fusion of the many components outlined above, the destination, through its Destination Marketing Organisation (DMO), will seek to develop a destination image that, with associated brand and logo(s), defines its key selling propositions (Buhalis 2000). It is the image, brand and logos generally conveyed through the media that allow consumers, and the travel trade, to develop perceptions that in turn inform the consumer during their destination selection process (Tasci and Kozac 2006; Morgan *et al.* 2002). Of course, and as will be demonstrated in Figure 3.4, consumer perceptions are influenced by many other factors that are beyond the control of the DMO, including wider political events, disasters, climate and so on (Murphy *et al.* 2000).

Developing destination competitiveness

The ability of any destination to retain competitiveness in national and international marketplaces relies on a range of factors including a positive destination image, the quality of products and experiences on offer, how successfully it is in enticing tourists to select it from the many alternatives available, its ability to compete with a range of other goods and services that vie for the consumers' disposable income and how it is able to surmount any political or geographic impediments. As Buhalis (2000) reminds us, destinations are not able to match all forms of demand and as a consequence must either focus on specific geographic markets and/or focus on specific market subsets. Researchers (e.g. Richie and Crouch 2003) have suggested a number of factors that affect destination competitiveness, including:

- destination image – ideas and impressions of a place that are available for consumption by consumers (Branwell and Rawding 1996);
- psychological distance – perceived distance between the destination and the consumer;
- comparative advantage – i.e. human resources, physical resources, size of economy;
- competitive advantage – i.e. efficiency, effectiveness, value-added;
- destination management – including organisation, marketing, visitor management, crisis management;
- core resources and attractions – i.e. culture, climate, special events, entertainment; and
- support factors and resources – i.e. infrastructure, enterprise, accessibility, political will.

To these may be added internal factors that shape the destination and its products including guest/host relations, responsiveness of the business sector to new ideas and demands, support from the political sector, innovativeness of destination businesses, organisation of promotional bodies, capacity and health of infrastructure and the life-cycle position of its main attractions. Furthermore, there are external forces that affect development, include generating markets, current level of competitiveness based on current exchange rates, attractiveness to investors, transport infrastructure, media commentaries and international political and security issues.

Each of these are important elements that collectively define the level of competitiveness of each destination relative to its competitors. One of the factors identified by Richie and Crouch (2003) is the role of price which is a major but not the only element of competitiveness and may or may not be a major element in the consumer's final destination choice. Competitiveness also includes both tangible (such as the quality of attractions and hotels) and intangible (consumer's perceptions of destination quality) factors.

A destination's resources base and its location relative to its main markets are also important determinates of competiveness. Resources include a wide range of factors such as landscapes, cultural attractions, built resources and human resources. Collectively these determine the type of products that can be offered and the opportunities that are available for value-adding. Within the resource base it is often possible to identify resources that have yet to be developed, others that may be overdeveloped and finally resources directed to inefficient uses. Location is also important because ease of access reduces costs and time of travel. As a number of researchers have pointed out (e.g. Hall and Boyd 2005) destinations located on the periphery face a relative disadvantage compared to destinations that are located near to their main markets.

Another element of destination competitiveness is related to the physical and psychological size of the destination. There is no hard and fast rule that determines the physical size of destinations, which can range in size from a small coastal island to country size in area. In most cases the definition of size is a product of the supply-side as it develops a destination product range and to some extent the demand-side based on location relative to the destination and their familiarity with it. Physical size may or may not be a factor. For example Macau, a former Portuguese enclave at the mouth of the Pearl River in China, had very little presence in the international marketplace prior to its handing back to China in 1999. After regaining control the Chinese government designated Macau as a Special Economic Zone and authorised the Macau Administration to greatly expand its gambling industry. Within a decade, Macau had emerged as the world's largest gambling destination. Psychological distance may also be an important factor in developing a destination's presence in the marketplace. Prior to its development as a major international gambling destination Macau could be described as occupying a psychologically distant place in the mind of Chinese gamblers but as its gambling sector grew the sense of distance retreated encouraging even greater interest in the destination.

Future drivers of competitiveness

Competitiveness once gained cannot be assumed to be retained over the long term. Numerous forces in the external as well as the internal destination environment have the potential to affect the level of competitiveness in the future and need to be continually monitored. The following are a range of factors that create change and in so doing have the ability to alter a destination's level of competitiveness. While not in any way exhaustive the following list illustrates the range of factors that impact on destination competitiveness. Although listed separately, many of these factors are indeed interrelated.

- Innovation. Probably the most powerful of all forces of change, innovation has created new technologies and provided the basis for economic growth that has underpinned the rapid growth in tourism since the second half of the twentieth century.
- Technology. New technologies such as the internet have fundamentally changed many aspects of the tourism industry. Recent examples include electronic sales of airline seats and online hotel bookings.
- The growth of the service economy. Economies that have transitioned from manufacturing to service dominated have become key generators for new tourism demand.
- World economic growth. Increasing global GDP has underpinned the rapid growth of tourism in the last 60 years. Rapid economic growth in China, for example, has added tens and will in the future add hundreds of millions new tourists. Further growth in India and Latin America will accentuate this process.
- Increasing number and variety of destinations. An outcome of the factors outlined above, new destinations have stimulated competition and offer consumers a wider choice of destinations to select from.
- Future factors. In the near future climate change, and it consequences, will force a radical redefining of the manner in which economies operate. This in turn will have a significant impact on the tourism industry, how it is organised and will operate (Gössling *et al.* 2010).
- Changing consumer demands. Consumer demand is never static and is often driven by changes in taste, fashion, new technologies and style.
- Political realignment. The collapse of the former USSR in 1989, for example, opened enormous opportunities for travel by Russian citizens. Reforms in China have had a similar effect.
- Unplanned crises and disasters (e.g. tsunamis, volcanic eruptions, global financial crises, pandemics). Crises of the nature of the recent global financial crisis have the potential to exercise significant short-term impacts on travel patterns. Largely unpredictable, crises will continue to impact on destination competitiveness in the future.

Collectively, these and other factors have a significant impact on demand for tourism services and the ongoing competitiveness of destinations supplying these services.

Changes in consumer demands

At the consumer level the impact of the forces of change outlined above will continue to shape and reshape consumer demand for tourism products and experiences.

Consumer demand is influenced by a range of drivers including technology, the rate at which technology is adopted, personal incomes, the opportunity to travel based on annual holidays and family commitments, personal preferences, life-cycle position and generation membership, and issues relating to the global economy and global security. The number of influences is potentially enormous and only a small number of potential changes are highlighted. One factor underlying rapid change in consumer demand is the willingness of consumers to accept that change is a normal condition of life and not something to resist. This acceptance creates a consumer mindset that welcomes rather than resists change, and in many cases a mindset that seeks out and embraces change. Another significant factor driving changes in consumer demand is generation membership (Glover and Prideaux 2009). For example, travel by post-war Baby Boomers has defined travel demand for some time and to some extent made travel fashionable. However, the Baby Boomer generation is rapidly ageing and while continuing to travel in very large numbers will eventually be replaced by members of Generation X and Generation Y. New generations of tourists will have different travel consumption demands forcing the tourism industry to manage a long period of generational change. Destinations that recognise this aspect of the contemporary consumer will be able to innovate and remain competitive; those that do not will experience reduced competitiveness.

Modelling change

Figure 3.1 brings together three models in a linked framework to explain a range of the forces that affect destination competitiveness. The approach taken here differs from that taken by Ritchie and Crouch (2003) in that it places a greater emphasis on the need for constant vigilance of changes in consumer perceptions and for new markets that have or are about to emerge. The framework has as its anchor the demand and elements of the Push–Pull Model (Figure 3.2) and plugs in new market opportunities (Figure 3.3) and changes in consumer perspectives (Figure 3.4) to illustrate the dynamic consumer and market forces that affect the relationship between demand and supply. In Figure 3.1 changes in consumer perceptions drive both the opportunities for new markets and changes to the demand and supply relationships within the destination (Figure 3.2). After outlining the function of each model the discussion will show how collectively they represent the dynamic and evolutional forces that operate in destinations and have a significant impact on long-term demand.

At its most basic level, a destination will only succeed if it has a product that it can sell. One of the simplest yet most effective models to explain this relationship is the Push–Pull Model. The Push–Pull Model (Usal and Jurowski 1994; Dann 1977; Crompton 1979) provides a useful method to explain, and measure, the various factors that *push* tourists to engage in travel and the factors that a destination uses to *pull*, or attract, tourists to its suite of experiences and products. In this way destinations are able to match the destination's supply propositions with consumer demand propositions. The significance of the Push–Pull Model is that it provides destinations with a useful inventory of the factors that

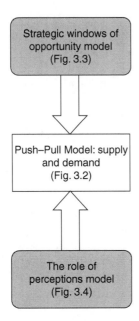

Figure 3.1 Framework explaining destination competitiveness.

stimulate travel by various groups of tourists and provides the opportunity to identify the specific attributes that should be promoted to attract tourism segments. From a destination perspective a key element in maintaining competitiveness is developing a positive destination image based on positive perceptions that the destination will meet consumer expectations and offer an exceptional holiday experience. However, the ability to match push and pull factors is not always as straightforward as it is illustrated in Figure 3.1. Various factors (e.g. access, language barriers, visa restrictions) may inhibit a destination from taking full advantage of its pull factors. From time to time other factors, termed 'repelling factors' (political unrest for example) will also reduce the ability of a destination to exploit the push attributes of various markets. Collectively, inhibiting and repelling factors may generate poor perceptions that will distract the consumer from the other positive factors a destination is able to offer. Managing perceptions is therefore an important element of destination management which will be discussed in more detail later in the chapter. Added to these factors is the influence of competing factors, including other forms of consumer consumption, that also vie for the consumer dollar.

The six step Evolved Strategic Window of Opportunity Model (modified from Prideaux *et al.* 2012) outlined in Figure 3.3 highlights how a destination can proactively utilise environmental scanning or similar tools, to identify new markets that, based on the destination's suite of pull factors, offer a strategic window of opportunity for new product and experience development. A strategic

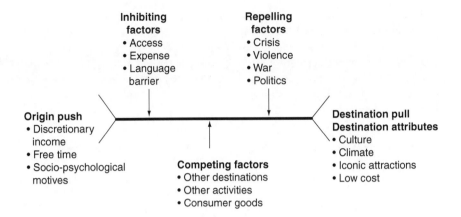

Figure 3.2 The Enhanced Push–Pull Model.

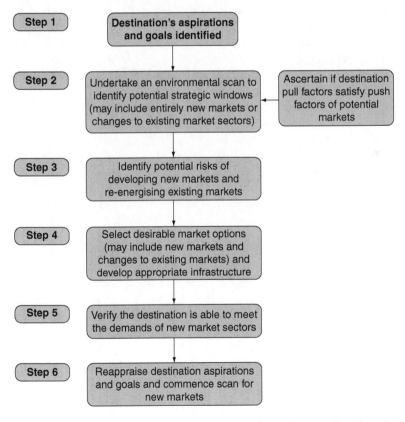

Figure 3.3 Evolved Strategic Window of Opportunity Model (modified from Prideaux *et al.* 2012).

window of opportunity is described as a situation where a destination has an opportunity to fit its key skills and/or resources with the needs of a target market (Wilson and Gilligan 2008), thereby offering the destination (or firm) an opportunity to enter new markets. However, to be able to exploit an identified strategic window, a destination has to first recognise that a strategic window has opened (Stahl and Grigsby 2001; Hunger and Wheelen 2003). This does not always occur.

As the discussion on push–pull factors and strategic windows has demonstrated, destinations need to be proactive in creating tourism products, identifying new markets and maintaining their level of competitiveness. A third model illustrated in Figure 3.4 is used to amplify the previous discussion and illustrate another important element of competitiveness. As Liu (2003) has noted, perceptions play an important part in creating demand for specific tourism products and experiences. Perceptions, here described as those ideas or beliefs people have of a destination, are dynamic and subject to rapid change (Leisen 2001). The model also highlights the role of external and internal factors, and the media in shaping consumer perceptions which generate new expectations. Perceptions are influenced directly and indirectly by the consumer's first-hand experiences; destination marketing and promotional information disseminated by the tourism industry; information filtered through the media; and from other sources such as the word-of-mouth of friends and relatives and social media (e.g. TripAdvisor or Facebook). Whether perceptions are influenced positively or negatively depends on how the message was received by consumers, the source of the information (within or outside of the industry), and the perceived reliability of the information source (Baloglu and McCleary 1999). For example, internally the manner in which the destination organises and delivers wellness products will influence consumer satisfaction (Chen *et al.* 2008). The media acts as a filter for both external and internal factors and has significant potential to assist in this process through positive stories in travel reviews. The model recognises two key elements that influence perceptions, the *level of control* over perceptions able to be exercised by the destination and shown as the y axis, and *time* represented by the x axis.

Compared to internal factors, the destination has little control over the external factors that generate perceptions (Hankinson 2004). For example, where a destination may be able to identify and manage internal factors such as training, marketing and product development, it has relatively little or no control over visitors' motivations, or global issues such as climate change and natural disasters. To gain, and retain, a competitive advantage in the wellness sector, and influence the perceptions of potential tourists, destinations that market wellness products need to focus on marketing and promoting directly to target markets, through print, electronic and social media, and addressing concerns about external factors where possible.

The advantage of linking models in this manner (see Figure 3.1) is that the researcher is able to bring together multiple perspectives to bear on the subject under investigation and in this way can have a richer understanding of the factors

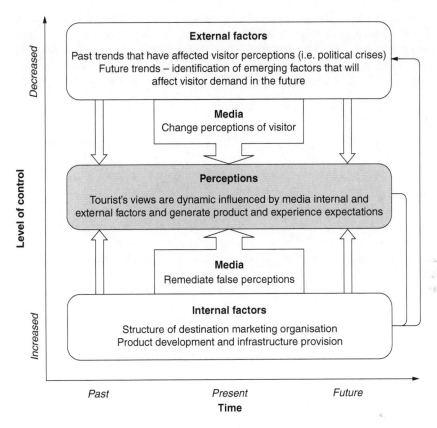

Figure 3.4 The role of external and internal factors in creating tourists' perceptions (source: Michelle Thompson).

being investigated. While only three models are used here there is potential to employ other related models to enhance our understanding of the plethora of dynamic forces that influence the destination system. As the following case studies demonstrate, wellness destinations that understand how the factors outlined in the Models Framework are interlinked will have a significant advantage over other destinations attempting to develop or retain their wellness sectors.

Case studies

Two case studies demonstrate how the Models Framework may be applied to understand destination competitiveness. In this case the two elements of destination competitiveness examined are comparative and competitive advantages and how these impact on product development and image formulation in destinations that offer a wellness product. The first case looks at the Indian state of Kerala and examines how it has been able to use its comparative advantage in traditional medicine to develop both a comparative and a competitive advantage in wellness products. The second example examines how Palm Cove, the self-proclaimed Spa Capital of Australia, has been able to overcome the lack of physical resources that are normally related to spa resorts and develop a comparative advantage at least in the Australian market for spa experiences.

Kerala

The traditional vision of wellness based on health has been used by the Indian state of Kerala to develop an internationally recognised wellness product based on Ayurveda, a system of traditional Indian medicine. Ayurveda originated in India at least 2,000 years ago (Hannam 2009) and is based on the belief that health relies on a balance of three humours, or elements, namely *vatha* (wind/air), *pitha* (fire), and *kapha* (water/earth) (Hannam 2009). Ailments are considered an imbalance of these elements, thus Ayurvedic treatments focus on restoring balance through massages, diet and lifestyle changes, among other approaches.

Kerala was one of the first Indian destinations to recognise that the emerging market for wellness products had created a strategic window of opportunity which offered the potential to turn the state's comparative advantage based on existing resources into a competitive advantage. To leverage the opportunity that had become available the state launched a strategy to develop its product base and market its wellness products domestically and abroad. The promotion of Ayurveda became the central theme in its destination branding (Hannam 2009; Dasgupta 2011). Largely unknown as a tourism destination until the 1980s, the state government proclaimed tourism as a major industry sector in 1986 and funded a successful branding campaign throughout the 1990s. The campaign raised awareness both domestically and internationally and was able to capitalise on growing consumer perceptions that wellness-related products offered opportunities to improve personal health and happiness. As a consequence of the branding campaign the state was able to attract significant private sector investment in tourism in addition to public sector investment and to position the state as an international destination. Aside from wellness tourism the state's major attractions are hill stations, beaches, heritage and nature-based tourism experiences. Competitive prices, access to international markets via three international airports and successful exploitation of other tourism resources have enabled the state to develop a major presence in the international tourism industry. The wellness tourism sector has been able to build on these resources and the state's positive international image to create a sector that draws its clients from both domestic and international sources. Kerala Tourism, funded by the State Department of Tourism, operates an accreditation system for operators providing Ayurveda services. As of January 2013 Kerala Tourism had accredited 103 Ayurveda providers ranging from hospitals to hotels and resorts. The scale of the Ayurveda sector is significant and according to the official website of Kerala Tourism there are over

12,000 Ayurveda doctors practicing in the state. In addition, there are over 100 government-run Ayurveda hospitals with 2,700 beds and about 750 dispensaries offering Ayurveda medicines (Kerala Tourism 2013).

Kerala's success in developing a reputation for wellness tourism is a good example of how a destination can turn its comparative advantages, in this case based on natural resources and traditional medicine, and growing consumer perceptions that wellness products offer a significant health advantage, into a powerful competitive advantage. It also confirms the need to constantly monitor the external environment for new opportunities, to understand the role of customer perceptions as a fundamental force influencing demand and the necessity of continually adjusting the destination's pull factors to meet changing customer push factors.

Palm Cove

Palm Cove, a beach-front sub-destination located in northern Australia is a good example of a destination that, while not having a comparative advantage in traditional forms of wellness resources, has been able to develop a strong wellness product based on day spas. In effect the destination has replaced experiences based on tradition medicine, mineral waters and hot springs with products based on skilled staff who offer a range of wellness experiences in up-market resort settings.

Palm Cove emerged in the 1990s as a destination able to offer a warm year round climate, access to rainforests and the Great Barrier Reef, and a beach-front location. The local government authority encouraged the construction of up-market resort properties that blended into the area's natural vegetation with capped building heights of three storeys. The result was a destination that successfully utilised its comparative advantages of landscape, position and climate to build a destination experience that had considerable appeal in the US and European markets.

In the early 2000s many of the destination's hotels and resorts recognised that the growth in demand for wellness products offered a window of opportunity and began investing in day spas that offered lifestyle and beauty products. The destination was able to overcome its lack of natural wellness-related resources by basing its products on purpose-built therapy facilities and human skills. The destination's wellness providers also recognised that to retain their level of competitiveness they needed to constantly monitor changes in customer perceptions and expectations to guide them in changes to the range of wellness products offered. Compared to the wellness products offered in Kerala, those offered in Palm Cove are designed to appeal to the lifestyle and beauty sector of the wellness market, not the medical sector of wellness.

Together, the Kerala and Palm Cove case studies represent the two contrasting types of health tourism providers illustrated in Figure 2.1 of this book. Palm Cove can be classed as a pure wellness tourism destination while Kerala can be classed as an example of a pure medical tourism provider though in the case of

Kerala the broadening of its product base to embrace lifestyle and spirituality has slowly moved it towards the overlap position postulated in Figure 2.1. Both cases also indicated how consistent monitoring of changes in consumer expectations are reflected in changes in consumer demand and how changes of this nature offer opportunities to develop new products.

Discussion and conclusion

The objective of this chapter was to explore aspects of destination competitiveness and how this may affect the ability of destinations to develop various wellness products. As part of the discussion the chapter demonstrated how linking a number of models is able to provide a more comprehensive understanding of the relationships that operate and how they are interlinked. At its most basic level competitiveness refers to the ability of a destination to successfully attract tourists over time in a marketplace where numerous other destinations are competing for the same or similar target markets. At first glance managing competitiveness appears relatively straightforward; however, this is far from the case. Competitiveness is not only linked to opportunities for growth. A failure to retain competitiveness can quickly lead to destination decline.

The chapter has also demonstrated that comparative advantage does not necessarily confer a competitive advantage on a destination. Rather, it is the manner in which destination resources are used that will determine the level of competitiveness. As the Palm Cove example has highlighted a destination that lacks a comparative advantage in key wellness resources such as mineralised water may not be competitive in all areas of wellness but may be able to develop product offerings in areas of the wellness market that lie in the lifestyle and beauty spa resorts end of the wellness product spectrum.

From a consumer perspective, competitiveness refers to the attractiveness of one destination relative to all other destinations based on a set of personal criteria (e.g. price, travel time, attractions) and the ability of the destination to offer specific products that appeal to tourists. As the chapter has demonstrated, consumer demand is dynamic and influenced by changes in consumer perceptions. Destination competitiveness is therefore a function of matching consumer demand with appropriate supply, understanding the dynamic nature of this interaction and, through understanding how changes in consumer perceptions open new opportunities and close others, developing a suite of appropriate products. The ability of destinations to maximise the opportunities afforded to them by this process is in part a function of their ability to utilise appropriate models and concepts such as comparative and competitive advantage.

References

Baloglu, S. and McCleary, K.W. (1999) 'A model of destination image formation', *Annals of Tourism Research*, 26: 868–97.
Branwell, B. and Rawding, L. (1996) 'Tourism marketing images of industrial cities', *Annals of Tourism Research*, 23: 201–21.

Buhalis, D. (2000) 'Marketing the competitive destination of the future', *Tourism Management*, 21: 97–116.

Chen, C., Chen, S. and Lee, H. (2011) 'The destination competitiveness of Kinmen's tourism industry: exploring the interrelationships between tourist perceptions, service performance, customer satisfaction and sustainable tourism', *Journal of Sustainable Tourism*, 19: 247–64, online, available at: http://dx.doi.org/10.1080/ 09669582.2010.517315 (accessed 16 February 2013).

Crompton, J. (1979) 'Motivations for pleasure vacation', *Annals of Tourism Research*, 6: 408–24.

Dann, G. (1977) 'Anomie, ego-enhancement and tourism', *Annals of Tourism Research*, 4: 184–94.

Dasgupta, D. (2011) *Tourism Marketing*, India: Pearson Education.

Dwyer, L. and Kim, C. (2003) 'Destination competitiveness: determinants and indicators', *Current Issues in Tourism*, 6: 369–414.

Dwyer, L., Forsyth, P. and Rao, P. (2000) 'The price competitiveness of travel and tourism: a comparison of 19 destinations', *Tourism Management*, 21: 9–22.

Glover, P. and Prideaux, B. (2009) 'Implications of population ageing for the development of tourism products and destinations', *Journal of Vacation Marketing*, 15: 25–37.

Gössling, S., Hall, C.M., Peeters, P. and Scott, D. (2010) 'The future of tourism: a climate change mitigation perspective', *Tourism Recreation Research*, 35: 119–30.

Hall, C.M. and Boyd, S. (2005) 'Nature based tourism in peripheral area: introduction', in C.M. Hall and D. Boyd (eds) *Nature-Based Tourism in Peripheral Areas: Development or Disaster*, Clevedon: Channel View.

Hankinson, G. (2004) 'The brand images of tourism destinations: a study of the saliency of organic images', *Journal of Product & Brand Management*, 13: 6–14, online. available at: http://dx.doi.org/10.1108/10610420410523803 (accessed 16 February 2013).

Hannam, K. (2009) 'Ayurvedic health tourism in Kerala, India', in M.K. Smith and L. Puczkó (eds) *Health and Wellness Tourism*, Amsterdam: Elsevier/Butterworth-Heinemann.

Hassan, S. (2000) 'Determinants of market competitiveness in an environmentally sustainable tourism industry', *Journal of Travel Research*, 38: 239–45.

Hunger, J. and Wheelen, T. (2003) *Essentials of Strategic Management*, 3rd edition, Boston, MA: Addison-Wesley.

Kerala Tourism (2013) Official website, Department of Tourism, Government of Kerala, India, online, available at: www.keralatourism.org (accessed 18 January 2013).

Leisen, B. (2001) 'Image segmentation: the case of a tourism destination', *Journal of Services Marketing*, 15: 49–66, online, available at: http://dx.doi.org/10.1108/ 08876040110381517 (accessed 17 February 2013).

Liu, Z. (2003) 'Sustainable tourism development: a critique', *Journal of Sustainable Tourism*, 11: 459–75, online, available at: http://dx.doi.org/10.1080/ 09669580308667216 (accessed 17 February 2013).

Messerli, H. and Oyama, Y. (2004) 'Health and wellness tourism – global', *Travel and Tourism Analysis*, 4: 1–54.

Morgan, N., Pritchard, A. and Piggott, R. (2002) 'New Zealand, 100% pure: the creation of a powerful niche destination brand', *Journal of Brand Management*, 9: 335–54.

Murphy, P., Pritchard, M. and Smith, B. (2000) 'The destination product and its impact on traveller perceptions', *Tourism Management*, 21: 43–52.

Prideaux, B. (2009) *Resort Destinations: Evolution, Management and Development*, Oxford: Butterworth-Heinemann.

Prideaux, B., Cave, J., Thompson, M. and Sibtain, J. (2012) 'Recognising new market opportunities and selecting appropriate segments: targeting Chinese outbound tourists', *Journal of Vacation Marketing*, 18: 287–99, online, available at: http://dx.doi.org/10.1177/1356766712461102 (accessed 17 February 2013).

Ritchie, J.R.B. and Crouch, G.I. (2000) 'The competitive destination: a sustainability perspective', *Tourism Management*, 21: 1–7.

Ritchie, J.R.B. and Crouch, G.I. (2003) *The Competitive Destination: A Sustainable Tourism Perspective*, Wallingford: CABI.

Scott, N., Baggio, R. and Cooper, C. (2008) *Network Analysis and Tourism: From Theory to Practice*, Clevedon: Channel View.

Stahl, M. and Grigsby, D. (2001) *Strategic Management: Total Quality and Global Competition*, Oxford: Blackwell Publishers.

Tasci, A.D.A. and Kozac, M. (2006) 'Destination brands vs destination images: do we know what we mean?' *Journal of Vacation Marketing*, 12: 299–317.

Usal, M. and Jurowski, C. (1994) 'Test the push and pull factors', *Annals of Tourism Research*, 21: 844–6.

Wilson, R.M.S. and Gilligan, C. (2008) *Strategic Marketing Management: Planning, Implementation and Control*, 3rd edition, Oxford: Butterworth-Heinemann.

Part II

The role of stakeholders in wellness tourism destinations

4 An examination of the extent of collaboration between major wellness tourism stakeholders in Australia

Cornelia Voigt and Jennifer Laing

Introduction

Worldwide, wellness tourism represents one of the fastest growing tourist niche markets and competition between wellness tourism destinations is growing fiercer. Destinations rather than single businesses increasingly compete to attract tourists. A destination can be understood as a complex network of more or less interdependent private and public stakeholders (e.g. Baggio *et al.* 2010). The importance of stakeholder collaboration in attaining or maintaining destination competitiveness has been progressively emphasised in the tourism literature. This chapter examines stakeholders that play a crucial role in the supply (i.e. development, marketing and management) of the actual wellness tourism product and the extent to which they collaborate. Australia is the geographic focus of this chapter and the analysis will be based on qualitative and quant-itative data from a nationwide scoping study of Australian wellness and medical tourism (Voigt *et al.* 2010). A nationwide census database with all Australian wellness tourism operators (N=590) was created. On this basis, a mail-out survey was sent to all operators and 152 surveys were returned. Additionally, 18 in-depth stakeholder interviews were conducted and produced five detailed case studies were produced, which also included site visits and in-depth interviews.

This chapter commences with an overview of tourism stakeholder collaboration and focuses particularly on previous research of wellness tourism development where collaboration was directly or indirectly discussed. It continues by discussing the following major Australian stakeholders of wellness tourism supply: (1) three core types of wellness tourism providers (i.e. beauty spa hotel/resorts, lifestyle resorts and spiritual retreats); (2) federal and state destination management organi-sations (DMOs); (3) wellness industry and accreditation associations; (4) the media; (5) the educational sector; and (6) the mainstream health care sector.

Benefits and challenges of stakeholder collaboration in (wellness) tourism

The tourism sector is heterogeneous and consists of a high percentage of small and medium-sized businesses (SMEs). Within a destination, tourist experiences are created by a bundle of services generally supplied by more than one organisation. Thereby services are not only provided by private, commercial businesses, but also by publically operated information facilities, attractions and infrastructure. For the tourist, the perceived value of his or her experience is a cumulative result of all contacts made with stakeholders at the destination. Consequently, it should be in the interest of all stakeholders to cooperate, because a single business may be only as strong as the weakest link in the value chain in which experiences are co-supplied.

Stakeholders in a destination face the challenge of coordinating their resources and competencies in a way that enables them to supply experiences that outperform alternative destination experiences. Moreover, a collaborative, tightly connected network of tourism stakeholders ideally leads to a sharing of knowledge, competencies, resources and technologies, which in turn are essential prerequisites for innovation at a destination level (Pechlaner et al. 2008). In summary, the fragmented nature of tourism, increasing competition and the need for constant innovation are all powerful arguments in support of researching collaboration between tourism stakeholders. In fact, collaboration has been referred to as a, if not the, key factor for destination competitiveness and long-term survival (Bramwell and Lane 2004; Jackson and Murphy 2006; Pechlaner et al. 2008), as well as an essential factor for competitive wellness tourism destinations (Sheldon and Park 2009).

On this basis, a significant body of tourism literature has paid attention to stakeholder collaboration, networks and tourism clusters (e.g. Jackson and Murphy 2006; Jamal and Getz 1995; Pforr 2006; Sheehan and Ritchie 2005). Although collaboration is not a tightly defined concept, it has been described as 'a process of joint decision-making among autonomous, key stakeholders ... to resolve planning problems ... and/or to manage issues related to the planning and development [of tourism products]' while stakeholders have been defined broadly as 'actors with a common interest in a common problem or issue' (Jamal and Getz 1995: 188). Frequently cited benefits of stakeholder collaboration for all involved partners include:

- cost savings through economies of scale and scope;
- higher quality products through faster communication and a better understanding of the locality;
- the possibility of product innovation and diversification through shared resources and knowledge;
- the possibility of a quicker response to environmental changes;
- enhanced market visibility and global positioning through cross-marketing activities;
- stronger commitment to put agreed upon policies into practice; and
- being more sensitive towards non-economic issues (Bramwell and Lane 2004; Novelli et al. 2006).

The issue of stakeholder collaboration has been discussed directly or indirectly in relation to wellness tourism. Particularly in Europe, where wellness tourism has a long tradition, several efforts have been made to either create wellness tourism destinations, or strengthen their positioning. Most recently, the Nordic Well-Being project explored the possibility of developing a specific Nordic Well-Being brand across five Nordic countries as well as in laboratory areas within each country (Hjalager 2011; Hjalager *et al.* 2011; Huijbens 2011). Another attempt at transnational geographic branding involved an EU-funded project in which two Austrian regions (Styria, Burgenland) as well as Slovenia and Hungary made an effort to collaboratively developing the brand European Spa World (ESW) (Lebe 2006). Through aggressive promotion, the project wanted to position ESW at the heart of quality European wellness tourism. Perhaps the best-known example of transnational collaboration and wellness product development is Alpine Wellness where Alpine regions in Germany, Austria, Switzerland and Italy promote the Alps as a uniquely attractive wellness tourism destination (Pechlaner and Fischer 2006). A final, more regional example, is East Sussex in Great Britain, where the aim was to build a collaborative cluster around the notion of healthy lifestyle as a means of revitalising the earlier concept of spa tourism and collaborating with non-tourism SME businesses – the Healthy Lifestyle Tourism Cluster (HLTC) (Novelli *et al.* 2006).

Stakeholder collaboration in wellness tourism can be difficult, a situation which is also echoed in the generic tourism literature and which will be outlined in the following in more detail. The challenges involved in successful collaboration can be well illustrated with the example of Iceland. While Iceland is not officially marketed as a wellness tourism destination, some tourists may already perceive it as one. This is because there is a long bathing tradition in Iceland and because the geothermal, natural Blue Lagoon spa is one of the most visited Icelandic tourist attractions. However, interviews with entrepreneurs in Mývatn, another Icelandic destination where bathing facilities exist around geothermal steam and water, indicated that entrepreneurs seemed to be unwilling to collaborate to develop a regional or Icelandic brand, let alone a transnational Nordic Well-Being brand (Huijbens 2011). There seems to be a lack of trust and an over-emphasis on rivalry and competition, as well as a lack of a strategic vision and leadership in developing a wellness tourism product among stakeholders in Mývatn (Hjalager *et al.* 2011; Huijbens 2011). Trust issues may intensify when multiple destinations across geographic boundaries are involved. As in Iceland, the four ESW regions share an existing product based on geothermal springs and with the Pannonian basin, they also share the same geographical features. While the ESW was initially successful in developing a brand logo and internet portal, it ultimately failed. Collaboration problems were visible from the outset, consisting of mistrust, language barriers, hostile political systems, strongly varying expectations, and unequal financial participation (Lebe 2006). These challenges are not unique to wellness tourism collaboration though since different levels of power, commitment and values, and disagreement among stakeholders about shared goals and how to split costs and benefits are commonly cited barriers to tourism stakeholder collaboration (Bramwell and Lane 2004; Haugland *et al.* 2011).

Convincing stakeholders to participate and making them recognise that significant benefits will result from cooperation, was also problematic in the British example of the Healthy Lifestyle Tourism Cluster (HLTC). Here, the aim was to achieve collaboration across industry and public sectors (e.g. tourism, agriculture, local government) to package healthy lifestyle products and services.

SMEs often lack time and the managerial capacities necessary for collaboration, which is why there might be a general unwillingness to cooperate (Pechlaner *et al.* 2008). Moreover, tourism researchers coined the term 'lifestyle entrepreneurs' by noting that some SME managers are not motivated by a desire to maximise profits and might even consciously reject economic growth and destination development in favour of ideological values (Ateljevic and Doorne 2000; Shaw 2003). In the case of the above-cited HLTC, keeping stakeholders motivated and convincing them of the value of the project would not have been possible without the provision of infrastructure and the enormous effort of a facilitating steering committee, showing the importance of strong leadership in collaborative endeavours. Adopted joint marketing and enhanced visibility through a brand logo and creation of an internet portal were signs of short-term success of the collaborative initiative. However, this portal does not exist anymore and one can only speculate whether the SMEs were able to achieve the long-term benefit of creating new, innovative products. Nevertheless, the case of the HLTC shows that strong leadership is one of the key prerequisites for stakeholder collaboration and, drawing it a step further, leadership has also been suggested as key factor for innovation (Keller 2002 in Pechlaner *et al.* 2008).

Providing leadership in destinations frequently falls to destination management organisations (DMOs) which are generally non-profit organisations, located in the public sector. In addition to their traditional role of promoting the destination, DMOs increasingly fulfil the task of facilitating a network of stakeholders and gathering stakeholders' consensus regarding the destination's strategy (Sheehan and Ritchie 2005). In the example of the HLTC, however, the DMO was bypassed and leadership was taken up by a steering group consisting of local entrepreneurs and local authorities, perhaps suggesting that the DMO did not engage in or did not share the innovative vision to develop the HLTC. In contrast, the DMO *VisitVejle* of the Southern Danish Nordic Well-Being laboratory area was the lead stakeholder in initiating collaboration with the strategic objective to transform Southern Denmark into a wellness tourism destination. While the collaboration process has been described as highly transparent, inclusive and open and characterised by a willingness to share, the project has unfortunately failed to establish Southern Denmark as a wellness tourism destination (Hjalager 2011). While a brand has been created, it was not taken seriously by the stakeholders. The underlying reason is that Southern Denmark lacks unique selling points and strong resources that unify the region around the concept of wellness (Hjalager 2011; Hjalager *et al.* 2011).

Thus, existing assets (Smith and Puczkó 2009), substance (Hjalager 2011), or resources (Pechlaner and Fischer 2006; Sheldon and Park 2009) which share an identifiable unique link to wellness seems to be crucial when planning and developing a wellness tourism destination. Examples of natural core wellness resources are geothermal and mineral springs, medicinal mud and plants, climate and wilderness areas that are of therapeutic and/or spiritual value. Examples of cultural/heritage core wellness resources are historically anchored wellness traditions (e.g. sweat bathing in saunas or *hammams*, spiritual/religious practices such as yoga), historic wellness architecture such as Roman baths, as well as alternative healing philosophies and modalities (e.g. Traditional Chinese Medicine, Hawaiian Lomi Lomi massage or Kneipp therapy). In addition, supporting resources also play an important role. Examples are skilled staff that know about and are able to deliver wellness (Smith and Puczkó 2009) and the intangible resource consisting of the community mindset at the destination (Hjalager 2011).

In the case of Alpine Wellness, several important prerequisites of stakeholder collaboration were fulfilled. Stakeholders have been willing to collaborate, a special interest group was formed which assumed leadership, all the regions shared similar economic and cultural backgrounds and the product could be based on unique core resources (e.g. the Alps and their health-beneficial altitude and climate, healthy local culinary produce, traditional Alpine cures and herbal medicine such as hay bathing). As a result, a distinctive Alpine Wellness brand and promotional material could be developed. An additional outcome was a catalogue of strict quality standards in order to certify wellness tourism operators and to ensure the high quality of the brand. Accreditation standards reassure both (potential) customers and wellness tourism operators of the quality of the product, which may be particularly important in wellness tourism, where a lack of market transparency and the fuzzy nature of the wellness product has created customer confusion (Voigt *et al.* 2010).

Stakeholder collaboration evolves over time and can take many forms: relatively simple or complex, temporary or long-lasting; and with or without formal rules. It is important to remember that tourism clusters can also emerge organically by a concentration of similar firms in a specific geographic location and without any conscious effort on the part of individual businesses or regulators. There may be a synergy between firms because of their geographic proximity and interdependence regarding supply and infrastructure, rather than particularly active collaboration. Examples of organically emerged wellness tourism destinations referred to by Smith and Puczkó (2009) include Goa in India and Chiang Mai in Thailand. In contrast, in the examples cited earlier in this chapter, clustering was attempted to be forced through lobbying and regulation (a 'development push').

Additionally, one can distinguish *specialised collaboration*, where the same type of tourism firms collaborate and *complementary collaboration* where organisations collaborate across different sectors. In the former case, the aim of collaboration mostly consists of higher customer reach through marketing, and a careful balance between competing for customers and cooperating to stimulate tourist demand at the destination needs to be found. Marketing alliances among wellness tourism operators to promote a regional destination are common: examples are *WellVital®* in Bavaria, Germany, *Seen Wellness®* (Wellness Lakes) in Carinthia, Austria, or the Wellness Nelson-Tasman cluster in New Zealand. In some of these alliances, regional DMOs play a central role in facilitating such collaborative marketing.

Innovative destination development, however, seems to require tighter links between stakeholders and needs to include information and knowledge sharing (Pechlaner *et al.* 2008). Moreover, innovation may be particularly successful through merging knowledge and skills across industries. In the case of Alpine Wellness, researchers acknowledge that there is much more potential for development if organisations across sectors were to cooperate further, for instance the religious sector could move Alpine Wellness beyond its physical emphasis to include spiritual wellness dimensions (Pechlaner and Fischer 2006).

This chapter now takes a geographical focus and moves on to analyse the issue of collaboration amongst key wellness tourism stakeholders in Australia. In the following section, Australia's wellness tourism sector is briefly outlined before the core actors in the supply chain of Australian wellness tourism are introduced and the extent of their collaboration discussed.

A snapshot of Australia's wellness tourism

The Australian wellness industry has not been in existence for very long. The vast majority of surveyed wellness service providers (78 per cent) are less than ten years old. Our research shows that, similar to many other countries, wellness tourism providers mainly cater to the domestic market (only 6 per cent of their market consists of international visitors). Our research estimates that wellness tourism operators cater to 2,209,300 wellness clients annually, which by far exceeds previous data from the National Visitor Survey. According to our estimate, the Australian wellness service industry (including day spas) generates in excess of AU$277 million per annum.

Australia's wellness tourism industry has not taken advantage of existing large deposits of mineral or geothermal springs. The exceptions are two areas in Victoria (Daylesford and the Mornington Peninsula) where (wellness) tourism operators have clustered around these natural resources. It has been argued that indigenous spiritual and/or healing practices generally provide a strong competitive advantage for wellness tourism destinations (Sheldon and Park 2009). Some Australian wellness tourism operators and cosmetic suppliers have begun to draw on Australian Indigenous health philosophy and healing ingredients. However, our survey and interviews shows that some industry stakeholders think that those operators largely exploit Indigenous culture without sharing the benefits arising from this utilisation. As will be discussed in the following section, very few destinations within Australia are actively marketed as wellness tourism destinations.

Australian wellness tourism providers

Major types of wellness tourism operators

Wellness tourism operators are the most obvious stakeholders in wellness tourism and the focal point for tourists in delivering wellness tourism experiences. In regard to wellness tourism operators, we have developed a provider typology consisting of three core categories: (1) beauty spa resorts/hotels; (2) lifestyle resorts; and (3) spiritual retreats (Voigt *et al.* 2010).

The main focus of beauty spa hotels/resorts is on body and non-medical beauty treatments such as massages, body wraps and facials. Some beauty spa providers have an intrinsic geographic advantage as they are based on or around mineral or thermal pools. Spas that do not have this advantage can also offer water-based treatments, for instance in the form of steam rooms, saunas, whirlpools, hot tubs and wet treatments rooms. A rather unique Australian feature is that less than half of beauty spa hotels/resorts offer any form of water treatments. It is often claimed that water is the central defining element of spas, which is clearly not the case in Australia. On the contrary, spas often emphasise that they use water sparingly, which reflects the increasing water scarcity in Australia. In Australia, spa resorts/hotels constitute the largest group of wellness tourism operators; our database analysis disclosed 201 operators, including 28 lifestyle resorts and 83 spiritual retreats.

Beauty spa visitors are passive recipients of treatments from therapists. In contrast, lifestyle resort visitors actively participate in a comprehensive program which focuses on health-promoting behaviour changes in areas such as nutrition, exercise and fitness, personal goals, and stress management. Most lifestyle resorts offer a vast range of alternative medicine treatments. The cuisine at lifestyle resorts tends to be very healthy. Amenities that are normally part of every hotel or resort room such as televisions, internet access and telephones are generally not provided and the consumption of alcohol, coffee, non-herbal teas and cigarettes is usually prohibited.

The emphasis of spiritual retreats is on people's spiritual development. Spiritual retreats can be religious or non-religious but always include meditation in various forms. Many spiritual retreats are based on some specific teachings or philosophy and/or focus on the study of a specific mind/body technique such as yoga, T'ai Chi, Reiki or particular forms of meditation, and accommodation and facilities tend to be basic and austere.

Despite the distinct differences between service offerings, there are also similarities across the three types of providers. The Australian Bureau of Statistics uses employment to define business size and under its definition, small business consists of those that employ fewer than 20 people. Accordingly, the vast majority of wellness tourism providers can be defined as small or even micro businesses. Spiritual retreats tend to employ the lowest number of full-time staff (four on average) and lifestyle resorts the highest (13.7 on average compared to 6.5 beauty spa full-time staff).

Another similarity between all types of providers is that the majority (73 per cent) have a retail section where health and wellness products are sold. A surprising 33 per cent offer their own products using local ingredients. Wellness tourism operators can increase brand loyalty to a specific place as customers are able to transfer their experience to their homes by reliving smells, textures or sounds. Furthermore, Hjalager and Konu (2011) point out that the use of local or national ingredients in cosmetics may strengthen a destination brand and create a unique selling point. The high proportion of providers developing retail products with local ingredients also point to strong connections between operators and particular suppliers in a certain region.

The majority of all wellness tourism providers (72 per cent) are located in regional areas. While mostly not particularly marketed as such, wellness tourism operators cluster in certain regions. Beauty spa hotels and resorts are often found in areas where luxurious accommodation properties are generally clustered (e.g. Tropical North, Gold Coast and Sunshine Coast). In our interviews, Byron Bay in northern New South Wales was often named as the unofficially leading Australian wellness tourism destination. Byron Bay is a very good example of an organically emerged wellness tourism cluster (Wray *et al.* 2010; see also Chapter 5 in this volume). The online directory *Byron Body & Soul* does not have a distinct tourism focus but collates all wellness services provided in the Byron Bay Shire by organisations and individuals. Competitive resources of Byron Bay include a beautiful environment, a large diversity of wellness operations, which are generally based around more alternative wellness services, and a local community that is laid-back, creative and enjoys an alternative lifestyle. On a much smaller scale, there are other Australian destinations with similar alternative lifestyle values where entrepreneurial wellness, spiritual and environmentally conscious local organic producers are clustered, and where places may be even known for their eco-spiritual value already long known by Indigenous people, for instance Margaret River (Western Australia), the Blue Mountains (New South Wales) and the Flinders Ranges (South Australia). Several stakeholders in the interviews mentioned that Australians are already generally perceived as laid-back, friendly and relaxed and that these lifestyle values, combined with the abundant pristine nature and state-of-the-art sustainable business practices, could be drawn upon to create a distinct *barefoot luxury* image of Australian wellness tourism. Fittingly, a great majority of respondents across all providers (85 per cent) indicated that they had implemented eco-friendly and socially sustainable practices in their businesses.

Some interviewees pointed out that the reconciliation between the business philosophy and a sustainable, holistic wellness philosophy is one of the greatest challenges of the wellness industry. However, specifically in the spiritual retreat category (27 per cent compared to 2 per cent of beauty spa resort/hotels and 4 per cent of lifestyle resorts), some providers operate on a non-profit or donation basis and are thus not really concerned with profit-making.

Australian federal and state DMOs and their role in the promotion and development of wellness tourism

Federal and state tourism bodies can play an important role through encouragement of stakeholder collaboration, destination branding and destination development. Federal DMOs all over the world are increasingly recognising wellness tourism as a key product in their national and international tourism development strategies (e.g. *Swiss Health*; *Wellness Croatia*; *Hungary – A garden of well-being*). Our research, however, revealed that representatives from Tourism Australia, the country's peak tourism marketing authority, showed no great interest in promoting and developing wellness tourism.

Out of all Australian states and territories, only Tourism Victoria is currently actively involved in the strategic development and promotion of wellness tourism, particularly in the Daylesford/Hepburn Springs region, where a tourism cluster has historically evolved around mineral springs since the 1850s and substantially revived and diversified since the 1990s. It has been strongly supported by the Victorian government, Tourism Victoria and the Hepburn Shire Council, both financially and through the creation of necessary infrastructure (e.g. refurbishment of the public bathhouse and upgrading of roads to increase accessibility). Tourism Victoria is invaluable in providing leadership, fostering collaboration and acting as an ambassador for the Daylesford/Hepburn Springs region (Voigt *et al.* 2010). Recently, a coordinated strategic tourism plan has been developed, involving all important stakeholders in this strategy (Lawrence and Buultjens 2008). Furthermore, Tourism Victoria has recently launched the AU$7.3 million *Lead a double life* advertising campaign, including TV and cinema spots, print advertising in women's and food magazines as well as PR to showcase Daylesford as the leading Australian spa and wellness destination.

Despite these developments in Victoria, half of the respondents to our survey did not think that the Australian wellness industry is well supported by federal and state tourism bodies and 40 per cent had no opinion, perhaps indicating that many wellness tourism operators do not have the perception that they belong to the tourism industry and therefore are not interested whether their type of business is promoted through DMOs or not. Additionally, almost 70 per cent of respondents thought that consumers are not well informed about wellness services offered in Australia.

In some destinations where there is little support from the DMOs to promote wellness tourism, stakeholders have collaborated and formed marketing alliances to promote wellness tourism at their destination. In the south-west of Western Australia stakeholders involved in wellness in all its guises (e.g. tourism providers, organic food providers, counsellors, massage therapists) created an online and print directory *Wellness Margaret River* (see also Chapter 11 in this volume). On the Mornington Peninsula, 13 day and hotel beauty spas collaborated, creating a website,[1] and developing a Spa Pass system, offering different types of spa packages.

Wellness industry and accreditation organisations

The professionalisation of the wellness industry has increased in recent years through the establishment of international, national and regional industry and accreditation organisations. Most of these organisations operate independently from tourism organisations and are non-profit organisations where member pay a fee to gain certain benefits (e.g. best practice business models, job opportunities, networking events, industry-relevant research). Another important task, where the involvement of wellness industry associations has been vital in some destinations, is the development and monitoring of certification standards. In addition, other organisations have developed accreditation or benchmarking indicators with a strong emphasis on sustainability (e.g. Green Spa Network, Green Globe benchmarking indicators for spas). The Australasian Spa Association (ASpa) was founded in 2000–2001. ASpa's achievements include the organisation of an annual conference, networking events and lobbying to include day spas as separate entry in the Yellow Pages. In 2011, they also produced a brochure, promoting participating members. There have been several attempts by ASpa to develop an accreditation scheme, but so far these attempts have failed. At this point in time, no accreditation schemes exist in Australia, but they are strongly demanded by many stakeholders. Some of the stakeholder interviewees were critical of ASpa. Several thought that ASpa's focus on beauty was too narrow and that there was a lack of lobbying and not enough advice on operational issues. In 2007, ASpa had over 460 members, whereas the current number has dropped to 280 (as of January 2012). Indeed, a look at current members reveals a high proportion of day spas and no lifestyle resorts or spiritual retreats. Thus, there is currently no industry body that represents the latter categories of wellness tourism operators.

The media

Research has been conducted on the promotion and advertising channels Australian wellness tourists use when choosing and booking their wellness tourism holidays. Data from the Australian National Visitor Survey (NVS) suggests that after the internet (57 per cent), the second-most likely source of information stemmed from a previous visit (23 per cent), followed by recommendations from friends or relatives (i.e. word-of-mouth, 18 per cent). Travel agents (5 per cent), travel guides or brochures (7 per cent) and advertising/editorials (2 per cent) did not play as important a role as a source of information for wellness tourists. Likewise, our research revealed that the vast majority of Australian wellness providers rely on the direct-to-consumer business model and the internet plays a very important role as a promotion and distribution channel.

Online and print directories have been increasingly developed. International examples are the *Spa Finder* or *Healing Hotels of the World* directories. A national example of an online directory is the *New Zealand Wellness Escapes Travel Portal*. These directories tend to focus mainly on beauty spa hotel/resorts and day spas. However, some directories have also been developed that specialise on spiritual retreats (e.g. *Retreatfinder*). Currently, there are no Australian-specific directories concerning any types of wellness tourism operators.

While magazines and newspapers may not be used as often as promotion channels by the operators, the media is influential in forming the general image that people have about wellness tourism. Industry-specific magazines have recently sprung into existence which include the Australian *Spa Life* and *Spa Australasia*. Unfortunately, the images used to portray wellness tourism by the media, as well as by many DMOs, are highly stereotypical, generally showing very young and pretty women who lie passively around, often with closed eyes or facial masks. This does not foster a diversified and educational understanding of wellness. However, recent, more generic healthy lifestyle magazines such as the Australian-based *Well-Being*, *Good Health* or *Australian Natural Health* and newspaper editorials such as the *Body and Soul* magazine of the *Herald Sun*, may indirectly promote a more diversified picture of wellness tourism, including promoting broad wellness principles and emphasising that health is more than the absence of disease.

The educational sector

The quality of staff is one of the most important factors determining the success of a wellness provider (Cohen and Russell 2008). For Australian wellness providers, employment accounts for one of the largest expenditures and, with the exception of the United States, wellness-related industry staff earn the highest wages in the world (ibid.). More than half of our survey respondents indicated that it is difficult to find and employ well-trained staff in Australia, and that there is a high turnover rate. In addition, 64 per cent agreed that there is a high burnout rate of Australian wellness staff. Because the industry has grown so fast, educational opportunities have lagged behind. Moreover, there is the problem that managers and staff need to be multiskilled. Managers from business and tourism industries may lack understanding of the wellness concept, while alternative medicine practitioners may lack necessary communication and business skills. In an interview, a stakeholder described the wellness industry as a 'hard industry' to work in, because people are often very isolated and need to be calm and patient in front of customers and listen to their worries even though they may not feel like it.

The majority of survey respondents (71 per cent) agreed that Australia needs to have wellness industry-specific training programs. At the moment, there is an extensive and confusing array of schools, colleges and private individuals offering vocational qualifications, courses or training in alternative medicine, New Age and beauty therapies. However, there is a need for all-encompassing, educational programs where people obtain a deep understanding of wellness principles and therapies as well as skills on how to pass on this knowledge to customers. An Australian exception where education has had an interdisciplinary focus on wellness and health-promoting areas such as positive psychology, nutrition and body/mind therapies is the online *Master of Wellness* offered by the Royal Melbourne Institute of Technology in Victoria.

The mainstream health-care sector

As in most countries, Australian politicians, insurance companies and orthodox health professionals mainly use the term 'health' to refer to the absence of illness and do not support or fund health promotion. Most stakeholders in our inter-views emphasised that much progress of the industry lies in a collaborative future with the mainstream health-care sector and that wellness services should be eligible for reimbursement by health insurances. However, 80 per cent of survey respondents agreed that medical practitioners currently do not recognise the importance of the wellness industry and 74 per cent agreed that government health bodies do not recognise the role that the wellness industry plays in health promotion.

Nevertheless, our survey uncovered that on average 10 per cent of customers visited a wellness service operator because of a medical practitioner's recommen-dation and 6 per cent of wellness service operators referred clients back to a general practitioner, indicating only minimal acknowledgement and collaborative effort on both sides. One way to increase acceptance with health policymakers and main-stream health professionals may be to further develop scientifically based evidence that shows the health effectiveness of wellness services, the therapeutic value of nature and/or particular wellness architecture and the effectiveness of a prolonged stay away from home at a wellness tourism operator.

Discussion

The above discussion of Australian stakeholders shows that the Australian well-ness tourism industry is fragmented and characterised by little collaboration between major groups of stakeholders. There is some evidence of collaboration among wellness tourism operators (e.g. Mornington Peninsula Spa Pass) or well-ness tourism providers and other wellness service businesses (e.g. Wellness Mar-garet River), but this is limited in scope to certain areas. This finding is in accordance with previous research on purposefully created or developed well-ness tourism destinations outside Australia, where stakeholder collaboration has proven very difficult and destination development has mostly failed.

With the exception of Tourism Victoria, there are no efforts by the national and state DMOs to take up leadership in promoting Australian wellness tourism. Addi-tionally, the wellness industry association ASpa focuses too narrowly on the spa sector and, in the perception of many stakeholders, has not yet been able to effect-ively support wellness tourism. There are also few signs of exchange between the three different types of wellness tourism providers. While beauty spa resorts and hotels have obvious connections to hospitality, managers from lifestyle resorts and spiritual retreats often come from outside the hospitality or business domains and may even operate on a non-profit basis. Therefore, owners or managers of some lifestyle resorts and spiritual retreats can be considered as 'lifestyle entre-preneurs' who do not see themselves to be part of a tourism or wellness industry. With ASpa or marketing alliances such as the one on the Mornington Peninsula, there are at least some indications of promotional collaborative linkages between beauty spa hotel/resort operators. It is interesting to note, however, the lack of any obvious promotional collaboration among lifestyle resort or spiritual retreat opera-tors. More research is clearly needed to understand this lack of connectedness as well as the perceived disconnectedness of lifestyle resorts and spiritual retreat operators to the wellness tourism industry.

Despite the lack of wellness tourism stakeholder collaboration, wellness tourism is a reality in Australia. Our research has shown that wellness tourists comprise a much larger niche than previously thought. Due to increasing consumer demand, wellness tourism providers have grown exponentially and in 2010 there were 590 organisations in Australia specifically designed to enable and enhance people's physical, psychological, spiritual and/or social wellbeing. While lifestyle resorts and spiritual retreats may not see themselves to be part of the wellness industry, their customers perceive themselves to be wellness tourists (Voigt *et al.* 2010).

Currently, there is only one officially marketed Australian destination with a core positioning on the basis of wellness tourism, namely Daylesford/Hepburn Springs. Ironically, this destination's positioning strategy is mainly based around its natural resource of mineral springs which diametrically contrasts with the typical provision of Australian wellness tourism where water does not play an important role. The Australian wellness tourism product differs from neighbouring New Zealand and also Europe, where water is often seen as the defining element of wellness tourism. It also differs from many Asian countries in that the staff–guest ratio is much smaller because of the expensive wages but with a more stable, safe and hygienic infrastructure. There are some unique natural and cultural resources that Australian wellness could be based upon, which has already happened in some destinations such as Byron Bay, albeit in an unplanned manner. Australia has an abundance of pristine, beautiful and awe-inspiring scenery and some locations with a perceived therapeutic or spiritual value linked to Indigenous culture. At some destinations, communities lead an alternative, sustainable lifestyle which can be easily connected to overarching Australian lifestyle values of being laid-back and friendly as well as the outdoor sporty 'Aussie coastal lifestyle' already promoted by Tourism Australia. The fact that the majority of all Australian wellness providers have implemented sustainable business practices and that many collaborate with local suppliers to create wellness products for their retail section could become important factors supporting the uniqueness of an Australian 'barefoot luxury' wellness tourism image.

The media, DMOs and perhaps even some of the wellness providers themselves unfortunately create an image of wellness tourism based on the passive relaxation of beautiful women soaking in water, ignoring the far more encompassing notion of active wellness and health promotion. It is arguably not the pampering delivered in beauty spas that increases wellness, but the provision of deep relaxation, stress relief and a nurturing human touch. In lifestyle resorts and spiritual retreats, tourists are (additionally) actively involved in gaining higher wellness levels. Tourists, DMOs and wellness tourism operators need to truly understand what wellness stands for and that they are already an active player in health-care provision. The education sector also plays an important role in this context as it needs to take on a leading role in teaching people about wellness and creating a skilled work force that is currently urgently needed.

Conclusion

Previous research has shown that it is very difficult to purposely foster collaboration and create or strengthen a wellness tourism destination. Accordingly, the present examination of Australian wellness providers confirms a general lack of collaboration between major stakeholder groups. The following strategies are outlined that could be used to foster collaboration and increase transparency of an integrated, unique Australian wellness tourism product:

- stakeholders across all three wellness tourism provider sectors and wellness experts need to be brought together and synergies surrounding the notion of wellness need to be explored;
- national and regional DMOs need to take a more active, leadership role and incorporate wellness tourism as a component into their strategies;
- a unique Australian wellness product, consisting of a 'barefoot luxury' image, unique natural landmarks with therapeutic/spiritual benefits, the importance of sustainability and local produce and a distinct natural outdoor focus should be promoted;
- an online and print directory featuring all three wellness tourism providers should be developed;
- a comprehensive accreditation scheme which incorporates environmental and social sustainability indicators should be developed;
- the inclusion of wellness and health promotion theories in general tourism and hospitality degrees and funding for the specific development of educational programs for wellness coaches or wellness facility managers;
- more research into the health effectiveness of wellness tourism could bring together tourism operators as well as alternative and mainstream health professionals.

Note

1 www.morningtonpeninsulaspas.com.au

References

Ateljevic, I. and Doorne, S. (2000) ' "Staying within the fence": lifestyle entrepreneurship in tourism', *Journal of Sustainable Tourism*, 8: 378–92.

Baggio, R., Scott, N. and Cooper, C. (2010) 'Network science: a review focused on tourism', *Annals of Tourism Research*, 37: 802–27.

Bramwell, B. and Lane, B. (2004) 'Collaboration and partnerships in tourism planning', in B. Bramwell and B. Lane (eds) *Tourism Collaboration and Partnership: Politics, Practice and Sustainability*, Clevedon: Channel View Publications.

Cohen, M. and Russell, D. (2008) 'Human resource management in spas: staff recruitment, retention and remuneration', in M. Cohen and G. Bodeker (eds) *Understanding the Global Spa Industry: Spa Management*, Oxford: Butterworth-Heinemann.

Haugland, S.A., Ness, H., Grønseth, B.-O. and Aarstad, J. (2011) 'Development of tourism destinations: an integrated multilevel perspective', *Annals of Tourism Research*, 38: 268–90.

Hjalager, A.-M. (2011) 'The invention of a Danish well-being tourism region: strategy, substance, structure, and symbolic action', *Tourism Planning and Development*, 8: 51–67.

Hjalager, A.-M. and Konu, H. (2011) 'Co-branding and co-creation in wellness tourism: the role of cosmeceuticals', *Journal of Hospitality Marketing and Management*, 20: 879–901.

Hjalager, A.-M., Konu, H., Huijbens, E.H., Björk, P., Flagestad, A., Nordin, S. and Tuohino, A. (2011) *Innovating and Re-Branding Nordic Wellbeing Tourism*, Oslo: Nordic Innovation Centre.

Huijbens, E.H. (2011) 'Developing wellness in Iceland: theming wellness destinations the Nordic way', *Scandinavian Journal of Hospitality and Tourism*, 11: 20–41.

Jackson, J. and Murphy, P. (2006) 'Clusters in regional tourism: an Australian case', *Annals of Tourism Research*, 33: 1018–35.

Jamal, T.B. and Getz, D. (1995) 'Collaboration theory and community tourism planning', *Annals of Tourism Research*, 22: 186–204.

Lawrence, M. and Buultjens, J. (2008) *Destination Daylesford Strategic Tourism Management Plan 2008 to 2018*, East Lismore: Southern Cross University, Australian Regional Tourism Research Centre.

Lebe, S.S. (2006) 'European Spa World', *Journal of Quality Assurance in Hospitality and Tourism*, 7: 137–46.

Novelli, M., Schmitz, B. and Spencer, T. (2006) 'Networks, clusters and innovation in tourism: a UK experience', *Tourism Management*, 27: 1141–52.

Pechlaner, H. and Fischer, E. (2006) 'Alpine Wellness: a resource-based view', *Tourism Recreation Research*, 31: 67–77.

Pechlaner, H., Fischer, E. and Hamman, E.-M. (2008) 'Leadership and innovation processes: development of products and services based on core competencies', *Journal of Quality Assurance in Hospitality and Tourism*, 6: 31–57.

Pforr, C. (2006) 'Tourism policy in the making: an Australian network study', *Annals of Tourism Research*, 33: 87–108.

Shaw, G. (2003) 'Entrepreneurial cultures and small business enterprises in tourism', in M.C. Hall, A. Lew and A. Williams (eds) *Blackwell Companion to Tourism Geography*, Oxford: Blackwell.

Sheehan, L.R. and Ritchie, J.R.B. (2005) 'Destination stakeholder: exploring identity and salience', *Annals of Tourism Research*, 32: 711–34.

Sheldon, P.J. and Park, S.-Y. (2009) 'Development of a sustainable wellness destination', in R. Bushell and P.J. Sheldon (eds) *Wellness and Tourism: Mind, Body, Spirit, Place*, New York: Cognizant Communication Corporation.

Smith, M. and Puczkó, L. (2009) *Health and Wellness Tourism*, Oxford: Butterworth-Heinemann.

Voigt, C., Laing, J., Wray, M., Brown, G., Howat, G., Weiler, B. and Trembath, R. (eds) (2010) *Wellness and Medical Tourism in Australia: Supply, Demand and Opportunities*. Gold Coast: CRC for Sustainable Tourism.

Wray, M., Laing, J. and Voigt, C. (2010) 'Byron Bay: an alternate health and wellness destination', *Journal of Hospitality and Tourism Management*, 17: 158–66.

5 Wellness tourism

The factors and processes that drive sustainable regional destinations

Meredith Wray and Betty Weiler

Introduction

The aim of this chapter is to identify the resources, factors and processes that may be used to develop and enhance wellness tourism as a tool for competitive advantage and for the sustainability of regional tourism destinations. The chapter begins by briefly examining the potential of wellness tourism as a strategy to distinguish and position some regions within the highly competitive tourism environment. Several bodies of literature related to destination competiveness, sustainable tourism and stakeholder cooperation are then reviewed to identify a set of five factors and processes that may potentially influence the sustainability of wellness tourism destinations. Integrated in this review are important findings, related to the development of wellness tourism for regional destinations, derived from a scoping study undertaken and funded by the Cooperative Research Centre for Sustainable Tourism (STCRC) for the Australian Commonwealth Government in 2009 that examined the demand for and supply of wellness and medical tourism in Australia.

The chapter presents case studies of two significant and distinctive regional wellness destinations in Australia: Daylesford/Hepburn Springs (located in central Victoria), and Byron Bay (located on the far north coast of New South Wales). Both destinations are endowed with natural resources and other ingredients thought to be important to both wellness tourists and destinations. Case-study findings are analysed against the five factors and processes determined from the literature review.

For the purposes of this chapter, the term 'wellness' includes spa tourism and holistic/spiritual forms of tourism that encompass a positive and holistic understanding of health that incorporates physical, psychological, social and spiritual dimensions (the typology and variety of wellness tourism is discussed in Chapter 2). Furthermore, a 'wellness tourist' is defined as a tourist whose primary motive is to maintain or improve his/her health and wellbeing (adapted from Voigt *et al.* 2010).

Wellness tourism as a tool for regional development

Tourism is well accepted as an important contributor to the economy and to the sustainable development of many regions. The recent global financial crisis has, however, created turmoil within world financial markets that has resulted in decline in tourist demand for many regional destinations. This is new for an industry that has experienced significant growth for many years. As a result, the domestic and international tourism environment continues to be aggressively competitive and increasingly volatile. The positive news for many regional tourism destinations that rely on domestic tourism is that due to the unpredictability of the global economic environment, consumers have tended to travel closer to home (UNWTO 2010). Given the significance of tourism to many regional economies, it is imperative that regional tourism organisations are poised to develop and act on strategies that maintain and enhance tourism as an economic driver for local communities (Wray *et al.* 2010).

Wellness tourism may offer a way to distinguish and position some regions within this highly competitive environment, particularly as a regional development strategy to attract domestic markets, extend tourism product and experience offerings, attract off-season visitors, increase visitors' length of stay, and rejuvenate and refresh destination image. As will be shown in this chapter, wellness tourism also has the advantage of attracting visitors who are seeking well-being and lifestyle experiences, thus potentially aligning more easily with host community values in comparison with other forms of tourism.

Factors and processes for sustainable regional development in a wellness tourism context

This section reviews concepts related to destination competiveness, sustainable tourism, and stakeholder cooperation that may contribute to the development of wellness tourism for regional destinations. Five factors and processes that potentially influence the sustainability of wellness tourism destinations are identified and discussed. Integrated in this review are findings derived from a scoping study that examined the demand for and supply of wellness and medical tourism in Australia during 2009.

1 Significance of historical antecedents and existence of natural resources

In reviewing the factors that may influence the development of wellness tourism for regional destinations, it is important to acknowledge at the outset that destinations differ with respect to their combinations of natural, built and human resources, the levels of support they receive from governments and their capacities to innovate and compete for visitors and tourist dollars (Wray *et al.* 2010). In particular, the historic context such as the complex and dynamic relations between community members, business interests and government can facilitate or constrain the sustainable development of wellness tourism in a region (Wray *et al.* 2010).

As part of the historical antecedents, an environment that is healthy and rich with significant natural resources is also recognised as representing a core element of the competitiveness and sustainability of a destination region (e.g. Ritchie and Crouch 2003; Leiper 2004; Weaver and Lawton 2010). In particular, the diversity, uniqueness, abundance, accessibility and attractiveness of scenic, ecological, recreational and other natural physical features often represent a primary motivation for travel and a key source of competitive advantage (Ritchie and Crouch 2003).

To achieve competitive advantage, destination managers need to plan and manage their distinctive combinations of resources effectively over the long term (Ritchie and Crouch 2003). As argued by Ritchie and Crouch (2003: 308) 'like any child, destinations might commence life with certain "gifts", but these gifts are neither sufficient determinants of a child's nor a destination's development and success'. As Poon (1993 in Ritchie and Crouch 2003: 25) points out, it is important that destinations 'put the environment first' if they are to be competitive and sustainable. Traditionally, wellness tourism facilities have been built around natural sources of geothermal and mineral springs. Wellness tourism locations that do not include mineral and/or hot springs are typically located in 'aesthetically pleasing [and] environmentally lush' settings (Smith and Kelly 2006: 15). As discussed by Voigt *et al.* (2010), some research undertaken by health geographers has recognised place as a determinant that can contribute to health and wellbeing, and other authors have referred to spas, yoga centres and retreats as 'therapeutic landscapes' (e.g. Frost 2004; Gesler 2003; Hoyez 2007; Lea 2008). More research is needed on the degree to which the environment drives the sustainability of wellness tourism regions (Voigt *et al.* 2010). The relationship between the natural environment and wellness is further examined in Chapters 9, 10 and 11 in this volume.

2 Values of host populations with respect to natural environments and wellbeing

A common theme in tourism research is that a sustainable approach to tourism requires attaining some level of harmony among stakeholder groups to develop a desirable quality of life that lasts (Lawrence 2006). Thus, in a regional tourism context, sustainability requires long-term conservation of not only the natural but also the region's human (sociocultural) resources to ensure quality of life for host communities as well as visitor satisfaction (Ahn *et al.* 2002). As explained by Gnoth (2007), it is the values and meanings as expressed in the cultural, social, natural and economic dimensions of people's lives that comprise the assets or *capital* of the destination, which attract and serve tourists. These values are relational and living, and form the core of what makes up the uniqueness of the place (ibid.).

Furthermore, regional destination marketing and branding research has advocated for processes that are value-led (Wheeler *et al.* 2011) and, in particular, driven by the values held by local communities and networks, rather than a more limited consumer-based value set that is usually economically driven and imposed upon a destination. A values-based approach to regional destination marketing proposes that brand identity, sense of place and community and stake-holder values are interrelated concepts (Wheeler *et al.* 2011). This interrelation-ship, and the roles of values in branding and positioning are yet to be fully explored in destination marketing literature. For wellness tourism, there has been some acknowledgement of but no research examining the importance of local values to the sustainability of wellness tourism regions (Voigt *et al.* 2010).

3 Diversity of destination experiences and wellness tourism practices

In addition to a destination's inherited natural assets, factors such as a region's knowledge, capital, infrastructure and tourism superstructure (created tourism assets), historical and cultural resources, and the size of the economy also con-tribute to a destinations 'comparative advantage' (Ritchie and Crouch 2003: 21). Ultimately, a destination that offers a *diversity of visitor experiences* is in a better competitive position than one that has a limited mix of activities (Ritchie and Crouch 2000). Research undertaken by Wray *et al.* (2010), of 21 regional tourism destinations in Australia, determined that successful destinations recog-nise that in addition to their iconic natural and built attractions there is a need to provide and promote a diversity of appropriate tourism product and experiences to enhance the visitor experience, improve yield, increase length of stay through-out the year, and encourage repeat visitation.

Research undertaken by Voigt *et al.* (2010) determined that places that offer wellness tourism services are more likely to succeed when planned as a com-ponent of a broader service offering. It has been recommended that wellness tourism product be developed and marketed with complementary activities such as those associated with fitness, nutrition or relaxation; and that regions take advantage of local resources which may be linked to naturally occurring water supplies, local plants or produce in ways that assist the development of allied wellness services. The resultant product mix can be used to establish an appro-priate place-branding strategy that is founded upon the locally based wellness theme (Voigt *et al.* 2010), and that is linked to broader tourism product and experiences offered by the destination.

4 Strategic initiatives to plan and achieve sustainable tourism development

An important issue that is influencing the economic future of regional Australia is the global trend for decision-making to be devolved to local and regional levels of government, and the emerging policy related to this trend (Bycroft *et al.* 2007). This places local government and local communities in the position of having to take a leadership role to achieve sustainable outcomes for their regions. Sustainable tourism planning and development has been increasingly advocated as a means to balance environmental, community and economic values (Wray 2011). The aim of sustainable tourism planning is to collaborate with government, business, community stakeholders with a *stake* in tourism and its environments to achieve a level and style of tourism that protects and enhances the natural and built features upon which it is based, and is consistent with community values and aspirations over the short and longer terms (Wray *et al.* 2010). Furthermore, effective planning processes are considered to require a partnership composed of planners, managers, scientists and various constituencies representing different tourism players (McCool 2009).

Wellness tourism has often developed organically in response to consumer demand and other influences drivers outlined earlier in this chapter, rather than being planned strategically or sustainably. Tourism policies and practices that are driven by sustainability principles and stakeholder engagement are yet to be examined comprehensively in the wellness tourism literature. It is, however, clear that governments can play a significant role in facilitating the growth and professionalism of this sector (Voigt *et al.* 2010).

5 Stakeholder cooperation in planning for wellness tourism

To provide a diversity of tourism products and services for visitors, destinations have to effectively coordinate destination resources and capabilities of participating businesses, which requires both cooperation and competition (Wang and Krakover 2008). Regional areas are well recognised as comprising multiple communities and thus a diversity of stakeholders with an interest or a *stake* in tourism (Wray 2009). Interests, expertise, knowledge and availability of these stakeholders result in different levels of interaction and engagement for different destination contexts (Wray 2009). Fostering cooperation, let alone harmony, through engagement of stakeholders across government, business and community interests in tourism for regional destination contexts is acknowledged as being problematic in practice (Wray 2011). One of the complexities of sustainable tourism development is that natural resources used for tourism are common pool resources, involving diverse stakeholders with differing value systems (McDonald 2009). Furthermore, the fragmentation of the tourism industry and complexity of regional destination management and marketing demands a collective approach that balances cooperation and competition amongst stakeholders for the long-term competiveness and success of the destination (Wheeler *et al.* 2011).

Understanding and leveraging these working relationships among tourism businesses is considered to be critical to the success of collaborative destination-marketing programs (Terpstra and Simonin 1993 in Wang and Krakover 2008). Halme (2001: 100) has proposed the establishment of a 'sustainability network', comprising a group of actors (stakeholders) that are orientated towards sustainable development in all or some of its dimensions – environmental, social, cultural and economic. These networks further 'imply cooperative efforts among businesses, governmental bodies organisations, persons or other entities that are interconnected in some way' (Smith-Ring 1999 in Halme 2001: 102). Timur and Getz (2008) contend that engaging with sustainability networks and fostering the interconnectedness of diverse destination stakeholder groups can improve the process of sustainable destination development.

For regional destinations with existing wellness tourism providers, and those that are seeking to develop wellness tourism as part of their tourism product and experience offerings, it is important that stakeholders across governments, businesses and the community with an 'interest' in wellness tourism be consulted in planning processes. The establishment of wellness networks or cooperatives is important for the enhancement and development of wellness tourism as a viable industry sector, destination sustainability, and for the provision of excellent and engaging wellness experiences for visitors. Findings of a survey of supply undertaken as part of the Australian scoping study by Voigt *et al.* (2010), however, found little evidence that wellness tourism product was distributed through traditional travel distribution networks, nor was there much evidence of cooperation amongst wellness providers. This could be due to operations and practices being mainly small scale.

Methodology

A case-study methodology is acknowledged as useful to develop an in-depth understanding of the complex social phenomenon and unfolding processes within contextual situations (Yin 2009). Due to their distinctive natural environments, well-established wellness tourism practices, commitment to sustainable tourism planning processes, and comparative advantage over other regional destinations the cases of Daylesford/Hepburn Springs, and Byron Bay were selected.

Multiple data collection methods were used to inform the case-study analyses including: (1) analysis of archival sources (e.g. academic literature, reports and consultancies, policy and planning documents, and media reports); (2) in-depth interviews undertaken with knowledgeable informants engaged in alternative health, wellness and spiritual experiences within the destinations; and (3) a product audit of all wellness tourism experiences undertaken within both destinations in August 2009.

The interview process used a purposeful sampling technique (Merriam 1998) to select informants with significant knowledge of wellness tourism in both destinations. The interviews were conducted by a case-study researcher who was familiar with both cases as a result of involvement in developing strategic tourism management plans for both destination regions during 2009. The interviewer used open-ended questions within a semi-structured format to minimise researcher bias.

To determine the diversity of wellness operations that offer and promote their services to visitors (and residents), a comprehensive audit of beauty, spa, health, wellness and spiritual services in both case-study destinations was undertaken in August 2009 as part of this research. The audit involved identifying and categorising, through the analysis of secondary data sources (internet and brochures) and field observation, all practices and services that were promoted to visitors. A profile of both case-study destinations is presented in Table 5.1.

Table 5.1 Profile of case study destination regions

	Byron Bay	Daylesford and Hepburn Springs
Location	New South Wales far north coast, one hour south of the Gold Coast, east coast of Australia	Victoria rural inland, one hour north-west of Melbourne, inland south-east Australia
Environment	Sub-tropical	Temperate
Significant natural resources	Geological (volcanic) World heritage listed rainforests National parks Coastal and beach Marine sanctuary	Mineral springs Rural landscapes National and state parks
Population of town(s):	5,000 (approx.)	3,100 (approx.)
Population of shire (2006 census):	28,000 (approx.)	13,700 (approx.)
Annual visitor numbers International: Domestic overnight: Day visitors:	181,000 416,000 812,000	5,000 234,000 520,000
Number of wellness tourism operators	144	94

Sources: Australia Bureau of Statistics (2013), Tourism Research Australia (2009).

Case analyses

This section draws on a collation of the various data sources and methods to present the case analysis for Byron Bay, followed by the case analysis for Daylesford/Hepburn Springs. The five factors and processes derived from the destination competitiveness, sustainable tourism and stakeholder literatures are used as a framework to examine if and how these have contributed to the development of wellness tourism in these destinations.

Case study one: Byron Bay

Significance of historical antecedents and existence of natural resources

Byron Bay is situated on the far north coast of the state of New South Wales and less than an hour south of the Queensland border, which is the start of Australia's well-known and highly urbanised Gold Coast. The Byron Bay/North Coast region is diversified with World Heritage-listed rainforests, an extensive coastal zone, tropical agriculture and distinctive geological formations. Byron Bay has one of the few north-facing beaches on the east coast of Australia, providing excellent surf and swimming conditions.

The Cape Byron Headland Reserve, located five kilometres east of the Byron Bay township, is the most easterly point of the Australian mainland, offers leisure and recreation opportunities provided by its rainforests and beaches and more adventurous recreation activities such as hang-gliding. In addition, Byron Bay is the site of Australia's first marine sanctuary, the Cape Byron Marine Park, which provides a high quality scuba diving environment (Green 1997). As such, Byron Bay hosts a wealth of natural assets, provided by its rainforest, coastal and marine environments, which are important both ecologically and for tourism and leisure purposes. At the year ending December 2008, it was estimated that there were 416,000 domestic overnight visitors, 181,400 international overnight visitors and 812,000 day visitors to the destination (Tourism Research Australia 2009).

Important historical antecedents that have influenced the development of wellness tourism in Byron Bay and its surrounds include wellbeing values and practices related to socio-demographic changes from the 1960s. This included the arrival of surfers and alternative lifestylers with strong environmental values, and growth in the number of health and wellness practitioners that evolved from the 1980s (including New Age and spiritual practices). Major tourism development in Byron Bay then occurred from the 1990s. Wellness tourism therefore emerged organically as a result of the expertise, interests and values of local residents rather than being imposed on the community. Thus, the wellness tourism focus has been an added layer that sits comfortably within the region rather than acting as a substitute.

Values of Byron community with respect to both the natural environment and wellbeing

Given the significance of both its terrestrial and marine environments, the Byron Bay community has traditionally had a strong concern for the environment. Evidence of Byron Bay residents' policy activism can be traced back to 1909 with the establishment of the Byron Bay and District Citizens Association that formed to act as a conduit of public opinion to Byron Shire Council (Ryan and Smith 2001). Ryan and Smith (2001: 30) believe that this legacy has been passed down to current residents of Byron Bay 'who are not backward in relaying their opinions to government authorities'. A particular feature of the area's social environment is the presence of vocal community groups that formed to vigorously defend the area's high environmental qualities (Essex and Brown 1997). 'Alternative lifestylers' have influenced community attitudes and more conservative members of the community have adopted their views on environmental conservation and preservation of lifestyle. Byron Bay is further described by Tatray (2002: 131) as 'an experimental community at the epicentre of alternative living in Australia, particularly in relation to spirituality and environmental activism'.

A number of studies and consultancy reports over the past decade provide further evidence of these distinctive local values. A consultancy study undertaken for Byron Shire Council in 1983 showed that the 'relaxing lifestyle' was the most valued feature about living in the area. This was followed by the 'pleasant climate' and 'attractiveness of the coastal location' (Planning Workshop 1983 in Essex and Brown 1997: 275). This lifestyle attribute can be considered an important foundation to the development of wellness tourism.

Diversity of destination experiences and wellness practices

Byron Bay is a well-established domestic and international destination in Australia offering a diversity of experiences associated with its natural and built environments. The development of wellness and New Age practices and experiences in Byron Bay largely emerged from these historical antecedents and values. The wellness product audit, undertaken in August 2009 as part of this case-study research, demonstrates the diversity and spectrum of practices across beauty, health and wellness, and spiritual services (see Figure 5.1). Overall, the audit determined that there were 139 business operations offering beauty, spa, health, wellness and spiritual services in Byron Bay. Most are small operations indicating that wellness tourism need not be on a large commercial scale. The audit further revealed that the wellness services in Byron Bay are mainly concentrated within the central business district, thus allowing easy access of these practices for tourists (both overnight and daytrip). More importantly, this means that visitors can stay in traditional accommodation establishments (e.g. holiday apartments, houses, motels, guesthouses and hostels) and seek these practices and services without having to stay in dedicated spa, health and spiritual resorts and retreats. Visitors can therefore choose and package their own wellness holiday. As such Byron Bay and the broader

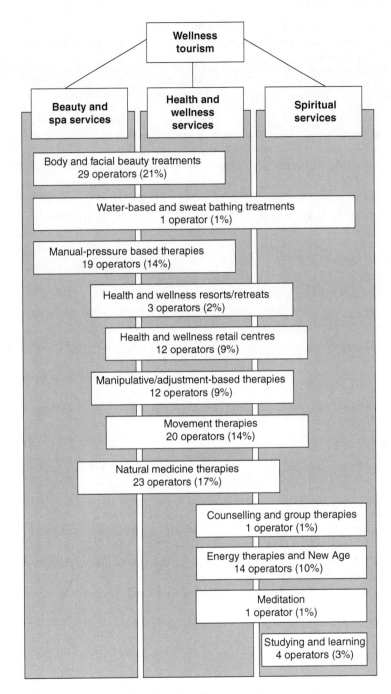

Figure 5.1 Byron Bay health and wellness operations.

Note
Percentages do not total 100 per cent because of rounding.

Byron Shire can be considered a well-established New Age destination given that the destination provides a concentration of 'new, exotic and transformational experiences' (Sutton and House 2003).

Strategic initiatives to plan and achieve sustainable tourism development

It can be argued that proactive planning toward sustainable tourism development has come very late to Byron Bay. The popularity of Byron Bay as a domestic and international tourist destination coupled with its attractiveness as a lifestyle locality has placed strains on the town's infrastructure and service facilities, and these have been exacerbated by a lack of planning for infrastructure, traffic and parking congestion. In 2007, Byron Shire Council identified the need for a tourism management plan that would help ensure the sustainable development, management and marketing of tourism for Byron Shire over the next ten years (Lawrence and Buultjens 2008a). The *Byron Shire Tourism Management Plan (BSTMP) 2008 to 2018* was developed comprising 13 strategies to guide the management, development and marketing of tourism for the Shire (Lawrence and Buultjens 2008a). These strategies have been considered within Council's sustainability framework and advocate protection of the natural environment and community values through improved destination management and sustainable tourism development.

Furthermore, the Plan recommends a consistent brand and image for Byron Shire and its destinations related to their unique natural environment, relaxed atmosphere, spiritual and cultural diversity, health and wellbeing experiences and innovative enterprises. This demonstrates the important role played by ecological and community values in underpinning destination branding (Wheeler *et al.* 2011) and as a tool to foster sustainable development.

Stakeholder cooperation in planning for wellness tourism

During 2009 and 2010, Byron Shire Council employed a Tourism Officer and established a Tourism Advisory Group to better manage local government involvement in tourism. However, there has been no substantial attempt by Council to engage with broader government, business and community stakeholders in a process that would ultimately harmonise their interests in tourism. This is mainly due to Council influence on the composition and process to establish a Tourism Advisory Group that engages adequately with tourism and business stakeholders. These stakeholders still function independently of Council's destination management initiatives. There is also no cooperative network of wellness practitioners operating within the destination region.

Case study two: Daylesford/Hepburn Springs

Significance of historical antecedents and existence of natural resources

The twin towns of Daylesford/Hepburn Springs are located in the local government area of Hepburn Shire, in the Central Highlands district of the Australian state of Victoria. The destination region is inland, just over an hour's drive from the city of Melbourne. The region is known as 'Spa Country' and contains over 80 per cent of Australia's mineral water reserves. The Hepburn Mineral Springs Bathhouse was established as Australia's original spa experience in 1895. The area is also renowned for its natural beauty, historic architecture, innovative and quality tourism enterprises, dynamic creative industries and diverse communities. At the year ending December 2008, it was estimated that there were 234,000 domestic overnight visitors (about half that of Byron Bay), 5,000 international overnight visitors (compared to 181,000 to Byron Bay) and 520,000 day visitors (similar to the numbers visiting Byron Bay) (Tourism Research Australia 2009).

Bathing in (balneotherapy) and drinking geothermal and natural mineral water have long been associated with mental and physical health benefits (Tourism Victoria 2007). The natural mineral water resources in the Daylesford/ Hepburn Springs area are naturally pure products that have been formed by hydro-geological processes (Tourism Victoria 2007). They contain varied and unique concentrations of minerals that cannot be artificially replicated by heating or treating normal fresh surface or reticulated water (ibid.). Most mineral water springs reserves in the area are small parcels of land that are subject to urbanisation and mixed rural development (VMWC 2009). All of the springs are situated in parks and reserves and are generally accessible to all. Many of the reserves also have picnic facilities, whilst the largest have the full range of visitor services (VMWC 2009).

Balneotherapy services have been provided by the Hepburn Springs Bathhouse since 1895, and since the 1990s a number of day spa operations, wellness and spiritual services have been established within the destination. Visitors can tour the region by car and sample different waters at each spring. The springs are well signposted from the main roads and are generally within one hour's drive of each other and all have subtle differences in flavour and effect (VMWC 2009). Each spring is either a bore, equipped with a hand pump, or a naturally flowing spring where the emerging mineral water has been captured and directed to an outlet within a retaining wall.

Historically, Daylesford/Hepburn Springs have been popular daytrip and lifestyle tourism destinations for over 130 years and have retained the character of their early Victorian heritage when people travelled to 'take the waters' and Swiss and Italian and other immigrants settled there.

Values of the community with respect to the natural environment and wellbeing

Strong environmental values and community activism have underpinned the protection and conservation of the mineral springs reserves in Daylesford/Hepburn Springs from the late 1800s through to the 1980s. The late 1970s and 1980s were considered to be the beginning of a renaissance of health, fitness and natural therapies as important values (Regional Development Victoria n.d.). From this time, a number of significant tourism and hospitality operations were established in Daylesford/Hepburn Springs that reinvigorated the area as an attractive wellness tourism destination. Daylesford's international and national award-winning Lake House Resort and Salus Day Spa were established on the edge of Lake Daylesford in 1984. As these developed, a pool of local trainees and apprentices grew and other significant attractions evolved as other entrepreneurs moved to Daylesford for lifestyle reasons and developed enterprises including: Central Springs Inn, Lavandula (a restored Swiss–Italian farm), Harvest 1 Organic Bakery, and the Convent Gallery (a restored and expanded Catholic convent) (Hollick 2007). Peppers Springs Retreat, at Hepburn Springs was developed in the late 1990s.

These new settlers and entrepreneurs were considered to share similar local attachment to community values and a commitment to quality (Hollick 2007). As a result the residential and weekender population expanded, as did the number of stores and services meeting their needs. Agriculture also revived, with a focus on olives, grapes, herbs and organic produce, fuelled by the demand of local eateries (ibid.). During this period, some migrant descendants also returned to the area, restoring the former Italian stone buildings and reinstating the Italianate gardens in Hepburn (ibid.).

The Bathhouse redevelopment (1992) proved to be an effective strategy to stimulate further development in Hepburn and Daylesford (Hollick 2007). There was considerable growth in the number of beauty, health, wellness and spiritual practitioners with experience and qualifications. As one study participant said, 'they cluster together because they all believe in each other and value each other's therapies … people come here for a lifestyle, they want to live cleaner and greener lives themselves'.

Diversity of destination experiences and wellness practices and tourism experiences

Visitors to Daylesford/Hepburn Springs can experience a wide range of tourist attractions and services including spa and wellness facilities, local restaurants, cafes and specialist retail outlets, galleries and other attractions. As in Byron Bay, the development of spa and wellness practices and experiences largely emerged from these historical antecedents and values. Figure 5.2 provides the results of the audit of beauty, spa, health, wellness and spiritual services promoted to visitors to Daylesford and Hepburn Springs in 2009. There are 94 business operations offering beauty, spa, health, wellness and spiritual services. Most services are clustered around the central business district of Daylesford and near Peppers Springs Retreat and the Hepburn Springs Bathhouse at Hepburn Springs. While the Hepburn Springs Bathhouse, Peppers Springs Retreat and the Lakehouse are principal commercial operations, individual practices and small operations account for the majority of providers within the destination. There are also some mobile operators that provide services to visitors at their place of accommodation, and there are nine dedicated retreat centres offering health, wellness and spiritual retreats.

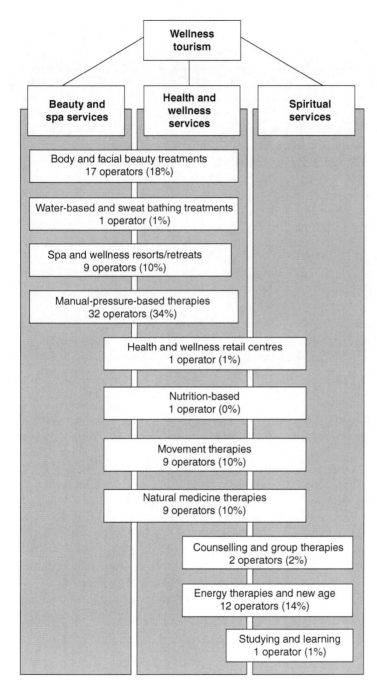

Figure 5.2 Daylesford/Hepburn Springs health and wellness operations.

Note
Percentages do not total 100 per cent because of rounding.

Strategic initiatives to plan and achieve sustainable tourism development

Until 2008, there was little evidence of planning toward sustainable development of tourism in the region. In terms of the sustainable management of the mineral water resources, the Victorian Mineral Water Committee (VMWC) provides advice to the Victorian Minister for Environment on the management of the mineral water resources and the disbursement of funds collected through a mineral water surcharge. The role of the VMWC is to ensure appropriate policies, plans, strategies and guidelines are in place to preserve the mineral water resources for the maximum benefit of the whole community. The Committee supports an extensive program of renovation and reticulation of public springs, many of which are old and degraded, and regularly undertakes technical studies to ensure the ongoing safety of the mineral water resources. In 2009, the VMWC released an updated Master Plan (originally prepared in 2000) that outlines capital works and management directions that address a range of physical and functional issues and opportunities for each Reserve to be achieved over the next ten years. These works focus on protection of the mineral water resource, presentation of the mineral water via public springs and general public access and use of the Reserves (Land Design Partnership 2009).

From a tourism planning perspective, Tourism Victoria has developed a number of plans and strategic initiatives to expand the tourism sector within Victoria to an $18 billion industry that employs 225,000 people by 2016 (Tourism Victoria 2009), the most recent being *Victoria's Spa and Wellbeing Tourism Action Plan 2011 to 2015* (Tourism Victoria 2011). In addition to its infrastructure investment in Hepburn Springs, the Victorian government has contributed considerable funding and strategic planning expertise to better position Daylesford/Hepburn Springs and the Macedon Ranges region as the Spa Capital of Australia.

Coinciding with the commencement of the Bathhouse redevelopment process, Tourism Victoria identified the need for a strategic tourism plan for Daylesford, Hepburn Springs and Surrounds to, among other things, 'assure the ongoing sustainability of the local tourism industry' and 'enhance and protect the well-being and uniqueness of this special place for visitors and its residents' (Lawrence and Buultjens 2008b). The *Destination Daylesford Strategic Tourism Plan 2008 to 2018* provided the first coordinated strategic and integrated approach to the sustainable management, development and marketing of tourism for Daylesford, Hepburn Springs and Surrounds. The following vision for tourism was developed through consultation with government, industry and community stakeholders:

> To position Daylesford, Hepburn Springs and Surrounds as an internationally and nationally renowned mineral water and wellness centre, sharing and celebrating its unique heritage, cultural diversity, community lifestyle, rural landscapes, natural resources, and built attractions with visitors. Over the next ten years and beyond tourism will be developed and facilitated by

appropriate, balanced, sustainable, inclusive and visionary policies which ensure social, economic and environmental benefits for the community and offer best practice experiences for visitors.

(Lawrence and Buultjens 2008b: 15)

Stakeholder cooperation in planning for wellness tourism

In contrast to the development of sustainable tourism planning initiatives led by local government for Byron Shire, the process of sustainable tourism planning for Daylesford/Hepburn Springs has been driven and supported mainly by the Victorian state government. From a marketing perspective, the area has been identified as a Level-One[1] destination region by Tourism Victoria which, along with the Daylesford and Macedon Ranges Campaign Committee, provides considerable marketing and professional support to achieve this status. A participant to this case study explained that Tourism Victoria played a vital role in marketing the destination given that Council's taxpayer base was so small and that there were few large tourism operations in the area.

An AU$7.3 million advertising campaign was launched by Tourism Victoria in August 2009 that aimed to position Daylesford/Hepburn Springs and Victoria as the nation's leading wellness destination. Tourism Victoria's Chief Executive explained that the campaign was developed to move Baby Boomers, who are attracted to Melbourne for its romance and style, to regional Victoria, given their growing interest in health. Don Richter, Marketing Director Tourism Victoria, explained that the 'Daylesford Lead a Double Life' campaign is about achieving balance in life. He explained that there are two sides to the Daylesford experience, indulgence with beautiful food and nightlife, the other side about restoring your inner wellbeing through massages, spas and mineral water experiences (Tourism Victoria 2009a).

The Bathhouse Business and Community Group was established in 2006 as an advisory committee to Hepburn Shire Council to consider how to maintain visitation to the area and to ensure the ongoing delivery of spa and wellness services within the destination during the closure of the Bathhouse (Hepburn Shire Council 2006). The Group was a ten-member committee that represented a range of business and community interests. The Group established an Action Plan to engage and inform interested stakeholders of the redevelopment process and develop initiatives to ensure the ongoing delivery of wellness services within the destination (ibid.).

Around this time, the Spa Therapy Group was also established as a cooperative network of spa and wellbeing practitioners within the area. It had considerable membership of smaller operators but was also well supported by larger operations. A participant to the study explained that the Group had an important role as a network for practitioners but needed the ongoing support of the larger operators. The Group, however, disbanded in 2009 following the opening of the redeveloped Bathhouse.

Discussion of findings

Factors and processes that have contributed to the sustainable tourism development of wellness tourism

In the two case studies, there was considerable evidence for four of the five factors derived from previous literature: the influence of historical antecedents and existence of natural resources; complementary values held by their host populations with respect to natural environments and wellbeing; adequate scale and diversity of tourism wellness tourism products and experiences; and strategic initiatives being undertaken to foster sustainable tourism development. With regard to this latter factor, despite both case studies demonstrating the implicit link between sustainable tourism development and wellness tourism, evidence of ongoing stakeholder cooperation in wellness tourism has been limited. The recent development of long-term strategic and sustainable tourism plans, since 2008, has sought to establish destination management frameworks to guide and inform the sustainable development of tourism and to better position both regions as important wellness tourism destinations. However, policies and practices recommended or underway to foster sustainable development are still immature.

Furthermore, stakeholder involvement for both planning processes has been largely driven by government interests rather than a more cooperative and sustained approach to engaging and harmonising all stakeholder interests. In the case of Daylesford/Hepburn Springs region, planning, management and marketing are very much top-down and have been driven and supported by state and local governments. Planning for sustainable tourism in Byron Bay has been initiated by local government. While such government support has played a positive role, both case-study regions show a lack of presence of 'sustainability networks' to foster cooperative efforts among businesses, governmental bodies, non-government organisations, persons or other entities that are interconnected in some way (Smith-Ring 1999 in Halme 2001: 102). As proposed by Timur and Getz (2008), sustainability networks and the interconnectedness of diverse destination stakeholder groups can improve the process of sustainable destination development. It should be acknowledged, however, that there is considerable evidence of strong environmental values and activism by particular stakeholder groups in both case-study regions that has influenced the ongoing conservation of natural resources that have helped to support the development of wellness tourism.

As discussed in the literature review and evidenced in the case-study analyses (in particular Daylesford/Hepburn Springs), a strategic approach to branding and positioning of regional destinations as *wellness* or *sustainable* destinations that are integrated with other destination products experiences is important. As explained by Voigt *et al.* (2010) destinations are more likely to succeed when planned as a component of a broader service offering. Moreover, the benefits and multiplier effects will be greatest where opportunities are created for local suppliers.

Further research is needed to explore whether the literature-derived factors are key contributors to sustainability of wellness tourism regions elsewhere. Quantitative modelling of their relative contribution to sustainable outcomes is probably still a long way off, but research that fosters a better understanding of the relative importance of each would be a contribution to the literature as well as of practical value when allocating resources to planning actions such as stakeholder engagement.

Conclusion

This chapter has sought to identify the resources, factors and processes that can be and have been used to develop and sustain wellness tourism as a tool for competitive advantage and for the sustainability of regional tourism destinations. Concepts derived from the destination competiveness, sustainable tourism and stakeholder literatures were used to create a framework for identifying the processes and factors that contribute to the sustainability of regional tourism destinations. Two Australian wellness destinations were used as case studies to identify and assess the importance of these factors, including the significance of the destinations' historical context and natural resources, the values held by their host populations with respect to both the natural environment and wellbeing, the scale and diversity of their wellness tourism products and experiences, initiatives undertaken to foster sustainable tourism development, and processes for engaging and harmonising the interests of stakeholders. Evidence for the first four of these five factors was found in both case studies. More research is however needed with respect to these five factors and processes in a wellness tourism context.

This chapter also provides some evidence that wellness tourism supports sustainable (tourism) development and may prove particularly useful for regional tourism destinations to attract domestic markets, extend their tourism product and experience offerings, attract off-season visitors, increase visitors' length of stay, and rejuvenate and refresh their image. Finally, in attracting visitors who are seeking wellbeing and lifestyle experiences, wellness tourism potentially aligns more easily with host community values in comparison with other forms of tourism, further enhancing its capacity to contribute to sustainability.

Note

1 A Level-One Destination is defined as those destinations that attract a strong mix of international, interstate and intrastate visitors and particularly demonstrate international appeal matched to Victoria's key product strengths.

References

Ahn, B.Y., Lee, B. and Shafer, C.S. (2002) 'Operationalizing sustainability in regional tourism planning: an application of the limits of acceptable change framework', *Tourism Management*, 23: 1–15.

Australian Bureau of Statistics (2013) *Australia Census 2006*, online, available at: www.censusdata.abs.gov.au (accessed 17 January 2013).

Bycroft, P., Dyer, P. and Nash, P. (2007) 'Serious business beyond tourism: attracting and retaining high value low impact industries to regional economies', *Australasian Journal of Regional Studies*, 13: 205–20.

Essex, S. and Brown, G. (1997) 'The emergence of post-suburban landscapes on the north coast of New South Wales: a case study of contested space', *International Journal of Urban and Regional Research*, 21: 259–85.

Frost, G.J. (2004) 'The spa as a model of an optimal healing environment', *The Journal of Alternative and Complementary Medicine*, 10: 85–92.

Gesler, W.M. (2003) *Healing Places*, Lanham, MD: Rowman & Littlefield Publishers.

Gnoth, J. (2007) 'The structure of destination brands: leveraging values', *Tourism Analysis*, 12: 345–59.

Green, R. (1997) 'Community perception of town character: a case study', unpublished thesis, Queensland University of Technology.

Halme, M. (2001) 'Learning for sustainable development in tourism networks', *Business Strategy and the Environment*, 10: 100–14.

Hardy, A., Beeton, R. and Pearson, L. (2002) 'Sustainable tourism: an overview of the concept and its position in relation to conceptualisations of tourism', *Journal of Sustainable Tourism*, 10: 475–96.

Hepburn Shire Council (2006) *Hepburn Springs Bathhouse: Brochure No. 1*, Hepburn Shire Council and Bathhouse & Community Liaison Group, 25 July.

Hollick, M. (2007) 'Sustainable regional tourism destinations project: Daylesford case study', unpublished report, Gold Coast: Sustainable Tourism Cooperative Research Centre.

Hoyez, A.-C. (2007) 'The "world of yoga": the production and reproduction of therapeutic landscapes', *Social Science and Medicine*, 65: 112–24.

Land Design Partnership (2009) *Victorian Mineral Springs Reserves Master Plan Review: Draft Consultation Press Release*, online, available at: www.hepburnshire.com.au/Page/page.asp?Page_Id=950&h=1 (accessed 20 October 2009).

Lawrence, M. (2006) 'Unravelling the complexities of tourist destination systems: policy networks and issue cycles in Byron Bay 1988 to 2005', unpublished thesis, Southern Cross University.

Lawrence, M. and Buultjens, J. (2008a) *Byron Shire Tourism Management Plan 2008 to 2018*, Lismore: Australian Regional Tourism Research Centre.

Lawrence, M. and Buultjens, J. (2008b) *Destination Daylesford Strategic Tourism Plan 2008 to 2018*, Lismore: Australian Regional Tourism Research Centre.

Lea, J. (2008) 'Retreating to nature: rethinking "therapeutic landscapes"', *Area*, 40: 90–8.

Leiper, N. (2004) *Tourism Management*, 3rd edition, Sydney: Pearson Education.

McCool, S.F. (2009) 'Constructing partnerships for protected area tourism planning in an era of change and messiness', *Journal of Sustainable Tourism*, 17: 133–48.

McDonald, J. (2009) 'Complexity science: an alternative world view for understanding sustainable tourism development', *Journal of Sustainable Tourism*, 17: 455–71.

Merriam, S.B. (1998) *Qualitative Research and Case Study Applications in Education*, San Francisco, CA: Jossey-Bass.

Regional Development Victoria (n.d.) *Hepburn Mineral Springs Bathhouse Refurbishment*, Victorian Government, online, available at: www.rdv.vic.gov.au (accessed 20 October 2009).

Ritchie, J.R.B. and Crouch, G. (2000) 'The competitive destination: a sustainability perspective', *Tourism Management*, 21: 1–7.

Ritchie, J.R.B. and Crouch, G. (2003) *The Competitive Destination: A Sustainable Tourism Perspective*, Wallingford: CABI Publishing.

Ryan, M. and Smith, R. (2001) *Time and Tide Again: A History of Byron Bay*, Lismore: Northern Rivers Press.

Smith, M. and Kelly, C. (2006) 'Holistic tourism: journeys of the self?' *Tourism Recreation Research*, 31: 15–24.

Sutton, P. and House, J. (2003) *The New Age of tourism: Postmodern tourism for post-modern people?* online, available at: www.arasite.org/pspage2.htm (accessed 4 April 2010).

Tatray, D. (2002) 'Alchemy, real estate and the culture of conservation in Byron Bay (visualising place and space)', *Journal of Australian Studies*, 72(January): 131–42.

Timur, S. and Getz, D. (2008) 'A network perspective on managing stakeholders for sustainable urban tourism', *International Journal of Contemporary Hospitality Management*, 20: 445–61.

Tourism Research Australia (2009) *National Visitor Survey and International Visitor Survey: January to December 2008*, Sydney: TRA.

Tourism Victoria (2007) *Victoria's Geothermal and Natural Mineral Water Tourism Investment Opportunities*, online, available at: www.tourism.vic.gov.au/images/ stories/ Documents/StrategiesandPlans/Geothermal-natural-spa-tourism.pdf. (accessed 13 August 2009).

Tourism Victoria (2009) *Regional Tourism Action Plan 2009–2012*, online, available at: www.tourism.vic.gov.au/component/edocman/?view=document&id=119: regional-tourism-action-plan-2009-2012-1-41-mb (accessed 10 July 2013).

Tourism Victoria (2011) *Victoria's Spa and Wellbeing Tourism Action Plan 2011 to 2015*, online, available at: www.tourism.vic.gov.au/component/edocman/ ?view=document&id=250:victoria-s-spa-and-wellbeing-tourism-action-plan-2011-2015-939-kb (accessed 10 July 2013).

UNWTO (United Nations World Tourism Organization) (2010) *International Tourism on Track for a Rebound after an Exceptionally Challenging 2009* (media release 18 January 2010), online, available at: www.unwto.org/media/news/en/ press_det. php?id=5361 (accessed 9 February 2010).

VMWC (Victorian Mineral Water Committee) (2009) *Business Plan 2009 to 2012*, formerly available online at: www.mineralwater.vic.gov.au/resources (accessed 24 October 2010).

Voigt, C., Laing, J., Wray, M., Brown, G., Howat, G., Weiler, B. and Trembath, R. (2010) *Health Tourism in Australia: Supply, Demand and Opportunities*, Brisbane: Sustainable Tourism CRC.

Wang, Y. and Krakover, S. (2008) 'Destination marketing: competition, cooperation or coopetition?' *International Journal of Contemporary Hospitality Management*, 20: 126–41.

Weaver, D. and Lawton, L. (2010) *Tourism Management*, 4th edition, Sydney: John Wiley & Sons.

Wheeler, F., Frost, W. and Weiler, B. (2011) 'Destination brand identity, values and community: a case study from rural Victoria, Australia', *Journal of Travel and Tourism Marketing*, 28: 13–26.

Wray, M. (2009) 'Policy communities, networks and issue cycles in tourism destination systems', *Journal of Sustainable Tourism*, 17: 673–90.

Wray, M. (2011) 'Adopting and implementing a transactive approach to sustainable tourism planning: translating theory into practice', *Journal of Sustainable Tourism*, 19: 605–27.

Wray, M., Dredge, D., Cox, C., Buultjens, J., Hollick, M., Lee, D., Pearlman, M. and Lacroix, C. (2010) *Sustainable Regional Tourism Destinations: Best Practice for Management, Development and Marketing*, Brisbane: Sustainable Tourism Cooperative Research Centre.

Yin, R.K. (2009) *Case Study Research: Design and Methods*, 4th edition, Thousand Oaks, CA: Sage Publications.

6 Health regions

Building tourism destinations through networked regional core competencies

Christof Pforr, Harald Pechlaner, Cornelia Locher and Judith Jochmann

Introduction

The driving forces for the emerging health tourism market match those observed for the entire health-care industry and include demographic and psychographic changes with a growing health awareness creating demand for a new range of health-related products and services in a leisure setting. This chapter highlights the growing importance of health as a regional development strategy and introduces the concept of a 'health region'. Not much research has yet been carried out on these newly established health regions to capture their operations and effectiveness. This chapter will discuss some of these issues. First, the growing importance of health as a regional development strategy is discussed. Then the development of health regions and the role tourism can play in their establishment is outlined. With the case example of the Health Region Kneippland Unterallgäu in Bavaria, Germany, the issues surrounding the development of one particular health region, which is founded on medical and wellness tourism, are presented. The case-study research is based primarily on a series of interviews with key representatives from the health tourism sector, as well as secondary data sources such as newspaper articles, government publications and specialist reports complemented by observation inquiry during a site visit to the Health Region Kneippland Unterallgäu in January 2010.

The structure of the health economy

The health sector has emerged as a significant economic plank on a regional, national and also international level. Indeed, in some countries, it has even developed into one of the most important economic activities. For instance, in Germany this sector occupies 13.8 per cent of the total employment, which is on a par with other key sectors like the automotive industry. This trend resonates at a global level where it is expected that over the next decade or two the health economy will develop into the largest growth sector (Hilbert and Kluska 2010). Along with this goes a change in the perception of health care in developed countries, which is no longer necessarily seen as a burden but rather as an opportunity for the national economy. Over the past three decades

Germany's health economy has been in a period of significant change, moving away from its traditional function as an important column of the German welfare state into a more independent role as a dynamic motor for new economic and social growth. One of the drivers of this extraordinary development is demographic change in the form of an increasingly ageing society. Consequently, there is a significant increase in the demand for medical and other health-related services. However, it is not only the ageing population that has fuelled this trend. Today, good health and wellbeing are core values for all sectors of society, a shift in attitude commonly known as psychographic change (Forschungsgemeinschaft Urlaub und Reisen 2008; see also Chapter 16 in this volume).

The complex health economy includes a wide range of goods and services conducive to the preservation and restoration of health which can be depicted in a multilayered so-called *Onion Model*, developed by the Institute for Work and Technology (Institute for Work and Technology 2010). This model adopts a value-chain perspective and illustrates how products and services on its periphery benefit from cross-sectoral expansion into the health economy and ultimately lead to a much more diverse product mix (Fretschner *et al.* 2002). One can visualise the model as consisting of three layers. At its core are primary health-care providers delivering inpatient and outpatient services, such as hospitals and general practitioners as well as preventive care and rehabilitation centres. Therapeutic, diagnostic and custodian ancillary services including the pharmaceutical industry and medical technology constitute the next layer. On the periphery health-orientated services such as sport and leisure activities, healthy nutrition and lifestyle as well as medical and wellness tourism are found. Hence, from this perspective the health-care industry takes on a more holistic view on health, incorporating products and services outside the traditional core primary health-care sector. This reflects an understanding of health as 'a state of complete physical, mental and social wellbeing and not merely the absence of disease or infirmity' (World Health Organization 2010).

The various sectors of the health-care industry demonstrate increased levels of interconnectedness as they bring together and offer much scope for collaboration between a wide range of health-service providers, for instance from the medical, pharmaceutical, but also the tourism, leisure and hospitality industries. These network clusters and the resulting leverage effects are more and more recognised in political debate and their significance acknowledged for future socio-economic development. In some instances partnerships have already formed in regional network structures to be able to capitalise on this trend. These networks are often formalised in the form of 'health regions' which are characterised by an active collaboration of service providers and industry sectors in a defined regional setting. The aim is to develop a competitive advantage over other regions through capacity building, know-how transfer, creation of competencies, regional marketing initiatives and the initiation of local projects.

The development of health regions

The maintenance or restoration of health is of crucial importance for most people, and hence society as a whole, and therefore constitutes an important objective of public provision. Since the Universal Declaration of Human Rights countries have a political and often legal obligation to gradually realise the right to the highest attainable standard of people's health (Backman *et al.* 2008). Health-care services are generally very widely used and the market volume of the health-care sector can be expected to continue to grow considerably in industrialised national economies in the years to come (Roland Berger 2008; Henderson 2009). Next to hospitals and practitioners, in- and outpatient health care as well as rehabilitation centres, which form the basis of the primary health-care sector, the health-care industry has made significant efforts to promote additional offers and services to specific target groups. This has initiated the development of a self-funded, so-called 'Second Health-Care Market'. It includes, for instance, privately funded wellness and fitness offerings, over-the-counter medication, alternative medical treatments, preventive health measures, spa treatments, cosmetic surgery and functional foods as well as health tourism activities. This increasing integration of products and services from the periphery of the health economy provides for new cross-linkages within the sector and opens up new avenues for migration of a growing number of customers into the sector.

The role of locations in this context is twofold. On the one hand they provide the primary health-care services on a local and regional level. Hospitals, for instance, as a traditional platform of primary health-care services, continue to play an important role in a location due to their local competence. On the other hand, as a result of increased regional competition in terms of economic investments, new companies, human resources, infrastructure and attraction points, regions are trying to develop and promote additional services with the aim of making the region particularly attractive to specific target groups (Pechlaner *et al.* 2006). Locations are thus now increasingly developed into attractive settings for Second Health-Care Market offerings for residents, visitors and investors alike.

Next to the so-called hard (economic) location factors such as infrastructure, human and natural resources, soft location factors including general living conditions and environmental quality as well as cultural and leisure offerings, play an increasingly important role in the competitiveness of regions (Grabow 2005). In this context *quality of life* features prominently in academic and public discourse (Kämpf 2010). Dissert and Deller (2000: 144) highlight that

> because of higher income levels, a shift to a service and technology-based economy, and growing environmental awareness, quality of life plays and will increasingly play a significant role in the various dimensions of places, human migration, firm location, and economic growth.

Thus, location-based quality of life has developed into an increasingly important factor in regional competitiveness. Florida (2005, in Jochmann 2010: 91) aptly highlights that 'certain regional factors appear to play a role in creating an environment or habitat that can produce, attract and retain talent or human capital'. Soft location factors do not only play an increasingly important role in attracting or retaining residents and companies in a region, but visitors and guests alike.

Empirical studies have demonstrated that a well-balanced relationship between economic, environmental and social indicators is a decisive factor in the perception of quality of life. In this context, health (next to education services, security and leisure offerings) is an important constituent of the social perspective on quality of life (Kämpf 2010; Jochmann 2010). Thus, the availability of high-quality products and services in the first but also the Second Health-Care Market goes hand in hand with the perceived attractiveness of a region. Based on their profiles and local resources, regions can be seen as competitive units which are capable of attracting special target markets (Bieger and Beritelli 2006). The range and quality of health products and services on offer can provide such a cross-sectoral focal point for regional development and ultimately lead to the emergence of so-called health regions.

In their progression towards this, regions with a strategic approach towards specialisation on health services offerings need to first take stock of their endogenous resources and potentials and with this create a particular health-focused regional profile. The aim must be to establish a network of health-focused regional knowledge, competences, abilities and resources. Such competence-orientated competitive advantages can occur both at the micro level (e.g. individual companies or public institutions) as well as at the macro level, in other words at the regional network level. Network-specific resources as well as their effective steering and control therefore represent the foundation for a (regional) competitive advantage (Dyer and Singh 1998; Duschek 2002, 2004). Focal points for regional development based on health as the primary competence factor are commonly found in the areas of aged-care services, medical technology, rehabilitation, biotechnology or the pharmaceutical industry. However, regional health competence can also be built on prevention, medical tourism, sport and fitness as well as wellness products and services (Illing 2009).

The foundation for any successful regional and destination development is based on quality and cost advantages in the context of regional proximity as well as the interaction of different factors (Porter 1993; Smeral 1998). For health regions, an attractive landscape, proximity to water, clean air or a favourable climate can all play a major role as factor conditions. These are complemented by local resources, the type, quality and cost of the available infrastructure and also any cultural resources in the sense of cultural heritage. Knowledge, human resources and the availability of trained personnel complete the range of factor conditions which are all important to increase the attractiveness of a location.

Health regions have emerged in many parts of Germany since the early 2000s. According to the Bundesministerium für Wirtschaft und Technologie (2011) there are currently 60 health regions in the country which try to raise their profile and market themselves as a health region in an increasingly competitive health economy. As Hilbert (2007, translated by authors) comments, 'there is hardly a week without a city, region or a state announcing that the health economy has become a focus for regional development'. These health regions differ considerably, however, in regards to their structure and size as well as the specific priorities attached to their approach to regional development.

Generally, health regions develop around primary health-care providers and/ or companies and institutions specialised in products and services in the periphery of the health economy. In the following section, some core health competences will be briefly discussed that can facilitate the development of health regions when supported by appropriate governance structures (Figure 6.1).

Health regions based on research and the education sector

For tertiary-education providers and research institutes specialising in the growing field of health economics and management, cooperation and partnerships with hospitals and other health-care providers might provide a competitive advantage as the underlying network structures and associated exchange in information and knowledge allow them to respond effectively to a growing demand for more information on health-related issues. This will allow them to promote health awareness in the region in line with the previously outlined more holistic understanding of health encompassing all socio-economic aspects. Such an emphasis on a *healthy* region can certainly serve as a soft location factor contributing to the region's quality of life which, in turn, is of crucial importance for the attraction of a range of other, complementary industries to the region.

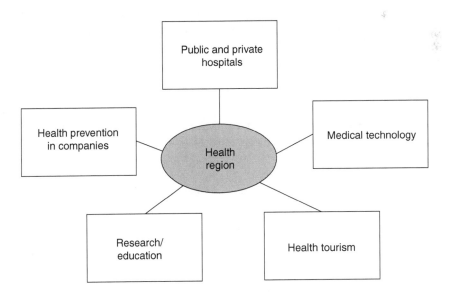

Figure 6.1 Major driving forces for the development of health regions.

Health regions based on health prevention within companies

Considering the interconnectedness of health and productivity from an employer's perspective, prevention in terms of prophylaxis and sensitisation but also appropriate workload management are important constituents of regional value creation through a safe and healthy work environment (Ahlers 2009). Since the health of their employees constitutes an important element in the development of human resources, companies from different sectors and industries have, thus, started to show strong interest in the development of healthy regions (e.g. the German car manufacturer Audi). Their support of regional development initiatives focusing on health is obviously also based on the realisation that healthy regions serve as an attractive pull factor for highly qualified professionals and thus aid in the recruitment of personnel.

Health regions based on medical technology

The medical technology and also the pharmaceutical industry sectors require a very specific location-based infrastructure such as high-end research and development institutions and a highly qualified workforce. Furthermore, they often benefit from close contact with primary health-care providers such as public and private hospitals. Therefore, hosting well-known companies in these fields often serves as the seed for regions to develop a particular health platform.

Health regions based on hospitals and specialised primary health-care providers

Hospitals and specialised clinics are often also an engine for the development of health regions as their specific infrastructural requirements promote technology-driven innovation, development and research. In this case medical clusters, thus, form the basis of regional health competence.

Health regions based on health tourism

Tourism and leisure offerings with a particular medical and/or wellness focus, such as thermal spas and health resorts commonly in combination with sport and fitness products and services, often form the basis of health tourism development in a destination. In this case health competence is established in a network which brings together a variety of medical and/or wellness providers with specialised product and service offerings based on unique local resources. This core competence in health in the form of medical and wellness tourism then forms the basis for the development of a health region. In the case-study section below, the establishment of such a health region with a particular tourism focus will be discussed in greater detail.

Health tourism in the form of wellness and medical tourism has become a significant dimension of tourism in a number of new and long-established destinations. As outlined in more detail in Chapter 2 in this volume, health tourism can be classified as a form of special interest tourism which comprises distinct niche markets such as medical and wellness tourism. Although the definitions of medical tourism and wellness tourism frequently overlap as a result of strong convergences, the underlying motivations differ. Medical tourism aims to treat or cure a particular medical condition, whereas wellness tourism is driven by the desire to maintain or promote health and wellbeing (Voigt *et al.* 2010; Berg 2008). As Müller and Lanz Kaufmann (2001: 6) emphasise, wellness is 'a state of health, featuring the harmony of body, mind and spirit, with self-responsibility, physical fitness/beauty care, healthy nutrition/diet, relaxation (need for distressing)/meditation, mental activity/education and environmental sensitivity/social contacts as fundamental elements.'

Case study – Health Region Kneippland Unterallgäu

There are more than 250 officially recognised spas and health resorts in Germany (Deutscher Heilbäderverband 2011; Forschungsgemeinschaft Urlaub und Reisen 2008). Based on their particular natural resources (e.g. soil, sea, climate), they are classified in six categories as (1) mineral, thermal and mud spa resorts; (2) healing climate health resorts; (3) seaside spas and resorts; (4) health resorts with healing caves and radon therapy; (5) aerotherapy health resorts and (6) Kneipp spas and health resorts (see Chapter 12 in this volume). A particular feature of all of these spas and health resorts is the *Kur*, a specific medical prevention, reconvalescence and rehabilitation program or treatment for particular chronic diseases. These *Kur* treatments of three or more weeks duration have to a large, but recently diminishing, degree been funded by the various German health insurance funds when recommended and prescribed by a general practitioner (Deutscher Heilbäderverband 2009a). About one-third of all visitor nights in Germany are spent in those spas and health resorts (Deutscher Heilbäderverband 2009b) which highlights the importance of health tourism for the country, not only in terms of economic significance but also with respect to employment and regional development. Within Germany the state of Bavaria is not only the Number One tourism destination in general (20.5 per cent of all tourist nights in 2011), but also the top destination for medical and wellness tourism (Kurdirektion Bad Wörishofen 2011). In 2010, 24 per cent of all domestic health tourists, for instance, opted to visit one of the state's officially recognised spas and health resorts which generated 24 per cent of all visitor nights within Bavaria. The sector's importance for Bavaria's health economy is also reflected in its contribution of €3.7 billion to the state's economy and also the more than 100,000 jobs it generates (Bayerischer Heilbäder-Verband 2011).

Amongst the officially recognised Bavarian spas and health resorts, Kneipp spas and resorts account for 11 per cent of all guest nights and 15 per cent of all visitor arrivals (Kurdirektion Bad Wörishofen 2011). As discussed in detail in Chapter 12, they specialise in traditional Kneipp water treatments based on the teachings of Sebastian Kneipp (1821–1897) and combine hydrotherapy with exercise, phytotherapy and appropriate nutrition to reinstate a balanced, healthy lifestyle (Deutscher Heilbäderverband 2009a).

The case example presented here, the Health Region Kneippland Unterallgäu, includes three traditional *Kur* resorts, Bad Wörishofen, Bad Grönenbach and Ottobeuren which constitute important pillars of the region's health economy. Recent developments in the Unterallgäu region have to be seen against the backdrop of a drastic reduction in visitor numbers and nights triggered in the main by a range of reforms to the German health-care system in the late 1990s and early 2000s. These health-care system reforms resulted in a substantial decline in the length and frequency of health insurance funded *Kur* visits. Consequently, the number of visitor nights spent in the region decreased steadily from around 1.5 million in 1994 with particularly significant downturns in 1997 and 2002 (Figure 6.2). Obviously, this downward trend posed a serious threat to the region's health economy (Unterallgäu Aktiv GmbH 2007; Neukam 2008).

These developments, however, were not unique but observed across many officially recognised German spas and health resorts. To overcome this crisis many of these, based on their existing infrastructure, expertise and reputation, started to develop health promotion and wellness offerings as a second business platform alongside the more traditional *Kur* treatments. In doing so, they have since claimed a share of the Second Health-Care Market and joined the growing number of newly emerging wellness tourism destinations within the country (Deutscher Heilbäderverband 2009b). In 2007, for instance, two-thirds of the traditional *Kur* destinations had already successfully complemented their offerings with holistic wellness programs (Kliegel 2007). Thus, their image has been rejuvenated in successfully combining tradition with innovation. The strategy to become less dependent on health insurance scheme funded traditional *Kur* treatment seems to be successful, since in many *Kur* destinations the majority of visits nowadays is self-funded.

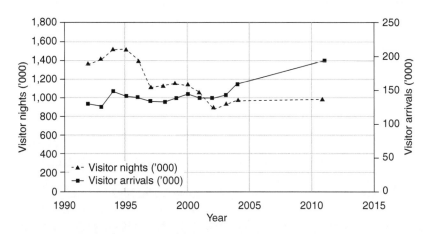

Figure 6.2 Visitor nights/arrivals in the Health Region Kneippland Unterallgäu (source: Unterallgäu Aktiv GmbH 2007, 2012a).

Confronted with these developments and in order to remain competitive, the Unterallgäu region also acknowledged the need for change towards a more holistic understanding of health beyond the traditional image of a *Kur* destination. Consequently, since the end of the 1990s a shift away from *Kur* tourism towards a stronger focus on wellness tourism could be observed in the Unterallgäu region. This culminated in the development of the Health Region Kneippland Unterallgäu by the Unterallgäu Aktiv GmbH, a regional organisation which was founded in 2002 to manage the health region's various activities. It has since played a unique coordinating role in developing opportunities, bringing together various stakeholders, identifying and promoting real and potential future win–win scenarios, and in overseeing the many regional projects which are considered crucial activities for a successful health region. A key task of the Unterallgäu Aktiv GmbH has been to provide leadership and to ensure good communication and effective dissemination of information amongst the various public and private stakeholders within the health region (Unterallgäu Aktiv GmbH 2007, 2009; Neukam 2008; Unterallgäu Aktiv GmbH pers. comm. 27 January 2010). Grounded in the traditional health competence of the region and local resources, the regional organisation has facilitated an active collaboration of various services providers and industry sectors under an overarching health theme with the aim of developing a competitive advantage within the medical and wellness tourism market. New products and services have emerged, and in associated areas like sport, leisure, fitness and nutrition. Quality control measures were also put in place to ensure a high standard in the health region's products and services and thus a satisfactory visitor experience.

Under the leadership of the Unterallgäu Aktiv GmbH, which has fostered many personal ties and initiated frequent communication amongst the various stakeholders, a range of very successful local projects and products have been initiated over the past ten years.

For example, in 2003 a competence centre for culture, health and tourism was established in Bad Grönenbach, which has since developed into a regional information hub. For the past decade the region has also hosted the very popular annual Unterallgäu Health Week. It has also started to market the various Kneipp activities it has on offer into a package known as Aktiv Park Kneippland Unterallgäu, which aims to attract locals and visitors alike (Unterallgäu Aktiv GmbH 2012b). The Unterallgäu Aktiv GmbH's initiatives towards know-how transfer, development of competencies in the emerging health network and various regional marketing initiatives have thus brought about a significant diversification in products and services (e.g. wellness) and ultimately resulted in a rebound of the region. Through this innovation the Health Region Kneippland Unterallgäu is now well positioned to capitalise on the growing wellness tourism market. The success of using the concept of a health region with a particular focus on health tourism as a regional development strategy is evident in an impressive growth of 29 per cent in visitor arrivals to the Health Region Kneippland Unterallgäu between 2002 and 2006. In 2011, the region welcomed around 195,000 visitors and registered 984,000 visitor nights which contributed around

10 per cent to the region's gross domestic product and offered direct and indirect employment to 25 per cent of its workforce. With 74 per cent of total visitation to the region and 79 per cent of all visitor nights, the three traditional Kneipp spas and health resorts Bad Wörishofen, Bad Grönenbach and Ottobeuren thus continue to play a very prominent role in the region's health economy. Amongst them, Bad Wörishofen is the region's top performer accounting for 690,000 guest nights (Bayerisches Landesamt für Statistik und Datenverarbeitung 2013; Unterallgäu Aktiv GmbH 2012a).

Conclusion

Flowing on from the predicted expanding market volume of health-related services, considerable future growth opportunities for medical and wellness tourism can be expected (Roland Berger 2008; Lohmann and Aderhold 2009). In the early 2000s Bennett *et al.* (2003) for instance, had already predicted that this market segment was likely to experience continued growth well into the future. The driving forces for the emerging health tourism market match those observed for the entire health-care sector and include demographic and psychographic change with a growing health awareness creating demand for a new range of health-related products and services in a leisure setting. Reform agendas for national health-care systems towards a greater emphasis on prevention, medical-technological advancements and newly emerging networks of cooperation across the health economy also facilitate this trend (Projekt M 2010).

Considering the growing demand for but also supply of health tourism products and services, competence management regarding the core issue health will play an increasingly important role for a destination or region in order to achieve sustainable competitive advantages. A prerequisite is the identification and integration as well as the development and utilisation of partnerships in the form of regional network structures (Fischer 2011; Duschek 2004; Dyer and Singh 1998; Pforr and Megerle 2006, 2010). Likely contributors to this health-related cooperative core competence of a region include actors from the field of medical technology, preventive and primary health care as well as research institutes who can share their know-how and competences in a more formalised way in form of a health region. The establishment of a health region primarily based on tourism has been outlined in greater detail in the discussion of the case study Kneippland Unterallgäu.

References

Ahlers, E. (2009)'Wertschöpfung durch präventiven Gesundheitsschutz – aktuelle Ergebnisse der bundesweiten PARGEMA/WSI-Betriebsrätebefragung 2008/09', paper presented at Kompetenzforum Regionalmangement, Wolnzach, October 2009.

Backman, G., Hunt, P., Khosla, R., Jaramillo-Strouss, C., Fikre, B.M., Rumble, C., Pevalin, D., Acurio Páez, D., Armijos Pineda. M., Frisancho, A., Tarco, D., Motlagh, M., Farcasanu, D. and Vladescu, C. (2008) 'Health systems and the right to health: an assessment of 194 countries', *The Lancet*, 327: 2047–85.

Bayerischer Heilbäder-Verband (2011) *Positive Jahresbilanz und große Herausforderungen*, Munich: Bayerischer Heilbäder-Verband.

Bayerisches Landesamt für Statistik und Datenverarbeitung (2013) *Statistik kommunal 2011 – Unterallgäu*, München: Bayerisches Landesamt für Statistik und Datenverarbeitung.

Bennett, M., King, B. and Milner, L. (2003) 'The health resort sector in Australia: a positioning study', *Journal of Vacation Marketing*, 10: 122–36.

Berg, W. (2008) *Gesundheitstourismus und Wellnesstourismus*, Munich: Oldenbourg.

Bieger, T. and Beritelli, P. (2006) 'Grundkonzept des virtuellen Dienstleistungsunternehmens', in T. Bieger and P. Beritelli (eds) *Dienstleistungsmanagement in Netzwerken. Wettbewerbsvorteile durch das Management des virtuellen Dienstleistungsunternehmens*, Bern: Haupt.

Bundesministerium für Wirtschaft und Technologie (BMWi) (2011) *Innovativer Gesundheitstourismus in Deutschland*, Berlin: BMWi.

Deutscher Heilbäderverband (2009a) *Die Kur in Deutschland*, Berlin: Deutscher Heilbäderverband.

Deutscher Heilbäderverband (2009b) *Jahresbericht 2009*, Berlin: Deutscher Heilbäderverband.

Deutscher Heilbäderverband (2011) *Jahresbericht 2011*, Berlin: Deutscher Heilbäderverband.

Dissert, J.-C. and Deller, S.C. (2000) 'Quality of life in the planning literature', *Journal of Planning Literature*, 15: 135–61.

Duschek, S. (2002) *Innovation in Netzwerken: Renten, Relationen, Regeln*, Wiesbaden: DUV.

Dyer, J.H. and Singh, H. (1998) 'The relational view: cooperative strategy and sources of inter-organizational competitive advantage', *Academy of Management Review*, 23: 660–79.

Fischer, E. (2011) 'Die Identifikation der kooperativen Kernkompetenzen am Beispiel der "Gesundheits- und Wellness-" Destination Bayern', in: H. Pechlaner, E. Fischer and M. Bachinger (eds) *Kooperative Kernkompetenzen – Management von Netzwerken in Regionen und Destinationen*, Wiesbaden: Gabler.

Forschungsgemeinschaft Urlaub und Reisen (2008) *Reiseanalyse 2008*, Kiel: Forschungsgemeinschaft Urlaub und Reisen.

Fretschner, R., Grönemeyer, D. and Hilbert, J. (2002) 'Die Gesundheitswirtschaft – ein Perspektivenwechsel in Theorie und Empirie', in Institut Arbeit und Technik (ed.) *Jahrbuch 2001/2002*, Gelsenkirchen: Institut Arbeit und Technik.

Grabow, B. (2005) 'Weiche Standortfaktoren in Theorie und Empirie – ein Überblick', in F. Thießen, O. Cernavin, M. Führ and M. Kaltenbach (eds) *Weiche Standortfaktoren. Erfolgsfaktoren regionaler Wirtschaftsentwicklung* (Volkswirtschaftliche Schriften, 541), Berlin: Duncker & Humboldt.

Henderson, J.W. (2009) *Health Economics and Policy*, Mason: Cengage Learning.

Hilbert, J. (2007) 'Gesundheitsregionen im Vergleich – auf der Suche nach erfolgreichen Entwicklungsstrategien', online, available at: www.iatge.de/aktuell/veroeff/2007/hilbert04.pdf (accessed 12 January 2013).

Hilbert, J. and Kluska, D. (2010) 'Boombranche Gesundheitswirtschaft: "frische Rückenwinde" für die Zukunft der Sozialen Arbeit', *Diakonieunternehmen*, 7: 21–4.

Illing, K. (2009) 'Region, Gesundheit und Qualität. Zur Entwicklung eines Qualitätsgütezeichens für Gesundheitsregionen', paper presented at Kompetenzforum Regionalmangement, Wolnzach, October 2009.

Institute for Work and Technology (2010) 'Structure of the health economy', online, available at: www.iatge.de (accessed 10 October 2011).

Jochmann, J. (2010) 'Standortfaktor Lebensqualität – Die subjektive Wahrnehmung Hochqualifizierter in der Region Ingolstadt', in H. Pechlaner and M. Bachinger (eds) *Lebensqualität und Standortattraktivität. Kultur, Mobilität und regionale Marken als Erfolgsfaktoren*, Berlin: ESV.

Kämpf, R. (2010) 'Die Rolle der Lebensqualität im Standortwettbewerb: Theoretische Ausgangslage – Messkonzept – empirische Ergebnisse', in H. Pechlaner and M. Bachinger (eds) *Lebensqualität und Standortattraktivität. Kultur, Mobilität und regionale Marken als Erfolgsfaktoren*, Berlin: ESV.

Kliegel, I. (2007) 'Der Markt der Gesundheit. Daten, Fakten, Trends', *Focus Markt Analysen*: 1–43.

Kurdirektion Bad Wörishofen (2011) *Kur- und Tourismusbericht 2011*, Bad Wörishofen: Kurdirektion Bad Wörishofen.

Lohmann, M. and Aderhold, P. (2009) *Urlaubsreisetrends 2020*. Kiel: Forschungsgemeinschaft Urlaub und Reisen.

Müller, H. and Lanz Kaufmann, E. (2001) 'Wellness tourism: market analysis of a special health tourism segment and implications for the hotel industry', *Journal of Vacation Marketing*, 7: 5–17.

Neukam, A. (2008) 'Gesundheitswirtschaft als regionale Profilierungschance', unpublished thesis, Universität Bayreuth.

Pechlaner, H., Fischer, E. and Hammann, E.-M. (2006) 'Wettbewerbsfähigkeit von Standorten – Die Rolle der Kernkompetenzen', in H. Pechlaner, E. Fischer and E.-M. Hammann (eds) *Standortwettbewerb und Tourismus. Regionale Erfolgsstrategien*, Berlin: ESV.

Pforr, C. and Megerle, A. (2006) 'Geotourism: a perspective from Southwest Germany', in R. Dowling and D. Newsome (eds) *Geotourism: Sustainability, Impact and Opportunities*, Oxford: Butterworth-Heinemann.

Pforr, C. and Megerle, A. (2010) 'Management of geotourism stakeholders – experiences from the Network History of the Earth', in R. Dowling and D. Newsome (eds) *Geotourism: The Tourism of Geology and Landscape*, Oxford: Goodfellow Publishers Limited.

Porter, M.E. (1993) *Nationale Wettbewerbsvorteile – Erfolgreich konkurrieren auf dem Weltmarkt*, Wien: Überreuter.

Projekt M (2010) *Innovativer Gesundheitstourismus in Deutschland. Handlungsempfehlungen zur Entwicklung und Implementierung erfolgreicher gesundheitstouristischer Angebote (Ergebnisprotokoll der Zukunftskonferenz Bayern in Bad Wörishofen, 1 July 2010)*, Berlin: Lüneburg.

Roland Berger (2008) *Der Gesundheitsmarkt*, München: Roland Berger Strategy Consultants GmbH.

Smeral, E. (1998) 'The impact of globalisation on small and medium enterprises: new challenges for tourism policies in European countries', *Tourism Management*, 19: 371–80.

Unterallgäu Aktiv GmbH (2007) *Regionales Entwickungskonzept LAG Kneippland Unterallgäu*, Bad Wörishofen: Unterallgäu Aktiv GmbH.

Unterallgäu Aktiv GmbH (2009) *Geschäftsbericht*, Bad Wörishofen: Unterallgäu Aktiv GmbH.

Unterallgäu Aktiv GmbH (2012a) 'Unterallgäu: Tourismus und Freizeit', online, available at: www.unterallgaeu-aktiv.de/tourismus.html (accessed 3 November 2012).

Unterallgäu Aktiv GmbH (2012b) '10 Jahre Innovative Regionalentwicklung', online, available at: www.unterallgaeu-aktiv.de/download/10jahre-unterallgaeuaktiv.pdf (accessed 12 January 2013).

Voigt, C., Laing, J., Wray, M., Brown, G., Howat, G., Weiler, B. and Trembath, R. (2010) *Health Tourism in Australia: Supply, Demand and Opportunities*, Gold Coast: ST CRC.

World Health Organization (2010) 'About WHO', online, available at: www.who.int/about/en/ (accessed 17 January 2012).

7 Identification and development of core competencies as a basis for regional development with special focus on health tourism

Harald Pechlaner, Christopher Reuter and Monika Bachinger

Introduction

The German health care system is very elaborate, but also expensive when compared to other OECD countries. The total health expenditure as a share of the German GDP reached 11.6 per cent in 2010, being surpassed only by the Netherlands which reached 12.0 per cent of GDP the same year (OECD 2012: 123). The press release for the recent OECD report *Health at a Glance: Europe 2012* in Germany reads as follows:

> The per capita health expenditures decreased on average by 0.6% in the European Union for 2010 while in Germany they kept growing despite the economic downturn. This is even more astonishing when considering that the average yearly increase between 2000 and 2009 was at 2.0% for Germany, but has jumped to 2.7% for 2010. Germany keeps moving against the trend.

Today the health-care sector is already one of the most important branches in the German economy when it comes to value creation and number of employees. It is also an industry that is a core area for applying new technologies. This is closely related to the fact that the dynamics of the health-care sector are well above the average growth rates of the general economic development (Prognos AG 2007). For entire regions the health industry has become one of the areas with the greatest future potential for regional growth and development (Hilbert and Kluska 2011). Therefore, regional brand and image effects generated through networking such as cluster development and concentration processes among certain industries need to be discussed. A good example for the historical development of such effects is the so-called 'Medical Valley' of the European Metropolitan Region of Nuremberg (EMN) which has among others at its core several important educational institutions, hospitals, as well as major research and production facilities of the Siemens Healthcare division (EMN 2011).

Generally, health care as a science is composed of several basic as well as applied areas of research, including medicine. However, the business side is also highly diversified: it is not only about hospital treatment and outpatient care, but also includes component suppliers like pharmaceutical companies, medical technology and different segments of wholesaling and specialised retailing. Even peripheral areas like sports and recreation as well as wellness and medical tourism can be added to that sector. Changing political and economic conditions and frameworks as well as societal change are the driving factors for the growing importance of the entire field. In Germany the federal government has pulled out of the financing of many health-care benefits, the demography is changing rapidly and the competition between regions has become fiercer in recent years (Freyer 2011). Therefore, regions are trying to concentrate on the most promising industries while considering their impact on sustainable development especially when it comes to the use of natural resources, since producing medical equipment or providing health-care services is considered to be less strenuous on natural resources than classical industrial sectors like the chemical industry or the automotive sector. Therefore health care is becoming an even more appealing alternative.

In addition, due to the increasing health awareness among the population, which calls for the local availability of all kinds of health products and services, the demand-side is also changing.

Hence, regional brokers and platforms are needed to evaluate the demand of the different stakeholders and organise the integration of suitable suppliers into the regional health network. Furthermore, service orientated offers like health tourism, sports, leisure, wellness, nutrition and assisted accommodation are fields that are forming the basis for a high quality of life which in turn makes regions especially attractive and therefore becomes an important unique selling proposition (USP) when competing for new industrial settlements, inhabitants and tourists (Bachinger and Pechlaner 2011).

This chapter will therefore concentrate on two booming sample regions within the so-called European Metropolitan Region of Munich (EMM) and will analyse the relations among the local stakeholders that could potentially lead to new proposals in the health tourism industry, what kind of fields could be interesting for such projects and who should be involved in implementing them. The chapter starts with giving a brief overview of health tourism in Germany, before discussing the theoretical framework of cooperative core competencies and introducing the overarching EMM which subsumes the regions of Ingolstadt and Garmisch-Partenkirchen.

Health tourism in Germany

Health tourism in Germany today

Health tourists are a very attractive customer segment for the German tourism industry since they spend €124 per night on average while the overall average spending lies at €80 per night (IPK International 2010). Health tourism has become a 'hot topic' in Germany since the decline of the traditional spas, that nevertheless dominate the market, is being compensated for by the booming new forms of health tourism, especially the segments of wellness and medical tourism. While the traditional climatic spas in Germany, of which some have been attracting visitors seeking recreation and health improvement for more than 150 years now, have been stagnating at around 3.3 million arrivals during the last decade, other segments like wellness tourism have seen their arrivals grow by more than a third during the same time span (DHV 2011). When looking at the number of overnight stays in Table 7.1 the situation appears to be similar. The climatic spas had to cope with a drop in overnight stays from around 17.5 million per year in 1999 to less than 14 million in 2010, which equates to a loss of 21.4 per cent during the first decade of the century, while other segments have seen their market share rising by 4.5 per cent (for mineral spas) and 16.3 per cent (for seaside spas) respectively. This means the seaside spas have gained about 5.1 million overnight stays and have reached a level of almost 36.4 million annually during those ten years, which in turn has brought them on a level with the mineral spas (41 million overnight stays per year in 2010). The statistics of the DHV in Table 7.1 also show that the sector has not been shielded from the general decline in the duration of stay seen throughout the tourism industry. While the duration of stay almost reached one week (6.88 overnight stays) for mineral spas in 1999, this number declined to 5.3 in 2010 and climatic spas only had an average length of stay of 4.1 in 2010.

Spas are only one part of the industry, but they are an important indicator for this general development in which the topic health has become a megatrend in the German economy and especially in the tourism industry in recent years (Tödter 2011). This development has been supported by the national and state governments through accompanying measures like research and marketing initiatives leading to the publication of several studies by the German Federal Ministry for Economics and Technology (FMET 2011a, 2011b) and according marketing strategies on the national level by the German National Tourism Board (GNTB). The most important among those measures and initiatives has been the decision to make health tourism the annual theme for the GNTB in 2011.

Table 7.1 Statistical data for German spas (1999/2010)

		Mineral spas	Climatic spas	Seaside spas	Kneipp spas
Arrivals	1999	5,700,857	3,312,442	4,788,909	1,837,148
	2010	7,667,580	3,371,706	6,630,696	2,435,271
	Δ	+1,966,723	+59,264	+1,841,787	+598,123
Overnight stays	1999	39,238,947	17,534,352	31,342,372	10,347,391
	2010	41,017,692	13,780,131	36,439,195	11,631,495
	Δ	+1,778,745	−3,754,221	+5,096,823	+1,284,104
Duration of stay	1999	6.88	5.29	6.54	5.63
	2010	5.30	4.10	5.40	4.70
	Δ	−1.58	−1.19	−1.14	−0.93

Source: Adopted and amended from DHV 2011.

The topic has also seen growing attention from scholars which has led to a great amount of studies and literature on that topic in the German tourism research community (e.g. Barth and Werner 2005; Berg 2008; Fischer 2009; Illing 2009; Nahrstedt 2008a; Brittner-Widmann and Rulle 2012). The federally funded studies as well as the generated publications have sparked a discussion about the structure and prospects of health tourism in Germany.

The structure of health tourism in Germany

When looking at tourism in a health context a differentiation into categories has taken place over the last few years (see Figure 7.1). First of all is wellness tourism, which includes the beauty and fitness offerings of premium segment hotels; second, medical tourism which relies on specialised hospitals and clinics to combine medical treatment with rehabilitation facilities and the local hotel industry.[1] These two mark the end of the entire spectrum while spas, sports facilities and other products combine elements from medical as well as wellness tourism and can be based on resources like high air or water quality.

This health tourism spectrum depicted in Figure 7.1 is part of an greater entity – the health economy – which in turn can be categorised into several different layers of segments, themes and industries (Pforr *et al.* 2011; see also Chapter 6). The core of this part of the health economy is made up of hospitals and direct health-care providers, while rehabilitation, the pharmaceutical industry, biotech companies, pharmacies, wellness hotels etc. form the outer layers. Actors of these different industry sectors interact with each other and establish their own network ties, but this does not necessarily lead to a directional network. The heterogeneity of the field makes it difficult for actors from completely different sub-segments to interact with each other, which in turn leads to a necessity for coordination on different geographical levels, especially in regional (or destination) contexts.

The health economy on the whole, and health tourism in particular, are under the influence of strong macro-level factors that lead to the formation of a 'New Health Tourism', depicted in Figure 7.2.

Not all of the factors that are included in the model can be discussed in depth, but demographic change should be accentuated here, since it will shape the development of the health sector and the tourism industry (e.g. Klemm 2007; Keck *et al.* 2012). There will be great changes on the demand-side as well as on the supply-side, since customers will be in different age groups and accordingly

Figure 7.1 The health spectrum (own illustration based on Nahrstedt 2008b).

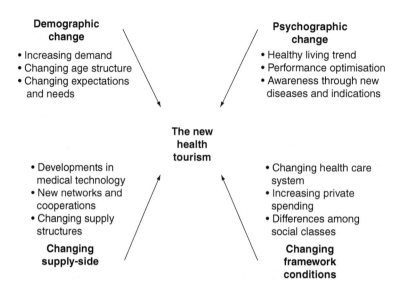

Demographic change
- Increasing demand
- Changing age structure
- Changing expectations and needs

Psychographic change
- Healthy living trend
- Performance optimisation
- Awareness through new diseases and indications

The new health tourism

- Developments in medical technology
- New networks and cooperations
- Changing supply structures

Changing supply-side

- Changing health care system
- Increasing private spending
- Differences among social classes

Changing framework conditions

Figure 7.2 The New Health Tourism (source: translated by authors from Kreilkamp 2011).

need specific offers and facilities. Therefore theme networks that foster regional and tourism development in that segment will be of utmost importance in order to enable the local and regional stakeholders to participate in the development. Regional platforms help to evaluate the demand of the different stakeholders and organise the integration of suitable suppliers into the regional health network. Furthermore, service orientated offers like health tourism, sports, leisure, wellness, nutrition and assisted accommodation are fields that are forming the basis for a high quality of life which in turn makes regions especially attractive (Bachinger and Pechlaner 2011).

The following section will provide the theoretical background to understanding such network processes and thereby laying the foundation for the cases – two booming sample regions within the so-called European Metropolitan Region of Munich (EMM). The study will analyse the relations among the local stakeholders that could potentially lead to new proposals in the health tourism industry, what kind of fields could be interesting for such projects and who should be involved in implementing them.

Theoretical framework

From the resource-based view to the relational view

According to the resource-based view it is the specific combination of resources that accounts for a company's success (Amit and Schoemaker 1993; Barney 1986, 1991, 1995, 2002; Collis 1991; Hall 1992; Helfat 1997; Rumelt 1984,

1991; Wernerfelt 1984, 1995). This view postulates that physical resources like machines and raw materials, as well as human resources and organisational resources, play a decisive role (Barney 1991).

However, aside from these resources, the specific way of their use – the way they are interlaced with each other – is important (Hamel and Prahalad 1996; Sanchez and Heene 2004). At this point the term 'competence' needs to be explained. Competencies may be understood as a 'firm's capacity to deploy resources, usually in combination, using organisational processes, to effect a desired end' (Amit and Schoemaker 1993: 35). They provide for resources to become concrete products or services which offer distinct value to customers and contribute to high company competitiveness.

Competencies, however, are not always unique and can rather be found in a great number of companies. The difference between these ordinary competencies and core competencies is that the latter qualifies the company to dominate the competition, whereas the former are just a pre-condition to take part in the market (Hamel and Prahalad 1994: 206). Core competencies are able to generate a high degree of value to the customer (Prahalad and Hamel 1996). They also help to coordinate plenty of resources; that is they can be understood as coordination routines, which are characterised by a high degree of aggregation (Amit and Schoemaker 1993; Grant 1991). It is important that competencies depend on their application. Competencies become 'core competencies' when they enable a company to act in different markets and segments: 'A firm's competence is a set of differentiated technological skills, complementary assets, and organisational routines and capacities that provide the basis for a firm's competitive capacities in one or more businesses' (Teece *et al.* 1994: 18). Core competencies thus form the basis for more than one product or service. They may be the origin of a great variety of different products and therefore secure the sustainability of a company's success (Grant 1991; Prahalad and Hamel 1990).

Furthermore core competencies may not only be found in single companies. They also exist in networks of cooperating firms (Duschek 2004; Dyer and Singh 1998). In this case they are called 'cooperative core competencies' (Duschek 2004). These competencies include the coordination of the employment of resources and capabilities between independent firms. They also make sure that resources are pieced together in such a way that competitive products or services are generated. In contrast to the situation in a single firm, cooperative core competencies are formed either by the combination of the competencies and resources of the participating firms or as a result of network processes (Dyer and Singh 1998). In the latter case cooperative core competencies are a product of the network itself and consist of interaction routines and shared knowledge of the partners. Cooperative core competencies therefore can be defined as a 'result of network relations' as well as 'resources brought into a network' (Duschek 1998: 333). When cooperative core competencies are employed, the network's customers profit as well as their partners. This is because cooperative core competencies provide for the generation of relational returns according to the relational view, which also states that the returns come into existence by the cooperation of partners and can only be appropriated collectively (Duschek 2004). Therefore, the existence and functioning of networks become decisive in order to stay competitive. The following section discusses what this theoretical framework means in the context of tourism destinations.

Cooperative core competencies development in health tourism

Summarising the findings from the previous section, it becomes clear that: (1) core competencies are the basis for a sustained competitive advantage; (2) this is true for networks as well; and (3) such cooperative core competencies are either competencies brought into a network or they are the result of network relations. Networks are then able to dominate the market in case they dispose of such cooperative core competencies. To put it the other way round: in case that the provision of a product or service depends on more than one firm, it is crucial for the involved partners to develop network-based cooperative competencies in order to keep their goods competitive, to be able to diversify successfully and to enter new markets (Dyer and Singh 1998). Figure 7.3 gives an overview of this context.

For touristic destinations this leads to the necessity to develop interorganisational competencies based on interorganisational relationships in order to maximise the competitiveness of the destination service network. In other words, the competitiveness of a tourism destination can be improved though the development of cooperative core competencies. These are in turn developed through interorganisational learning processes. It needs to be acknowledged that there can be substantial barriers to beneficial network development such as the heterogeneity of the supply-side (Flagestad and Hope 2001) or the problem of free-riders (Pechlaner and Tschurtschenthaler 2003); however due to space restrictions these cannot be discussed in detail.

Regional development in this context means establishing networks among different stakeholders on the basis of predefined goals in order to activate health-relevant resources of the region so that the stakeholders and businesses can

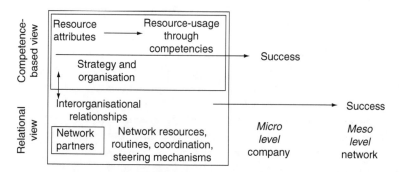

Figure 7.3 Components of the competitive business view and relational view (source: own illustration based on Freiling 2001 and Fischer 2009).

profit. The overall goal would be the enhancement of the attractiveness of the entire region; giving it a differentiation factor in the inter-regional competition. Different paths can lead to such a development of the health-care sector on a regional level. For example, health-care regions can be based on technological competencies in the medical field. Another basis can be the existence of diversified clinical and/or spa providers within the region.

A good example for a fully developed regional health-care sector based on technological competencies is the so-called 'Medical Valley' cluster in the European metropolitan region of Nuremberg (EMN) which consists of 40 hospitals, 60 academic chairs and professorships and 20 extra-faculty research facilities closely linked to medical engineering. The 180 medical engineering companies in the region employ approximately 16,000 employees. The cluster is concentrated in a formally structured network that was initiated with public funds and is organised in the legal form of an association (EMN 2011). The core of the network is focused on medical engineering, but there are also cross-industry product development and innovation initiatives, as well as projects to develop strategies to tackle issues related to demographic change (EMN 2011).

Before concretely discussing health tourism in the overarching Munich Metropolitan Region and introducing the regions, the methodologies will be explained briefly.

Two cases from the Munich Metropolitan Region (EMM)

Case design and methods used

Two cases located in the Metropolitan Region of Munich (EMM) are presented in the following, namely the case of the Ingolstadt region (IN) and the case of the Garmisch-Partenkirchen region (GAP). The conducted research relies on the theoretical foundations of the resource-based view with its later developments in the formation of core competencies as combinations of resources, capabilities and competencies on a regional level (Teece *et al.* 1997; Wernerfelt 1984) that have been previously described. The core competency development through network interaction and the formation of cooperative core competencies, especially, has been discussed in depth (Duschek 2004; Fischer 2009), providing the needed framework to discuss the empirical data from the two regions.

Research for both case studies has been conducted recently by the Chair of Tourism of the Catholic University of Eichstaett-Ingolstadt with varying partner institutions. The research projects have been conducted in order to answer the questions of how health tourism is developing in the two regions and how health tourism may act as a basis for the development of regional core competencies in the future. The cases are therefore descriptive and explorative in the sense that the status quo in health tourism on the regional level was assessed as well as the potential of its future development in regional network contexts.

The cases rely on different methodologies. The case for the Ingolstadt region is based on a quantitative approach including a social network analysis which visualises social and/or economic ties by asking selected interview partners to disclose their business ties in order to understand the structure and quality of the network.

The main source of data of the second case is qualitative and includes results from five major stakeholder workshops held in 2010 and 2011. These are the main sources for the two cases, providing the needed data according to the understanding of Eisenhardt (1989) and Yin (2003) who state that case-study research can lead to mid-range theory development by describing and explaining the specific circumstances of the presented cases. However, since both quantitative as well as qualitative data (statistics, documentation of stakeholder interaction) was analysed in both cases, the approaches can also be understood in the context of mixed methods research in tourism (Jennings 2010).

The quantitative social network analysis for the Ingolstadt region consists of results from 407 actors that have responded to a questionnaire either by mail or online and additional workshops that have been conducted afterwards. The workshops at Garmisch-Partenkirchen included 21 local actors while the final meeting was open to public discussion and included 47 interested inhabitants of Garmisch-Partenkirchen. Additionally a local opinion poll (n=1,140) was conducted by one of the project partners, which included questions about economic development as well as tourism. The results were used to prepare the final public discussion.

Health tourism in the Munich Metropolitan Region

The European Metropolitan Region of Munich (EMM) encompasses a total of 51 municipalities including 25 Bavarian counties which equals an area of 24.094 km² and is populated by 5.5 million inhabitants that generated a GDP of close to €210 billion in 2010 (EMM 2012). Backed by these numbers the EMM states about itself on its homepage:

> With its extraordinary dynamism the Munich Metropolitan Region (EMM) is one of the leading economic regions in Europe. The core competences of this region are to be found in the concentration of knowledge on a level that is top in Europe, a very broad technological basis with a diversity of future-oriented industries as well as the highest quality of life in a charming landscape in conjunction with top quality infrastructure.
>
> (EMM 2012)

Figure 7.4 depicts the Munich Metropolitan Region and its basic traffic infrastructure, including the major highways, train lines and its international airport. The airport alone counted for 34.5 million arrivals in 2010, turning it into the second most important travel hub in Germany.

The map at Figure 7.4 also shows the two case-study regions. Garmisch-Partenkirchen is located on the border with Austria and is part of the Bavarian Alps encompassing Germany's highest mountain, the famous Zugspitze (2,962 m above sea level). The Ingolstadt region lies half way between Nuremberg and

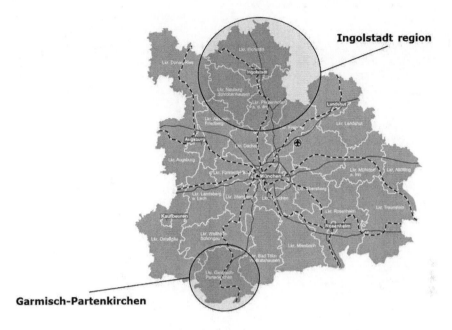

Figure 7.4 The European Metropolitan Region of Munich and its traffic infrastructure (based on EMM 2012).

Munich and comprises the city of Ingolstadt and the three neighbouring counties of Eichstaett, Pfaffenhofen and Neuburg-Schrobenhausen. The EMM is one of the most popular destinations for both domestic and foreign travellers and tourism is considered one of the most comprehensive cross-sectoral industries for Munich as it consists not only of the hotel and catering trades, but also encompasses other areas of the service sector, for example leisure, sport or cultural activities, traffic and retail, plus the event and health-care fields (EMM 2012). The City of Munich occupies the first place within the Munich Metropolitan Region in terms of city tourism. A number of other cities and regions complement the range of offers, for example in the form of attractions that vary according to the season or sporting and cultural events, as well as traditional festivals.

The EMM alone is home to 19 so-called spas which in the German context means entire communities based on health tourism; employs more than 300,000 people in the health care industry and attracts 1.2 million health tourists every year (EMM 2012). Because of the sophisticated clinical structure and the high degree of specialisation among the providers of health care services, Munich has become a hub for medical tourism on an international level. This development affects mainly the city of Munich and its close surroundings, but the cases presented in the following will focus on the regions of Ingolstadt and Garmisch-Partenkirchen on the northern and southern periphery of the metropolitan region where the health-care sector is beginning to develop into an important pillar of the local economy.

The case of Ingolstadt region (IN)

The Ingolstadt region with its approximately 500,000 inhabitants can be characterised by its strong urban–rural contrast. The city itself is dynamic, but has a mono-structured focus on the automotive sector and its surroundings are still shaped by a rural background and culture. The region counts for more than 800,000 arrivals and 1.5 million overnight stays per year. Tourism, which concentrates on the nearby Altmuehl Valley and the city of Ingolstadt itself, with its strong influx of business tourists, is therefore only of medium importance for the region's economy today, but the numbers have been steadily rising for the last five years with growth rates of up to 7 per cent (Stadt Ingolstadt 2012). The case relies on findings from a network study that was conducted in 2010/2011 which analysed the potential of other industries to become a much needed additional pillar for the local economy and therefore to enrich the local value chains, thereby enhancing the region's attractiveness for employers, inhabitants and tourists. Figure 7.5, which depicts the entire economic network of the region, clearly shows the potential hazard that lies within the structure of the regional economic network with its strong focus on one core company. The circles depict businesses as well as institutions (especially the two universities and the main hospital of Ingolstadt). The bigger the circles the more links they have to other network partners. In this figure one can see that one company forms a network core (the biggest circle – in this case a well-known premium segment carmaker which has its headquarters in Ingolstadt) while additional sub-networks appear to be only of minor importance in terms of cooperation and interlinkages.

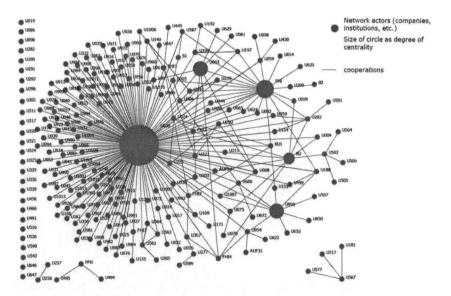

Figure 7.5 The economic network of the Ingolstadt region (source: Thierstein *et al.* 2011).

This strong focus and the low diversification pose a threat to sustainable development in the region. Another conclusion from the conducted study was that the health sector and also health tourism could have the potential to lead to a more balanced economic structure even though the industry is only of average importance today and there are no spas or health resorts of more than regional attraction. The clinics and hospitals in the area (which are depicted in the sub-networks geriatrics and care) also have only intraregional importance and reputation, and the region has not developed a clear image as a health or wellness destination yet. Despite these issues Figure 7.6 shows that some small-scale networks have already emerged that could be the basis for further development. What is still missing is coordination and interconnectedness as can be seen in the low level of linkages between the different segments. There is also no clear concept yet to make use of those existing structures to develop and promote health tourism products on a regional level while some of the local actors are already active in that field.

Furthermore, the network analysis revealed a dominance of geriatrics and care. There are also some specialised clinics operating in the nearby Altmuehl Valley national park. Nevertheless there is a strong need for entrepreneurial activities in health care and especially in health tourism. Only small- and mid-scale improvements have taken place and only products of local and regional importance have been developed. Additionally no clear cooperative core competencies have been created yet which is also due to the fact that there have been

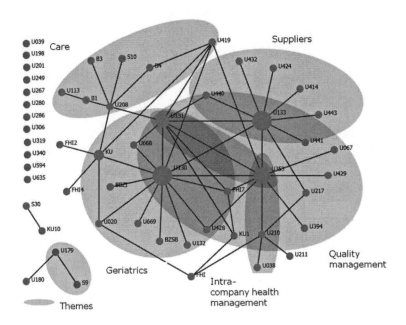

Figure 7.6 The network of the Ingolstadt region health sector (source: Thierstein *et al.* 2011).

no resources or competencies clearly defined that could become the basis for developing competitive products that add unique selling propositions. In that context cross-industry cooperation, especially, could have the potential to improve the diversification of the regional economic structure thereby increasing the regional resilience against possible crisis. A functioning network core would be the first step to improve situation, tap the existing resources and enable the region to develop the needed cooperative core competencies for successful health tourism on a regional level.

The case of the Garmisch-Partenkirchen region (GAP)

The second case concerns Garmisch-Partenkirchen which is located in the Alps on the border with Austria where summer as well as winter tourism prevail. Garmisch-Partenkirchen hosted the 2011 FIS World Ski Cup and relies heavily on its tourism structures and competencies. It is also a climatic health resort (pollen-free starting 1,000 m above sea level) and offers 300 km of hiking trails to its visitors. There are two major clinics in the area and additional treatment centres. Demographic change, the attractiveness of the landscape and its proximity to Munich has turned GAP into a hotspot for retirement homes with an accordingly high proportion of the elderly (LfStaD 2011). GAP has been neglecting its potential for innovation for some time now and also struggles with a migration of companies to the core of the EMM. These general developments and the according tourism-specific issues have been identified during a study on regional sustainable development that has been conducted in 2010/2011. GAP has been called a mature destination with stagnating tourism business (BAK Basel Economics 2010) and suffers from low quality perception (Brand:Trust 2010). There is only a low perception of GAP as a climatic health resort and the provided medical services are highly diversified but uncoordinated. The major institutions in the health sector are not interconnected and there is no clear linkage to the tourism sector, including the wellness resorts. The hospital of Garmisch-Partenkirchen and the private clinics in the area provide health-care services as well as health-service products for foreign clients, but do not see themselves as active participants in health tourism on a regional level. This lack of identification and cooperation between medical and wellness service providers as well as a need for additional educational facilities in the health sector have been identified as major hindrances to a more successful development that could be the starting point for the promotion of health tourism on a national or even international level (GAP 2006).

The starting point for the conducted research was a major project study for a sustainable development strategy that encompassed the entire community of Garmisch-Partenkirchen as part of the combined 2018 Winter Olympic Games bid of Munich and Garmisch-Partenkirchen where mainly the skiing competitions were supposed to be held. The project was supported by the Bavarian state government as well as the community of Garmisch-Partenkirchen and encompassed five areas of development, ranging from mobility and traffic, demographic change and social issues, economic and tourism development to energy and climate change as well as landscape conversation (Seiler and Stappen 2012). Each topic was worked on by a group of 10–25 local experts and the workshops were conducted by scientists from different fields of interest, e.g. traffic management and nature conservation, as well as specialised consultants. The entire project was coordinated by Wolfgang Seiler (Karlsruhe Institute of Technology, retired) and Ralf-Klemens Stappen (SP Group) who have worked as scientists and consultants in the field of sustainable development and climate-change research. The findings presented below were collected during the workshop phase from February 2010 to July 2011 in the group for economic and tourism development which was coordinated by the Chair of Tourism of the Catholic University of Eichstaett-Ingolstadt. Together with the local experts a SWOT-analysis was conducted and goals and strategies for sustainable economic development were defined. The combination of tourism and health products, especially, was seen as a major chance for future development which led to the proposal of a new institution that could help to bring people from fields like nutrition, sports, tourism and medical services together. Based on this discussion and the identification of health care as part of health tourism as a potential core competency an Academy for the Health Care Industry was proposed during the workshops in order to establish a close-knit network that helps to overcome the high dependency on classic leisure tourism within the region (Pechlaner and Reuter 2012).

The following objectives would define the operational arrangement of such an institution:

- To become an integrated centre for the megatrends health and wellness.
- To interconnect the topics health, nutrition, wellness, sports and related fields.
- To develop education and training capacities for intra- and extra-regional demand.

This goal was defined along with internal marketing and a concept for the congress centre as the three most important issues to be tackled in the near future in order to promote tourism as well as to stabilise and improve the economic situation of GAP. In order to realise such an educational institution the regional stakeholders that are already active in the health industry would need to be brought together to enable an exchange between the still separated fields of health care and tourism. Again a working network core is needed as a basis for the development of cooperative core competencies on a regional level, but with the proposed academy and its management a concrete network core could already be defined. The academy must then be integrated into inter-regional tourism theme networks which would increase marketing efficiency and enable the development of cross-sectional health-related tourism products.

Conclusion and outlook

The quantitative and qualitative empirical results from the cases show today's lack of interorganisational cooperation as a possible basis for the development of cooperative core competencies. Quantitative network analysis can help to understand the local and regional situation and become a platform for strategy formulation and cooperative core competency development. In the case of Garmisch-Partenkirchen a possible development has been initiated by proposing the foundation of an integrated academy for the highly diversified health sector which includes health tourism. Key issues for the selected regions within the EMM will be the creation of functioning network cores that will activate the networks and improve cooperation among the fragmented network members, since cooperative core competencies depend on the resources and competencies brought into the network as well as the competencies that result from the network activities. This is especially true for the Ingolstadt region where health tourism could help to diversify the mono-structured economy and improve cross-sectional linkages by creating new ties between the different segments of the health industry. Health tourism can act as an umbrella to combine those activities as well as provide the much needed network core in order to coordinate and promote the different activities and newly created products.

Further research is needed to analyse similar/completely different health care and health tourism regions in order to support or falsify the notion that the health industry and especially health tourism play an integral part in future regional development (as it has been formulated for GAP and Ingolstadt region).

Note

1 There are no official numbers available for Germany, but the growing importance of medical tourism can be seen when looking at the neighbouring Czech Republic, which is the leading provider of medical services to foreigners (so-called exports of health-related travel) in relation to the size of its health sector. According to the OECD (2012: 131) 4.17 per cent of all medical expenditures within the Czech Republic in 2012 have been consumed by foreigners which is triple the rate of Luxembourg, the number two in the OECD statistics.

References

Amit, R. and Schoemaker, P.J.H. (1993) 'Strategic assets and organizational rent', *Strategic Management Journal*, 14: 33–46.
Bachinger, M. and Pechlaner, H. (2011) 'Regionale Kernkompetenzen. Ein netzwerkbasierter Definitionsansatz', in H. Pechlaner, E. Fischer and M. Bachinger (eds) *Kooperative Kernkompetenzen. Management von Netzwerken in Regionen und Destinationen*, Wiesbaden: Gabler, pp. 57–92.
BAK Basel Economics (2010) *Tourism Benchmarking – die Schweizer Tourismuswirtschaft im internationalen Vergleich*, Basel: BAK Basel Economics.
Barney, J.B. (1986) 'Strategic factor markets: expectations, luck and business strategy', *Management Science*, 42: 1231–41.

Barney, J.B. (1991) 'Firm resources and sustained competitive advantage', *Journal of Management*, 17: 99–120.

Barney, J.B. (1995) 'Looking inside for competitive advantage', *Academy of Management Executive*, 9: 49–61.

Barney, J.B. (2002) *Gaining and Sustaining Competitive Advantage*, Upper Saddle River, NJ: Prentice-Hall.

Barth, R. and Werner, C. (2005) *Der Wellness-Faktor: modernes Qualitätsmanagement im Gesundheitstourismus: mit dem Qualitätsgütezeichen von Best Health Austria und Einführung in die Bewertungskriterien*, Wien: Relax Verlag Werner.

Berg, W. (2008) *Gesundheitstourismus und Wellnesstourismus*, München: Oldenbourg.

Brand:Trust (2010) *TOP 40 der begehrtesten deutschsprachigen Wintersport-Destinationsmarken der Alpen 2010*, Nürnberg: Brand:Trust.

Brittner-Widmann, A. and Rulle, M. (2012) *Gesundheitstourismus, Grundlagen, Marktstrukturen, Potenziale*, München: Oldenbourg.

Collis, D.J. (1991) 'A resource-based analysis of global competition: the case of the bearings industry', *Strategic Management Journal*, 12, 49–68.

DHV (Deutscher Heilbäderverband e.V.) (2011) *Gäste- und Übernachtungszahlen in den deutschen Heilbädern und Kurorten 1999–2010*, Berlin: Deutscher Heilbäderverband e.V.

Duschek, S. (1998) 'Kooperative Kernkompetenzen. Zum Management einzigartiger Netzwerkressourcen', *Zeitschrift Führung & Organisation*, 67: 230–6.

Duschek, S. (2004) 'Inter-firm resources and sustainable competitive advantage', *Management Review*, 15: 53–73.

Dyer, J.H. and Singh, H. (1998) 'The relational view, cooperative strategy and sources of inter-organizational competitive advantage', *Academy of Management Review*, 23: 660–79.

Eisenhardt, K. (1989) 'Building theories from case study research', *Academy of Management Review*, 14: 532–50.

EMM (Europäische Metropolregion München) (2012) *The Munich Metropolitan Region's Health Sector: The Regional Competencies at a Glance*, Munich: Europäische Metropolregion München.

EMN (Europäische Metropolregion Nürnberg) (2011) 'Medical Valley: Europäische Metropolregion Nürnberg', presentation by Medical Valley EMN e.V., Munich, 13 December 2011.

FMET (Federal Ministry of Economics and Technology) (2011a) *Innovativer Gesundheitstourismus in Deutschland. Leitfaden*, Berlin: Federal Ministry of Economics and Technology.

FMET (Federal Ministry of Economics and Technology) (2011b) *Innovativer Gesundheitstourismus in Deutschland. Branchenreport 'Gesundheitsregionen und Gesundheitsinitiativen'*, Berlin: Federal Ministry of Economics and Technology.

Fischer, E. (2009) *Das kompetenzorientierte Management der touristischen Destination: Identifikation und Entwicklung kooperativer Kernkompetenzen*, Wiesbaden: Gabler.

Flagestad, A. and Hope, C.A. (2001) 'Strategic success in winter sports destinations: a sustainable value creation perspective', *Tourism Management*, 22: 445–61.

Freiling, J. (2001) *Resource-Based View und ökonomische Theorie. Grundlagen und Positionierung des Ressourcenansatzes*, Wiesbaden: Gabler.

Freyer, W. (2011) *Tourismus. Einführung in die Fremdenverkehrsanalyse*, Munich: Oldenbourg.

GAP (Garmisch-Partenkirchen Tourismus) (2006) '6-Jahresplan. Garmisch-Partenkirchen Tourismus. Ziele, Strategien und Massnahmen', unpublished study.

GNTB (German National Tourism Board) (2011) 'Medizinreisen im DZT-Themenjahr 2011', presentation held at Garmisch-Partenkirchen on 18 March 2011.

Grant, R.M. (1991) 'The resource-based theory of competitive advantage, implications for strategy formulation', *California Management Review*, 33: 114–35.

Hall, R. (1992) 'The strategic analysis of intangible resources', *Strategic Management Journal*, 13: 135–44.

Hamel, G. and Prahalad, C.K. (1994) *Competing for the Future*, Boston, MA: Harvard Business School Press.

Hamel, G. and Prahalad, C.K. (1996) *Competing for the Future*, 2nd edition, Boston, MA: Harvard Business School Press.

Helfat, C.E. (1997) 'Know-how and asset complementarity and dynamic capability accumulation: the case of R&D', *Strategic Management Journal*, 18: 339–60.

Hilbert, J. and Kluska, D. (2011) 'Gesundheit als Zukunftsfaktor in Regionen', in M. Bachinger, H. Pechlaner, and W. Widuckel, W. (eds) *Regionen und Netzwerke*, Wiesbaden: Gabler.

Illing, K.-T. (2009) *Gesundheitstourismus und Spa-Management*, Munich: Oldenbourg.

IPK International (2010) *World Travel Monitor*, Munich.

Jennings, G. (2010) *Tourism Research*, Melbourne: John Wiley.

Keck, A., Creutzberg, C. and Bergelt, C. (2012) 'Konkreter Anpassungsbedarf der Kur- und Erholungsorte in Mecklenburg-Vorpommern an den demographischen Wandel – unter Berücksichtigung von ganzjährigen Mehrgenerationenangeboten', online, available at: www.projectm.de/project-m/downloads/PROJECT-M_KECK-Medical_Leitfaden-demographischer-Wandel-in-Kur-und-Erholungsorten-in-MV.pdf (accessed 9 January 2012).

Klemm, A. (2007) *Demographischer Wandel und Tourismus: zukünftige Grundlagen und Chancen für touristische Märkte*, Berlin: ESV.

Kreilkamp, E. (2011) 'Die Zukunft des Gesundheitstourismus – Was macht eine erfolgreiche Gesundheitsdestination aus?' presentation held at Bad Bevensen, 25 February 2011.

LfStaD (Landesamt für Statistik und Datenverarbeitung) in Bayern (2011) 'Interaktives Kartenverzeichnis des LfStaD', online, available at: www.statistik.bayern.de/ interaktiv/regionalkarten/archiv/home.asp (accessed 15 July 2011).

Nahrstedt, W. (2008a) 'Von Medical Wellness zu Cultural Wellness', in T. Fischer, and A. Schulz (eds) *Handbuch Gesundheitstourismus. Grundlagen in Gesundheit, Freizeit und Tourismus*, Aachen: Shaker.

Nahrstedt, W. (2008b) *Wellnessbildung: Gesundheitssteigerung in der Wohlfühlgesellschaft*, Berlin: ESV.

OECD (2012) *Health at a Glance: Europe 2012*, online, available at: www.oecd.org/health/HealthAtAGlanceEurope2012.pdf (accessed 16 November 2012).

Pechlaner, H. and Reuter, C. (2012) 'Teilstrategie "Wirtschaft und Tourismus"', in W. Seiler and R.K. Stappen (eds) *Garmisch-Partenkirchen 2020: Nachhaltigkeitsstrategie Garmisch-Partenkirchen*, online, available at: http://energiewende-oberland.de/hp1086/Nachhaltigkeitsstrategie-Garmisch-Partenkirchen.htm.

Pechlaner, H. and Tschurtschenthaler, P. (2003) 'Tourism policy, tourism organizations and change management in alpine regions and destinations: a European perspective', *Current Issues in Tourism*, 6: 508–39.

Pforr, C., Pechlaner, H., Locher, C. and Jochmann, J. (2011) 'Health regions as tourism destinations: a new approach to regional development?' paper presented at the International Conference on Tourism – tourism in an era of uncertainty, Rhodes, 27 April 2011.

Prahalad, C.K. and Hamel, G. (1990) 'The core competence of the corporation', *Harvard Business Review*, 68: 79–91.

Prognos AG (2007) *Die Gesundheitsbranche: Dynamisches Wachstum im Spannungsfeld von Innovation und Intervention*, Basel: Prognos AG.

Rumelt, R.P. (1984) 'Towards a strategic theory of the firm', in R.B. Lamb (ed.) *Competitive Strategic Management*, Englewood Cliffs, NJ: Prentice-Hall.

Rumelt, R.P. (1991) 'How much does industry matter?' *Strategic Management Journal*, 12: 167–85.

Sanchez, R. and Heene, A. (2004) *The New Strategic Management, Organization, Competition and Competence*, New York: Wiley.

Seiler, W. and Stappen, R.K. (eds) (2012) 'Garmisch-Partenkirchen 2020. Nachhaltigkeitsstrategie Garmisch-Partenkirchen', Garmisch-Partenkirchen: unpublished study.

Stadt Ingolstadt (2012) *Statistischer Vierteljahrsbericht der Region 10 Ingolstadt*, Ingolstadt: Stadtplanungsamt.

Teece, D.J., Pisano, G. and Shuen, A. (1997) 'Dynamic capabilities and strategic management', *Strategic Management Journal*, 18: 509–33.

Teece, D.J., Rumelt, R.P., Dosi, G. and Winter, S. (1994) 'Understanding corporate coherence: theory and evidence', *Journal of Economic Behavior and Organization*, 23: 1–30.

Thierstein, A., Bentlage, M., Pechlaner, H., Doepfer, B., Brandt, A., Drangmeister, C., Schrödl, D., Voßen, D., Floeting, H. and Buser, B. (2011) 'Wertschöpfungskompetenz der Region Ingolstadt', unpublished study.

Tödter, N. (2011) 'Medizinreisen im DZT-Themenjahr 2011', presentation held at Garmisch-Partnekirchen, 18 March 2011.

Wernerfelt, B. (1984) 'A resource-based view of the firm', *Strategic Management Journal*, 5: 171–80.

Wernerfelt, B. (1995) 'The resource-based view of the firm: ten years after', *Strategic Management Review*, 16: 171–4.

Yin, R. (2003) *Case Study Research. Design and Methods*, 3rd edition, Thousand Oaks, CA: Sage.

8 Fit for purpose

Delivering wellness tourism through people

Tom Baum and Leonie Lockstone-Binney

Introduction

The focus of this chapter is on people and the workplace as part of the management of wellness tourism businesses and destinations. As such, this is an agenda-setting chapter because this is a neglected area for research. The chapter aims to identify key themes and issues in the area of people management in wellness tourism and propose these as a focus for future research and reflection. Wellness tourism, in common with other sectors of the industry, depends heavily on human intervention and mediation in the delivery of its services. The people who work in wellness tourism are, arguably, every bit (and a bit more) as vital to the success of the industry as their counterparts within the wider sector. Yet, their role is largely unsung and, certainly, under-researched in terms of theoretical analysis and practical management application. The purpose of this chapter is, first, to conceptualise the people who work in wellness, recognising the location of such work in relation to other related areas of professional, vocational and allied tourism activity across a number of service areas and, second, to identify themes and issues that merit both conceptual and empirical analysis and thereby to set a research agenda which will prepare the ground for serious academic and practitioner consideration of this area.

Conceptualising wellness tourism and its people

Wellness tourism can be located within two discrete contexts and its relationship with neighbouring components within each context plays a major role in shaping the nature of work and the experience of employees and their customers in wellness tourism. Figure 8.1 recognises that wellness, in its broadest interpretation, is part of a wider context which draws on health, sport, fitness and spirituality, among other areas. Each of these contributes a dedicated workplace culture and expectations in terms of skills and services which set them apart from each other but also exhibit attributes that highlight much that exists in common.

Locating wellness tourism in Figure 8.1 places it within a context which is of increasing social and political importance in many countries and cultures where recognition of the consequences of medical advances and lifestyle changes have

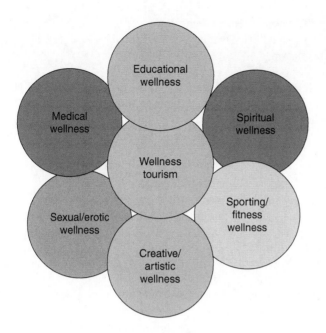

Figure 8.1 A conceptual positioning of wellness tourism within a wellness paradigm.

increased the interest of the state and society in the personal and collective management of the individual's health agenda (see, for example, Backett and
Davison 1995; Contoyannis and Jones 2004; Cockerham 2005). Wellness and
lifestyle issues are increasingly pervasive across many walks of working (see
Madsen 2003; Baiker *et al.* 2010; Jensen 2011) and non-working lives (Payne *et
al.* 2010; Singh 2011) and the emergence of wellness tourism and the workplace
it creates can be seen in the context of these trends.

Wellness tourism can also be seen as a growing subset of the broader field of
health tourism (Müller and Lanz Kaufmann 2000; Smith and Puczkó 2009) and
has been generally examined from the consumer (Kelly 2012; Konu and
Laukkanen 2010; Mak *et al.* 2009; Pesonen *et al.* 2011) and destination (Huijbens 2011; Kucukusta and Heung 2012; Wray *et al.* 2010) perspective. Whilst
health tourism as an overarching concept that includes medical tourism, people
travelling for a health-related cure or treatment; wellness tourism as Smith and
Puczkó (2009: 40) note is 'more preventative than curative'. Nevertheless, the
authors contend that wellness as a term has received increasing recognition internationally, despite its subjective meaning and varying cultural interpretations.

Concurrently, wellness tourism can be located with a broader set of interrelationships within wider tourism, coexisting with, and depending upon, a range of
allied tourism sub-sectors. The current paper adopts Voigt *et al.*'s (2011)
succinct definition of wellness tourism in recognition of the terminological

confusion that has arisen surrounding the health and wellness tourism domains, while recognising that the concept is contestable and is subject to alternative scoping or definitions (Hall 2003; Sheldon and Bushell 2009). Voigt *et al.* (2011: 17) define wellness tourism

> as the sum of all the relationships resulting from a journey by people whose motive, in whole or in part, is to maintain or promote their health and well-being, and who stay at least one night at a facility that is specifically designed to enable and enhance people's physical, psychological, spiritual and/or social wellbeing

This definition encompasses the aspects of mind, body and spirit; with Kelly (2010: 109) highlighting research evidence that suggests all three are essential for 'optimal wellness'. This definition allows us to position wellness tourism indicatively in relation to other facets of the wider tourism industry context in order to gain further understanding of the workplace consequences of its relationship to these areas (Figure 8.2). We do recognise that the parameters of wellness tourism which we describe in Figure 8.2 can be debated in terms of what is and what is not included and, in a sense, such debate will always be contextually and culturally bound. Previous definitions, for example, have not included sex tourism in this context but we believe that the intimacy of wellness services creates a blurred border with sex tourism in some contexts. The key point, in this

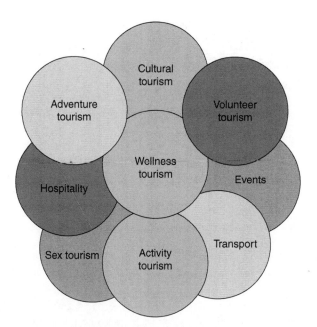

Figure 8.2 An indicative positioning of wellness tourism within a tourism industry paradigm.

chapter, is the location of wellness tourism work in close proximity to other aspects of tourism.

Researchers highlight the importance of studying wellness tourism experiences to better understand customer motives and needs (Smith and Puczkó 2009; Voigt *et al.* 2011). It is important to recognise that the field of wellness seeks to cater for diversity in this regard. At a relatively crude level, we have classified the wellness market in terms of the following groups:

- Guests who attend wellness facilities during the post-operative stage, where the main driver is recovery and a focus on convalescence.
- Guests for whom the main driver is enhancing general health, hence the focus is on prevention.
- Guests for whom the main driver is fitness and health and is part of a lifestyle regime.
- Guests for whom the main driver is recreation as part of wider lifestyle choices.
- Guests who attend facilities such as sanatoria on medical advice, indeed, where they have little choice.

Each of these groups has differing personal and technical service requirements and, as a consequence, influences the roles and responsibilities of those who work within the sector.

In contrast to demand-side considerations, less research attention has been afforded to the supply-side of wellness tourism, particularly at the micro level; Kelly's (2010) study of retreat operators is one exception. Within this, specifically, the role of frontline human resources in facilitating wellness tourism provision has been neglected of research inquiry. This chapter is intended to start a process of addressing this gap.

In common with tourism and allied areas of hospitality, leisure and events, wellness tourism engages people in a multitude of roles and scripts in the delivery of services that span time, space and focus in a way that makes generalisation challenging (Baum 2006). The particular workplace environment of each of these areas creates a relatively *closed* context for many of those who work in them. At the same time, each of the workforce contexts in question also includes some common skills areas, generally in areas of lowest status and remuneration, for example, those responsible for cleaning, security and administration. These commonalities relate to the nature of the predominantly weak labour market within which tourism and its allied fields are located.

Classifying work and workers in wellness tourism, therefore, is complex and includes work areas that relate to specific wellness functions in the delivery of therapeutic, fitness, dietary and spiritual services; generalised wellness/health/medical areas where there is overlap with related fields; tourism-specific functions that are also offered within other areas of travel and tourism services; general support roles found across a range of business sectors; and general management functions for which no specific wellness attributes are essential.

In identifying key issues facing the wellness tourism sector, in terms of employment, it is evident that these relate to a broad range of considerations that are common with allied areas, including the impact of stochastic demand on employment opportunities and stability; widely held perceptions of the hospitality employment as primarily consisting of *low*-skilled jobs; challenging workplace conditions in requiring what is often demanding work undertaken at antisocial times; negative lifestyle issues including a substantial percentage of hours worked outside normal business hours; the social stigma of working in this industry in some cultures; a (often young) transient workforce with poor utilisation of 'Gen Y' labour (Solnet and Hood 2008); low relative pay; and a high ratio of female, minority, student, part-time and casual workers (Deery and Shaw 1999; Deery 2002) with a consequent failure to compete in the recruitment of talent and skilled personnel; high levels of labour turnover at all levels (Baum 2006, 2007; Richardson 2009; Duncan *et al.* 2013); low levels of training and development within the sector and a perceived and real lack of formal qualifications at all levels; and a general inflexibility within the workforce in responding to changing demand. Each of these concerns is manifest in differing ways within each of the sub-sectors that may be associated with tourism – travel, transport, heritage, hospitality, events and, of course, wellness. Cohen and Russell (2008: 379) suggest that, perhaps, some aspects of wellness work (in spas) have changed in terms of status and recognition. They note that

> [i]n many parts of the world the status of spa employees has changed dramatically. In the past, working in a spa would have been considered by many as a low status job. A career as a beauty therapist may have been seen being similar to that of a hairdresser of [*sic*] cabin crew; suitable for school leavers with little or no qualifications. A massage therapist in many parts of the world would also have been considered low status and may even have had connotations of akin to working in the sex industry

Cohen and Russell (2008) continue by arguing that the contemporary situation is rather different – an optimistic assessment for which they provide little by way of evidence.

In contrast to the other specialist areas of tourism activity, wellness tourism offerings draw upon a number of the allied areas identified in Figure 8.1 in order to provide a framework for their workplace environment. Working in wellness draws on these in differing ways and to varied extents, depending on the particular focus of the wellness tourism offering and the cultural and economic traditions within which it operates. In addition, wellness tourism also calls upon an additional veil of human resource requirements, drawn from its tourism context, relating to areas such as service delivery and service operations, cultural engagement, tourism marketing and an array of links into other areas of the tourism experience within its destination – accommodation, food, attractions, events and the like. These in turn, create demands in workforce terms.

Locating the character and characteristics of work in wellness tourism requires recognition of the inter-relatedness of the field within the two contexts of wellness and wellness tourism which we have described in Figures 8.1 and 8.2, each of which poses challenges in terms of its own traditions, practices and skills demands. As we have noted, Figure 8.1 locates wellness tourism in relation to six allied wellness domains, which also exist as independent strands both within tourism (medical tourism, religious tourism, sex tourism, sports tourism, creative/artistic tourism, educational tourism) and external to it – wellness in relation to medicine and health, religion and belief, commercial sex, arts and culture, organised sport and formal education. Alongside this, Figure 8.2 locates wellness within the context of selected tourism industry sub-sectors, with which there is a mutual dependence.

Each set of these related areas exhibits its own characteristics in terms of the workforce that populates it and this impacts directly upon the work, workplace and organisational culture; the status of work and careers/opportunities; the extent to which the labour market is open or closed; the nature of work and work routines within the area; the level and demands of skills; perceptions of vocational commitment, professional status and professionalism; the role of professional bodies and their regulation; workplace organisation and industrial relations; employee turnover, tenure and workplace security; the nature and extent of formative education and training; and requirements for in-service education and training.

Setting a research agenda

The dynamics of the interactions developed above raise a number of key issues for wellness tourism industry stakeholders – employees, their managers, business owners, customers and, in some areas, legislators and the wider community. Equally important for an emergent and complex field are the research areas that require addressing in order to better inform stakeholder debate and theoretical engagement. Key emergent themes addressed in this chapter will survey the underdeveloped body of work in the field, and raise questions which call for research consideration. The authors recognise that this emergent agenda is one which includes areas of sensitivity, of some overlap and, in some respects, contradiction. It is driven by a process which frames the workforce environment in wellness tourism in terms of a number of key issues, namely:

- ethical standards and practice
- professional roles and scripts
- aesthetic and emotional dimensions to work
- skills, training and qualifications
- cultural considerations
- diversity issues
- duty of care beyond the fun zone
- personal health and safety for both employees and customers.

Some of these drivers of the wellness tourism workforce have attracted partial attention from researchers in the past but, generally, such work has not taken into consideration wider contexts and linkages. Elaborating on these drivers it is noted that, in substantial part, these relate to concerns which are unique to the wellness and tourism nexus.

Ethical standards and practice

The ethics of embodied work in wellness tourism raises issues of sensitivity and challenges employees, management and customers in terms of their expectations, their responsibilities and the parameters which are drawn around highly interactive physical work, placing both the workforce and their customers in potentially ambiguous and difficult situations. These issues are recognised by Bjurstam and Cohen (2008: 365) when they argue that the 'very personal nature' of wellness services means that the workforce is likely to be more engaged emotionally and spiritually than staff from other industries. Therefore, compared to related fields in tourism, wellness undoubtedly provides some of the most physically and emotionally intimate workplace interactions that demand the drawing of carefully prescribed parameters and recognition of clear, unambiguous 'rules of engagement'. Smith and Puczkó (2009: 186) note that 'a certain level of sensitivity is required on the part of those administering services, treatment or courses', with examples provided of massage therapists preserving client modesty and fitness staff dealing with the emotional and physical stress caused to clients as a result of injuries incurred in a session. This discussion raises wider issues, which draw on the work of Trethewey (1999), Smith Maguire (2002, 2008), Wolkowitz (2002) and McDowell (2009) and consider both the professional management of intimate work and its border zones with other areas of embodied work such as sex tourism. At its outermost borders, the physical proximity of wellness in the form of, for example, the massage suite in a spa, in a tourism context, may be misinterpreted as a consensual precursor to other forms of intimacy, especially in cultural contexts where sex tourism is widely practiced. Sex work, in turn, exposes employees to vulnerabilities in terms of exploitation and violence (Sanders and Campbell 2007). Sex tourism, itself, is an emergent field for research interest and this emanating discourse throws some light on the nature of such work, the role of sex workers themselves and the customers who patronise their services (Brents *et al.* 2010; Dorfman 2011). Little is known about how boundaries between wellness and sex tourism are patrolled by management and by wellness workers themselves or, indeed, what the expectations of tourists are when approaching this context.

Bridges over uncomfortable waters

Wellness tourism brings to the fore issues of professional identity and the crossover realms between the delivery of medical, paramedical, wellness, leisure, tourism and hospitality services. These areas do not have traditions of collaboration and can, on occasion, operate in counter directions. Management themes that emanate from such tensions are of particular interest in terms of future research. In particular, concurrent management of cohorts of relatively high- versus low-skilled staff and management of locally sourced versus imported staff. Professionalism is important to medical identity and forms the basis for the trust that exists between professionals and their patients (Stern 2006). This trust has to transfer into the wellness tourism context where medical services form part of the offering, imposing implications largely absent from the rather more informal and casualised business settings that are normal within tourism. Recognising professional status in tourism work is a challenge inhibited by both the nature of activities undertaken and by structural and demographic inhibitors (Sheldon 1989). Indeed, the predominance of women working in wellness and the employment choices made by many females further reduces professional recognition for their work (Marlow and Carter 2004).

Aesthetic and emotional dimensions

Aesthetic and emotional dimensions lie at the heart of work in wellness tourism and pose organisational and management challenges which require serious analysis beyond the initial contribution of Sayers and Bradbury (2004) and others in this area. Wellness tourism work is highly demanding in emotional (Hochschild 1983) and aesthetic (Nickson *et al.* 2003) and, by extension, sexualised labour terms (Warhurst and Nickson 2009). Hochschild's work, relating to emotional labour, inspired recognition of what Westwood (2004) notes are commonly referred to as 'soft skills' and, in doing so, highlights less tangible dimensions in the bundling of skills. These represent skills (see below) which are at the heart of work in the wellness sector. Bolton (2004) argues a strong case for recognition of the skills dimensions within emotion work. She argues that emotional inputs are inherently skilled elements within the work routines, control processes and socially constructed demands that typify much service work. Some aspects of wellness tourism, where the field borders on spiritual and faith-healing experiences, take the demands of emotional engagement into relatively uncharted waters in an organisational management sense. To the requirements of emotional labour in wellness tourism can be added the skills demands of what Warhurst *et al.* (2000) describe as aesthetic labour, the skills required to look, sound and behave in a manner that is compatible with the requirements of the job and with the expectations of the customers. Both Snoj and Mumel (2002) and Alén *et al.* (2006) highlight the aesthetic expectations and demands of spa customers with respect to staff employed within the sector – unless masseurs, for example, meet customers' aesthetic criteria, they will not be employed, irrespective of their skills levels. In many cases, aesthetic labour involves staff demonstrating the ability to respond to fashion and trend imperatives in the consumer marketplace in a way that can be socially exclusive of many groups and cultures within society. Understanding the complexity of both emotional and aesthetic skills in the varying contexts of wellness is an area that merits further investigation. Indeed, Bjurstam and Cohen (2008: 364) go a step further in describing spas as 'spirituality in the workplace' and, in arguing that those working in the industry require emotional attunement to their work in order to empathise with their clients' needs, note that '[i]t is difficult for a therapist to give advice, provide empathy, or truly "be" with a client and explore their emotional life unless they have undertaken a similar exploration within themselves'. Articulating this requirement, within a job specification, would appear to present some interesting challenges for the human resource manager!

Skills, training and qualifications

Wellness tourism brings together an amalgam of skills requirements that draw on very different worlds in terms of education and training, both formative and within the workplace, worlds that operate to divergent learning cultures and traditions, qualifications and professional requirements (Lloyd 2005). At the same time, there is a global shortage of professionals with the appropriate skills and attributes for employment within wellness tourism (Voigt *et al.* 2010). Managers and frontline staff alike can have varying skill levels and attitudes to formal training. Kelly's study (2010) of retreat operators noted that many were entrepreneurs of small to medium-sized businesses with more informal approaches to training and quality assurance. This finding was noted in contrast to the spa sector, which as Kelly points out has more advanced regulatory schemes established by industry bodies (e.g. The International Spa Association) and large hotel chains that increasingly provide spa offerings. Smith and Puczkó (2009: 180) highlight the sector's requirement for trained staff stating 'most of the services and treatments offered in these health institutions require special skills, trainings and maybe years of experience' before going onto lament a lack of adequate training and qualifications across the wellness tourism field. They highlight that 'damage can be done to body, mind or spirit through neglectful or uninformed practice' (Smith and Puczkó 2009: 189). The authors further suggest qualification suites need to catch up to the growing trend of staff multitasking, particularly in spas and wellness centres, where they may provide a range of services, instead of just one specialisation. In recognition of the specialist nature of wellness industry skills, Buchner *et al.* (2008) point to the emergence of bespoke education programs for the spa sector, noting however the considerable disparity in duration and complexity of such educational initiatives.

Cultural considerations

Cultural aspects of work in wellness tourism means that there is need for recognition that wellness plays differing roles in social and economic terms across time and space and that these divergences have implications for the work undertaken within the industry and the people who undertake it (Laing and Weiler 2008). Striking among these differences are the origins and consequent traditions which underpin the sector in, for example, central Europe and North America. In the former, traditions have a strong curative base whereas the latter has evolved with stronger lifestyle and leisure drivers. These differing traditions impinge on the status, conditions and remuneration of wellness work in differing locations. Wellness tourism, along with other areas of interactive service work, increasingly reflects multiculturalism in its workforce. Aspects of this reflect specialist areas of work within wellness where both skills demands and customer expectations make the employment of Thai workers for Thai massage treatments, for example, a necessity in many operations. There is scope for extended research consideration of the impact of culture on wellness tourism work across differing contexts.

Diversity issues

Diversity issues are significant in wellness tourism in terms of role, opportunities and management (Aitchison *et al.* 1999). Smith and Puczkó (2009: 155) highlight the 'resource intensive' nature of the sector and some of the challenges of sourcing and managing staff in this environment. These challenges include importing staff into local economies to service wellness tourism developments, particularly in areas where there is a limited workforce or the host community does not have the necessary skills base to provide guests with specialised or high-quality service. This may lead to wage disparities between the imported and local staff and a certain level of resentment. This problem may be further exacerbated where locals are employed in more lowly skilled roles, as Kelly (2010) found in her study, and are offered little access to career progression opportunities. Smith and Puczkó (2009) further note that locals may struggle to deal effectively with management, particularly where chains are involved in the operation of large resorts. On a more positive nature, Smith and Puczkó (2009) also highlight that the wellness sector is less prone to the vagaries of seasonality, thereby negating the impact of temporal fluctuations to workforce numbers.

Duty of care

After-care issues are also an under-researched area in wellness tourism and have implications for the workforce within the sector. Kelly (2010: 108) notes that 'wellness tourism brings with it many new, potentially loaded responsibilities, not just for the normal touristic concerns of transport, accommodation and restaurant standards, but perhaps also for the care of the psyche'. This added layer of care and attention in some cases extends beyond the immediate wellness tourism experience, in acknowledgement that wellness holidays can be in some cases powerful, life-altering experiences (Smith and Puczkó 2009). Kelly's (2010: 114) study of retreat operators noted that 60 per cent provided some form of after-care service to their clients, in recognition that 'the nature of certain personal development programs can release emotions that require more care than regular tourism activities, particularly when the visitor leaves the "safe place" of the retreat to return home'. Wellness staff, if not aware of the longer-term ramifications of their immediate interactions with clients, may also inflict unintended damage.

Health and safety issues

Health and safety issues are highlighted by Hall (2011) who discusses the risks to health professionals and tourists alike arising from health and, by extension, wellness tourism as a subset. Whilst not generally involving invasive medical procedures, the wellness sector still brings staff and client in close contact, presenting health and safety risks to both resulting from the use of unhygienic equipment and facilities, tainted food provision, wet surfaces, and a range of other sources, potentially leading to infection and illness. Researchers have considered the relationship between tourism and a range of HIV-related issues (see, for example, Padilla *et al.* 2010; Rice *et al.* 2012) but the issues relating to wellness tourism extend beyond high-profile medical conditions such as HIV and require consideration from an organisational/management context as well as from medical perspectives.

Conclusion

There is little dispute that wellness tourism is one of the fastest growing sub-sectors within the wider tourism environment and that it is manifest in a wide range of formats, offering guests a diversity of opportunities and experiences. Wellness tourism is, from a conceptual and theoretical perspective, an emerging field with limited research engagement and the opportunity to develop new and innovative areas for investigation. In the context of the theme of this paper, wellness tourism is labour intensive and demands the management of a wide range of employees with skills which draw on traditions that cross tourism, hospitality, health, healing, fitness, sport and spirituality. This chapter aspired to identify key areas that merit consideration within a wellness tourism people-management research agenda in the hope that this will be of value to both academic researchers and practitioners in engaging with the challenges of people management in the wellness tourism sector. The proposed agenda is by no means conclusive or definitive; neither does it seek to prioritise issues that require consideration in engaging, empirically and conceptually, with human resource management issues as they pertain to wellness tourism. Rather, this chapter has sought to highlight some of the valuable work undertaken to date but also to focus on the limitations of relatively narrow and specific research within a field that incorporates complex and interdependent dimensions, drawn from wider contexts of both wellness and tourism.

References

Aitchison, C., Jordan, J. and Brackenridge, C. (1999) 'Women in leisure management: a survey of gender equity', *Women In Management Review*, 14: 121–7.

Alén, E., Fraiz, J.A. and Rufín, R. (2006) 'Analysis of health spa customers' expectations and perceptions: the case of Spanish establishments', *Polytechnical Studies Review*, 3: 245–62.

Backett, K. and Davison, C. (1995) 'Lifecourse and lifestyle: the social and cultural location of health behaviours', *Social Science and Medicine*, 40: 629–38.

Baiker, K., Cutler, D. and Song, Z. (2010) 'Workplace wellness programs can generate savings', *Health Affairs*, 29: 304–11.

Baum, T. (2006) *Human Resource Management for Tourism, Hospitality and Leisure. An International Perspective*, London: International Thomson.

Baum, T. (2007) 'Human resources in tourism: still waiting for change', *Tourism Management*, 28: 1383–99.

Bjurstam, A. and Cohen, M. (2008) 'Spas and the future leadership climate', in M. Cohen and G. Bodeker (eds) *Understanding the Global Spa Industry: Spa Management*, Oxford: Butterworth-Heinemann.

Bolton, S. (2004) 'Conceptual confusions: emotion work as skilled work', in C. Warhurst, I. Grugulis and E. Keep (eds) *The Skills that Matter*, Basingstoke: Palgrave, 19–37.

Brents, B., Jackson, C. and Hausbeck, K. (2010) *The State of Sex: Tourism, Sex and Sin in the New American Heartland*, New York: Routledge Press.

Buchner, D., Snelling, A. and Cohen, M. (2008) 'Spa-related education and training', in M. Cohen and G. Bodeker (eds) *Understanding the Global Spa Industry: Spa Management*, Oxford: Butterworth-Heinemann.

Cockerham, W. (2005) 'Health lifestyle theory and the convergence of agency and structure', *Journal of Health and Social Behavior*, 46: 51–67.

Cohen, M. and Russell, D. (2008) 'Human resource management in spas: staff recruitment, retention and remuneration', in M. Cohen and G. Bodeker (eds) *Understanding the Global Spa Industry: Spa Management*, Oxford: Butterworth-Heinemann.

Contoyannis, P. and Jones, A. (2004) 'Socio-economic status, health and lifestyle', *Journal of Health Economics*, 23: 965–95.

Deery, M. (2002) 'Labour turnover in international hospitality and tourism', in N. D'Annunzio-Green, G. Maxwell and S. Watson (eds) *Human Resource Management: International Perspectives in Hospitality and Tourism*, London: Thomson.

Deery, M. and Shaw, R. (1999) 'An investigation of the relationship between employee turnover and organisational culture', *Journal of Hospitality and Tourism Research*, 23: 387–400.

Dorfman, R. (2011) 'A Foucauldian analysis of power and prostitution: comparing sex tourism and sex work migration', *Polis Journal*, 5, online, available at: www.polis.leeds.ac.uk/about/student-life/journal/polis-journal-summer-2011.php (accessed 2 February 2013).

Duncan, T., Scott, D. and Baum, T. (2013) 'The mobilities of hospitality work: an exploration of issues', *Annals of Tourism Research*, 4: 1–19.

Hall, C.M. (2003) 'Spa and health tourism', in S. Hudson (ed.) *Sport and Adventure Tourism*, New York: Haworth Hospitality Press.

Hall, C.M. (2011) 'Health and medical tourism: a kill or cure for global public health?' *Tourism Review*, 66: 4–15.

Hochschild, A.R. (1983) *The Managed Heart: Commercialisation of Human Feeling*, Berkley, CA: University of California Press.

Huijbens, E.H. (2011) 'Developing wellness in Iceland: theming wellness destinations the Nordic way', *Scandinavian Journal of Hospitality and Tourism*, 11: 20–41.

Kelly, C. (2010) 'Analysing wellness tourism provision: a retreat operators' study', *Journal of Hospitality and Tourism Management*, 17: 108–16.

Kelly, C. (2012) 'Wellness tourism: retreat visitor motivations and experiences', *Tourism Recreation Research*, 37: 205–13.

Konu, H. and Laukkanen, T. (2010) 'Predictors of tourists' wellbeing holiday intentions in Finland', *Journal of Hospitality and Tourism Management*, 17: 144–9.

Kucukusta, D. and Heung, C.S. (2012) 'The problems of developing wellness tourism in China: from supply perspective', *Journal of China Tourism Research*, 8: 146–58.

Jensen, D. (2011) 'Can worksite nutritional interventions improve productivity and firm profitability? A literature review', *Perspectives in Public Health*, 131: 184–92.

Laing, J. and Weiler, B. (2008) 'Mind, body and spirit: health and wellness tourism in Asia', in Cochrane, J. (ed.) *Asian Tourism: Growth and Change*, Oxford: Elsevier.

Lloyd, C. (2005) 'Competitive strategy and skills: working out the fit in the fitness industry', *Human Resource Management Journal*, 15: 15–34.

Madsen, S. (2003) 'Wellness in the workplace: preparing employees for change', *The Organization Development Journal*, 20: 46–55.

Mak, A.H.N., Wong, K.K.F. and Chang, R.C.Y. (2009) 'Health or self-indulgence? The motivations and characteristics of spa-goers', *International Journal of Tourism Research*, 11: 185–99.

Marlow, S. and Carter, S. (2004) 'Accounting for change: professional status, gender disadvantage and self-employment', *Women In Management Review*, 19: 5–17.

McDowell, L. (2009) *Working Bodies: Interactive Service Employment and Workplace Identities*, Chichester: Wiley-Blackwell.

Müller, H. and Lanz Kaufmann, E. (2000) 'Wellness tourism: market analysis of a special health tourism segment and implications for the hotel industry,' *Journal of Vacation Marketing*, 1: 5–17.

Nickson, D., Warhurst, C. and Witz, A. (2003) 'The labour of aesthetics and the aesthetics of organization', *Organization*, 10: 33–54.

Padilla, M., Guilamo-Ramos, V., Bouris, A. and Matiz Reyes, A. (2010) 'HIV/AIDS and tourism in the Caribbean: an ecological systems perspective', *American Journal of Public Health*, 100: 70–7.

Payne, L., Ainsworth, B. and Godbey, G. (2010) *Leisure, Health and Wellness: Making the Connections*, State College, PA: Venture Publishing Inc.

Pesonen, J., Laukkanen, T. and Komppula, R. (2011) 'Benefit segmentation of potential wellbeing tourists', *Journal of Vacation Marketing*, 17: 303–14.

Rice, B., Gilbart, V., Lawrence, J., Smith, R., Kall, M. and Delpech, V. (2012) 'Safe travels? HIV transmission among Britons travelling abroad', *HIV Medicine*, 13: 315–17.

Richardson, S. (2009) 'Undergraduates' perceptions of tourism and hospitality as a career choice', *International Journal of Hospitality Management*, 28: 382–8.

Sanders, T. and Campbell, R. (2007) 'Designing out vulnerability, building in respect: violence, safety and sex work policy', *The British Journal of Sociology*, 58: 1–19.

Sayers, J. and Bradbury, T. (2004) 'Let the music take your mind: aesthetic labour and "working out" to music', paper at the Work, Employment and Society conference, Manchester, 1–3 September 2004.

Sheldon, P. (1989) 'Professionalism in tourism and hospitality', *Annals of Tourism Research*, 16: 492–503.

Sheldon, P.J. and Bushell, R. (2009) 'Introduction to wellness and tourism', in R. Bushell and P.J. Sheldon (eds) *Wellness and Tourism: Mind, Body, Spirit, Place*, New York: Cognizant Communication Corporation.

Singh, P. (2011) 'The changing patterns of work and leisure: revolutions in leisure behaviours: health and wellness', *African Journal for Physical Health Education, Recreation and Dance*, 17: 69–80.

Smith, M. and Puczkó, L. (2009) *Health and Wellness Tourism*, Oxford: Butterworth-Heinemann.

Smith Maguire, J. (2002) 'Body lessons: fitness publishing and the cultural production of the fitness consumer', *International Review for the Sociology of Sport*, Special Issue on Media and Sport, 37: 449–64.

Smith Maguire, J. (2008) 'The personal is professional: personal trainers as a case study of cultural intermediaries', *International Journal of Cultural Studies.* 11: 203–21.

Snoj, B. and Mumel, D. (2002) 'The measurement of perceived differences in service quality: the case of health spas in Slovenia', *Journal of Vacation Marketing*, 8: 362–79.

Solnet, D. and Hood, A. (2008) 'Generation Y as hospitality employees: framing a research agenda', *Journal of Hospitality and Tourism Management*, 15: 59–68.

Stern, D. (2006) *Measuring Medical Professionalism*, New York: OUP USA.

Trethewey, A. (1999) 'Disciplined bodies: women's embodied identities at work', *Organization Studies*, 20: 423–50.

Warhurst, C. and Nickson, D. (2009) ' "The look?" Emotional, aesthetic and sexualized labour in interactive services' *Gender, Work and Organization*, 16: 385–404.

Warhurst, C., Nickson, D., Witz, A. and Cullen, A.M. (2000) 'Aesthetic labour in interactive service work: some case study evidence from the "New Glasgow" ', *The Service Industries Journal*, 20: 1–18.

Westwood, A. (2004) 'Skills that matter and shortages that don't', in C. Warhurst, I. Grugulis, and E. Keep (eds) *The Skills That Matter*, Basingstoke: Palgrave, 38–54.

Wolkowitz, C. (2002) 'The social relations of body work', *Work, Employment and Society*, 16: 497–510.

Wray, M., Laing, J. and Voigt, C. (2010) 'Bryon Bay: an alternate health and wellness destination', *Journal of Hospitality and Tourism Management*, 17: 158–66.

Voigt, C., Brown, G. and Howat, G. (2011) 'Wellness tourists: in search of transformation', *Tourism Review*, 66: 16–30.

Voigt, C., Laing, J., Wray, M., Brown, G., Howat, G., Weiler, B. and Trembath, R. (2010) *Health Tourism in Australia: Supply, Demand and Opportunities*, Gold Coast: Sustainable Tourism Cooperative Research Centre.

Part III

Relationships between nature, wellbeing and destinations

9 Researching the links between parklands and health

Michael Hughes

Introduction

The concept for this chapter was derived from research into the development and subsequent expansion of a program in Australia and New Zealand known as *Healthy Parks, Healthy People*. This program is based on the notion that access to parkland is an important means of improving the health of individuals and communities. This includes promoting the benefits of outdoor activities as well as the benefits of interactions with nature.

For the purposes of this chapter, the term 'health' is used in the context of the World Health Organization's (WHO) definition as a 'state of complete physical, mental and social wellbeing, and not merely the absence of disease or infirmity' (WHO 1946). This definition is based on an ecological theory of public health recognising that health is influenced by many interrelated factors. This is a holistic view of health that encompasses the wellness paradigm, in terms of the presence of wellbeing as well as the absence of illness. That is, the WHO definition includes a positive construction of health that encompasses concepts such as happiness and quality of life. The World Health Organization identified that all settings of society and activity should provide greater opportunities for promoting health, including provision of parklands for public access. 'Parklands' refer to public open green space such as urban parks, national parks and other natural areas managed for recreation and tourism use. This includes managed areas with elements of nature ranging from contrived manicured gardens and lawn through to nature reserves with some or all endemic ecosystem processes intact.

Background: *Healthy Parks, Healthy People*

Tourism is, in part, an activity people undertake to escape the daily routine of life and encounter new or exotic experiences as a means of restoring wellness. In this context, it is no coincidence that parklands are a significant point of focus for tourism and leisure-related activities (Eagles 2002; Kuo 2002; Nyaupane *et al.* 2004). The popularity of natural areas as tourism and leisure destinations seems to relate to a normative awareness of the beneficial health effects of experiencing nature to counteract the stress associated with modern living. For example, Heimstra and McFarling (1974) postulated that visiting natural areas was born from an instinctive need to escape from urban living and re-connect with nature to restore a sense of wellbeing. Similarly, Rolston (1998) commented on the human urge to connect with and experience nature based on the idea that the human experience of nature provided a sense of wellness. To explain this urge, Wilson (1984) put forward the 'Biophilia Hypothesis'. Wilson argued that humans have a fundamental affinity for nature which is genetically engrained as a result of our natural evolutionary origins. Living in isolation from nature thus has negative health effects. Contact with nature is thus connected with a sense of revitalising physical and mental health, that is, wellness. This inherent connection between humans and nature perhaps explains why wellness tourism products commonly feature elements of nature or are located in destinations featuring parkland settings. Therefore, accessing parklands, as nature-based tourism destinations, could be classified in part as an activity intended to restore wellness. That is, parklands could be classified as a type of wellness tourism destination.

Linking public health to parklands access is officially identified as a priority concept by the various state-based parks management agencies in Australia as well as New Zealand. This imperative was originally identified in Australia by the state of Victoria more than a decade ago. Subsequently, the Victorian state government agency directly responsible for management of public parklands, Parks Victoria, developed a concept labelled *Healthy Parks, Healthy People* as a core component of a public campaign to encourage park access based on highlighting the associated health benefits. *Healthy Parks, Healthy People* (HPHP) is essentially a branding exercise conceived as a result of the more entrepreneurial approach to parkland management in Victoria. The perceived success of the campaign encouraged Parks Victoria to give the use of the HPHP brand to the Western Australian agency responsible for parks management, the Department of Environment and Conservation. Following on from this, Parks Victoria then sub-licensed it in 2007 to the regional parkland management peak body, Parks Forum. This enabled the use of the HPHP brand concept to expand across the various Australian and New Zealand parks management agency members.

HPHP was initially devised as a promotional campaign to increase awareness of parklands as tourism and recreation destinations that were beneficial to health, and hence grow park visitor numbers. It also triggered government-sponsored reviews of available research to lend further substance to the health destination orientated brand. Branding is about providing imagery and information that helps build product recognition, loyalty, value and market share. Success of a brand is based on the ability to deliver its promise and, hence, encourage repeated consumption. Consequently, the development of the HPHP brand was followed by an effort to gather additional supporting research-based evidence to lend it further substance. Fortunately, a substantial body of literature exists on the relationship between public access to green or natural environments (parklands) and human health, both at the individual and community level. However, little is known about the underlying mechanisms for this relationship and the extent to which natural environments themselves influence health. Further, much of the research design is based on correlation rather than causal relationships, so it is generally unclear whether healthy people tend to access parklands or whether parklands improve health. Also, it is not certain as to what extent health benefits accrue from secondary factors associated with parklands, such as participation in physical exercise, organised programs or socialisation. This chapter presents a review of published research on the relationship between parklands and health in terms of methodology and the subsequent types of knowledge created. From this review some potential research directions are suggested that could contribute to understanding the key factors in the relationship between accessing parklands and health.

Measuring the health effects of parklands

There are a range of methods for measuring health. The method selected depends on what aspect of health is being measured and why it is being measured. For example, Ware *et al.* (1981) described five broad reasons including determining the effectiveness of interventions; assessing quality of care; estimating the needs of the population; improving clinical decisions; and understanding causes and consequences relating to health. Each reason requires a different method and approach. Many of these are applied in research on the influence of parklands on health. Consequently, the research outlined in this chapter includes a wide range of health measurement techniques.

Broadly speaking, measures of health may be described in terms of being subjective or objective. Subjective assessment, in the context of this chapter, usually involves participants self-reporting their health status using a questionnaire while objective assessment generally involves some sort of clinical measurement of bodily functions. Self-reporting could be based on quantitative or qualitative techniques. Quantitative methods require participants to rate their responses to statements using a scale or range of options (agree–disagree; good–bad and so on). This type of approach seems to dominate the literature with a proliferation of self-reporting scales gaining popularity amongst medical researchers in the 1970s. The quantitative approach to self-reported health gained acceptance over the following decades as research functioned to improve reliability and validity of the scales used (McDowell 2006). Qualitative health assessment might include interviews and focus groups, requiring textual analysis of narrative responses that afford a greater understanding of the reported health status of an individual or group. However, the quantitative, subjective health measures enable greater ease of comparison between participants and groups as well as enabling more rapid data gathering to capture a larger sample within a given time frame.

The literature on the health effects of parklands and nature appears to be dominated by quantitative, subjective health measures. There is a wide range of questionnaires and scales available for self-reporting health status. The scale selected is determined by what is being measured and why it is being assessed. These subjective health scales can be broadly divided into positive and negative measures. The latter relates to reporting the presence of illness, stress and other physical and mental conditions that impede everyday life. Positive scales focus on reporting the presence of good health, happiness and wellbeing that enriches everyday life. Chapter 10 in this book provides a discussion of positive health measures in relation to parklands in the context of a specific case study. In terms of determining types and acuteness of health conditions, subjective or self-reported measures of health are prone to significant margins of error determined by factors such as lifestyle, participant knowledge of health, demographics and socio-economic status (Baker *et al.*1980). As a consequence, subjective health measures are considered by some to be weak measures of actual physical health condition (Ambrasat *et al.* 2011). However, subjective health measures can usefully indicate intangible concepts such as quality of life and level of happiness or satisfaction in connection to assessed physical and mental health. This can provide a more holistic understanding of health compared to objective, physiological measures (Streiner and Norman 2008). That is, subjective measures may also indicate why people have responded in a certain way in addition to their reported health status.

Objective measures of health include monitoring of physiological indicators such as heart rate, blood pressure, body temperature and hormone levels that are influenced by physical health or emotional state. It may also include measurement of cognitive function, such as reaction times and time taken to complete certain tasks as an indicator of fatigue, stress and rate of mental or physical restoration. Objective measures at the community level may include statistical data such as crime rates, hospital admissions and education participation. Objective measures are considered to be more reliable than subjective measures in terms of physical health condition as they are not reliant on the opinion or perception of the observer or participant (Baker *et al.* 2001). A number of studies into the effect of parklands on health have used these objective measures. For example Pretty *et al.* (2005) measured blood pressure response to scenery and Takano *et al.* (2002) measured mortality in aged populations in relation to neighbourhood greenness. However, objective health measures are difficult to link to why an individual or group is responding in a given way. This is because there is a wide range of confounding factors and variables that may influence physiological functions such as diet and lifestyle and levels of stress in day-to-day living. Furthermore, objective measurement can include subjective influences that would not be accounted for unless the participant provides additional information to place the measurement in context. That is, the act of measuring medical status can also influence the result, introducing a subjective element that is difficult to control. This has been referred to as the 'white coat effect' where a person's emotional response to being in the presence of a medical practitioner or researcher can influence physiological functions. For example, having blood pressure measured can cause blood pressure to rise as a stress response to the act of measurement in a clinical setting (Myers *et al.* 2009). Given the multifaceted character of health, using a combination of objective and subjective measures can provide better insight into health and how it is influenced by interventions such as exposure to nature in parklands (Bowling 2009).

Research on parklands and health benefits

There is a considerable body of knowledge from a range of disciplines using various methods regarding the relationship between exposure to nature and its positive impact on human health. For example, research indicates a positive association between the amount of green space in an urban area and adults' self-reported general health (Maas *et al.* 2006, 2008; Mitchell and Popham 2008). Other research has found the availability of access to parklands to be inversely linked with self-reported stress levels and depression (Morita *et al.* 2007; Nielsen and Hansen 2007). In terms of recovery from ill health, Ulrich's 1983 objective study of hospital patient records was among the first to indicate a positive association between having a view of nature from the hospital ward and improved rates of recovery (Health Council of the Netherlands and Dutch Advisory Council for Research on Spatial Planning 2004). This study found that hospital patients with a view of a park with trees had faster physical recovery post-surgery than those with a brick-wall view. Parklands are also known to facilitate socialisation within a community, encouraging positive interactions and promoting stronger social networks among neighbours. A strong social network within a community has been shown to be conducive to better health (Berkman *et al.* 2000; Kawachi *et al.* 1999). It is thus apparent from research that parklands are linked to a wide range of physical, mental and social health-related effects.

Physical health benefits of parklands

It is well documented that provision of access to parklands encourages physical activity within a population. Physical activity as a factor in itself is known to be directly linked to health within a population (Jago and Bailey 2012). However, studies have indicated that the environmental setting for physical activity is associated with additional health benefits. Research suggests an association between physical activity in parklands may have greater physiological and psychological benefits than physical activity in other settings (Pretty *et al.* 2005; van den Berg *et al.* 2007). For example, Pretty *et al.* (2005) exposed subjects exercising on a treadmill in a laboratory to a sequence of rural and urban pleasant and unpleasant scenes. Viewing pleasant rural and urban scenes while exercising on a treadmill was linked to a positive effect on blood pressure (an indicator of cardiovascular health) and self-reported mood measures relevant to mental health compared to those viewing unpleasant scenes.

In terms of field-based research, a longitudinal study in Japan focused on measuring the association between walkable green space in a densely populated urban area and local resident senior citizens' survival rates over five years (Takano *et al.* 2002). Walkable green space included parkland and tree-lined streets. Results suggested there was a positive influence on survival for people living in neighbourhoods with walkable green spaces after controlling for age, sex, marital status, baseline health and socio-economic status. However, convenience sampling techniques were used as were very generic indicators for health while the extent to which surrounding green spaces were actually used for walking was not measured. This means that the associations found are correlational and cannot be casually determined. Along similar lines, a study by Sugiyama *et al.* (2008) also found a positive association between health indices and access to green environments. Respondents who perceived their neighbourhood as having a high level of accessible green space were more likely to show better self-reported physical and mental health compared with those who reported low levels of accessible green space in their neighbourhood. The researchers found that the level of recreational walking seemed to explain the relationship between greener neighbourhoods and self-reported physical health. They also concluded that the positive relationship between green space and mental health was partly explained by the restorative effects of natural environments.

Related to this, physical activity in parklands has been identified as being more restorative than in urban built environments and indoor settings (Bendell and Font 2004; Hug *et al.*2009; Wilson 1984; Zeng *et al.* 2010). Restorative quality is known to predict the frequency of exercise and thus acting as a further motivator to engage in physical activity on a regular basis (Hug *et al.* 2009). Research also indicates that people tend to engage in exercise for a longer duration in parklands (Health Council of the Netherlands and Dutch Advisory Council for Research on Spatial Planning 2004). This study suggests that readily accessible parklands are linked to a higher frequency of physical exercise for longer duration in the surrounding population. The frequency and duration of exercise are important for public health benefits. For example, the Australian National Physical Activity Guidelines for Adults recommends engaging in at least 30 minutes of moderate intensity physical activity on most, preferably all, days of the week in order to achieve health benefits (Australian Government Department of Health and Ageing 1999). The positive link between physical exercise and health is clear, while the link between green space and increased physical exercise is apparent. However, separation of the health effects of physical activity and that of parklands is more difficult.

Parklands are associated with increased levels of observed and self-reported physical activity within the nearby community which in turn is associated with healthier residents. It is difficult to establish a direction of cause and effect as research commonly involves *in situ* residential and parkland user sampling, cross-sectional and non-random design. Studies of communities and health in relation to parks access do not readily lend themselves to an experimental design where a population can be randomly assigned to residential areas with or without parklands. While not practical, random allocation of neighbourhood green space as part of a longitudinal experiment could enable a direction of cause to be established more clearly. In practice, it can be difficult to control for all factors and variables associated with the socio-economic differences that may exist in populations living in generally wealthier leafy suburbs compared to residential areas without green space. That is, part of the parkland effect may be explained by selective migration to or retention in particular living environments. Direct selection occurs when people's wellness influences their chances of living in a favourable environment whereas indirect selection occurs when people with particular attributes, such as a high income, that are related to wellness can afford to reside in a favourable environment (Groenewegen *et al.*2006). The field-based studies also tend to (out of necessity) use self-reported measures of health. Although there are validated and reliable instruments, self-reporting is potentially more prone to bias by the respondent than actual physical measurement of health. Thus, while access to parklands have been linked with improved health, it is not yet certain as to what extent the positive health benefits are accruing from other factors associated with living within proximity to and visiting parklands (Pretty 2004).

Mental health benefits of parklands

The World Health Organization (2001) defines mental health as 'a state of well-being in which the individual realises his or her own abilities, can cope with the normal stresses of life, can work productively and fruitfully, and is able to make a contribution to his or her community'. This specific definition is encompassed by the more general WHO definition of health cited earlier. The World Health Organization and the World Bank forecast that depression, a mental health issue, will become the second largest cause of disease burden worldwide (Walker *et al.* 2004). Further to this, it is recognised that treatment of the symptoms will not address the problem adequately. Walker *et al.* (2004) highlight the need for preventive measures to effectively reduce the rate of mental ill-health. Mental health is recognised as being closely associated with physical health and quality of life, and therefore is an important element when considering overall health. Evidence indicates that promoting mental health, through a focus on key determinants, could not only result in lower rates of some mental disorders, but deliver individual and community benefits such as improved physical health, enhanced educational performance, increased worker productivity, increased community safety and improved relationships within families (Walker *et al.* 2004).

Research on mental health has predominantly focused on recovery from stress and attention fatigue, as these are common issues in urbanised and industrialised societies (Health Council of the Netherlands and Dutch Advisory Council for Research on Spatial Planning 2004). There is a compelling accumulation of evidence from a large number of studies that indicate a positive association between exposure to parklands and recovery from stress and attention fatigue. Benefits are reported to include enhancement of mood, concentration and self-discipline and reduction of physiological stress. The research includes both laboratory and field studies.

Recovery from stress and attention fatigue occurs via the mechanism of restoration. Restoration is the 'process whereby a person returns to a state of unimpaired affective, cognitive, physiological and physical functioning' (Health

Council of the Netherlands and Dutch Advisory Council for Research on Spatial Planning 2004: 47). This could be in response to fatigue resulting from sustained direct attention to a task and active suppression of irrelevant information that affects cognitive performance. There are two dominant theories regarding the restorative effects of nature, Kaplan's (1995) attention restoration theory and Ulrich's Stress Reduction Theory (1983). Kaplan (1995) proposed four main components that could contribute to the restorative effects of a natural environment including:

- fascination – natural environments are rich with fascinating objects and processes which automatically attract the attention without requiring any effort;
- being away – natural settings provide opportunities to distance oneself from everyday life and thoughts, allowing for the resting of one's directed attention;
- extent – the environment must have extent, it must be rich enough and coherent enough so that it constitutes a whole other world. Even a relatively small area can provide a sense of extent; and
- compatibility – there should be compatibility between the environment and personal purposes and inclinations.

Ulrich's Stress Reduction Theory (1983) proposes that in addition to providing recovery from attention fatigue, natural environments also promote recovery from any form of stress. Ulrich postulates that people have an innate mechanism whereby experience of certain characteristics of natural settings triggers positive emotional reactions. These characteristics include a level ground surface, considerable spatial openness, the presence of a pattern or structure, curving sightlines and the presence of water. These reactions also ensure that humans are attracted by natural environments. This theory relates to the Biophilia Hypothesis put forward by Wilson (1984) mentioned earlier in this chapter. This in part could explain human attraction to nature and its positive cognitive and affective influence.

There has been very limited research to date about the particular components of the physical environment that support restoration (Nordh *et al.* 2009). That is, little is also known about the effect of different types of parklands on mental health. Kaplan's (1995) theory suggests that the influence of parkland type may be highly subjective and variable, dependent on the perceptions and purpose of individuals. Rolston (1998) and Collins (1995) noted that the type and extent of past experience in natural areas is a key factor affecting how nature is viewed and it subsequent influence on the individual. Similarly, Bixler and Floyd (1997) commented that childhood exposure to natural areas significantly increased the likelihood of nature-orientated career paths and strengthened positive association with nature later in life. While research suggests that people who believe nature to have a restorative effect tend to seek out parkland environments when they experience stress or fatigue, whether people with no connection, or a fear of nature, experience the same potential benefits is unclear. Louv (2005) noted that people living in urban environments, with little or no contact with natural places tend to harbour negative attitudes toward nature. Ironically they may also suffer mental and physical health problems due to lack of contact with nature.

The Health Council of the Netherlands and Dutch Advisory Council for Research on Spatial Planning (2004) note that the duration or frequency of exposure to nature that is necessary to prevent stress-related illness in the long term is unknown. However, studies regarding affective recovery show that short-term contact with nature is associated with a significant positive effect (Hartig *et al.* 1996; Hartig *et al.* 2003). However, it seems that contact with nature needs to be rather more prolonged for cognitive recovery (Taylor 1994).

Community benefits of parklands

Social relationships and community networks are important to all individuals across all cultures. This particularly holds true for older adults, where social integration and the strength of social ties have been found to be significantly important predictors of health (Kweon *et al.* 1998). Research has indicated that the availability of accessible urban parklands can facilitate social interaction and social coherence. This can function to strengthen social ties and sense of community which has been associated with better personal health (Berkman *et al.* 2000; Kawachi *et al.* 1999). Research has also found that urban housing developments with more greenery have fewer crimes reported to police while exposure to natural settings is associated with reduced aggressive behaviour (Australian Bureau of Statistics 2010; Soanes and Stevenson 2008). However, there have been limited studies which have explored the underlying mechanisms explaining the social factors involved in the neighbourhood greenness and health relationship. Other factors may also play a significant role in facilitating social contacts, such as social and psychological factors, the architecture and the level of maintenance of neighbourhoods, combined with individual factors such as age, sex, education and earlier life experiences. Characteristics of a particular public area, including its accessibility, proximity, safety, and design and layout (including comfort), also appear to influence the extent of social contact (Health Council of the Netherlands and Dutch Advisory Council for Research on Spatial Planning 2004).

Parklands as a wellness tourism destination?

The *Healthy Parks, Healthy People* campaign has used some of the above outlined information and knowledge as a foundation for promoting parklands as tourism and recreation destinations that are beneficial to health. This is essentially a tourism and recreation branding exercise where parklands are promoted as wellness tourism destinations.

Research into the relationship between access to parklands and health consistently indicates a positive association. However, there is limited evidence indicating the direction of cause between health and access to parklands (Bell *et al.*

2007; Health Council of the Netherlands and Dutch Advisory Council for Research on Spatial Planning 2004). This is generally because most research is cross-sectional in design, obtaining a snapshot at a given place and point in time. Sugiyama *et al.* (2008) note that longitudinal studies are required to explore the effects of environmental interventions on health outcomes to clearly establish the casual direction of the relationship between natural environments and health. In addition, many field-based research projects are not experimentally random in design. For example, researchers tend to locate an urban study area with a given level of greenness or select parkland locations and sample people who are present within that area. This means the results of the sample could be biased toward the types of people who tend to reside in a given type of urban area or who tend to use parks. These issues can demonstrate a relationship between health and parklands but cannot establish whether healthy people tend to access or live near parks or if parks generate healthy people.

Research in this field also tends to focus more on indirect connections, by looking at how parklands influence actions or mechanisms which in turn influence health; for example, research into links between public access to parklands and increased physical activity or social interaction that then lead to health benefits. In this regard, research is needed to identify the underlying mechanisms of these health benefits and the extent to which they each account for the nature–health relationship. Admittedly, separating the influence of physical activity, socialisation from the presence of nature itself is difficult. However the effects of physical activity and socialisation associated with access to parklands obscure how active and passive use of natural environments is conducive to health (Sugiyama *et al.* 2008). Separating these effects could provide a better understanding of the influence of the parkland destination itself and whether it could be substituted for other settings.

In addition to clarifying existing research findings, there are also areas requiring further understanding. For example, there is little knowledge regarding what frequency, duration and type of experience in what type of park optimises health benefits or represents the minimum threshold at which health benefits could occur. Essentially, what the research appears to be lacking is the identification of a relationship between dose of park experience and subsequent relative health benefits. This type of research could provide important insights into preventive health-care for particular target groups, such as children, older people and people with disabilities (Bell *et al.* 2007). Such knowledge would also provide guidance into the types of parks and experiences that result in the best health outcomes for communities.

Finally, there appears to be limited research into the influence of parklands in ordinary settings. Most research focuses on extreme settings, such as hospitals, prisons or extremely disadvantaged urban areas, where people are more prone to be highly stressed or frustrated. Research also commonly involves laboratory-based experiments. While this allows for better control of confounding factors and potentially enables clearer results, the artificial character of the setting and common focus on isolated elements of health may provide limited insight into real-life effects over time. This means that findings have limited application to a broader population context. Expanding the focus of research beyond these extreme or laboratory-based environments may increase the generalisability and applicability of findings (Groenewegen *et al.* 2006). That is, it could provide better understanding of the influence of parklands as a wellness destination for the general population.

In summary, the review of research into the health effects of parklands as a wellness destination indicates a need for further research to

- establish the direction of cause and effect;
- establish a dose relationship between access to parklands and health;
- establish relationships between types of parkland and positive influences;
- separate the influence of parklands from activities in parks;
- understand the longitudinal effects of parkland access on health; and
- understand the influence of parklands on health in ordinary settings.

The *Healthy Parks, Healthy People* brand is based on the premise that access to parklands and exposure to nature will create healthy people. As discussed above, while there is a growing body of evidence indicating a relationship between human health and access to parklands, a review of published research indicates the direction of this relationship is not clearly established. There is a lack of clarity in terms of whether healthy people tend to access parks or parks make people healthy. There is also a lack of clarity regarding the effect of providing access to different types of parkland in various urban and regional settings and the individual and community scale. The uncertainty as to the veracity of the HPHP claims could weaken the brand of parklands as a wellness tourism destination. Establishing a clear, evidence-based understanding of the relationship between parklands and health could help to lend additional substance to the *Healthy Parks, Healthy People* concept. This type of research could also work to clearly identify the role of parklands as destinations for preventive health care rather than the general focus of health care on remedial effects. Preventive health measures are most likely to reduce the rate of health problems such as obesity and depression to a greater degree than remedial care and treatment of symptoms (Walker *et al.* 2004). Establishing whether there are clear casual links between access to parklands and improved health could guide support for investment in establishing and maintaining parklands as an important component of the wellness tourism destination brand.

References

Ambrasat, J., Schupp, J. and Wagner, G.G. (2011) 'Comparing the predictive power of subjective and objective health indicators: changes in handgrip strength and overall satisfaction with life as predictors of mortality', *SOEP Papers on Multidisciplinary Panel Data Research*, Berlin: German Socio-Economic Panel Study.

Australian Bureau of Statistics (2010) *Mining Indicators, Australia*, Canberra: Australian Government, online, available at: www.abs.gov.au (accessed 12 October 2012).

Australian Government Department of Health and Ageing (1999) *An Active Way to Better Health: National Physical Activity Guidelines for Adults*, Canberra: Australian Government.

Baker, M., Stabile, M. and Deri, C. (2001) 'What do self-reported, objective, measures of health measure?' *Journal of Human Resources*, 39: 1067–93.

Bell, S., Montarzino, A. and Travlou, P. (2007) 'Mapping research priorities for green and public urban space in the UK', *Urban Forestry and Urban Greening*, 6: 103–15.

Bendell, J. and Font, X. (2004) 'Which tourism rules? Green standards and GATS', *Annals of Tourism Research*, 31: 139–56.

Berkman, L.F., Glass, T., Brissette, I. and Seeman, T.E. (2000) 'From social integration to health: Durkheim in the new millennium', *Social Science and Medicine*, 51: 843–57.

Bixler, R. and Floyd, M. (1997) 'Nature is scary, disgusting and uncomfortable', *Environment and Behavior*, 29: 443–67.

Bowling, A. (2009) *Research Methods in Health: Investigating Health and Health Services*, New York: McGraw-Hill International.

Collins, P. (1995) *God's Earth*, Melbourne: Harper Collins Religious.

Eagles, P.F.J. (2002) 'Trends in park tourism: economics, finance and management', *Journal of Sustainable Tourism*, 10: 132–54.

Groenewegen, P.P., van den Berg, A.E., de Vries, S. and Verheij, R.A. (2006) 'Vitamin G: effects of green space on health, well-being and social safety', *BMC Public Health*, 6: 149–59.

Hartig, T., Book, A., Garvill, J., Olsson, T. and Garling, T. (1996) 'Environmental influences on psychological restoration', *Scandinavian Journal of Psychology*, 37: 378–93.

Hartig, T., Evans, G.W., Jamner, L.D., Davis, D.S. and Garling, T. (2003) 'Tracking restoration in natural and urban field settings', *Journal of Environmental Psychology*, 23: 109–23.

Health Council of the Netherlands and Dutch Advisory Council for Research on Spatial Planning (2004) *Nature and Health: The Influence of Nature on Social, Psychological and Physical Well-Being*, The Hague: Health Council of the Netherlands and RMNO.

Heimstra, N. and McFarling, L. (1974) 'The natural environment and behaviour', in G. Holloway (ed.) *Environmental Psychology*, Belmont: Wadsworth Publishing Co. Inc.

Hug, S.M., Hartig, T., Hansmann, R., Seeland, K. and Hornung, R. (2009) 'Restorative qualities of indoor and outdoor exercise settings as predictors of exercise frequency', *Health and Place*, 15: 971–80.

Jago, L. and Bailey, G. (2012) *State of the Industry 2012: Full Report*, Canberra: Australian Government.

Kaplan, S. (1995) 'The restorative benefits of nature: toward an integrative framework', *Journal of Environmental Psychology*, 15: 169–82.

Kawachi, I., Kennedy, B.P. and Glass, R. (1999) 'Social capital and self-rated health: a contextual analysis', *American Journal of Public Health*, 89: 1187–93.

Kuo, I.-L. (2002) 'The effectiveness of environmental interpretation at resource-sensitive tourism destinations', *International Journal of Tourism Research*, 4: 87–101.

Kweon, B.-S., Sullivan, W.C. and Wiley, A.R. (1998) 'Green common spaces and the social integration of inner-city older adults', *Environment and Behavior*, 30: 832–58.

Louv, R. (2005) *Last Child in the Woods: Saving our Children from Nature Deficit Disorder*, Chapel Hill, NC: Algonquin Books.

Maas, J., van Dillen, S.M.E., Verheij, R.A. and Groenewegen, P.P. (2008) 'Social contacts as a possible mechanism behind the relation between green space and health', *Health and Place*, 15: 586–95.

Maas, J., Verheij, R., Groenewegen, P., deVries, S. and Spreeuwenberg, P. (2006) 'Green space, urbanity and health: how strong is the relation?', *Journal of Epidemial Community Health*, 60: 587–92.

McDowell, I. (2006) *Measuring Health: A Guide to Rating Scales and Questionnaires*, 3rd edition, Oxford: Oxford University Press.

Mitchell, R. and Popham, F. (2008) 'Effect of exposure to natural environment on health inequalities: an observational population study', *The Lancet*, 372: 1655–60.

Morita, E., Fukuda, S., Nagano, J., Hamajima, N., Yamamoto, H., Iwai, Y. and Shirakawa, T. (2007) 'Psychological effects of forest environments on healthy adults: shinrin-yoku (forest-air bathing, walking) as a possible method of stress reduction', *Public Health*, 121: 54–63.

Myers, M., Valdivieso, M. and Kiss, A. (2009) 'Use of automated office blood pressure measurement to reduce the white coat response', *Journal of Hypertension*, 27: 280–6.

Nielsen, T.S. and Hansen, K.B. (2007) 'Do green areas affect health? Results from a Danish survey on the use of green areas and health indicators', *Health and Place*, 13: 839–50.

Nordh, H., Hartig, T., Hagerhall, C.M. and Fry, G. (2009) 'Components of small urban parks that predict the possibility for restoration', *Urban Forestry and Urban Greening*, 8: 225–35.

Nyaupane, G., Morais, D. and Graefe, A. (2004) 'Nature tourism constraints: a cross-activity comparison', *Annals of Tourism Research*, 31: 540–55.

Pretty, J. (2004) 'How nature contributes to mental and physical health', *Spirituality and Health International*, 5: 68–78.

Pretty, J., Peacock, J., Sellens, M. and Griffin, M. (2005) 'The mental and physical health outcomes of green exercise', *International Journal of Environmental Health Research*, 15: 319–37.

Rolston, H. (1998) 'Aesthetic experience in forests', *The Journal of Aesthetics and Art Criticism*, 56: 157–66.

Soanes, C. and Stevenson, A. (eds) (2008) *The Concise Oxford English Dictionary*, 12th edition, Oxford: Oxford University Press.

Streiner, D. and Norman, G. (2008) *Health Measurement Scales: A Practical Guide to Their Development and Use*, 4th edition, Oxford: Oxford University Press.

Sugiyama, T., Leslie, E., Giles-Corti, B. and Owen, N. (2008) 'Associations of neighborhood greenness with physical and mental health: do walking, social coherence and local social interaction explain the relationships?' *Journal of Epidemiology and Community Health*, 62: 1–6.

Takano, T., Nakamura, K. and Watanabe, M. (2002) 'Urban residential environments and senior citizens' longevity in megacity areas: the importance of walkable green spaces', *Journal of Epidemiology and Community Health*, 56: 913–18.

Taylor, G.D. (1994) 'Sustainable tourism development: guide for local planners', *Tourism Management*, 15: 477–8.

Ulrich, R. (1983) 'Aesthetic and affective response to natural environment', in I. Altman and J. Wohlwill (eds) *Behavior and the Natural Environment*, New York: Plenum Press.

van den Berg, A.E., Hartig, T. and Staats, H. (2007) 'Preference for nature in urbanized societies: stress, restoration and the pursuit of sustainability', *Journal of Social Issues*, 63: 79–96.

Walker, L., Moodie, R. and Herrman, H. (2004) 'Promoting mental health and well-being', in R. Moodie and A. Hulme (eds) *Hands-on Health Promotion*, Melbourne: IP Communications.

Ware, J., Brook, R., Davies, A. and Lohr, K. (1981) 'Choosing measures of health status for individuals in general populations', *American Journal of Public Health*, 71: 620–5.

Wilson, E. (1984) *Biophilia: The Human Bond with Other Species*, Cambridge, MA: Harvard University Press.

World Health Organization (1946) *Constitution of the World Health Organization 22 July*, Official Records of the World Health Organization, 2: 100.

World Health Organization (2001) *Strengthening Mental Health Promotion*, Geneva: WHO.

Zeng, Y.P., Gu, D.P., Purser, J.P.T.P., Hoenig, H.M. and Christakis, N. (2010) 'Associations of environmental factors with elderly health and mortality in China', *American Journal of Public Health*, 100: 298–305.

10 Exploring visitor wellbeing in parks and nature reserves

Margaret Deery, Sebastian Filep and Michael Hughes

Introduction

This chapter reports on a study that examined individual wellbeing (feeling good and experiencing a sense of meaning) of visitors to parks and nature reserves. Chapter 9 in this book outlines the role of parks as wellness tourism destinations. This relates to the observed common need for people to escape from urban settings and daily routines and experience nature as a means of rejuvenating wellbeing. Past work indicates that it is possible to differentiate between individual wellbeing and wellbeing at a community or group level. Researchers in neurology have established motivational drivers of play and lust, which are common for all humans and which can be recognised in human brains (Panksepp 2005). Fredrickson's (2001) seminal work on positive emotions similarly points to four core universal emotions of love, interest, joy and contentment, which are experienced by all humans. This research is based on an underlying assumption that there is a difference between *what* is experienced and *how* something is experienced. While everyone may experience a positive emotion of joy, there are many different situations for experiencing this positive emotion. Similarly, when people find their park visits meaningful there are multiple contexts for those meaningful experiences (e.g. being in a park alone and appreciating nature or being with a partner). Hence, while a formulaic definition of wellbeing may not exist, there is a difference between the psychological, often universal, nature of the wellbeing experience (Seligman 2011) and situational circumstances (such as being with friends while experiencing wellbeing). Sociological and anthropological analyses may embellish our individual and almost clinical focus on wellbeing. These analyses are, however, outside the scope of this chapter.

Literature review

Many studies tend to investigate benefits of parks and nature reserves for communities as a whole rather than at the individual level. In examining the benefits of parks at the macro level, some of the studies have found that separation from nature as a symptom of urbanised modern living is detrimental to human development, health and community wellbeing (Frumkin 2001; Scull 2001;

Stilgoe 2001). Other studies have found that when given a choice, communities prefer natural environments (particularly those with water features, large old trees, intact vegetation or minimal human impact) to urban ones, regardless of nationality or culture (Herzog *et al.* 2002; Newell 1997; Parsons 1991). It seems that there are fewer in-depth studies of individual wellbeing. At an individual level, research has often focused on benefits of park visits to physical health. For example, it was found exposure to natural environments, such as parks, enhances people's ability to recover from illness and injury (Parsons 1991; Ulrich *et al.* 1991; Ulrich 1984). There is further evidence suggesting that a lack of exposure to parks and nature reserves is associated with physical harm. Specifically, it was found that artificial environments combined with a lack of exposure to natural environments, such as parks, can cause exhaustion and reduce vitality (Stilgoe 2001; Parsons 1991; Katcher and Beck 1987; Furnass 1979; Lewis 1996). New evidence is, however, needed on the extent, nature and process of the impact of parks on individual wellbeing (Wood *et al.* 2005; Ho *et al.* 2005; Louv 2005). This chapter addresses this knowledge gap.

There are two accepted conceptions of wellbeing in psychology – hedonic and eudaimonic (Ryan and Deci 2001). The first conception suggests wellbeing is mostly associated with pleasure and is explained by the subjective wellbeing theory (SWB). Literature on SWB has flourished since the 1970s (Diener 2009). SWB includes evaluations of people's moods and feelings and people's judgements of life satisfaction (typically on a scale from zero to ten) (Cummins 2009). While satisfaction-with-life scales touch on aspects of life's meaning in their assessments (e.g. a rank from zero to ten on satisfaction with spirituality; Diener 2009), the SWB theory suggests that wellbeing is mostly about what makes people feel good. As Layard (2005) points out in his examination of SWB, one can identify and talk about wellbeing in terms of feeling good or feeling bad.

On the contrary, the eudaimonic conception suggests wellbeing is about a deeper sense of purpose or meaning in life. Meaning in life can be defined as 'the sense made of, and significance felt regarding, the nature of one's being and existence' (Steger *et al.* 2006: 81). Collins (1995) highlights that nature experiences could facilitate an awareness of the fundamental life force that underlies human existence, represented in a tangible form by nature. Rolston (1998) also considered that nature provides a connection between humanity and its primeval origins, providing a sense of meaning and appreciation of the elemental forces of nature. Other authors have also noted the link between nature experiences, spirituality and meaning in life (e.g. Beringer 2000; McArthur and Hall 1993; Hughes 2004; Townsend 1999). This greater awareness of meaning in life contributes to a more enduring sense of wellbeing. Indeed, Kristjansson (2010: 300) argues that 'people would not in retrospect, count themselves as happy even if their brains had been connected to a machine that guarantee them uninterrupted flow of hedonistic pleasure'. So clearly both hedonic and eudaimonic wellbeing should be investigated in research concerning individual wellbeing in parks and nature reserves.

A fulfilling park experience is arguably one that is characterised not just by pleasure but also by the personal meaning tourists associate with their holiday activities. Laing and Crouch's (2011) research highlights the importance of meaning that tourists derive from their experiences in natural environments. Likewise, in research of independent female tourists and their experiences, Wilson and Harris (2006) show that meaningful travel centred around themes such as a search for self and identity and self-empowerment – themes that are clearly much less about pleasure and much more about the nature of one's being and existence-meaning (Steger *et al.* 2006).

The few tourism-related studies that have examined the impact of green space on individual wellbeing, primarily interpreted wellbeing in hedonic terms (feeling well-balanced and being in good mood or experiencing positive emotions). In a Swiss study of restorative effects of visits to city parks, respondents rated their levels of stress and how balanced they felt prior to and at the time of visiting the outdoor environment (Hansmann *et al.* 2007). Stress decreased significantly (the recovery ratio was 87 per cent in terms of improvement on a five-point scale). With respect to feeling well-balanced, the changes amounted to 40 per cent of the possible enhancement. In a study by Rappe (2005) the influence of a green environment on positive emotions of the elderly with dementia was considered in a nursing home environment. According to Rappe's observations, garden plants in a nursing home reduced the effects of dementia on the elderly by stimulating their senses and creating positive emotions. Karmanov and Hamel (2008) examined the 'natural versus urban dichotomy', finding, as did Pretty *et al.* (2005), that the unpleasant rural scenes in their experimental study had a greater negative effect on mood than unpleasant urban scenes. Rural areas that had been degraded significantly affected wellbeing negatively while attractive, well-kept natural environments significantly improved hedonic wellbeing. This work lends substance to the notion of parks as wellness tourism destinations, based on the demonstrated beneficial relationship between experiencing nature and wellbeing and the popularity of parks for tourism and recreation.

This current study further develops the body of knowledge on visitor experiences in natural settings by examining both hedonic and eudaimonic wellbeing. The key aims of this study were to:

- identify general levels of individual wellbeing (hedonic and eudaimonic) of visitors to parks and nature reserves;
- identify factors that relate to the subjective quality of the visitor experience in parks and nature reserves as wellness tourism destinations; and
- compare the findings with results from other related studies.

Research instruments

The research instruments used in this study were appropriate in ascertaining the general levels of individual wellbeing of visitors as they included assessment of both hedonic and eudaimonic wellbeing. Three established scales were employed. The instruments used were the Psychological Benefits of Green Space Questionnaire (Fuller *et al.* 2007), the Personal Wellbeing Index – PWI

(International Wellbeing Group 2006) and the Warwick-Edinburgh Mental Well-Being Scale – WEMWBS (Stewart-Brown and Janmohamed 2008).

The work by Fuller *et al.* (2007) examines the benefits of green space to human wellbeing, specifically focusing on the richness of the flora and fauna within the green space. Using factor analysis on data from parks in and around Sheffield (United Kingdom), Fuller *et al.* (2007) found four hedonic and eudaimonic factors namely reflection, attachment, distinct identity and continuity with the past. The researchers then used these factors to test their strength within different park locations with varying levels of biodiversity richness. They found the green space, and in particular the quality of the vegetation within the green space, positively impacted on the visitors' wellbeing. More importantly, they found that the benefits were related to the quality of the flora and fauna within the parks.

The PWI devised by Cummins and his colleagues (International Wellbeing Group 2006) is also used in this study to test any link between perceptions of life satisfaction and the impact of parks and natural environments. There are two approaches adopted in the scale, namely a single item asking respondents about their global life satisfaction and then a number of life domain scales to capture hedonic and eudaimonic wellbeing. Following substantial testing by Cummins and his colleagues of the scale items and numerous studies to refine the scale, the domains were reduced to one item each as shown in Table 10.1.

The instrument uses an 11-point response scale ranging from zero to ten, and it has been repeatedly tested across countries. It is used annually in Australia to obtain understanding of personal wellbeing.

The final instrument used for data collection in this study is the WEMWBS survey, developed in the United Kingdom (UK) and funded by the Scottish government's National Programme for Improving Mental Health and Well-Being. It is a 14-item scale of wellbeing covering both hedonic and eudaimonic functioning. The items are shown in Table 10.2.

The scale is scored by summing responses to each item on the one-to-five Likert scale and the results can range from 14–70. The WEMWBS is one of the best validated scales measuring mental wellbeing having been used over a number of years on the Scottish population in general and subgroups with the population. Findings from the use of this survey show that the Scottish population mean score is 50.7

Table 10.1 The Personal Wellbeing Index items

Questions focus on respondents' satisfaction with:
Standard of living
Health
Life achievements
Personal relationships
Safety
Community membership and participation
Future security
Religion/spirituality

Source: International Well Being Group, 2006: 13.

Table 10.2 Warwick-Edinburgh Mental Well-Being Scale

Rating*	Item
1 2 3 4 5	I've been feeling optimistic about the future
1 2 3 4 5	I've been feeling useful
1 2 3 4 5	I've been feeling relaxed
1 2 3 4 5	I've been feeling interested in other people
1 2 3 4 5	I've had energy to spare
1 2 3 4 5	I've been dealing with problems well
1 2 3 4 5	I've been thinking clearly
1 2 3 4 5	I've been feeling good about myself
1 2 3 4 5	I've been feeling close to other people
1 2 3 4 5	I've been feeling confident
1 2 3 4 5	I've been able to make up my own mind about things
1 2 3 4 5	I've been feeling loved
1 2 3 4 5	I've been interested in new things
1 2 3 4 5	I've been feeling cheerful

Notes
* 1 = none of the time; 2 = rarely; 3 = some of the time; 4 = often; 5 = all of the time.

with variations on levels of wellbeing depending on gender, age and work status. So, for example, women were found to have a mean of 51.3 while men averaged out at 50.3, showing that Scottish women have a slightly higher level of individual wellbeing. The lowest recorded mean in the Scottish analysis came from those who perceived themselves to have very poor physical health (40.9).

Data collection

Using the WEMWBS scale, the PWI and the Psychological Benefits of Green Space questionnaire, data collection was undertaken through a panel research company throughout the Australian state of Victoria. The respondents were approached by the panel research company via email and the questionnaire was answered online. The following screening question was used: 'Have you visited a park or a nature reserve in the last two weeks?'. Those respondents who answered no to this question were eliminated from the sample. The panel research company was asked to provide respondents from a random sample. Data collection was conducted in March 2010 from those visitors who answered yes to this question. In addition to the sense of individual wellbeing, demographic data such as gender, age and nationality were collected.

Sample

A sample of 270 participants (42 per cent male; 58 per cent female) was obtained, with the overall mean age of 57 years (19 – youngest; 81 – oldest). With regard to nationality, 72 per cent had been born in Australia and 19 per cent born in a European country (14 per cent UK; others were from Germany,

Sweden, Italy, Austria, Ireland, the Netherlands and Malta). The remaining respondents chose not to answer this question. The following section presents key results of the study.

Findings

Reasons for visiting and psychological benefits of green space

Both descriptive analysis and multivariate analyses were undertaken. One of the questions in the first part of the questionnaire inquired about the reason for visiting the park. Respondents indicated that the main reason was to go for a walk (55 per cent) and to relax (20 per cent). Only a small percentage (2 per cent) undertook a less involved and more passive activity by taking a drive through the park (Table 10.3).

As illustrated by the comments under 'Other Reasons', many of the reasons for visiting the park focused around family activities, which suggests that the park visits were psychologically relaxing while being physically rejuvenating.

In further examining the park visit, the responses to Fuller *et al.*'s (2007) individual wellbeing questions are informative. In examining the descriptive statistics for this scale, the first ten items illustrate the affection for the park and the hedonic qualities of happy, looking forward, connected to nature, safe and gaining pleasure from the visit (Table 10.4).

In their study, Fuller *et al.* (2007) found that their items could be reduced to four main constructs focusing on reflection, attachment, distinct identity and continuity with the past. This current study also conducted Principal Component factor analysis to examine the constructs with the sample and, again, four factors evolved, although with different labels from Fuller *et al.*'s (2007) findings. These are provided in Table 10.5.

The factor analysis explained 58 per cent of the variance with the factors showing both face validity and reliability. Factor 1 (Place Attachment) illustrates the ways in which people become attached to places such as parks with

Table 10.3 Reasons for visiting the park

What is your main reason for visiting the park?	N	Percentage
To go for a walk	142	55
To drive through the park	5	2
To go for a jog and do sport	13	5
To just sit around and relax	51	20
Other reason	48	18
Total	259	

Note
1 The *Other Reasons* category included 'to have lunch'; 'take two mothers somewhere pleasant'; 'Mothers' group hang out'; 'it was an animal sanctuary, so I went to relax and look at all the animals!!'; 'So children could play and run about with the dog'.

Table 10.4 The top ten items of the park experience

Item	N	Mean[1]	Std. deviation
1. I felt happy while at the park	266	4.30	0.761
2. I gained pleasure from using this park	270	4.25	0.838
3. I look forward to coming to this park in the future	266	4.24	0.734
4. I liked this park	264	4.22	0.594
5. I found it easy to get familiar with this park	267	4.01	0.710
6. I liked the sounds that I heard in this park	269	3.99	0.715
7. Being here made me feel more connected to nature	263	3.97	0.776
8. I felt safe in the park	263	3.96	0.626
9. I am proud of this park	267	3.96	0.779
10. This park is well known as a desirable place to visit	264	3.84	0.826

Note
1 Rating scale from 1 = strongly disagree to 5 = strongly agree.

memories of past experiences and a strong sense of belonging. The factor contains eudaimonic items suggesting a deeper relationship with the park. Factor 2 (Discomfort with the Park), expresses the hedonic items of unease and the feeling of being unsafe when in the park, together with some sense of disorientation when in the park and after visiting it. Factor 3 (Comfort with the Park) contrasts with Factor 2, as it contains positive, eudaimonic items, being able to clear one's thoughts by being in the park. These concepts potentially relate to eudaimonic items in Factor 4 that express the sense of reflection through the connectedness with the park. These factors are used in further examining the sample later in regression analysis. On the individual items in the PWI, respondents were most satisfied with their feelings of safety and their personal relationships and least satisfied with their future security.

In examining the final component of the study's questionnaire, the descriptive statistics on the WEMBWS scale show that being decisive, feeling loved and being interested in new things received the highest respondent wellbeing score, while lower individual wellbeing scores were found on feeling optimistic about the future, feeling relaxed and having energy to spare (Table 10.6).

The main analysis of the WEMWBS findings, however, focused around the summation of the scores. The findings from the WEMWBS showed a lower mean score for wellbeing for the study's sample than for the only other comparable sample, the Scottish population (Stewart-Brown and Janmohamed 2008). The summed score for the study's sample, with results that could range from 14 to 70 was 48.7. In comparison, the Scottish population mean was 50.7, again suggesting a lower level of individual wellbeing with the Australian sample. This lower level of individual wellbeing from the Australian sample may be explained by the effect of the global financial crisis (GFC). Although Australia's experience of the GFC was more like a recession, Tanton *et al.* (2010: 14) found that Australians felt 'their personal circumstances had declined'. The relevant summed scores are provided in Table 10.7.

Table 10.5 Factor analysis and reliability scores for the psychological wellbeing measures

Items	Factor Loadings				Eigenvalue	Percentage Variance	Cumulative %	Reliability
	1	2	3	4				Cronbach Alpha
Place attachment					9.67	38.68	38.68	0.91
When I was in this park, I felt strongly that I belonged here	0.813	–	–	–	–	–	–	–
This park almost felt like a part of me	0.812	–	–	–	–	–	–	–
I am proud of this park	0.774	–	–	–	–	–	–	–
Compared with other local parks, this park had many advantages	0.760	–	–	–	–	–	–	–
I've had a lot of memorable experiences in this park	0.742	–	–	–	–	–	–	–
I really miss this park when I am away from it for a long time	0.726	–	–	–	–	–	–	–
This park reflects the type of person I am	0.720	–	–	–	–	–	–	–
I gained perspective on life when I came here	0.683	–	–	–	–	–	–	–
This park is well known as a desirable place to visit	0.638	–	–	–	–	–	–	–
Lots of things in this park reminded me of past experiences	0.562	–	–	–	–	–	–	–

	F1	F2	F3	Eigenvalue	% Variance	Cumulative %	α
Discomfort with park				2.12	8.48	47.16	0.72
I was not satisfied with this park	0.734	—	—	—	—	—	—
It was difficult to find my way around the park	0.727	—	—	—	—	—	—
I found it hard to concentrate on difficult activities after being in the park	0.681	—	—	—	—	—	—
I didn't feel at home in this park	0.652	—	—	—	—	—	—
There were unsafe places in this park	0.590	—	—	—	—	—	—
Comfort with park				1.52	6.08	52.34	0.86
I felt happy while at the park	—	0.924	—	—	—	—	—
I gained pleasure from using this park	—	0.865	—	—	—	—	—
I look forward to coming to this park in the future	—	0.849	—	—	—	—	—
I found it easy to get familiar with this park	—	0.620	—	—	—	—	—
I liked this park	—	0.616	—	—	—	—	—
Coming here cleared my head	—	0.573	—	—	—	—	—
I felt safe in the park	—	0.508	—	—	—	—	—
Reflection				1.15	4.59	57.83	0.73
I could easily think about personal matters while at the park	—	—	0.796	—	—	—	—
Being here made me feel more connected to nature	—	—	0.767	—	—	—	—
I liked the sounds that I heard in this park	—	—	0.690	—	—	—	—

Table 10.6 Descriptive statistics on the WEMWBS

Item	N	Mean[1]	Std. deviation
I've been able to make up my own mind about things	269	3.89	0.833
I've been feeling loved	268	3.69	1.008
I've been interested in new things	267	3.61	0.904
I've been thinking clearly	268	3.54	0.854
I've been feeling useful	269	3.53	0.775
I've been feeling cheerful	269	3.53	0.892
I've been feeling interested in other people	269	3.49	0.929
I've been feeling good about myself	268	3.49	0.889
I've been feeling confident	269	3.47	0.896
I've been dealing with problems well	265	3.46	0.825
I've been feeling close to other people	269	3.45	0.895
I've been feeling optimistic about the future	269	3.38	0.849
I've been feeling relaxed	269	3.34	0.843
I've had energy to spare	269	2.88	0.966
Valid N (listwise)	260		

Note
1 1=none of the time; 2=rarely; 3=some of the time; 4=often; 5=all of the time.

The Scottish data analysis examined a number of demographic details from its sample and we compared the levels of wellbeing here between males and females in both studies. Again, the current study's sample from Australia exhibits a lower level of individual wellbeing than the UK counterpart (Table 10.8).

Further analysis

Further analysis was undertaken to examine the correlations between the various scales. Regression analysis using the summed WEMWBS score as the dependent variable and the factor scores from Fuller *et al.* (2007) found that the factor Comfort with the Park and Discomfort with the Park were the best predictors of wellbeing (Table 10.9)

Specifically, these findings show that wellbeing can be obtained through feeling safe and at home in a natural setting, being able to find your way around the area easily and being able to think clearly when in the park. Visitors will not gain improved wellbeing if these aspects are missing from the natural setting.

Table 10.7 Comparison of the current study's sample and the WEMWBS UK sample

		Current study sample (2010)	*WEMWBS Scottish sample (2008)*
N	Valid	260	1,749
	Missing	13	NA
Mean		48.74	50.70
Median		49.00	51.00

Table 10.8 Comparison of gender responses

	Gender	Mean	N	Std. deviation
Current study sample (2010)	Male	48.8	111	9.39338
	Female	48.7	149	8.97491
WEMWBS Scottish sample (2008)	Male	51.3	783	–
	Female	50.3	966	–

Table 10.9 Regression

Model	Unstandardised coefficients		Standardised coefficients	t	Sig.
	B	Std. Error	Beta		
1 (Constant)	48.615	0.590	–	82.457	0.000
Place Attachment	0.723	0.676	0.082	1.070	0.286
Discomfort with the Park	−1.518	0.600	−0.178	−2.530	0.012
Comfort with the Park	2.034	0.854	0.191	2.381	0.018
Reflection	−0.157	0.695	−0.017	−0.225	0.822
Dependent Variable: Sum					

Notes
1 F statistic 6.162[**].
2 R^2 0.333.
3 Adjusted R^2 0.093.
4 $**p < 0.05$.

Overall, these findings suggest that there is an association between individual wellbeing and the factors identified. Specifically, there was a statistically significant correlation between:

- Comfort with the park and individual wellbeing on both the WEMWBS scale and the life satisfaction scale; higher ratings of comfort are associated with higher individual wellbeing.
- Reflection, place attachment and individual wellbeing on the WEMWBS scale; higher levels of place attachment and reflection derived from parks are associated with greater individual wellbeing.

Implications for management and conclusions

The research study has uncovered the psychological benefits of park experiences in visitor settings. Despite research in the leisure field (Kaplan and Kaplan 1989; Kaplan 2001), limited works exist on individual hedonic and eudaimonic wellbeing of visitors in natural environments away from usual domiciles. While there is a long tradition of research on tourist and visitor satisfaction and experiences, much of this research has been dominated by theories and methods from consumer behaviour (Archer and Griffin 2005). Little knowledge exists on how methods of wellbeing from psychology (particularly eudaimonic measures) can help us better understand the quality of visitor experiences in natural environments. Methodologically, therefore, this study went beyond standard satisfaction appraisals of visitor satisfaction in parks. These standard appraisals ask respondents to rate their levels of satisfaction with parking facilities, signage, toilets and similar instrumental features on a seven-point Likert scale (Archer and Griffin 2005). While useful for park managers, these appraisals cannot uncover the eudaimonic and hedonic qualities which were investigated in this wellbeing study.

There are also practical implications of this study. Understanding intangible factors such as visitors' emotions or meanings is increasingly seen as more relevant for effective product development and promotion than merely understanding service quality issues (Oh *et al.* 2007). This is because the level of service quality in many visitor contexts can simply no longer be used to differentiate choices for visitors (Mehmetoglu and Engen 2011). Those who manage parks as tourist venues and destinations need to understand and develop a distinct value-added provision for services that have already achieved a consistent, high level of functional quality (Stamboulis and Skayannis 2003). Tourists tend to seek psychological rewards from an experience of a park that are influenced by more than the functional quality of a venue – such as signage or availability of parking. Reward is also derived from the individual meaning and sense of wellbeing taken from the experience (Vestpestad and Lindberg 2010). How parks are presented or packaged as venues influences the subsequent meanings derived from park experiences, and subsequently how often and in what capacity people engage with parks (Coffey 2001).

Understanding hedonic and eudaimonic wellbeing of visitors is however not only relevant for managers of parks and nature reserves but also for managers of other wellness tourism destinations, as these managers often claim to offer increased health and wellbeing for their customers. These findings suggest that park managers as wellness providers could influence visitor wellbeing levels by providing opportunities for reflection and for the development of place attachments. Managers could, for example, send out informal periodic emails to customers that contain fascinating wildlife footage or video clips describing humorous events that happened at their destination. By using such tools that encourage positive reminiscence, managers could informally provide their customers with opportunities for greater reflection and for building place attachments.

Despite the suggested practical implications and the methodological approaches utilised, there are perceived limitations of this visitor study. While there is an association between the subjective, psychological quality of park experiences and overall psychological wellbeing, no causal links can be inferred. As a consequence, there is a need to be cautious when assessing the relative wellbeing of the participants in the study by comparison to population means derived from other studies. Nevertheless, it is hoped the study serves as an exploratory evaluation of individual wellbeing derived from visitor experiences in Australian (Victorian) parks and nature reserves using these research methods. The research findings could open doors to further research of wellbeing, particularly eudaimonic wellbeing, in relation to parks as wellness tourism destinations.

References

Archer, D.J. and Griffin, A.R. (2005) *A Study of Visitor Use and Satisfaction in Mungo National Park*, Gold Coast: Sustainable Tourism Cooperative Research Centre.

Beringer, A. (2000) 'On ecospirituality: true, indigenous, western', *Australian Journal of Environmental Education*, 15/16: 17–22.

Coffey, B. (2001) 'National park management and the commercialization of nature: the Victorian experience', *Australian Journal of Environmental Management*, 8: 70–8.

Collins, P. (1995) *God's Earth*, Melbourne: Harper Collins Religious.

Cummins, R. (2009) 'The influence of tourism on the subjective wellbeing of host communities', Exploring Wellbeing Seminar, Melbourne: Victoria University.

Diener, E. (2009) 'Subjective well-being', *The Science of Well-Being: The Collected Works of Ed Diener*, New York: Springer.

Fredrickson, B.L. (2001) 'The role of positive emotions in positive psychology: the broaden-and-build theory of positive emotions', *American Psychologist*, 56: 218–26.

Frumkin, H. (2001) 'Beyond toxicity: human health and the natural environment', *American Journal of Preventative Medicine*, 20: 234–40.

Fuller, R., Irvine, K., Devine-Wright, P., Warren, P. and Gaston, K. (2007) 'Psychological benefits of greenspace increase with biodiversity', *Biology Letters*, 3: 390–4.

Furnass, B. (1979) 'Health values', in J. Messer and J.G. Mosley (eds) *The Value of National Parks to the Community: Values and Ways of Improving the Contribution of Australian National Parks to the Community*, Sidney: University of Sydney, Australian Conservation Foundation.

Hansmann, R., Hug, S.M. and Seeland, K. (2007) 'Restoration and stress relief through physical activities in forests and park', *Urban Forestry and Urban Greening*, 6: 213–25.

Herzog, T.R., Chen, H.C. and Primeau, J.S. (2002) 'Perception of the restorative potential of natural and other settings', *Journal of Environmental Psychology* 22: 295–306.

Ho, C., Sasidharan, V., Elmendorf, W., Willits, F.K., Graefe, A. and Godbey, G. (2005) 'Gender and ethnic variations in urban park preferences, visitation, and perceived benefits', *Journal of Leisure Research*, 37: 281–306.

Hughes, M. (2004) 'Influence of varying intensities of natural area on-site interpretation on attitudes and knowledge', unpublished thesis, University of Notre Dame, Fremantle, Western Australia.

International Wellbeing Group (2006) *Personal Wellbeing Index*, 4th edition, Melbourne: Australian Centre on Quality of Life, Deakin University.

Kaplan, R. (2001) 'The nature of the view from home: psychological benefits', *Environment and Behavior*, 33: 507–42.

Kaplan, R. and Kaplan, S. (1989) *The Experience of Nature: A Psychological Perspective*, Cambridge/New York: Cambridge University Press.

Karmanov, D. and Hamel, R. (2008) 'Assessing the restorative potential of contemporary urban environment(s): beyond the nature versus urban dichotomy', *Landscape and Urban Planning*, 86: 115–25.

Katcher, A. and Beck, A. (1987) 'Health and caring for living things', *Anthrozoos*, 1: 175–83.

Kristjansson, K. (2010) 'Positive psychology, happiness, and virtue: the troublesome conceptual issues', *Review of General Psychology*, 14: 296–310.

Laing, J.H. and Crouch, G.I. (2011) 'Frontier tourism: retracing mythic journeys', *Annals of Tourism Research*, 38: 1516–34.

Layard, R. (2005) *Happiness: Lessons Form a New Science*, London: Allen Lane.

Lewis, C.A. (1996) *Green Nature/Human Nature: The Meaning of Plants in our Lives*, Chicago, IL: University of Illinois Press, Urbana.

Louv, R. (2005) *Last Child in the Woods: Savings Our Children from Nature-Deficit Disorder*, Chapel Hill, NC: Algonquin Books of Chapel Hill.

McArthur, S. and Hall, C.M. (1993) 'Visitor management and interpretation at heritage sites', in C.M. Hall and S. McArthur (eds) *Heritage Management in New Zealand and Australia: Visitor Management, Interpretation and Marketing.* Auckland: Oxford University Press.

Mehmetoglu, M. and Engen, M. (2011) 'Pine and Gilmore's concept of experience economy and its dimensions: an empirical examination in tourism', *Journal of Quality Assurance in Hospitality and Tourism*, 12: 237–55.

Newell, P.B. (1997) 'A cross cultural examination of favourite places', *Environment and Behavior*, 29: 495–515.

Oh, H., Fiore, A.M. and Jeong, M. (2007) 'Measuring experience economy concepts: tourism applications', *Journal of Travel Research*, 46: 119–32.

Panksepp, J. (2005) 'Affective consciousness: core emotional feelings in animals and humans', *Consciousness and Cognition*, 14: 30–80.

Parsons, R. (1991) 'The potential influences of environmental perception on human health', *Journal of Environmental Psychology*, 11: 1–23.

Pretty, J., Peacock, J., Sellens, M. and Griffin, M. (2005) 'The mental and physical health outcomes of green exercise', *International Journal of Environmental Health Research*, 15: 319–37.

Rappe, E. (2005) 'The influence of a green environment and horticultural activities on the subjective well-being of the elderly living in long-term care', University of Helsinki, Department of Applied Biology, Publication no. 24. [Academic Dissertation] Helsinki: Yliopistopaino.

Rolston, H. (1998) 'Aesthetic experience in forests', *The Journal of Aesthetics and Art Criticism*, 56: 157–66.

Ryan, R.M. and Deci, E.L. (2001) 'On happiness and human potentials: a review of research on hedonic and eudaimonic well-being', *Annual Review of Psychology*, 52: 141–66.

Scull, J. (2001) 'Reconnecting with nature', *Encompass*, 5: 1–5.

Seligman, M.E.P. (2011) *Flourish*, Sydney: Random House.

Stamboulis, Y. and Skayannis, P. (2003) 'Innovation strategies and technology for experience-based tourism', *Tourism Management*, 24: 35–43.

Steger, M.F., Frazier, P., Oishi, S. and Kaler, M. (2006) 'The Meaning in Life Questionnaire: assessing the presence of and search for meaning in life', *Journal of Counseling Psychology*, 53: 80–93.

Stewart-Brown, S. and Janmohamed, K. (2008) *Warwick-Edinburgh Mental Well-being Scale (WEMWBS), User Guide Version 1*, Edinburgh: NHS Health Scotland, the University of Warwick and the University of Edinburgh.

Stilgoe, J.R. (2001) 'Gone barefoot lately?' *American Journal of Preventative Medicine*, 20: 243–4.

Tanton, R., Keegan, M., Vidyattama, Y. and Thurecht, L. (2010) *The Impact of the GFC on Australians*, Report for the Commonwealth Bank of Australia, Sydney.

Townsend, L. (1999) 'A spiritual place', *Terrain*, fall: 22–4.

Ulrich, R.S. (1984) 'View through a window may influence recovery from surgery', *Science*, 224: 420–1.

Ulrich, R.S., Dimberg, U. and Driver, B.L. (1991) 'Psychophysiological indicators of leisure benefits', in B.L. Driver, L.R. Brown and G.L. Peterson (eds) *Benefits of Leisure*, State College, PA: Venture Publishing.

Vestpestad, M. and Lindberg, F. (2010) 'Understanding nature-based tourist experiences: an ontological analysis', *Current Issues in Tourism*, 14: 563–80.

Wilson, E. and Harris, C. (2006) 'Meaningful travel: women, independent travel and the search for self and meaning', *Tourism*, 54: 161–72.

Wood, L., Giles-Corti, B. and Bulsara, M. (2005) 'The pet connection: pets as a conduit for social capital?' *Social Science and Medicine*, 61: 1159–73.

11 Nature-based wellness tourism

The case of the Margaret River region in Western Australia

Christof Pforr, Michael Hughes, Melanie Dawkins and Emma Gaunt

Introduction

The perception of health changed during the mid-twentieth century from simply being considered an absence of physical illness to including notions of wellness. As quoted in other chapters in this book, the World Health Organization (2010) states that health is 'a state of complete physical, mental and social wellbeing and not merely the absence of disease or infirmity'. Good health and wellbeing are promoted as important values in many societies and this has subsequently influenced the travel sector (Erfurt-Cooper and Cooper 2009). The integration of health and tourism has become a significant aspect of modern tourism in a number of new and long-established destinations. Health tourism is however a heterogeneous market segment embracing a variety of products and services that range from wellness tourism to medical tourism (Voigt *et al.* 2010). The focus of this chapter will be on nature-based wellness and spa tourism, including spa hotels as well as day spas in Margaret River, Western Australia. For the purpose of this chapter we adopted the definition of wellness tourism provided by Voigt *et al.* (2010: 8) as

> the sum of all the relationships resulting from a journey by people whose primary motive is to maintain or promote their health and well-being and who stay at least one night at a facility that is specially designed to enable and enhance people's physical, psychological, spiritual and/or social well-being.

In a broader sense, tourism is an activity that can contribute to wellness. Tourism involves experiencing something apart from the everyday routine of life, a way to experience the *other* or something perceived as exotic. It is an escape that enables a temporary removal of daily responsibilities and associated stress, arguably contributing to wellness (Pearce 2011). In particular, nature-based or rural tourism provides a means for escaping the stresses of increasingly urbanised environments where people live (Wilson 1984; Rolston 1998; Louv 2005). As described in Chapters 9 and 10 of this book, research has shown that experiences in natural and rural settings are linked to positive effects on mood, reduced blood pressure and associated indicators of stress, reduced irritability and improved cognitive functions. Nature-based or rural tourism in itself can therefore serve as a means of promoting physical and mental health and wellness, irrespective of whether this forms a specific motivation for travel. This is perhaps why nature-based tourism is a significant component of the tourism market (see Chapters 9 and 10 for a more detailed discussion).

However, the effect of nature on health and wellness of an individual is very much influenced by a tourist's personal tastes, social and cultural background as well as life experience (Bixler and Floyd 1997; Louv 2005). While some natural settings may seem attractive to one individual, another may find it unpleasant or even threatening. Similarly a natural environment that seems mundane or ordinary to one person may seem exotic and extraordinary to another. These different views of nature in a tourism context can be understood within the concept of the 'tourist gaze' (Urry 1992). The tourist gaze can be understood as a combination of a conscious decision to participate in tourism and experience the *other* and the individual's perception of nature and natural places form a lens through which a nature-based tourism destination may be viewed. A natural environment that is out of the ordinary in terms of what the tourist has previously experienced can function to promote a sense of wonder, exhilaration or similar positive affective responses.

While a nature-based tourism experience can function to improve wellness, the Western desire for a healthy lifestyle has resulted in a significant push for a range of new tailored tourism products, experiences and services (Hall 2003). Continuing growth in health awareness in industrial society coupled with demographic change, a shift towards prevention and complementary and alternative medicine, and a stronger focus on customised travel experiences contribute strongly to this increase in wellness tourism and the provision of new products and services in a leisure setting. According to Voigt *et al.* (2010), the current wellness tourism supply can be categorised into three different types of wellness tourism: beauty spas, lifestyle resorts and spiritual retreats. Beauty spas are defined as 'establishments that promote wellness through the provision of therapeutic and other professional services aimed at reviving the body, mind and spirit' (Ellis 2009). The main focus for spa visitation is on body and beauty treatments. Spa tourism products are often found within the vicinity of particular natural features, for instance natural mineral water springs or thermal pools. Lifestyle resorts constitute another category where the experience includes a comprehensive program focusing on lifestyle transformations. This might involve fitness programs, nutritional education, weight and stress management. The third category includes spiritual retreats with an emphasis on spiritual development and enlightenment. Spiritual retreats generally revolve around meditative elements such as yoga, T'ai Chi or Reiki. These are commonly located in nature-orientated settings, either gardens or rural and natural environments. The profile of visitors to the three types of wellness experience appears to differ significantly. In Australia, for example, spiritual retreats commonly attract so-called Best Agers (55+) with a higher proportion of males (26 per cent), Baby Boomers (45+) tend to visit spiritual retreats as well as lifestyle resorts in high numbers and the younger generation (25–44 years) prefers beauty spas (Voigt *et al.* 2010: 47).

Australian wellness tourism

Australia is a relatively new player in the wellness tourism market segment but is generally seen as having good future growth potential. For instance, there has been a reported increase in spa facilities of 142 per cent between 2002 and 2008. In 2008 there were 554 destination spas and resort spas in Australia with the majority of these (69 per cent) being day spas (Puczkó and Smith 2009; Voigt *et al.* 2010). Australian wellness tourism is an emerging tourism niche market. It is dominated by intrastate wellness tourists while interstate and international demand is limited (Voigt *et al.* 2010). Recent research (Voigt *et al.* 2010: 47) has identified the typical domestic wellness tourist as an affluent, highly educated female, aged between 24 and 45, who commonly travels with a friend, spouse or other family member. Spa tourism in Australia is dominated by mostly small- to medium-sized business operators. It is very much in line with the North American approach focusing on specialty spas offering pampering spa treatments such as detoxification, healthy habits and disciplined learning retreats (Puczkó and Smith 2009: 122).

Western Australia (WA) is home to about 12 per cent of Australian wellness service providers (Voigt *et al.* 2010). The state's wellness and spa industry is quite small and fragmented. The WA wellness and spa industry market includes a diverse range of visitors from teens and young adults to middle-aged travellers and the seniors market. The two most recognised tourism regions in Western Australia that feature wellness tourism experiences in their offerings include the state capital Perth with mainly day spa facilities and the Margaret River and the Great Southern regions in the south-west (Figure 11.1). These regions also include significant nature-based and rural tourism experiences that form an important part of the regional tourism brand identity.

To date very limited wellness tourism research has been carried out in Western Australia to better understand the various wellness markets and to explore how the emerging wellness destinations use their potential for sustainable growth in the sector in the future. This chapter reports on a study that aimed to better understand the nature and scope of the wellness tourism sector in Western Australia, particularly in the Margaret River region, which is well placed to develop into a significant wellness tourism destination.

Methodology

To better understand the emerging wellness tourism sector in Western Australia, the study set out to gain an insight into how important Western Australia's natural environment is for a wellness experience. It also captured some key characteristics of wellness tourists in WA. Adopting a case-study approach, the Margaret River region in the south-west of Western Australia (Figure 11.1) was chosen as the area to contextualise the research. Semi-structured interviews with 14 representatives from the region's wellness industry were carried out in the data collection phase in August and September 2010. Each of these interviews

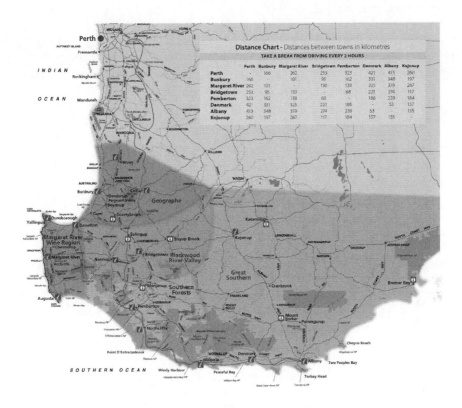

Distance Chart - Distances between towns in kilometres
TAKE A BREAK FROM DRIVING EVERY 2 HOURS

	Perth	Bunbury	Margaret River	Bridgetown	Pemberton	Denmark	Albany	Kojonup
Perth	-	166	262	253	323	421	413	260
Bunbury	166	-	101	95	162	331	348	197
Margaret River	262	101	-	150	139	325	379	267
Bridgetown	253	95	150	-	68	221	274	117
Pemberton	323	162	139	68	-	186	239	184
Denmark	421	331	325	221	186	-	53	157
Albany	413	348	379	274	239	53	-	155
Kojonup	260	197	267	117	184	157	155	-

Figure 11.1 Map of Australia's South-West (source: Australia's South West 2013: 5).

took on average one and a half hours, was audio recorded and subsequently transcribed. Interview data were augmented by a range of secondary data sources such as newspaper articles, government publications, specialist reports and media content on wellness tourism in Western Australia as well as observation enquiry during site visits.

Nature-based wellness tourism in Australia's South-West

Described as a pillar of the Western Australian tourism experience, nature-based tourism is the main platform of the marketing image of Western Australia presented worldwide by the state's peak tourism body, Tourism Western Australia. This is most certainly true for the south-west of Western Australia, one the world's top biodiversity hot spots of global significance, which hosts some of the state's most outstanding marine wildlife and natural landscapes. The region features tall karri forests, clean water and beach shores, migratory whales, rugged forests and bushland and fruitful soils. It is these distinct attributes coupled with clean air and a Mediterranean climate that form the basis of tourism attractions, products and services for visitors to the south-west of Western Australia (Margaret River Visitor Centre, n.d.).

Tourism Western Australia identified in its 2005–2010 Strategic Plan five iconic themes characterising a quintessential Western Australian holiday experience (Tourism Western Australia 2005: 5). These include wine and food, people and lifestyle, outback and adventure, forest and wildflowers and the marine environment, which also constitute core elements of the tourism products and services within Australia's South-West tourism region. Of these, wine and food are of great importance, particularly for the Margaret River sub-region, which is a key tourism destination within Western Australia. The value-adding character of the wine and food tourism industry creates employment opportunities and acts as a stimulus for local businesses (Tourism Western Australia 2010a). Next to premium wines and picturesque vineyards, spectacular beaches with world-class surf breaks, old growth forests, limestone caves and fertile farmlands also attract visitors. Not surprising, dining at local restaurants, surfing, swimming, snorkelling or diving or a visit to one of the area's national parks are the most popular tourist activities (Tourism Western Australia 2010a).

Case-study area Margaret River

Australia's South-West, including the Margaret River region, is a significant tourism destination for Western Australia. The Margaret River region (see Figure 11.1) in particular has been identified as a tourism icon, a region recognisable to the international and domestic tourism markets. The region received 1.7 million visitors in 2009, making it the second most visited WA destination after the state capital Perth (Tourism Western Australia 2010b). The natural environment is evidently the basis and foundation of all tourism offerings within the Margaret River region. The unique aspects of the South-West's natural environment are cross-linked with other local products and services, thus creating the foundation for a range of specialised tourism experiences. How the region's natural environment is used for these ultimately depends on demand and thus on visitor motivations. If the main reason for the visit is physical and mental relaxation, for instance, wellness offerings based on the region's spectacular natural resources can meet this demand. The majority of tourist activities and product offerings that can be experienced within the Margaret River region that are based on the region's natural resources are, although not necessarily formally recognised as such, forms of wellness tourism. Activities such as guided bush walking tours, surfing, canoeing, cave tours, wildflower tours, ocean swimming and native wildlife interaction can thus form the basis of a wellness tourism experience if they contribute to a state of physical and mental rejuvenation.

Wellness tourism in the region is a fairly new phenomenon that emerged as a niche market segment in the early 2000s. Since then, the Margaret River region has become the most prominent wellness and spa tourism destination in Western Australia.

The Western Australia state government tourism marketing organisation, Tourism Western Australia, has acknowledged the importance of niche market segments, such as wellness tourism, for Margaret River's tourism sector. Fuelled by recent growth in the demand for wellness products and services, there is also growing interest amongst the various local and regional stakeholders to advance Margaret River as a wellness destination. This has fostered collaboration between interested groups, resulting in the establishment of *Wellness Margaret River* in 2007, a marketing focused organisation of about 50 wellness providers, which aims to coordinate and promote the region's wellness products and experiences.

As outlined above, the region boasts many unique natural and rural features favourable to the development of a wellness tourism industry, which is serviced by several resorts, a number of day spas and a range of natural and alternative therapy providers within the town of Margaret River, where aromatherapy, naturopathy, massage, beauty therapy, yoga, meditation and acupuncture are offered. Several Margaret River region hotels also house day spa facilities as a complementary wellness tourism product (Voigt *et al.* 2010: 184).

Nature-based and rural–agricultural elements of the Margaret River brand form the basis of the region's wellness retreats. Its wellness products have a strong emphasis on a natural clean and green environment providing a beneficial and positive wellness experience. The range of products offered in the region demonstrates the strong focus on nature and natural or rural settings, including wilderness experiences and nature-based tourism activities (for example, wild-flower tours, whale watching, bush walking, surfing and diving). Local produce ranging from wine and cheese to chocolate, jams and berries also provide a strong foundation for product offerings, which can be integrated into a wellness experience. Indeed, these nature-based and rural experiences are increasingly cross-linked with wellness-orientated tourism products such as holistic therapies, spa pampering and specialised products and services, for instance grape massage, detox therapies and olive oil products.

The above discussion has highlighted the natural environment as an important aspect of the wellness product. This perception is evident in the interviews carried out for this study. According to the owner of an accommodation business, Margaret River offers forests, beaches and seclusion in a rather luxurious setting, and has been described as somewhat 'majestic' in nature. At night the forests light up, and the possums and bandicoots rise; tourists can experience first-hand and be one with the wildlife and nature.

The manager of another accommodation business within the region commented that the 'clean and green surroundings of Margaret River act as a natural relaxant; visitors say they get here and can just breathe out'. This view was supported by another accommodation provider who stated that 'a lot of people say they can interact with the local wildlife and native flora species and go back to their childhood. That is relaxation in itself'. This was a very common perception expressed during interviews. One industry representative referred to the region as 'something that is green, serene and relatively untouched', another stated that he is frequently approached by visitors to the region and 'asked about how they can integrate with nature; for example, where a beautiful place to walk is or where a tour operates to see nature in its element'. It was felt that 'the Margaret River region has the natural environment in place to strongly support wellness and spa tourism, and the sustainability of that type of tourism also'. During the interviews it was also commented by participants that the various shires through-out the region are 'very inclined and very much wanting to and always protect the natural environment and keep it as pristine as possible as for people to experience true wellness and at that conscious level of health, you need that pris-tine environment'. It can thus be argued that the reason why the Margaret River region is attractive to wellness tourists and operators is mainly due to the pos-itive perception of the nature-based setting. Interestingly, while the nature-based setting is seen as central to the wellness product in the region, convenience of access from urban centres is also considered important. According to an industry representative interviewed for this study, 'the rivers, oceans and trees provide that secluded and private setting, however the Margaret River region is still located relatively close to Perth so a traveller can get away quickly'. In other words, while the product itself is ideally situated in a seemingly idyllic nature-based setting, its success also relies on proximity to large urban areas and major transport hubs and corridors to ensure accessibility for key markets.

A snapshot of Margaret River's wellness tourists

The South-West region is significantly reliant on the intrastate visitor market. Tourism Western Australia (2010c) data reveal that 86 per cent of the region's visi-tors (averaged between 2007 and 2009) were from Western Australia with 8 per cent being interstate and 6 per cent international tourists. The Margaret River region much mirrors this visitation pattern although interstate and international vis-itors are slightly higher in proportion than the state average. On average (2001–2008) 69 per cent of the region's visitors came from within the state, 17 per cent from other Australian states and territories and 14 per cent from overseas (Tourism Western Australia 2010c). According to the data, most visitors came to holiday in the region and engaged in activities like dine out and visit vineyards, going to the beach or visit national parks. The most common type of visitor, regard-less of origin, were adult couples. However, visitors from Western Australia also included family groups whereas international tourists also often liked to travel on their own. The most common age groups visiting the region span across the 25–64 age bracket with younger travellers (15–24) featuring more prominently amongst the intrastate visitors. The senior market segment (65+) is mostly represented by interstate visitors (Tourism Western Australia 2010c).

From this general snapshot of visitors to the Margaret River region, the char-acteristics of those travelling specifically for a wellness experience were ana-lysed. It was then examined how their expectations are met by local tourism service providers. Based on interview results, it appears that wellness tourists aged 45+, the so-called Baby Boomers, tend to visit the lifestyle and eco resorts, and luxury retreats within the region. This is in line with findings by Voigt *et al.* (2010: 47) who state that spiritual retreats and lifestyle resorts tend to attract Best Agers (55+) and Baby Boomers. Younger people (25–44 years) prefer beauty spas. The latter has also been confirmed in this study since in particular day spa facilities within the region attract visitors in the 20–40 year age bracket. According to the views of an interviewed spa/health clinic operator 'there are generally more female than male clients, with a great deal of mothers and daughters, sisters and couples'. Other spa operators interviewed for this study confirmed that there are 'a significant number of people, especially from Perth, who come down for girls' weekends, hens and bridal nights'. A business stakeholder commented that

> a new upcoming market of ages between 25 to 45 years of age and mostly female will be the change within the region for wellness spa establishments over the next 10 to 20 years. This market of the young affluent female career women will further shift into male equality as well.

Thus, although females still outnumber male wellness visitors, based on the observations of the interviewed business owners, male numbers seem to have increased markedly in recent times. This includes either visiting alone or with a partner. The latter is especially the case for dual-income-earning couples seeking escape from stressful and demanding work responsibilities. As stated by the owner of a health clinic within the region, 'males are starting to take care of themselves and are no longer so embarrassed about wellness and spa treatments'. This broadening demand is currently met by a range of wellness tourism providers in the region. Even so, the wellness tourism and nature experience is still dominated by the female market. Voigt *et al.* (2010: 47) summarise the attributes of a typical domestic wellness tourist as female, 24–45 years old, highly educated and affluent. Identified as very important for wellness tourists within this particular age bracket were the aspects tranquillity, peace and quiet, outstanding natural beauty and overall atmosphere. Each of these characteristics, which are abundant in the Margaret River region, is conducive to evoking feelings of relaxation, rejuvenation and therefore an enhanced state of wellbeing. The elements that the region boasts, such as a relaxed and welcoming lifestyle, seclusion and remoteness from the busy city life, unspoilt beaches, a spectacular coastline and an abundance of green forests and bushland are thus the unique local resources that a wellness experience can be based on. This view is also captured well in the current marketing of the Margaret River region:

> There's perhaps no better destination in Australia to kick back and unwind surrounded by nature than the Augusta Margaret River region. With its prestigious luxury retreats, world-class wineries, stunning natural landscapes and relaxing spa treatments the Margaret River region lends itself perfectly to the ultimate getaway weekend.
>
> (Margaret River Visitor Centre n.d.)

Thus, the region's clean and green environment and natural elements appear important and imperative factors for its emerging wellness market. 'Due to people's fast pace lives, working longer hours resulting in not having as much time on recreation as they used to, the prime motivation of visitors to engage in a wellness experience', according to one of the interviewees, 'is the search for a better work and life balance'. Research on spa visitors by Mak *et al.* (2009) revealed similar findings, as in their study relaxation and relief as well as escape and self-reward and indulgence were ranked as the most important motivational factors for a wellness experience. Given that natural environments are associated with restoration of health and perceived to be healthy places to visit, the perceptions of Margaret River combined with its accessibility based on proximity to urban centres appears to make it an ideal region for further development of the wellness tourism product.

Where from here? Discussion and conclusion

Wellness providers and tourism industry representatives within the Margaret River region acknowledge the unique natural environment in which they operate and therefore the location-specific products and services available to visitors. Margaret River's unique and accessible local resources provide ample opportunities for original and authentic South-West wellness tourism products and services. This is especially when associated and integrated with other current tourism products, for instance food and wine, marine or eco and nature-based tourism. One of the interviewed industry representatives reinforced this view, explaining that

> Australia's and Western Australia's image as a natural clean and green destination for wellness tourism is an extremely important factor, especially for the Asian market, as it allows them to experience something different from their own understandings of wellness and form a connection with nature.

For a unique wellness profile it is important to develop authentic wellness products which are hard to imitate and therefore allow a region to remain nationally and internationally competitive. In this context Sheldon and Park (2009: 104) highlight that wellness tourism experiences should be 'generated from competitive advantages of the destination such as … unique natural features'. Also, Pechlaner and Fischer (2006), for instance, favour such a local resources-based perspective over traditional market-based approaches (see also Barney 1997; Pechlaner and Tschurtschenthaler 2003). In their view, in order to be able to use local resources effectively and in doing so develop them into competitive products, it is essential to bring together different stakeholders from the region, not only those from the tourism industry as such but also from other sectors. These combined location-specific resources and knowledge can then form the basis for innovation and new product developments (Pechlaner and Fischer 2006). In the Margaret River region, wellness providers should therefore ensure they partner with a range of providers, for instance, local wineries and vineyards in order to add value to the visitor's experience as well as promote and fuel the growth of the local wellness and spa industry. There are also many nature-based tour operators who could also help propel the wellness tourism sector by arranging packages and deals with various establishments, allowing the visitor to have an all-encompassing experience.

In terms of accommodation, it appears that the region would benefit from enhanced cross-linking between accommodation packages and wellness products. According to one industry representative, 'accommodation in Australia's South West is currently only selling a room and a bed, and not focusing on selling the visitor an experience'. Respective businesses and establishments could work more closely together in order to promote nature-based wellness tourism within the region. A more integrated approach would certainly help to progress the wellness tourism niche market further and create more awareness amongst potential wellness tourists for the products and services on offer in the Margaret River region. Better integration of accommodation and wellness products could also help to position the region on the global wellness tourism map. So far, according to an industry representative, these products and services are, however poorly marketed and promoted outside the Margaret River and South-West region:

> Inbound and wholesale brochures in Western Australia don't include any wellness tourism or related product offerings. The two biggest wholesalers in the state do not include wellness tourism in their packages. Therefore, there are no wellness tourism packages for travel agents themselves.

In conclusion, with our case-study research we were able to highlight the role of natural resources and the significance of the surrounding environment for the development of a successful wellness tourism destination. In the context of the Margaret River region wellness tourism is closely aligned with nature-based tourism, using natural resources such as climate, forests and water to attract travellers in pursuit of wellbeing.

In the future the strategic development and management of the destination will be crucial to further establish the Margaret River region as a unique, authentic, competitive and adaptable wellness tourism destination, nationally and internationally. It appears that the marketing and management of its specialised and differentiated wellness products, particularly those which are grounded in the region's unique natural assets, need to be enhanced. Further to this, effective relationships between accommodation providers, tour operators, winery owners and wellness practitioners need to be fostered in order to encourage the development of new products. This will help to attract additional visitors expanding the market segment beyond the current market of young female wellness tourists and prepare the region for future growth leading to a greater diversification within the wellness market in the Margaret River region.

Such an expansion must go hand in hand with effective quality control to ensure a high standard of the growing number of wellness products and services on offer. Moreover, these developments require the support and guidance from a coordinating organisation, for instance a regional wellness tourism association, supported by an appropriate government policy and planning framework. As mentioned above, first collaborative activities amongst a range of wellness providers in the Margaret River region have already taken place over the past decade, providing the foundations for the development of a much stronger, wider and denser network built on the region's endogenous potentials. Ultimately, the enhancement of a network of wellness-focused regional core competencies will make the region not only an attractive destination for wellness tourists but will also provide economic and social benefits for the local community and thus, in the long term, contribute to the sustainable development of the region.

References

Australia's South West (2013) *Your Holiday Guide to Australia's South West 2013/14*, Bunbury: Australia's South West.

Barney, J.B. (1997) 'Looking inside for competitive advantages', in A. Campbell, L. Sommers and K. Luchs (eds) *Core Competency-Based Strategy*, London/Boston, MA: International Thomson Business Press, pp. 13–30.

Bixler, R. and Floyd, M. (1997) 'Nature is scary, disgusting and uncomfortable', *Environment and Behavior*, 29: 443–67.

Ellis, S. (2009) ' "Spas" and "medical tourism": two booming industries with striking parallel paths and issues', online, available at: http://blog.spafinder.com/ medical-tourism/ spa-medical-tourism/ (accessed 2 October 2010).

Erfurt-Cooper, P. and Cooper, M. (2009) *Health and Wellness Tourism: Spas and Hot Springs*, Bristol: Channel View Publications.

Hall, C.M. (2003) 'Spa and health tourism', in S. Hudson (ed.) *Sport and Adventure Tourism*, New York: Haworth Hospitality Press, pp. 273–92.

Louv, R. (2005) *Last Child in the Woods: Saving our Children from Nature Deficit Disorder*, Chapel Hill, NC: Algonquin Books.

Mak, A., Wong, K. and Change, R. (2009) 'Health or self-indulgence? The motivations and characteristics of spa-goers', *International Journal of Tourism Research*, 11: 185–99.

Margaret River Visitor Centre (n.d.). *Margaret River*, online, available at: www.margaretriver.com (accessed 2 October 2010).

Pearce, P. (2011) 'Travel motivation: benefits and constraints to destinations', in Y. Wang and A. Pizam (eds) *Destination Marketing and Management: Theories and Application*, Wallingford: CABI.

Pechlaner, H. and Fischer, E. (2006) 'Alpine Wellness: a resource-based view', *Tourism Recreation Research*, 31: 67–77.

Pechlaner, H. and Tschurtschenthaler, P. (2003) 'Tourism policy, tourism organisations and change management in Alpine regions and destinations: a European perspective', *Current Issues in Tourism*, 6: 508–40.

Puczkó, L. and Smith, M. (2009) *Health and Wellness Tourism*, Oxford: Elsevier.

Rolston, H. (1998) 'Aesthetic experience in forests', *The Journal of Aesthetics and Art Criticism*, 56: 157–66.

Sheldon, P.J. and Park, S.-Y. (2009) 'Development of a sustainable wellness tourism destination', in R. Bushell and P.J. Sheldon (eds) *Wellness and Tourism: Mind, Body, Spirit, Place*, New York: Cognizant Communication Corporation.

Tourism Western Australia (2005) *Tourism Western Australia Strategic Plan 2005–2010*, Perth: Tourism Western Australia.

Tourism Western Australia (2010a) *Tourism Western Australia*, online, available at: www.tourism.wa.gov.au/Pages/welcome_to_tourism_western_australia.aspx (accessed 3 October 2010).

Tourism Western Australia (2010b) *Australia's South West – Tourism Development Priorities 2010–2015*, Perth: Tourism Western Australia.

Tourism Western Australia (2010c) *Australia's South West*, Perth: Tourism Western Australia.

Urry, J. (1992) 'The tourist gaze "revisited"', *The American Behavioral Scientist*, 36: 172–86.

Voigt, C., Laing, J., Wray, M., Brown, G., Howat, G., Weiler, B. and Trembath, R. (2010) *Health Tourism in Australia: Supply, Demand and Opportunities*, Gold Coast: Sustainable Tourism Cooperative Research Centre.

Wilson, E. (1984) *Biophilia: The Human Bond with Other Species*, Cambridge, MA: Harvard University Press.

World Health Organization (2010) *About Who*, online, available at: www.who.int/about/en/ (accessed 19 March 2010).

12 The Kneipp philosophy – a 'healthy' approach to destination development

Cornelia Locher, Cornelia Voigt and Christof Pforr

Introduction

Sebastian Kneipp was a German priest and naturopath, who advocated a holistic approach to health and wellbeing by embracing five principles, that of phytotherapy, hydrotherapy, healthy nutrition, exercise and a balanced lifestyle in harmony with nature. His teachings have strongly influenced medical wellness offerings in many certified spas and health resorts based on traditional water treatments known as *Kneipp Kur* (Kneipp cure). Kneipp's philosophy needs to be seen in the context of its time and also Kneipp's personal circumstances, which will be briefly outlined below before an overview of his philosophy and the way it has influenced complementary therapies to date is provided. This information will form the requisite background for the ensuing review of the development of Kneipp spas and health resorts. The final part of the chapter explores how Kneipp's philosophy can be translated into a broader destination context. Here, the Unterallgäu region in Bavaria (Germany), where the five Kneipp tenets have been used as guiding principles to promote regional development, will be discussed.

Sebastian Kneipp's life and the origin of the Kneipp therapy

Sebastian Kneipp, born on 17 May 1821 into a poor family of weavers, is seen by many as one of the Fathers of modern naturopathy (Helwig 2005; Whorton 2002). Whilst he is in particular known for his hydrotherapy treatments, his approach to health and healing was holistic and incorporated exercise, healthy nutrition, phytotherapy and guidance for a generally healthy lifestyle (Kneipp 1891). To be fully understood and appreciated, Kneipp's philosophy needs to be seen in the context of its time and also Kneipp's personal circumstances.

In the early nineteenth century controversial, yet inspiring figures to many, like Christof Wilhelm Hufeland and Samuel Hahnemann, promoted the body's self-healing powers which they saw as the force of life itself. For Kneipp to believe in this intrinsic power of self-healing was almost a last resort as he had been suffering from pulmonary tuberculosis, a disease which at that time was usually fatal. After commencing his theological studies in 1849 he was in a very poor physical state but drew inspiration from a book on the healing powers of water which had been published by Johann Sigmund Hahn nearly a century earlier (Helwig 2005). A series of self-experiments with cold water treatments in the icy Danube river followed which seemed to strengthen his immune system to such an extent that he was not only able to complete his studies, but to be ordinated as priest in 1852 with fully restored health (Whorton 2002). Assigned as priest to Wörishofen, a small Bavarian parish, he continued to experiment with a range of water treatments and soon had a big enthusiastic community of followers. He refined and expanded Vincent Priessnitz' hydrotherapy principles which mainly relied on cold water treatments and complemented them with exercise and the use of warm water. Typical Kneipp water applications consisted of cold, warm and steam baths as well as wraps and gushes to particular body parts (Winnewisser 2009). In Kneipp's (1891) view water was not only essential to the maintenance of a person's health and wellbeing, but also a very simple and natural cure.

The book *My Water-Cure* (Kneipp 1891) detailing his treatments was an instant success. To date, it has been published in 74 editions and translated into ten languages (WorldCat 2013). In this volume Kneipp did not only outline his use of water but emphasised the importance of a healthy nutrition. Kneipp was not an advocate of an ascetic lifestyle, he rather highlighted the importance of a balanced diet and moderation in eating habits (Kneipp 1897b). He also elaborated on the complementary use of herbal medicines as sole treatments or adjuvant to hydrotherapy. 'The longer I have to do with sick people, the more convinced I am that God, the Creator of all things, has bestowed upon us the means of Cure, viz. one half water the other half herbs' (Kneipp 1897b: 1). From 1890 onwards, Kneipp endowed his friend and pharmacist Leonhard Oberhäußler with lifelong exclusive rights to use his name and portrait for developing and marketing an expanding range of herbal remedies and personal care products (e.g. teas, plant juices, tinctures, bath oils). To date, these products are still manufactured and distributed by Kneipp International, a global company with its headquarter in Würzburg, Bavaria, and more than 30 branches worldwide (www.Kneipp.com). Kneipp is credited with being the first to introduce phytotherapeutic principles into the nature cure movement of his time (Kneipp 1894, 1897b) which is arguably one of his greatest contributions to modern naturopathy (Duda 2010). Despite his involvement in the creation of commercial products based on natural plant essences, Kneipp perceived the promotion of simple herbal remedies as a very useful way of providing the poor with easily accessible, yet effective, basic treatments. He emphasised,

No expensive stock-in-trade will be found here, for most of my medicines, infusions, extracts, oils, and powders are drawn from simple weeds and herbs, well known and much prized by our ancestors, but mostly now forgotten and despised. These may be found in almost every field and garden, on the common, and by the wayside; and as this little work is chiefly written for the poor, the greatest merit of my remedies lies in their very cheapness and vulgarity.

(Kneipp 1891: 71)

Kneipp's care for the underprivileged is well documented. Although he is reported to have successfully treated some members of the high society like the Archduke Johann of Austria-Hungary, he mainly cared for the poor and was able to open a children's hospital (*Kinderheilstätte*) and the foundations *Sebastianeum* and *Kneippianum*, which are still in operation and offer Kneipp treatments in Bad Wörishofen to date. He even published a book, *The Care of Children in Sickness and in Health*, giving young parents (mothers in particular) guidance on the upbringing of healthy and happy children and also on how to care for them when sick (Kneipp 1897a).

A further important element in Kneipp's approach to health and healing were physical exercises not only in combination with the various hydrotherapies he advocated (e.g. treading cold water) but also in form of brisk walks, home callisthenics, and other moderately intense physical activities on a daily basis (Kneipp 1897b).

Whilst each of the individual elements of his approach, hydro- and phytotherapy, exercise and a healthy nutrition, were acknowledged for their contribution to health and wellbeing, it was their combination and a general inner balance which in Kneipp's view made a healthy person. 'Besides the continued applications of water, it was, as I have already mentioned, my way of living, lodging, sleeping, dressing, which has kept me in excellent health now for more than forty years' (Kneipp 1894: x). Kneipp himself acknowledged that his physical self-treatments had only taken their full effect when he had started to also involve his soul in the process. With this holistic view on health and wellbeing Kneipp already foreshadowed what today is seen by many as the most appropriate definition of health, namely 'a state of complete physical, mental and social well-being and not merely the absence of disease or infirmity' (World Health Organization 2010). His emphasis of an emotional and spiritual dimension to health resonates in modern approaches to complementary and alternative medicines and also the concept of wellness. Similarly, he already called for treatments carefully tailored to an individual's particular circumstances, a trait of modern complementary and alternative medicine which often attract patients disillusioned with the anonymity of the mainstream health care system. He stressed, '[t]o discriminate, therefore, which applications are adapted to the disease in question, and furthermore to determine how these are to be varied according to the constitution of the patient, is the touchstone of the true physician' (Kneipp 1891: 5) and highlighted that '[t]o each new patient who comes to consult me I address certain questions, in order to avoid the danger of prescribing hastily and without sufficient knowledge' (Kneipp 1891: 6).

So what relevance does the teaching of Sebastian Kneipp have in the twenty-first century? As outlined earlier, with his holistic understanding of health, his consideration of not only the physical but also the emotional aspects of diseases, his promotion of hydrotherapy and phytomedicine, he laid the foundations for modern naturopathy. After having been cured himself by Kneipp's treatments, one of his early followers, Benedict Lust (1872–1945), returned to the United States in 1896 'to spread the Gospel of the Water Cure' beyond the German immigrant population. Ultimately he complemented Kneipp's teachings with other nature cure therapies such as massage and sunbathing, osteopathy and chiropractic, which eventually matured into the concept of naturopathy (Whorton 2002: 192). However, perhaps the most visible legacy of Kneipp's philosophy in the twenty-first century is the continued practice of offering his holistic therapy concept (known as *Kneipp Kur*) to countless of 'tourist-patients' in hundreds of spas and health resorts, particularly in German-speaking countries.

The development of Kneipp's spas and health resorts

The most famous Kneipp spa and precursor of all other Kneipp *Kurorte* (health resorts) is the southern German town of Bad Wörishofen near Munich where Sebastian Kneipp lived and promoted his *Kur* for 42 years. At first his parish was a very small settlement with about 1,400 inhabitants and 180 houses (Kneipp 1891). In a preface to the book *My Water-Cure* (Kneipp 1891), an anonymous male translator describes his visit to Wörishofen in 1889 and gives a very interesting account of its struggle with hosting the ever-growing numbers of sick people seeking a cure. The translator laments that he had to learn 'what a precious thing a room was in this little village of Wörishofen' (Kneipp 1891: x) and that the two existing village inns were not able to cope with the visitor influx (Kneipp 1891: xvi). Through his writings, the translator highlights the beginnings of a village progressively transforming into an internationally known healing and tourism destination. He describes entrepreneurial-minded peasants who started to rent out simple rooms in their dwellings. In the same vein he depicts the arrival of numerous sales booths and advertising boards offering unendorsed branded products such as 'Kneipp bread and linen' and 'Kneipp coffee and cigars' (Kneipp 1891: xxxiii). Souvenirs such as tin, silver and gold miniature watering-cans started to appear and a horde of photographers commenced offering their services, so that visitors were able to take home encoded memories of their experience (ibid.). According to the translator, Kneipp himself received more than 200 patients per day who were being admitted through a ticketing system in batches from five to ten people. Other necessary infrastructure was introduced little by little to handle the stream of visitors and improve living conditions, such as a sewage system in 1893, direct access to the railway network in 1895 and electricity in 1896 (Waltenberger 2012). As the translator describes Wörishofen as 'neither beautiful nor picturesque' and 'exceedingly commonplace' (Kneipp 1891: x), the parish initially did not seem to have much aesthetic appeal, nor did it boast any typical tourist amenities.

In order to attract more visitors and perhaps also to keep accompanying family members and friends occupied, several measures were introduced to increase the attractiveness of the destination. In 1888, the first restaurant in Wörishofen opened up and a bathhouse so central to Kneipp's hydrotherapies was established. In 1889 an Association for Beautification (*Verschönerungsverein*) was founded which conceptualised a landscaped spa garden (*Kurpark*). Subsequently entertainment venues for concerts, theatres and exhibitions were built, croquet and tennis courts were erected, and the village creek was dammed up so that visitors were able to go ice skating in winter (Eckart 2011). Major developments in Wörishofen such as easy access through the development of railways, entrepreneurship, the modernity of amenities, entertainment facilities and beauty of the surroundings do not only give evidence to the rising linkage between the therapeutic *Kur* and tourism, but also show that they are important factors to attract visitors. Visitor numbers to Wörishofen increased dramatically from 4,000 in 1889 to 33,130 people in 1893 (ibid.). Despite the availability of amenities facilitating pleasurable entertainment and consumptive behaviours, the Kneipp *Kurort* differed from other famous European health resorts such as Karlsbad (now Karlovy Vary), Wiesbaden or Baden-Baden which were elegant, extravagant places where aristocracy and wealthy upper-classes primarily sought pleasure and recreation rather than recuperation (Lempa 2008; Steward 2000). Kneipp advocated a lifestyle of simplicity and a return to nature, thus his *Kur* destination was intended to be less frivolous (Maretzki and Seidler 1985). Several of his treatments, like walking barefoot in the snow, were rigorous and harsh, and patients had to undertake a strict daily regimen of therapies. Thus, the emphasis on amusement and leisure was eclipsed by the therapeutic needs of predominantly sick visitors travelling to Wörishofen and Kneipp's care for the poor heralded the general turn towards more democratised and less elitist era of spa visitation all over continental Europe by the end of the nineteenth century.

Even during Kneipp's lifetime the translator of his book *My Water Cure* referred to Kneipp as a 'daily growing European celebrity' (Kneipp 1891: xvi) and 'a household word throughout Germany and Austria ... [with] his photograph displayed ... in every shop-window' (Kneipp 1891: viii). Moreover, other places started to take up his therapy approach and offered the Kneipp *Kur* to their guests. There are several factors why his philosophy and therapeutic practices spread out so successfully from Wörishofen throughout Europe. First, with 19 monographs and countless journal articles, Kneipp was a very active author. The strategically clever employment of Kneipp's secretary Vera Freifrau von Vogelsang, who spoke English, French, Italian and Spanish, ensured that translated works were distributed internationally (Waltenberger 2012). Second, Kneipp himself travelled extensively throughout Europe, promoting his therapeutic approach in form of lectures in which he displayed a strong charismatic presence (Steward 2002). Klofat (2009, in Waltenberger 2012) estimates that around a million visitors listened to Kneipp's lectures given during one of 32 tours he undertook between 1890 and 1896. Third, Kneipp's success story of healing himself as well as mounting reports of patients, who found their health much improved, added to the growing recognition of the Kneipp *Kur*. Some of his former patients shared their personal healing experiences by setting up similar Kneipp facilities in other towns or countries. One well-known example is the Viennese Sister Raphaela Freund who, after having met Father Kneipp and being cured twice from a serious disease in Wörishofen, started to promote the Kneipp *Kur* at her order of Sisters of Mary of Mount Carmel near Linz in Upper Austria. Today, the Sisters still run three Kneipp cure centres in Aspach, Bad

Kreuzen and Bad Mühlacken. As a similar result of Kneipp's growing popularity, former patients started to establish a number of Kneipp societies. In 1897 the German umbrella organisation *Kneipp Bund* (German Kneipp Association) was founded, which is still in existence today and subsumes 600 German Kneipp associations with about 160,000 members, thereby constituting one of the largest non-commercial health organisations in Germany. The Kneipp Association is a member of Kneipp Worldwide which was founded in 1962 and has become the international confederation of the Kneipp movement with 200,000 member associations or single members from over 40 countries (Kneipp Worldwide 2012).

One factor of the enormous growth of the German spa industry in the nineteenth century, which included Kneipp spa towns and facilities, was that a huge part of the *Kurort* development was professionally planned, funded and controlled by the state (Bacon 1997). Predominantly in the twentieth century state institutions commenced to award the prefix or suffix *Bad* to officially designate a destination as a spa town (e.g. Bad Ems, Wiesbaden). The *Bad* prefix was added to Bad Wörishofen in 1920, making this destination one of the earliest contenders signifying its official spa town status. Today, in order to claim to be a *Kurort*, destinations have to fulfil strict quality standards and obtain official accreditation by the Deutsche Heilbäderverband (German Spa Association). Currently, German spa destinations can be categorised in one of six broad categories (Deutscher Heilbäderverband 2005):

- *Mineral-, Thermal- und Moorheilbäder* (mineral, thermal and mud spa resorts)
- *Heilklimatische Kurorte* (healing climate health resorts)
- *Seeheil- und Seebäder* (seaside spas and resorts)
- *Heilbäder mit Heilstollen- und Radontherapie* (health resorts with healing caves and radon therapy)
- *Luftkurorte* (aerotherapy health resorts)
- *Kneippheilbad und Kneippkurorte* (Kneipp spas and health resorts)

The Kneipp category differs from the others because it is the only category not bound to certain localised conditions such as air, waters or moor mud. In contrast, to be certified as a Kneipp destination, the destination must offer a mixture of therapies based on the five pillars of Kneipp's therapeutic approach: (1) hydrotherapy; (2) phytotherapy or herbal remedies in form of bath additives, ointments, teas and juices; (3) nutritional therapy/dietetics; (4) exercise/kinesiology; and (5) lifestyle management, including emotional and spiritual health, relaxation techniques, and avoidance of health risk factors. Currently, out of the 350 accredited German spa destinations, there are around 20 certified *Kneippheilbäder* (Kneipp spas) and 40 *Kneippkurorte* (Kneipp health resorts). In more detail, these Kneipp certified destinations must include Kneipp-specific tourism superstructure, for example in form of spa/wellness hotels, clinics, bath houses and therapeutic centres which adhere to the five pillars, and which employ experts in all aspects of Kneipp therapy, including physiotherapists, nutritionists and qualified spa physicians. As for all other spa destination categories, a natural and quiet environment with limited traffic is extremely important and a core requirement to become certified. Besides extensive networks for walking, cycling or hiking, or a *Kurpark* (spa park), many Kneipp destinations have developed specialised Kneipp outdoor facilities. These include herb gardens, themed walks with stations for water treading and arm bath basins, or barefoot trails where walking on a wide variety of surfaces such as sand, pebbles, hay, pine cones, bark mulch and mud offer a sensory experience to get back to nature and provide a therapeutic form of self-reflexology. Recently, the Kneipp approach has experienced a renaissance in Germany with communities still striving to become a formally recognised Kneipp spa or health resort (e.g. Wendisch Rietz, Bad Schwalbach) and with some just recently having been officially certified after a year-long accreditation process (e.g. Tabarz).

The following section gives a short background on the relationship between the Kneipp *Kur* and orthodox medicine which alternates between rapprochement and divisiveness, thereby influencing how products and services are delivered at German spa destinations.

On the relationship between the Kneipp *Kur* and orthodox medicine in Germany

Kneipp developed his therapeutic approach on the basis of observation, reading about previous naturopathic health practices and his own practical experience, without ever having any orthodox medical training. Consequently, the majority of orthodox medical professionals were very sceptical towards Kneipp's therapeutic approach; they accused him of profiteering and called him a *Kurpfuscher* (quack or charlatan) (Eckart 2011). Some newspapers also agitated aggressively against Kneipp's work and a few people even expressed their resentment in the form of arson attacks on the *Sebastianeum* in Wörishofen (ibid.). Nevertheless, a number of orthodox physicians travelled to Wörishofen to experience and study the *Kneipp Kur*. The anonymous translator of *My Water-Cure* reports that at 'first doctors seemed inclined to pooh-pooh the whole thing' (Kneipp 1891: xix) before becoming curious and studying the methods and then finally sending patients to Wörishofen who they were not able to cure. About 150 doctors came to Wörishofen each year to be schooled in Kneipp's therapeutic approach (Ärztegesellschaft für Präventionsmedizin und klassische Naturheilverfahren, Kneippärztebund 2012). It was important to Kneipp to bridge the gap to orthodox medicine (*Schulmedizin*). At the time when physicians increasingly stirred up hostility against Kneipp due to his rising fame, he employed doctors to attend all his consultations for libel protection and to stimulate the creation of a scientific basis and research of his methods (Waltenberger 2012).

In 1884, 26 medical doctors founded the International Association of Kneipp Physicians. This happened at a time when the influence of science on the spa industry grew in general, making it increasingly medicalised. Licensed physicians, known as *Badeärzte* (spa doctors), established their practices in spa destinations and started to scientifically examine the healing properties of water, thus contributing to the establishment of the medical field of balneology (Maretzki 1987, 1989). To this day hydrotherapy constitutes a research area and has been demonstrated to be effective in the treatment of a number of medical conditions such as anxiety disorders (Dubois *et al.* 2010), chronic pain (Cimbiz *et al.* 2005), back pain (McIlveen and Robertson 1998; Barker *et al.* 2003) and osteoarthritis (Vaht *et al.* 2008; Hill *et al.* 1999), to mention only a few. The gradual incorporation of naturopathic methods such as hydrotherapy and the Kneipp approach into mainstream medicine laid the basis for German welfare legislation to cover its costs for patients in need of rehabilitation therapy. Consequently, in 1953 the *Kneipp Kur* became a legitimate form of therapy reimbursable through national health insurance and has remained so, albeit to a lesser extent, until today.

Nevertheless, the acceptance of spa therapies by orthodox medicine was not as straightforward as the foregoing discussion may suggest. Maretzki and Seidler (1985) highlight that physicians advocating the Kneipp cure have always formed a minority among orthodox health professionals. Moreover, the profession of the spa doctor as well as the entire field of balneology have a relatively low prestige in the overall hierarchy of medicine and tend to be ostracised (Maretzki 1987, 1989). The fact that many orthodox German health professionals still doubt the effectiveness of any type of *Kur* has fuelled the political demand for cutting back the involvement of the state in the spa industry. One of the political reactions to mounting economic difficulties in the nationalised spa industry was to privatise many *Kur* facilities and treatment costs, thereby creating a more consumer-orientated spa management in spa destinations and increasing their international competitiveness (Bleile 1985). Through health care reforms in 1997 and 2000, the German government, buckling under the weight of a growing deficit in their health care system, targeted the *Kur* as one area to significantly reduce public spending. Due to the reduction of financial support from the health care system, many traditional spa destinations such as Bad Wörishofen were faced with seriously declining visitor numbers, which forced them to strategically attract new consumer segments (Pforr and Locher 2012; Nahrstedt 2004; see also Chapters 6 and 16 in this volume). Besides international tourists, one consumer segment that plays an increasingly important role consists of wellness tourists who are primarily interested in promoting their health and in preventing future illnesses. Thus, besides or even instead of targeting patients seeking cures, many German spa destinations have turned towards tourists seeking a wellness experience. One could also argue that this development leads to a demedicalisation of spa destinations, at least from the perspective of orthodox medicine. The therapeutic approach by Kneipp is well suited for this reorganisation of traditional spa destinations, which also explains its current growing popularity. While the Kneipp *Kur* has initially mainly targeted sick patients with various acute and chronic diseases, most of Kneipp's methods can also be applied for rehabilitation and, more importantly, health promotion. From a tourism point of view it also plays a role that many of his treatments are intrinsically pleasurable or can be made enjoyable, hence they are very well suited to be part of a wellness tourism experience.

Kneipp's philosophy as a regional development strategy: Kneippland Unterallgäu

As mentioned earlier, it was in the rural district Unterallgäu in the south-west of Bavaria where Sebastian Kneipp lived and worked. His teachings and holistic approach to health to date still strongly influence the region's identity and are a significant aspect of its economy which is strongly focused on spa and health facilities in the three traditional *Kur* resorts Bad Wörishofen, Bad Grönenbach and Ottobeuren. These three spa towns are core tenets of the region's health economy which provides direct employment to 11 per cent of the 136,000 Unterallgäu residents (Unterallgäu-Aktiv GmbH 2007). In 2010/2011, for instance, the region counted around 225,000 visitor arrivals and approximately one million visitor nights which contributed around 10 per cent to the region's gross domestic product and offered direct and indirect employment to about 25 per cent of its workforce. With 96 per cent of total visitation to the region, the three traditional Kneipp spas and health resorts Bad Wörishofen, Bad Grönenbach and Ottobeuren continue to play a very prominent role in the region's health economy. Amongst them, Bad Wörishofen is the region's top performer accounting for 755,614 guest nights (Bayerisches Landesamt für Statistik und Datenverarbeitung 2012; Unterallgäu Aktiv GmbH 2012).

As a region that has been heavily reliant on the health care industry and has been particularly focused on *Kur* treatments that were traditionally funded by health insurance schemes, Unterallgäu was hit hard in the last decade by a string of reform measures which aimed to rein in the spiralling costs of the German health care system (Pforr and Locher 2012). In line with the strategy adopted by many of its competitors, the Unterallgäu region's response to the crisis was, as outlined above, a stronger focus on medical wellness with products and services geared specifically towards the growing self-funded wellness tourism market. Moreover, these initiatives to rejuvenate and strengthen the Unterallgäu's traditional health economy were embedded in an overarching vision for the region. Kneipp's philosophy was used as the guiding principle to develop a particular health focus for the entire region which was considered as its best potential for the future. The aim was not to restrict the health theme to the traditional Unterallgäu *Kur* destinations but to develop it into the region's guiding principle encompassing everything from its economy, to its natural environment and the wellbeing of its people. This holistic view on health has helped to demarcate the Unterallgäu region from other destinations and has led to innovation and the establishment of a network of health-service providers, and ultimately improved the region's competitiveness (Unterallgäu-Aktiv GmbH 2007; Neukam 2008; Pforr *et al.* 2011).

Back in 2002 this new health-focused regional development concept for the Unterallgäu region was initiated and has since been implemented by the Unterallgäu Aktiv GmbH, a regional organisation in charge of managing the evolving health region's various activities. Its development strategy for the region is based on Kneipp's approach to health and wellbeing and thus built on his five key tenets water, plants, exercise, nutrition and inner balance. The aim was to translate

Kneipp's philosophy into a broader regional context, the natural environment and the sociocultural fabric as well as the economic activities of the region. At its core are three development objectives: improved quality of life; regionalism; and better health, which it is aimed to implement via a stronger engagement of the local community, conservation of natural resources, sustainable economic activities and a holistic approach to health. The strategy links the region's natural assets, its landscape and also its tourism potential to the Kneipp's pillar *water*. The importance Kneipp assigned to *plants* is reflected in the region's agriculture and forestry which constitute core regional economic activities. Similarly, regional produce is linked to *healthy nutrition* and the region's mobility, for instance, to *physical exercise*. Finally, the concept of *inner balance*, Kneipp's overarching tenet, is reflected in the region's rural and urban development and cultural activities. The strong connection to Kneipp's philosophy is also evident in the region's marketing, referring to the region not only as Unterallgäu but to Kneippland Unterallgäu, which can be translated as Kneipp country Unterallgäu (Unterallgäu-Aktiv GmbH 2007).

Founded on the traditional health competence of the region and local resources, for the past decade the Unterallgäu Aktiv GmbH has facilitated an active collaboration of various service providers and industry sectors under the overarching Kneipp theme with the aim of developing a competitive advantage. How well this health theme has been entrenched in the various socio-economic activities in the region is evident, for instance, in the very popular Unterallgäu Health Week. This annual event, which is supported by more than 30 communities, showcases and promotes the various health facets the region has to offer not only to its visitors but also its residents (Unterallgäu-Aktiv GmbH 2007, 2009; Neukam 2008).

Conclusion

Sebastian Kneipp's philosophy and his approach to health and healing have had a profound impact not only on the wellbeing of countless individuals. He became a figurehead of the naturopathic movement of the nineteenth century and his parish in Wörishofen was the first to develop into a Kneipp spa. Today, officially accredited by the German Spa Association, Kneipp destinations are a hallmark of health tourism in Germany and other European countries. However, this case example of the Kneippland Unterallgäu region has shown that the five pillars of Kneipp's philosophy have been employed far beyond the context of health tourism. Kneipp's approach to health has guided broader regional strategies, bringing together different stakeholders and economic sectors to create a health-conscious, sustainable community.

References

Ärztegesellschaft für Präventionsmedizin und klassische Naturheilverfahren, Kneippärztebund (2012) 'A brief history of the Kneipp therapy', online, available at: www.kneip-paerztebund.de/de/english-version/ (accessed 3 March 2013).

Bacon, W. (1997) 'The rise of the German and the demise of the English spa industry: a critical analysis of business success and failure', *Leisure Studies*, 16: 173–87.

Barker, K., Dawes, H., Hansford, P. and Shamley, D. (2003) 'Perceived and measured levels of exertion of patients with chronic back pain exercising in a hydrotherapy pool', *Archives of Physical Medicine and Rehabilitation*, 84: 1319–23.

Bayerisches Landesamt für Statistik und Datenverarbeitung (2012) *Statistik kommunal 2011 – Unterallgäu*, München: Bayerisches Landesamt für Statistik und Datenverarbeitung.

Bleile, G. (1985) 'Kurorte und Heilbäder in der Bundesrepublik Deutschland: Struktur und Entwicklung', *Tourism Review*, 40: 9–14.

Cimbiz, A., Vayazit, V., Hallaceli, H. and Cavlak, U. (2005) 'The effect of combined therapy (spa and physical therapy) on pain in various chronic diseases', *Complementary Therapies in Medicine*, 13: 244–50.

Deutscher Heilbäderverband (2005) *Begriffsbestimmungen – Qualitätsstandards für die Prädikatisierung von Kurorten, Erholungsorten und Heilbrunnen*, 12th edition, Gütersloh: Flöttmann Verlag.

Dubois, O., Salamon, R., Germain, C., Poirier, M.-F., Vaugeois, C., Banwarth, B., al Mouaffak, F., Galinowski, A. and Olié, J.P. (2010) 'Balneotherapy versus paroxetine in the treatment of generalized anxiety disorder', *Complementary Therapies in Medicine*, 18: 1–7.

Duda, T.A. (2010) 'Review of natural health philosophy in support of understanding optimal health', unpublished thesis, University of Natural Medicine, Santa Fe, New Mexico.

Eckart, W.U. (2011) *Illustrierte Geschichte der Medizin: Von der französischen Revolution bis zur Gegenwart*, 2nd edition, Heidelberg: Springer.

Helwig, D. (2005) 'Kneipp Wellness: Gale Encyclopedia of Alternative Medicine', online, available at: www.encyclopedia.com/doc/1G2-3435100456.html (accessed 2 October 2012).

Hill, S., Eckett, M.J.H., Paterson, C. and Harkness, E.F. (1999) 'Effects of floatation spa treatment on patients with osteoarthritis', *Complementary Therapies in Medicine*, 7: 235–8.

Kneipp, S. (1891) *My Water-Cure as Tested Through More Than Thirty Years and Described for the Healing of Diseases and the Preservation of Health*, Edinburgh: Blackwood.

Kneipp, S. (1894) *Thus Shalt Thou Live: Hints and Advice for the Healthy and the Sick on a Simple and Rational Mode of Life and a Natural Method of Cure*, Kempten: Koesel Publisher.

Kneipp, S. (1897a) *The Care of Children in Sickness and in Health*, Kempten: Koesel Publisher.

Kneipp, S. (1897b) *The Codicil to 'My Will' for the Health and the Sick*, Kempten: Koesel Publisher.

Kneipp Worldwide (2012) 'The International Confederation of the Kneipp Movement', online, available at: http://kneippworldwide.kneippbund.de (accessed 8 December 2012).

Lempa, H. (2008) 'The spa: emotional economy and social classes in nineteenth-century Pyrmont', *Central European History*, 35: 37–73.

Maretzki, T.W. (1987) 'The Kur in West Germany as an interface between naturopathic and allopathic ideologies', *Social Science and Medicine*, 4: 1061–8.

Maretzki, T.W. (1989) 'Cultural variation in biomedicine: the Kur in West Germany', *Medical Anthropology Quarterly*, 3: 22–35.

Maretzki, T.W. and Seidler, E. (1985) 'Biomedicine and naturopathic healing in West Germany: a historical and ethnomedical view of a stormy relationship', *Culture, Medicine and Psychiatry*, 9: 383–421.

McIlveen, B. and Robertson, V.J. (1998) 'A randomised controlled study of the outcome of hydrotherapy for subjects with low back or back and leg pain', *Physiotherapy*, 84: 17–26.

Nahrstedt, W. (2004) 'Wellness: a new perspective for leisure centers, health tourism, and spas in Europe on the global health market', in K. Weimermaier and C. Mathies (eds) *The Tourism and Leisure Industry: Shaping the Future*, New York: Haworth Hospitality Press.

Neukam, A. (2008) 'Gesundheitswirtschaft als regionale Profilierungschance', unpublished thesis, Universität Bayreuth, Bayreuth.

Pforr, C. and Locher, C. (2012) 'The German spa and health resort industry in the light of health care system reforms', *Journal of Travel and Tourism Marketing*, 29: 298–312.

Pforr, C., Pechlaner, H., Locher, C. and Jochmann, J. (2011) 'Health regions as tourism destinations: a new approach to regional development?' paper presented at the International Conference on Tourism (ICOT2011) – Tourism in an Era of Uncertainty, Rhodes, 27 April 2011.

Steward, J. (2000) 'The spa towns of the Austro-Hungarian empire and the growth of tourist culture, 1860–1914', in P. Borsay, G. Hirschfelder and R.-E. Mohrman (eds) *New Directions in Urban History: Aspects of European Art, Health, Tourism and Leisure since the Enlightenment*, Münster: Waxmann Verlag.

Steward, J. (2002) 'The culture of water cure in nineteenth-century Austria, 1800–1914', in S. Anderson and B. Tabbs (eds) *Water, Leisure and Culture: European Historical Perspectives*, Oxford: Berg.

Unterallgäu Aktiv GmbH (2007) *Regionales Entwicklungskonzept LAG Kneippland Unterallgäu*, Bad Wörishofen: Unterallgäu Aktiv GmbH.

Unterallgäu Aktiv GmbH (2009) *Geschäftsbericht*, Bad Wörishofen: Unterallgäu Aktiv GmbH.

Unterallgäu Aktiv GmbH (2012) 'Unterallgäu: Tourismus und Freizeit', online, available at: www.unterallgaeu-aktiv.de/tourismus.html (accessed 3 March 2013).

Vaht, M., Birkenfeldt, R. and Übner, M. (2008) 'An evaluation of the effect of differing lengths of spa therapy upon patients with osteoarthritis (OA)', *Complementary Therapies in Clinical Practice*, 14: 60–4.

Waltenberger, S. (2012) 'Erinnerungsort Sebastian Kneipp', online, available at: www.umweltunderinnerung.de/index.php/kapitelseiten/verehrte-natur/38-sebastian-kneipp (accessed 3 March 2013).

Whorton, J.C. (2002) *Nature Cures: The History of Alternative Medicine in America*, New York: Oxford University Press.

Winnewisser, S. (2009) *Gesund mit Wasser*, Hannover: Humboldt.

World Health Organization (2010) 'About WHO', online, available at: www.who.int/about/en/ (accessed 3 March 2013).

WorldCat (2013) 'WorldCat Identities: Kneipp, Sebastian (1821–1897)', online, available at: http://worldcat.org/identities/lccn-n50-43458 (accessed 6 March 2013).

Part IV
Drivers of wellness tourism development

International experiences

13 Regional trends and predictions for global health tourism

Melanie Smith and László Puczkó

Introduction

The discussion on the future of health tourism will first be set in the context of a brief review of the meaning of health and wellness in different geographical and cultural contexts, followed by a short analysis of historical traditions. However, the main focus of the chapter will be to assess contemporary trends in health and wellness destination development around the world and to identify some of the most significant initiatives or products. In doing so, this chapter provides an overview of some of the latest developments in health tourism from around the world. The chapter aims to be as comprehensive as possible encompassing all regions and providing brief examples of destinations which are seen to be especially representative of a particular region. Emphasis will be placed on the need for destinations to promote what is unique and indigenous rather than supplying standardised treatments or activities which are becoming ubiquitous. This line of argument is supported by data derived from two research projects. The first was a project undertaken with and on behalf of the Global Spa Summit (GSS) in 2011 about the role of spas in wellness and medical tourism, and the second was The Tourism Observatory for Health, Wellness and Spa's (TOHWS 2012) research entitled *4WR: Wellness for Whom, Where and What? Wellness Tourism 2020*, which was supported by Hungarian Tourism plc. A more detailed methodology will be provided later in the chapter, but both projects had global reach and provide a robust representation of all regions and many countries of the world.

Geographical and cultural variations in health and wellness traditions

It is important to note that there are different historical, cultural and linguistic understandings of health and wellness. Interestingly, the term wellness was rarely used in an English-speaking context and seemed rather archaic until the 1950s. Indeed, until recently, it was hardly used in British English at all. In many languages there is no word for wellness (e.g. Hebrew, Finnish) and the term health or wellbeing is used instead. The German word *Wohlbefinden* reflects the exact translation of wellbeing, whereas *Wohlfühlen* means 'well feeling', which does not have much meaning in English. On the other hand, the word spa is rarely used in German-speaking countries where the preference is for *Bad* or *Therme* in addition to wellness, especially where mineral or geothermal water is used. However, it is perhaps less useful to discuss definitions and the use of these terms in this chapter as this has been done extensively albeit not yet conclusively in the wellness tourism literature. Instead, the analysis will focus on perceptions and understandings which tend to be geographically specific and culturally defined. Notions of health, wellness and spas tend to be affected by the natural resources of a country, their historical traditions and sometimes religious or other rituals.

One of the oldest health practices is Indian Ayurveda which goes back as far as 5000 BC. The earliest known writings about Chinese medicine go back to 1000 BC. The first reference to healing waters is about 1700 BC (Crebbin-Bailey *et al.* 2005). The word spa is thought to have originated from Latin and phrases such as *sanitas per aqua* which means health through water. Ancient Greeks and Romans focused on both cleanliness and fitness and understood the health benefits of various types of water treatments. The ancient civilisations of Asia and the Middle East and indigenous peoples all over the world have been aware of the benefits of massage, yoga, meditation, herbal medicines and other forms of healing and spiritual practice for many more centuries than is evident in Europe. Most regions of the world have traditions based on balance or holism, for example, the Four Elements in Europe, Tibb in the Middle East and Body–Mind–Spirit or Ying and Yang in Asia. Interestingly, the extent to which water was perceived to be an important element of healing appears to depend on the natural resources available. In Asia, Japanese *Onsen* culture has a long tradition both within spiritual and secular society. Water is also used for ritual purification by Hindus in India, for example the River Ganges. Some parts of China are rich in mineral springs, which are currently being developed for tourism. In other countries and regions (e.g. Europe, Middle East, New Zealand) hot springs played an important role in ritual bathing, often for religious or spiritual reasons as well as cleanliness. In many countries, the sea was also used as a resource for health enhancement. The medicines of indigenous tribal groups, witch doctors or shaman may also have been used extensively for health reasons, for example in Africa, Australia and South America.

Historical and cultural traditions, which are often based on natural resources, can have a significant impact on contemporary understandings and expectations of health and wellness customers or tourists. Many cultural preferences may also be linked to Hofstede's (1984), Trompenaars's (1993) or other similar cultural indices. For example, Hall and Hall's (1990) model mentions monochronic and polychronic cultures. Polychronic cultures tend to perform multiple tasks simultaneously and are less concerned about time, whereas monochronic cultures tend to follow linear time and are more task-orientated. Hofstede divides culture into four dimensions: power distance, individualism/collectivism, masculinity/femininity and uncertainty avoidance. Trompenaars developed seven value dimensions: universalism versus particularism; communitarianism versus individualism; neutral versus emotion; defuse versus specific cultures; achievement versus ascription; human–time relationship; and human–nature relationship. Not all of these are relevant to wellness practices of course, but they may affect whether people visit spas collectively or individually; their perceptions of and need for space; if they frequent spas with their bosses and work colleagues; their views on men and women sharing a wellness space; their feelings about nudity; the extent to which they trust doctors and conventional medicine, or their propensity to try new products and treatments. Western cultures tend to be more monochronic than Asian ones (Hall and Hall 1990). Monochronic cultures make a sharp division between work and personal life, which means that they may not want to associate with business contacts in a spa, for example. The opposite may be true of the Japanese. More feminine cultures (Hofstede 1984) like Scandinavians and Germans tend to be more comfortable with mixed male and female nudity in spas. This would be unthinkable in the Middle East or Muslim countries generally. In Asia, men and women might be naked, but they would not mix. More individualistic cultures may like to visit spas alone (e.g. Nordic visitors) whereas more collective ones see spas as a social space (e.g. Mediterranean visitors).

All elements of a destination or facility can be influenced by cultural preferences. For example, spas or wellness hotels in China may need to conform to feng shui specifications or in India to Vasati because energy flows are deemed so important. For Europeans, such issues may be unknown or simply unimportant. Japanese designers tend to favour a simple, clean *zen* style, the same is true of Scandinavians who may prefer neutral colours and natural materials. On the other hand, Middle Eastern or India cultures usually like more opulent decor. Muslims may need the whole facility to correspond to *halal* specifications (e.g. some of the new spa developments in the United Arab Emirates). Even colour can have various symbolic meanings in different cultures, for example, red is perceived as positive in Asia whereas white is not. Many contemporary global spas seem to adopt an Asian style with Buddha statues, incense and warm colours. However, a parallel trend seems to involve more simple, minimalist design with space, light and natural furnishings. This is especially popular in more sustainable and eco-friendly spas.

In terms of understandings and perceptions of services and treatments, visitors from Central and Eastern Europe, Russia or the Baltic States have a long tradition of medical spas based on healing waters in their own countries, where treatments tend to be curative for specific physical conditions. Therefore they may expect to see a medical practitioner for a consultation, or desire some kind of medical supervision during their stay (Smith *et al.* forthcoming). Western European visitors, especially from Northern and Western Europe often expect spas to afford them leisure, luxury, pampering and beauty. They would therefore not necessarily want to be confronted by a medical practitioner. This is true mainly for British, Dutch and some Scandinavians (e.g. Norwegians, Danish), although it may differ for Germans, Austrians and Swiss who are familiar with the concept of *Kur*, which has a medical basis even though treatments may take place in hotels or spas.

The globalisation of health and wellness

The health and wellness industries are becoming more globalised, especially as international tourism is growing. This has resulted in an inevitable standardisation of products, services and treatments; however, it can also affect the whole destination if there is no special natural resource to provide a unique selling proposition (e.g. a Dead Sea or Blue Lagoon). The main culprits are spa and wellness hotels, which tend to offer similar treatment menus with standard favourites like Swedish massage and aromatherapy massages (both of which are essentially placeless). Even more exotic offers like Indian Ayurvedic or Lomi Lomi Hawaiian massage tend to be somewhat decontextualised when offered outside the country of origin. It is not uncommon to see Thai massage or Ayurveda offered in a Hungarian spa, for example. Many ancient traditions are becoming ubiquitous but this somehow diminishes their uniqueness and place-specificity. Although some tourists may still choose to visit the home of a particular therapy or treatment, most may simply be offered a diluted, shortened or distorted version of the practice in another location. In the case of Ayurveda for example, practitioners may not be adequately trained (e.g. a full three-year training in India), correct preparatory procedures may not have been followed (e.g. changes of diet in advance of a treatment like an Ayurvedic enema), and the actual treatment may be given at the wrong time of day, because this is the only time when the guest could procure an appointment. The spa or hotel owners are relying on customer ignorance and lack of experience, but this is a risky strategy in the long-term. Indeed, the GSS (2011) report on *Wellness Tourism and Medical Tourism: Where do Spas Fit?* noted that there is a new trend of consumers looking for local, traditional and unique experiences, and recommended that there should subsequently be an emphasis on national or regional specialisms and signature treatments.

In order to provide these, it is necessary to have an understanding of natural resources and assets, historical traditions and cultural practices. To gather some of this information, the authors took part in two global research projects. The first was with and on behalf of the GSS (now the Global Spa and Wellness Summit) in February and March 2011 which partly aimed to redefine wellness tourism and medical tourism, as well as to provide an overview of worldwide developments. More specifically, the project focused on the role of spas in wellness tourism and medical tourism. The methodology was as follows:

- In-depth case-study research on 12 representative countries. This included data collection from official websites (e.g. government, tourist office and spa industry), including statistics about the nature of the sectors and the numbers and profiles of wellness and medical tourists.
- Web-based survey of spa industry leaders around the world (sample size 206). The majority were from North America, Europe and the Asia-Pacific region and mainly included day spas, resort or hotel spas and spa consultancy companies. Questions were asked about definitions, characteristics of tourists, and the role of spas in wellness tourism and medical tourism.

- Forty interviews with leading experts and stakeholders from around the world who are working in (or studying) the wellness tourism and medical tourism markets. Questions were mainly asked about the role of spas in wellness and medical tourism and how they viewed the present and future situation.

The second research project was undertaken in 2011 and was later published by TOHWS (2012) which was founded by the researchers. Information was collected from 140 visionaries representing stakeholders from wellness, tourism, spa and health-care industries in over 50 countries worldwide. The research aimed to provide an analysis of the greatest opportunities over the next ten years for policymakers and practitioners and to better define new product development strategies. The respondents were individually invited to participate in the survey through professional social media channels, such as TRINET, ATLAS and relevant LinkedIn groups (e.g. Global Spa Summit). Convenience sampling was used to invite key decision-makers and influential members of academic, scientific and professional networks. Those who accepted were included in the research.

The research aimed to be as representative as possible of what is happening worldwide in wellness, spa and medical tourism. The interviewees were chosen to reflect a diverse range of countries, organisations and initiatives. The researchers also carefully selected case-study countries which were perceived to represent to a great extent the regions in which they are located. This does not mean that they are necessarily more advanced in terms of medical tourism and wellness tourism (in fact, some of the countries were focusing only on one or the other) but they reflect typical trends and stages of development. Of course, it is impossible to mention all of the global developments in wellness tourism and medical tourism, but this study aims to represent all of the world's major regions and to reflect most of the current trends in these fields.

An analysis of regional trends

The results of the research projects are extensive and fascinating. A selection of key findings is presented here to indicate some of the main trends in different regions and their representative countries in the world. Both full research reports are publicly available (see GSS 2011; TOHWS 2012). Health tourism (including both wellness and medical tourism) seems to be one of the fastest growing forms of international and domestic tourism according to many of the respondents from the research. This trend is not expected to change in the coming five to ten years. Although the 4WR research (TOHWS 2012) is mainly aimed at wellness tourism services, medical tourism was also a minor focus of this research and a major focus of the GSS (2011) research.

The Medical Tourism Association (2011) definition was used for the 4WR research:

People who live in one country travel to another country or travel within their country to receive medical, dental and surgical care while at the same time receiving equal to or greater care than they would have in their own country, and are travelling for medical care because of affordability, better access to care or a higher level of quality of care.

Wellness tourism was defined by the present authors as:

Trips aiming at a state of health featuring the harmony of the body, mind and spirit, self-responsibility, physical fitness, beauty care, healthy nutrition, relaxation, meditation, mental activity, education, environmental sensitivity and social contacts as fundamental elements.

Of course, there are numerous services that are on the borderline, e.g. medical wellness. There is no clear-cut distinction between wellness and medical, since that very much depends on cultural, religious and other factors, such as the availability of natural healing resources. In fact information about medical travel can help us to understand the recent status and future opportunities of wellness tourism. It should be noted that several wellness approaches have very close links with mental and psychological health. Travellers in search of mental balance or a better psychological state often look for complementary or alternative approaches, many of which (e.g. Ayurveda, yoga retreats, faith, meditation) are closely related to medical treatments. However, most of these are not yet evidence-based and are therefore not always accepted officially by the medical industry or counted in official medical tourism statistics.

According to the findings of TOHWS (2012), 58 per cent of respondents consider traditional medical tourism services (i.e. travelling primarily for surgical interventions, dental services, rehabilitation) to be popular or very popular in the industry.

The definitions used in the GSS (2011) report made a clear distinction between wellness tourism and medical tourism. These definitions were refined during the research process (i.e. they were partly shaped by the data).

The medical tourism definition does not differ significantly from the Medical Tourism Association definition (GSS 2011: 33):

Medical tourism involves people who travel to a different place to receive treatment for a disease, ailment, or condition, and who are seeking lower cost of care, higher quality of care, better access to care, or different care than what they could receive at home.
Bottom line: undertaken by people who are sick

The wellness tourism definition emphasises place-specificity and uniqueness as these were deemed important for the future by the respondents:

Wellness tourism involves people who travel to a different place to proactively pursue activities that maintain or enhance their personal health and wellbeing, and who are seeking unique, authentic, or location-based experiences that are not available at home.

Bottom line: undertaken by people who are healthy

'Authenticity' is a relatively complex and contentious term within both anthropological and tourism literature. Beer (2012) provides a comprehensive analysis from a philosophical perspective. It is often considered from two sides: objective authenticity (e.g. Wang 1999) and existential authenticity (e.g. Steiner and Reisinger 2006a). Objective authenticity, which is genuine and consensual (i.e. everyone agrees on what it is), is arguably rare as most experiences or perceptions of authenticity are socially constructed and negotiable. Within a wellness context, authentic treatments may be said to be those which are undertaken ideally in the home location or country of a tradition or practice and which follow prescribed steps or procedures. However, these may have been changed or modified over the centuries and may be further adapted when practices are shifted from one context to another (i.e. Thai massage being practised in Hungary, for example). The notion of existential authenticity has been explored in a wellness context (e.g. Steiner and Reisinger 2006b; Smith 2013) but this relates more to the concept of developing an authentic sense of self through holistic practices, for example. (Authentic) self-development is becoming a growing preoccupation within the wellness industry.

Health and wellness services

In terms of wellness tourism services, the TOHWS (2012) research showed that the following facilities, treatments and activities are the most popular within the industry:

- beauty treatments (89 per cent of the respondents named them as very popular or popular)
- sport and fitness services (89 per cent)
- leisure and recreational spas (85 per cent)
- spa and wellness resorts (83 per cent, respectively).

These services can easily be considered as global products since most of the service offers and provision have a tendency to be standardised and are available in almost all parts of the world. Traditional and local products were considered to be less popular at the moment but were expected to grow in importance in the future. Some of the following services were considered less important or were even unknown:

- spa cruises (40 per cent of the responses considered it neither popular, nor unpopular)
- therapeutic recreation (38 per cent)
- nutritional and detox programmes (35 per cent)

- occupational/workplace/corporate wellness (19 per cent of respondents reported unfamiliarity with the term)
- thalassotherapy (19 per cent)
- New Age (15 per cent).

There is a growing trend, especially in medical tourism, towards evidence-based services which have been extensively researched and are proved to have health benefits (e.g. healing waters, muds). However, some visitors may not know about such research or could still be sceptical about the benefits (e.g. many British people are unfamiliar with the notion of using healing waters for medical reasons). They may also be quite risk averse, especially when high prices are involved. Some responses to the perceived popularity of treatments were either neutral or negative, but this could perhaps have been attributed to unfamiliarity with some of the terms used. Although a Glossary of Terms was provided in the report, it was not given to the respondents. In future research, this would be

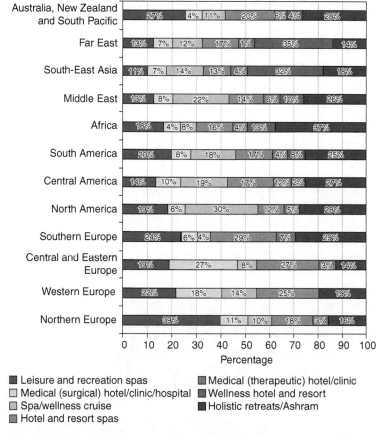

Figure 13.1 Most popular wellness services globally.

made available, as the research was not designed to be a test of knowledge, but a recording of perceptions and opinions.

Health and wellness assets and resources

As was found in the research, the most important assets vary from region to region, for example:

- there are a large number of leisure and recreation spas in Northern Europe;
- therapeutic medical hotels/clinics are typical of Central Europe;
- surgical medical clinics play an important role in North America;
- the number of wellness hotels and resorts is significant in Southern Europe;
- holistic retreats are numerous in the Far East; and
- spa and wellness cruises show moderate (but higher than average) importance in Central America.

Destination development is, of course, largely influenced by tangible resources as well as intangible traditions. According to the most popular services, the world's health and wellness tourism map is characterised by five main service groups:

1 *Wellness hotels and resort spas* that offer a wide range of wellness services from fitness, beauty, spa treatments, and often some water-based resources.
2 *Medical (surgical) services* refer to trips where treatments involve certain operation(s), e.g. dental or cosmetic work, or even life-saving operations.
3 *Leisure and recreation* is more related to everyday life and lifestyle than to tourism. A wide range of facilities and services are provided (e.g. water-parks) for visitors who are looking for relaxation, fun and rejuvenation.
4 *Spiritual and holistic tourism* services focus on the spiritual quest of the individual leading to transcendence or enlightenment. This may or may not have a religious affiliation, but it is often likely to include rituals, ceremonies and traditions that are derived from different religions
5 *Medical (therapeutic) services* are somehow different from surgical. They have similar elements, i.e. medical check-ups and diagnosis, but the difference lies in the fact that they often include a long stay or a repeat visit to the destination. Therapeutic tourism tends to use some natural assets that have a healing capacity and it has links to Therapeutic Recreation which focuses on rehabilitating people with illnesses or disabling conditions.

The detailed regional analysis reveals that there are significant differences in wellness tourism region by region. Marketers, developers and policymakers need to take these differences into consideration; especially considering that this research-based forecasts show that a growing number of travellers may be expecting more and more destination-specific services that complement globally available products and services in the future (GSS 2011).

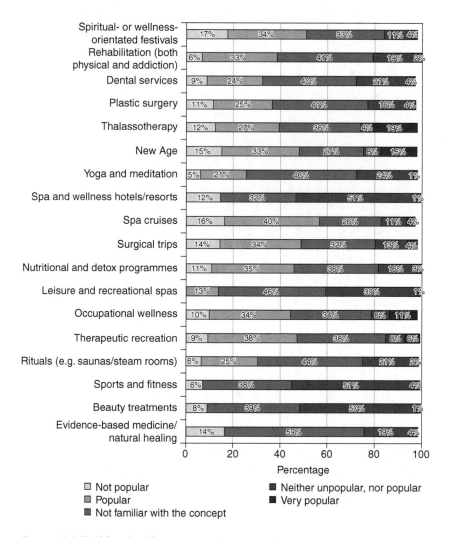

Figure 13.2 Health and wellness assets and resources by region.

Future regional trends in health tourism

The research shows that traditional, lifestyle-defining approaches (e.g. yoga) will become widely accepted in wellness tourism services in North America and Northern Europe. Wellness hotels and resort spas are already and are forecast to remain the most popular wellness tourism products in several continents and regions by 2020 including Africa, South America, Central America, Australia and New Zealand. In Central and Eastern Europe, therapeutic services and treatments are mainly based on the availability of natural assets (e.g. thermal waters) and will stay or become the most important.

Summarising the key trends we can say that *Africa* will show an increase in leisure and recreational segments, based on wellness products. Complementary services are seen as important but have not yet been fully developed and this cannot be expected in the near future. The focus should be placed on innovation and diversification. Morocco is an example of an African country which is developing fast in terms of its wellness tourism and spa industry (especially its *hammam*s and thalassotherapy), and to a lesser extent its medical tourism industry. Tunisia is also developing quickly in this respect. South Africa is quite unique in Africa because it has a tradition of hot springs tourism, a burgeoning spa and wellness tourism industry and high-quality medical tourism developments. In terms of landscape and spa developments, it perhaps has more similarities to other countries with a similar geography and climate (e.g. Australia) than to other African countries. South Africa has developed a number of luxury safari or bush spas which are located near to national parks where visitors can go on safari. Some spas or wellness centres also specialise in vinotherapy or wine therapy. Many of the spas offer global and especially Asian treatments, but a few specialise in African traditions, such as African wood massage and African raindrop treatment. However, one interviewee in the GSS (2011) research especially noted the potential to double the number of medical tourists because of the great facilities and infrastructure.

In *Australia, New Zealand and the South Pacific* leisure and recreational spas as well as wellness hotels and spas are predicted to be the most important in 2020 while the new lifestyle-based services (e.g. combination of physical fitness and nutrition) will gain ground. The region has basic assets in natural resources, which have not yet been fully captured. Standard, non-site-specific services will become available, but this is not necessarily the most successful approach. Australia has much in common with many other Western developed countries, for example the UK and the USA as well as much of continental Europe. The emphasis is mainly on wellness tourism and day spas, and holistic retreats also play an important role. Interviewees (GSS 2011) stated that there would be a 'significant increase in spa facilities, especially natural bathing spas and an evolution of hot spring spa culture', but that 'they will need to continue to innovate and develop new products that are uniquely Australian, to capture more of the international market'. New Zealand follows a similar trend except that there is perhaps a greater tradition of using the hot springs.

In the *Far East* holistic and spiritual approaches/services will still be the most important services with a strong wellness base. The region will undergo changes toward lifestyle-based and therapeutic services away from holistic and wellness tourism by capturing the important natural (e.g. thermal) and therapeutic resources. *South-East Asia* will still be the main centre for holistic and spiritual tourism but medical tourism will be important as well. India is one of the oldest countries in terms of wellness tourism and one of the leading countries now in medical tourism. Many Indian traditions are being exported to other countries and are featuring in wellness tourism and medical tourism programs worldwide (e.g. Ayurveda, yoga, meditation). However, India is also typical of many other

Asian countries which understand and practise body–mind–spirit balance and use holistic or integrated medical systems which are also based on lifestyle.

Like India, Thailand is very well developed in both medical tourism and wellness tourism. According to reports, Thailand currently holds a 38 per cent stake in the world's medical tourism market, the largest of any country in the world (Thaiways 2013). As it is well established as a tourism destination, many tourists stay in spa hotels and resorts and take advantage of the lovely landscapes, beaches and cultural activities, as well as enjoying some of the wellness traditions like Thai massage or Buddhist meditation, which have also been globalised in recent years. One Thai interviewee (GSS 2011) stated that 90 per cent of wellness tourism in Thailand is about relaxation and pampering rather than well-being. Another interviewee noted the growth of medical spas and especially those dealing with longevity. Other Asian countries have some very different traditions, for example, Traditional Chinese Medicine or Japanese *Onsen*, but these are also becoming popular elsewhere so people start to want to visit the home of these traditions. Korea is focusing heavily on medical tourism, but with some emergent specialisms like marine medical tourism (or thalassotherapy).

In the *Middle East* wellness as well as medical tourism will dominate the market. Wellness and leisure services play a dominant role in the region, but spiritual and holistic services can be expected to increase. Jordan is somewhat typical of the Middle East in that it mainly focuses on medical tourism and has a relatively long history of high-quality facilities, services and treatment. Most Jordanian health-care facilities are accredited by both domestic and international organisations. Dental tourism is one of the fastest growing sectors within medical tourism in Jordan (Al-Hammouri 2010). However, like Israel, Jordan also has the advantage of a unique resource – the Dead Sea – which is an ideal location for spa hotels and resorts. The Dead Sea also has some healing properties, therefore even the spas can promote evidence-based medical treatments (e.g. for skin conditions). The spa business in Jordan is currently growing at 12 to 15 per cent per year, with 11 per cent of room nights at the Dead Sea currently derived from spa and wellness visits. That market is expected to grow 10 per cent per year over the next ten years (USAID 2009).

South America and Central America remain strong in wellness tourism as well as in leisure and recreational spas. Surgical medical services seem to be the dominant tourism product, however natural resources and complementary treatments are the main assets. There are uncaptured resources in the area of developments connected to nature and complementary treatments (e.g. spiritual services, resorts, holistic retreats). Leisure and recreational facilities are already available in the region and will grow according to the forecasts; so will therapeutic medical services connected to complementary and alternative medicine. Brazil is fairly representative of both South and Central America in that there is more emphasis on medical tourism than wellness tourism, and especially on cosmetic surgery which is also popular amongst local people in these regions. Although there is a growth in the number of spas, the countries of Central and South America are tending to focus more on medical tourism at present. However, one interesting trend is the development of adventure spas which use the dramatic landscapes of Brazil, Argentina and Chile, for example, or eco-spas, which are located in the jungles of countries like Costa Rica and Ecuador.

In *North America* wellness and lifestyle services based on leisure and recreational spas and wellness hotels will gain importance. Medical services will be eclipsed by the focus on disease prevention. Canada is somewhat similar to the USA or many Northern European countries (especially Nordic countries) as the emphasis is mainly on wellness tourism, which has quite close connections to outdoor recreation and landscape. At present, there is very little medical tourism. The number of spas is growing, but they are used more by domestic than foreign tourists. There are large numbers of retreats in Canada that are located in beautiful tranquil landscapes. These focus on a number of activities, including yoga, meditation, occupational wellness and life-coaching.

Southern Europe seems to be the most dominant in leisure and recreational spas (with the highest rating in the world) as well as wellness hotels. Natural healing assets and complementary services have not yet reached their potential. Significant changes are not expected, so the region's innovation capacity and diversification of the product on offer should be enhanced.

In *Central and Eastern Europe* therapeutic medical services still dominate the market, but wellness and lifestyle-based services will become more important. The natural resources and healing assets are the key factors in the region, which will remain popular. The forecast for 2020 does not show any changes; however, there are new global trends, so the region should focus on its innovation capacity and product diversification. Hungary is typical of the Central and Eastern European region as it has a large number of thermal waters which have healing or medical properties. Thermal baths, which are sometimes called spas, tend to be developed in this region, but are often used simultaneously by domestic medical tourists and international wellness tourists (especially in the capital cities). Governments in these former Socialist countries (e.g. Czech Republic, Slovakia, Slovenia, Poland, Romania, Bulgaria, Serbia) still often subsidise domestic medical tourism to thermal baths.

The *Western European* health tourism market will be dominated by wellness hotels, but leisure and recreational spas remain popular. In German-speaking countries *Kur* or medical motivations are also likely to remain prominent. As an example of this region, Austria shares many characteristics with other Alpine countries as it uses its climate, fresh air, mountains and lakes as an inherent part of the wellness tourism product. Austria has a highly developed wellness tourism industry. About 12 per cent of all tourists make health-orientated holidays, so Austria is the European leader in this segment (Austrian Business Association 2011). There are large numbers of high-quality thermal baths and wellness hotels. One Austrian interviewee (GSS 2011) stated that 'sustainability and authentic marketing will be important. Tourists want to mix wellness with other experiences (not only thermal tourism)'. Other German-speaking countries like Germany and Switzerland are also very advanced in terms of their development of thermal resorts and baths. The facilities and services are incredibly sophisticated and of a high quality. The emphasis is more on wellness tourism than medical tourism, but the concept of medical wellness is also widespread (i.e. wellness and lifestyle-based activities which are advised by a medical practitioner).

Northern Europe will be the most important hub for wellness and lifestyle-based services with leisure and recreational spas. Nature and natural healing assets are the dominant resources of the region, but these so far are only partially used in wellness tourism. Wellness and lifestyle-based services will gain ground (e.g. Nordic Well-Being).

Globally available services are likely to lose their differentiating qualities by 2020 including beauty treatments, massages of any kind, sauna, day spas and some spiritual practices (e.g. yoga or meditation). Many fusion/crossover services (e.g. hotel-to-hospital conversions or medhotels) are not yet known or understood globally. Medhotels blend services and qualities of hospitals, hotels and spas. A medhotel offers various medical as well as wellness and spa services – without the hospital, clinic or sanatorium, or even a standard hotel feeling and image. This can manifest itself in either the form of an extended spa, modified hospital or even a cruise ship.

The research highlights the trend that there is a clear interest in the market to experience new services and products that differ from standardised services. The wellness tourism industry needs to better inform the market about the available assets and products, since many new products are not known and concepts are not yet generally accepted by the consumer. Figure 13.3 summarises some of the trends discussed above.

	Lifestyle	Leisure	Spiritual	Wellness	Therapeutic	Medical
Australia, New Zealand and the South Pacific	▲	•		•		
Africa		•	▲	•		
North and Central America	▲	▲		▲		▼
South America		•		•		•
Middle East			▲	•		•
South-East Asia			▲	•		•
Far East			▲	•		
Northern and Western Europe	▲	▼		•		
Central and Eastern Europe		•		•	•	
Southern Europe	▲	▲		•		

▲ Increase   ▼ Decrease   • No change

Figure 13.3 A predicted regional distribution of health and wellness trends by 2020.

Conclusions

One of the main points to emerge from the GSS (2011) research was that 'spas are an important part of wellness tourism, but wellness is about much more than just spas' (p. 9). Wellness goes beyond relaxation and is a key element of life-style, which is a significant opportunity for the tourism industry, since people following a wellness lifestyle will look for similar services when they are travel-ling. Wellness tourism includes healthy cuisine, specific fitness or body–mind–spirit regimes, active-ageing or longevity programs, learning, adventure, spiritual enlightenment, personal growth and the ability to enhance quality of life. The industry appears to be dominated by wellness destinations and hotel spas; however, other attractions and facilities are becoming more popular with con-sumers (e.g. wellness retreats, outdoor recreational activities, lifestyle centres, thermal treatment centres). There will be a proliferation of new, crossover and fusion services and products which will support the development of wellness tourism in countries and regions that are not yet on the global map of wellness tourism. These need to position themselves in a distinctive way so as not to dis-appear in a competitive environment. The research revealed that most regions have a number of unique assets that can and should be developed for wellness tourism. This will help to create unique selling propositions, distinctive brands and competitive destinations. Several ubiquitous wellness services (e.g. saunas, massage) may lose their differentiating power and become entry-level services without which no wellness provider can (or should) operate. However, they are not enough to guarantee an appealing destination and other newer or unusual services should be offered in parallel (e.g. rituals, traditions, signature treatments).

Spirituality remains important in countries where there is a strong spiritual tra-dition (e.g. Asia). However, the growing interest in non-religious spiritual prac-tices in increasingly secular societies (e.g. Europe) means that such products and services need to become more widely available. There are also many European monasteries or nunneries offering spiritual retreats. Consumers are becoming more attuned to the importance and value of green, eco, sustainable and organic practices and products. These should become more of a norm than an exception in wellness facilities, and the products and services should merit the label.

Evidence-based wellness is becoming more important, i.e. consumers need to know that the treatments or rituals that they are receiving have been adequately researched and are safe and beneficial. This could include healing waters, muds, cosmetics and nutrition. Similarly, wellness practices and practitioners should be regulated properly. Wellness tourism tends to be fairly exclusive, especially when it is based on wellness hotels and spas. In the future, there is likely to be a democratisation of wellness (especially if young people are being targeted), for example, budget spas, basic retreats and nature-based activities. Wellness tourism is likely to be seen as contributing to long-term wellbeing and quality of life, especially if there is a focus on the whole person and their entire life span in the form of active ageing and longevity.

Finally, although the chapter has mainly focused on countries and cultures, the importance of segments based on other demographic variables should also be considered. Although one facility cannot be all things to all people, a health-focused destination has the ability to provide enough variety of services to meet the needs of multiple target segments. There is significant potential in targeting the growth segments men, singles, families and youth (Gen Y). Men have different needs and expectations from women. Single people may feel uncomfortable surrounded by families and need tailor-made programs. Young people have few physical health problems compared to the elderly. Parents with children need relaxation but can rarely achieve this.

Overall, a competitive health or wellness destination needs to adopt a multi-layered approach to development and promotion, which reflects an awareness of unique resources and assets, as well as an understanding of history, culture and traditions. This includes the perceptions and needs of different nationality groups, as well as multiple segments differentiated increasingly according to their lifestyle.

Acknowledgement

This chapter was based on the findings of the research titled 'The adaptation and ICT-supported development opportunities of regional wellbeing and wellness concepts to the Balkans' (ref: KTIA_AIK_21-1-2013-0043).

References

Al-Hammouri, F. (2010) *Medical Tourism: The Fastest Growing Industry Overview with a Focus on the Jordanian Experience*, online, available at: www.treatment-abroad.ru/files/4IAl-HammoriIJordanPHAInew.pdf (accessed 25 July 2013).

Austrian Business Association (2011) *Wellness/Tourism*, formerly available at: http://aba.gv.at/EN/Home/Sectors/WellnessTourism/WellnessTourism.aspx (accessed 4 March 2011) and quoted in GSS (Global Spa Summit) (2011) *Wellness Tourism and Medical Tourism: Where do Spas Fit?* New York: GSS.

Beer, S. (2012) 'Philosophy and the nature of the authentic', in M.K. Smith and G. Richards (eds) *The Routledge Handbook of Cultural Tourism*, Abingdon: Routledge.

Crebbin-Bailey, J., Harcup, J. and Harrington, J. (2005) *The Spa Book: The Official Guide to Spa Therapy*, London: Thomson.

GSS (Global Spa Summit) (2011) *Wellness Tourism and Medical Tourism: Where do Spas Fit?* New York: GSS.

Hall, E. and Hall, M. (1990) *Understanding Cultural Differences*, New York: Intercultural Press.

Hofstede, G. (1984) *Culture's Consequences: International Differences in Work-Related Values*, London: Sage.

Medical Tourism Association (2011) *Medical Tourism FAQs*, online, available at: www.medicaltourismassociation.com/en/medical-tourism-faq-s.html (accessed 15 November 2011).

Smith, M.K. (2013) 'Wellness tourism and its transformational practices', in Y. Reisinger (ed.) *Transformational Tourism: Tourist Perspectives*, Wallingford: CABI.

Smith, M.K., Tooman, H. and Tomasberg, K. (forthcoming) 'Cross-cultural issues in health and wellness services in Estonia', in J. Kampandully (ed.) *Service Management in Health and Wellness Services*, Dubuque: Kendall Hunt.

Steiner, C.J. and Reisinger, Y. (2006a) 'Understanding existential authenticity', *Annals of Tourism Research*, 33: 299–318.

Steiner, C.J. and Reisinger, Y. (2006b) 'Ringing the fourfold: a philosophical framework for thinking about wellness tourism', *Tourism Recreation Research*, 31: 5–14.

TOHWS (The Tourism Observatory for Health, Wellness and Spa) (2012) *4WR: Wellness for Whom, Where and What? Wellness Tourism 2020*, Budapest: Xellum Ltd/Hungarian National Tourism plc.

Thaiways (2013) *Thailand – A Hub of Asia's Health Services*, online, available at: www.thaiwaysmagazine.com/health/medical_service.html (accessed 25 July 2013).

Trompenaars, F. (1993) *Riding the Waves of Culture: Understanding Cultural Diversity in Business*, Bath: Bath Press.

USAID (2009) *Market Assessment and Demand Forecast for the Jordan Dead Sea Development Zone*, Amman: Jordan Economic Development Program.

Wang, N. (1999) 'Rethinking authenticity in tourism experience', *Annals of Tourism Research*, 26: 349–70.

14 Fantasy, authenticity and the spa tourism experience

Jennifer Laing, Cornelia Voigt and Warwick Frost

Introduction

In a world of increasing connectivity and relentless schedules, holidays that calm the mind and soothe the soul are sought-after commodities. The growing popularity of spa tourism worldwide has led to the need to understand these experiences in greater depth, including the nature of their appeal and how they are marketed to tourists. Spa tourism remains under-researched in terms of its experiential value, despite its ubiquity in many, if not most destinations, and the premium paid for these experiences by growing numbers of tourists (Erfurt-Cooper and Cooper 2009). It has been noted that these experiences present 'more choices than ever' and can be eclectic and highly personal (Burt and Price 2003: vii). There are, however, common elements or features within spa tourism experiences, which warrant further exploration.

One of these hallmarks appears to be the blend of authentic and fantasy elements. While seemingly contradictory, they are often seen in tandem in the context of spa tourism experiences, with dreams or fantasies adding to or reinforcing feelings of authenticity, and high levels of authenticity, often connected to heritage, contributing to a sense of fantasy. The background to this paradox is postmodernist thinking about authenticity. Urry (1990, 2002) suggests that postmodern tourists have a predilection for playfulness, rather than seeking authentic tourist experiences. However, these ludic episodes and the search for novelty may incorporate authentic elements. Authenticity is not necessarily an objective construct, but something which is emergent (Cohen 1988) and can be linked to an individual's sense of self; discovering who they really are and what they are made of (Reisinger and Steiner 2006; Wang 1999, 2000). Fantasy can also be understood as an element of 'deep play', where the tourist acts out narratives or imagine themselves in different roles (Gyimóthy and Mykletun 2004). In the spa tourism context, this might involve playing at being royalty or a pampered celebrity, where authentic elements add to the drama or heighten the sense of liminality, as the tourist 'transitions from the ordinary to the extraordinary' (Ryan 2010: 12).

Authenticity and the spa tourism experience

Three forms of authenticity might be relevant in this context – intrinsic, existential and corporeal. *Intrinsic authenticity* suggests that there is one objective determination of 'genuineness, actuality, accuracy, originality, or truth' (Reisinger and Steiner 2006: 69), rather than multiple realities. *Existential authenticity*, by contrast, is determined by the visitor, who perceives an opportunity to be their true or authentic selves (Wang 1999, 2000). *Corporeal authenticity* refers to authenticity with respect to the senses – sight, smell, touch, taste and sound.

According to Reisinger and Steiner (2006), intrinsic authenticity is impossible to articulate, given the myriad of meanings or realities that can be attached to artefacts or events and the fact that there is no common ground amongst scholars in relation to this concept. Others argue that it is a personal construct, which is measured in the eye of the beholder (Bruner 1994; Cohen 1988). Thus, if the tourist believes something to be real, then it has intrinsic authenticity from their standpoint, even if others might argue that it has been staged for tourist consumption (Boorstin 1964) or is a fantasy. Intrinsic authenticity is potentially associated with spa tourism experiences built around traditional therapies, rituals and treatments, particularly those originating in or linked to the country of origin and its culture. Examples include Balinese or Thai massage, Indian Ayurvedic practices and the use of products based on Australian indigenous ingredients (Laing 2009). Intrinsic authenticity might then be the result of tangible cues, such as heritage features, interpretation and decor, and/or intangible elements, such as traditions or stories linked to the spa or the forms of treatments being provided. In some cases, the nexus is tenuous and the visitor is told that their spa tourism experience is *inspired by* traditional therapies. Authenticity might not be a matter of importance for some tourists, who simply desire some services, no matter how genuine they are and however loosely they are connected to the country in which the treatment is being sought.

While there appear to be a number of motivations for engaging in spa tourism, the overarching theme involves a desire for transforming the self (Voigt 2010; Voigt *et al.* 2011). This could be argued to constitute a form of existential authenticity, in that through engaging with wellness tourism, the visitor might feel a more authentic version of themselves (Wang 1999, 2000). This might be particularly the case where there is a spiritual overtone to the experience or alternatively some form of enhancement of the appearance or shape (Cook 2010). This sense of the authentic self might be linked to fantasy elements, making the tourist feel that this is a lifestyle which they aspire to and deserve, whatever the reality of their financial circumstances or social status.

Wang (1999, 2000) has developed a framework of 'intra-personal existential authenticity', which distinguishes between two aspects of this phenomenon, 'bodily sources of authentic self' and 'self-making' (Wang 2000: 67). The latter concerns the achievement of self-awareness and identity construction, through the tourist experience. A visit to a spa might give the tourist time to contemplate or meditate on who they really are. However, it is the *bodily* form of authenticity, which is particularly interesting in this context, given the appeal of spa treatments to the senses, especially the use of touch. Voigt (2010: 82) notes with respect to these bodily feelings that 'intense relaxation or recuperation, excitement, fun, and sensation seeking, can become the source of feeling authentic'. This suggests that highly hedonic tourist experiences, rather than being merely self-indulgent or pleasurable, have a role to play in making people feel a more authentic version of themselves (Voigt 2010).

Existential authenticity can also be conceptualised as 'inter-personal' (Wang 1999, 2000). This occurs when a tourist's interactions with other people, such as travel companions or people met along the way, engender a sense of authenticity. The visitor to the spa might feel freer and more who they really are, as a result of meeting with and interacting with the staff, including finding out more about their heritage and culture.

The third type of authenticity relevant in this context is corporeal authenticity involving the senses, which would include smells (i.e. essential oils, incense), sounds (i.e. music, the noises of nature such as wind, bird calls), sights (i.e. colours, natural surroundings) and touch, through treatments such as massages and facials. This may overlap with the concept of intra-personal existential authenticity discussed above, where it concerns bodily feelings. Spa tourism involves bodywork, which 'is closely linked with pleasure and emotional intimacy' (Twigg 2000: 391), and the sense of touch is an important component of this (Pearce *et al.* 2010). The tourist may find the experience less than satisfying or even *inauthentic*, if the therapist does not appear to be sufficiently engaged, either physically or emotionally, or the requisite tactile quality is absent. It might also affect the sense of fantasy that is being created, where tourists feel that they are not being treated with the requisite dignity or sense of worth that they equate with a pampering, luxurious experience. Authenticity might also be affected if the music doesn't fit with the ambience or visual cues, or where the fragrances used jar with the culture on display. Visitors to a Balinese spa, for example, might expect to smell traditional fragrances like frangipani, jasmine or sandalwood or hear gamelan music, rather than rock or pop.

The spa tourism experience appears to be a useful context for exploring these various forms of authenticity. We next consider aspects of fantasy and heritage within spa tourism and how they interplay with elements of authenticity.

Fantasy and heritage

Aspirational or *fantasy* elements of the spa tourism experience may be linked to issues of authenticity. Some spas are designed around exotically beautiful landscapes with names such as Mandalay or Shangri-La, redolent of myth and literary associations of escape. While these ludic experiences might involve the tourist playing at being royalty or a pampered celebrity, albeit for a brief period, this could be based, at least in part, on the authentic history of the spa as a magnet for the rich and famous. Royalty, including British kings and queens and Habsburg emperors, patronised the famous European spa towns (Corak and

Ateljevic 2008), while their modern equivalents – pop stars, models, top sports-people and actors – are photographed for glossy magazines and websites in luxury spa resorts such as Chiva Som or the Banyan Tree, Phuket in Thailand (Laing and Weiler 2008).

Tourism can be conceptualised in these cases as a form of performance, leading to the enactment of fantasies or 'dreamwork' (Light 2009). The tourist might feel a more authentic sense of self (Wang 1999, 2000) through this role play. Dann (1976: 22) notes that travel provides an environment for acting out psychic needs, and the playing of certain roles which cannot be fulfilled at home. Smith and Puczkó (2009: 71) refer to societal trends that encourage this, 'where fantasy relationships can seem easier than real ones in a world where fragmentation of society and communities is becoming more common'.

Gyimóthy and Mykletun (2004: 865–6) see this fantasy element manifested in travellers such as Arctic trekkers, who 'invent substitute worlds, supplement versions of reality, or inscribe themselves into the new identities' in their case, the explorer or pioneer. This type of fantasy can form shared narratives within a community of travellers, as identified by Belk and Costa (1998: 220) with their focus on recreated mountain rendezvous: 'Certain fantasies have the benefits of scripts and motifs'.

This chapter explores the nexus between fantasy and heritage in spa tourism through a comparative case study of three international beauty spas – the Gellért Baths in Budapest, Hungary; the Thermae Spa in Bath, United Kingdom; and the Polynesian Spa in Rotorua, New Zealand. Each exemplifies a different form of heritage – Secessionist/Art Nouveau (Gellért Baths), Georgian (Thermae Spa, Bath), and mock-Tudor heritage, Spanish mission/art deco and indigenous heritage (Rotorua). A qualitative approach was adopted in this study, given the exploratory stage of the research, and to enable these issues to be examined from an in-depth perspective (Jennings 2010). Data for the case studies was gathered from participant observation during site visits, and a thematic analysis of websites and promotional material generated by the three spas. This type of analysis groups data around a common theme; 'capturing the phenomenon being studied' (Denzin 1989: 75). The authors looked for text, images or offerings associated with themes of fantasy and authenticity.

A typology of beauty spa experiences

Each spa examined in this study has its own source of natural mineral water and offers water-based treatments. Each, however, provides a distinctive type of experience, using the typology identified by Voigt and Laing (2010). This typology, developed in an Australian context, groups beauty spa hotels or resorts into the following three types:

- *European* or traditional European style spas. There may be an ambience redolent of a sanatorium or medical facility, with white decor, or alternatively a luxurious setting reminiscent of the iconic spas of the nineteenth century, with columns or statues. Water-based treatments are standard, such as the Vichy shower, and European beauty products are commonly used, such as the Decléor and Thalgo brands from France.

- *Asian*, **where the spa theme is based on Asian healing techniques and philosophies.** These might include Traditional Chinese Medicine, Ayurveda from India, or the Japanese Reiki. These spas aim for a mystical and nurturing atmosphere, with furniture made of local stone and wood, particularly bamboo; statues and artefacts of deities such as Buddha; exotic plants; the heavy use of essential oils or incense; and traditional music.
- *Indigenous*, **where the spa theme is based on Indigenous cultural elements and healing philosophies.** This is epitomised by spas in Australia and New Zealand, where treatments draw upon Aboriginal and Māori cultural rituals and practices, including prayers, and knowledge of the healing properties of many local species of plants, such as lilly pilly and lemon myrtle (Australia) and acacia and manuka (New Zealand).

We would add a further type of beauty spa, which offers a *fusion* of the different experiences outlined above. Their offerings are not necessarily specific to a location or culture. Instead, they borrow what are perceived to be the best offerings from around the world or those that they perceive are in demand by their current and prospective clientele. Bodeker and Burford (2008: 426) refer to this as a 'smorgasbord approach'. Occasionally, there are attempts to reconcile this diversity though 'syncretism' – 'the fusing of diverse or disparate philosophies and practices into an overarching framework that focuses on commonalities by referencing a unifying philosophy' (Bodeker and Burford 2008: 426).

Case studies

The Gellért Baths, Budapest, Hungary

Budapest is a World Heritage site, partly with reference to its spa (*fürdő*) culture. It can be argued that these spas are 'part of the historic city fabric' (Smith and Puczkó 2009: 173). Budapest was a centre for wellness in the time of the Roman Empire, when it was known as *Aquincum*, the capital city of the province of Lower Pannonia, although there is evidence that the Celts and Dacians also used these springs during the earlier Neolithic period (Erfurt-Cooper and Cooper 2009). The archaeological ruins of *Aquincum* were excavated in the nineteenth century, including the public thermal baths. The Ottoman occupation was also marked by the development of a number of Turkish baths in the sixteenth and seventeenth centuries (Erfurt-Cooper and Cooper 2009; Smith and Puczkó 2009), notably the Rác, Rudas and Király Baths.

The next heyday of spa development in Budapest occurred in the late nineteenth and early twentieth centuries, during the dual monarchy of the Austro-Hungarian Empire, and the Golden 1920s and 1930s, when Budapest was considered the Paris of the East. The Széchenyi Baths, with their neo-Baroque colonnades and statues and chess-playing patrons, were constructed just before the start of the First World War and are the largest spa complex in Europe. The other iconic spa from this era is the Gellért Hotel and Baths (Figure 14.1).

The Gellért Baths illustrate the European spa model. They were built in Secession style, which is related to Art Nouveau and characterised by natural motifs of flowers and plants, and curved lines. The Baths, which opened their

Figure 14.1 The Géllert Baths in Budapest (photo by Cornelia Voigt).

doors to the public in 1927, nestle at the foot of Gellért Hill – a site with a history of healing practices going back to the thirteenth century, but also a locale for the Turkish bathing tradition of the Ottoman occupation. The baths were bombed during the Second World War, but were restored thereafter (Burt and Price 2003). Entering the foyer, one is struck by the brightly coloured mosaic floors, the fairytale quality of the stained glass and air of faded grandeur. The complex includes a hotel, with Turkish-like turrets; indoor and outdoor swimming pools with artificial waves in the latter; separate thermal baths for men and women; single-sex nude sunbathing areas; saunas; steam rooms; and treatment rooms. This emphasis on separating the sexes follows the Turkish model, rather than the more liberated mixed bathing that was popular in Georgian Bath and nineteenth-century German resorts such as Baden-Baden. The indoor pool is bedecked with Roman style marble columns and a domed roof, which Burt and Price (2003: 108) describe as 'a sybaritic fantasy right out of a Fellini movie'.

The Baths are used for medical treatments based on water therapy, including physiotherapy, healing gymnastics, and inhalation (to help patients with respiratory problems). Visitors can also avail themselves of a carbonic acid tub-bath or an underwater water-beam massage. These offerings are aligned with the idea of the spa as a medical-orientated facility (Voigt *et al.* 2010). A dental surgery is also available in the complex, leveraging off Hungary's reputation as a centre of expertise for dental care, which attracts many medical tourists to Budapest for treatment (Smith and Puczkó 2009).

The fantasy element may be shattered for some tourists when they are asked to take their clothes off for massages, alongside total strangers, unless this is their cultural norm, such as in many European countries. In the latter case, this might add to the authenticity, as it conforms to what is expected from a European spa. The atmosphere created by the treatments at the Gellért is perfunctory rather than exclusive or luxurious. Corporeal authenticity may also be absent for some visitors, when treatments are performed roughly or over-vigorously and/or without the expected soothing manner. This might be a cultural notion, as locals might feel that treatments that are administered too gently are not therapeutic enough. The spa offers some treatments that make an attempt at pampering the client, such as a Thai massage, which is not a traditional Hungarian offering. Thai massage is now available, which does not appear to correspond with the fanciful elegance of the Gellért's architecture and the image of old Budapest it conjures up for the visitor. This attempt at a *fusion* of experiences might diminish the objective authenticity of the Gellért Baths or make visitors feel less than their true self by affecting their bodily feelings and thus notions or levels of intra-personal existential authenticity. It might lead to a confusing jumble of sensory experiences, which could weaken perceptions of corporeal authenticity.

The Thermae Spa, Bath, UK

Like Budapest, Bath was settled by the Romans for its natural hot springs (when it was known as *Aquae Sulis*). Both cities are World Heritage listed, replete with heritage assets across a number of different eras and popular tourist destinations. Tourists to Bath can visit the Roman Baths, which were not just a place for recreation but also a sacred site with a temple to Minerva, the goddess of health and wisdom. This site was previously used by the Celts for their water cults linked to the goddess Sul (Burt and Price 2003) and there are stories of the mythical Celtic King Bladud who was cured of leprosy by bathing in the springs (Erfurt-Cooper and Cooper 2009). This Celtic past was acknowledged by the Romans, who juxtaposed Minerva's name with *Sulis*, a derivative of *Sul* (Erfurt-Cooper and Cooper 2009). The spa became a fashionable place for socialising in the eighteenth and nineteenth centuries, although the perceived health benefits of taking the waters was also a factor in their popularity (Smith and Puczkó 2009). The other major spa-related attraction in Bath dating from this period is the Pump Room, where today's visitors are still able to try a glass of mineral water from the spring and dine in neoclassical splendour.

The Thermae Spa in Bath (Figure 14.2), while housed in a Georgian building and leveraging off the city's Roman spa heritage, provides treatments from a broad range of cultures, including Asian healing techniques and philosophies and those more traditionally associated with the European spa. It is an example of a fusion of treatments, but also a fusion in the way they are *delivered*; juxtaposing the traditional Bath spa experience, described by Jane Austen in *Northanger Abbey* (1818) as a ritual of parading and being seen, with modern spa treatments, which take place behind closed doors in private sanctuaries. Paradoxically, despite Austen's association with Bath, she deeply disliked the city, as do many of her literary characters. Even the architecture is a synthesis of Georgian honey brick with a twenty-first century glass and steel facade designed by Sir Nicholas Grimshaw (Arfin and Lee 2008). There are two buildings – the New Royal Bath and the Cross Bath. The complex is the result of a partnership between the local council (Bath and North East Somerset) and a development company and was the recipient of funding from a lottery grant from the Millennium Commission.

The rooftop swimming pool within the multistorey New Royal Bath provides a view over the chimney pots and roofs of Bath, as well as a panorama of the surrounding hills. More modern facilities include multisex changing suites, with their own private cubicles, steam rooms infused with fragrances such as eucalyptus and lavender, showers simulating rainfall, complete with fibre optic lighting, and foot baths. Children under 16 years are not permitted in this spa complex. The Minerva Bath within the Thermae Spa is a tribute to its spiritual past. The Cross Bath is an oval-shaped thermal pool which is open to the elements. This facility is not open to children under 12, while youth between 12 and 16 years must be accompanied by an adult on a ratio of 1:1. Its spring has been recognised as 'an official sacred site' according to the latest brochure produced by Thermae Spa, and thus also has spiritual and perhaps existentially authentic associations for visitors.

There is an eclectic selection of treatments on offer at the Thermae Spa. Many are linked to Asia, including Pantai Luar massages, based on techniques from eastern Asia and using limes, coconuts and warm oils; Japanese Reiki massage;

Figure 14.2 Entrance to the Thermae Spa in Bath (photo by Jennifer Laing).

and Indian head massages. There are also Moroccan body wraps using minerals pertaining to that country. The spa staged a Malaysian Spa Festival in 2009, where visitors were attended to by therapists from the Spa Village in Malaysia. Offerings were described as 'authentic spa treatments' in the festival brochure and included Malay traditional massages to stimulate energy points, and a Pandan and coconut hair mask, which 'testifies to the rich culture of hair treatment in Malaysia'. This fusion approach might affect perceptions of objective authenticity, but perhaps also elements of corporeal or intra-personal existential authenticity, by not specialising in any one tradition and mixing so many cultural and multisensory elements, none of which are plausibly linked to the Roman spa tradition or the Georgian bathing heritage at Bath.

Other treatments have a more distinctly rural European association, such as Kraxen Stove therapy involving an Alpine hay chamber, where herbs are used to warm the back and shoulders, and the bath and foot massage using peat from the Salzburg region of Austria. In contrast, some beauty treatments, particularly the facials, are reminiscent of a high-end European spa, such as the Vichy showers with thermal water, body polishes and salt glows, and facials using the luxurious Pevonia range. These perhaps evoke greater perceptions of objective, corporeal and intra-personal existential authenticity amongst visitors, given the obvious connection with European heritage and the emphasis on pampering.

Other treatments are promoted using language and imagery that emphasises both authenticity and fantasy. The Cleopatra bath and foot massage will allow the guest to 'follow in the footsteps of the famous Egyptian Queen', while there are luxury facials made with 'caviar and pearl extract', a 'tropical escape' wrap and a 'chocolate indulgence' floatation. These treatments, with their emphasis on luxury and sensuality might evoke the bodily form of existential authenticity identified by Wang (1999, 2000), but also corporeal authenticity, as they fit with what might be expected from a high-end spa. Photographs of the spa on its website either show couples or single women, with no one else in sight, a far cry from the busy reality of a popular facility where there can be queues to enter. The image they aim to create is that of serenity and privacy within an intimate space; a luxury in this hectic and connected world. This occurs within the treatment rooms, even if the public areas are more noisy and bustling, and might allow the visitor to discover their true self within such a tranquil setting. The age of the therapies is also emphasised in the brochure, which is a nod to objective authenticity. For example, massage treatments are introduced with the phrase 'For thousands of years the ancient art of massage has been used to bring benefits to health and wellbeing'.

The heritage of Bath is alluded to with statements that the Thermae Spa is 'in the heart of the World Heritage site', but also that it is part of a tradition which harks back to the ancient past: 'You can now bathe in Britain's only naturally warm, mineral-rich waters, as the Celts and Romans did over 2,000 years ago'. The Cross Bath is described as 'surrounded by centuries of history'. Thus, heritage is central to both perceptions of authenticity and fantasy at this site.

The Polynesian Spa, Rotorua, New Zealand

The Polynesian Spa in Rotorua, New Zealand (Figure 14.3) is a contemporary spa based on Māori heritage. The city of Rotorua is famous for its geysers, mud pools and mineral springs, and the smell of sulphur is heady and pervasive. It is also an interesting melding of European and Māori influences, with tourism contributing to a more affluent Māori populace compared to the rest of the country (Ryan and Crotts 1997). The Māori were attracted to the region for its geothermal resources, which they used domestically for cooking, heating, bathing and laundry as well as for medical reasons and as an element of sacred and cultural rituals, such as preparation for battle or for childbirth (Barrick 2007; Erfurt-Cooper and Cooper 2009; Pohatu *et al.* 2010). The spa is however named after their ancestors, the Polynesians, who are believed to have arrived in New Zealand around the thirteenth century (Hogg *et al.* 2002).

Commercial spa tourism in Rotorua became a reality in the nineteenth century as a result of the availability of tours through Thomas Cook and articles, poems and books extolling 'the healing properties of the natural springs in the Rotorua area ... establishing a mythology of New Zealand as a scenic wonderland' (Corak and Ateljevic 2008: 132). Rotorua was planned as a European spa town; a recreation of Bath or Carlsbad in the colonies (Corak and Ateljevic 2008; Pike 2008).

The Māori heritage was not always celebrated in connection with spa development. In an ironic twist, while the Māori were made to use different pools from the European settlers (Erfurt-Cooper and Cooper 2009), their indigenous heritage is now celebrated and bestows a level of objective authenticity upon the Rotoruan spas, which is marketable and a source of competitive advantage.

The Polynesian Spa has a family pool or spa, accessible to children, as well as cascade pools and private pools that are reserved for adults. There are 26 pools in total: seven are reserved for adults, including three Priest spa pools, named after a nineteenth-century Catholic priest who, according to the Spa website (www.polynesianspa.co.nz), was said to have used the spring water to help his arthritis. The site of the spa has been registered by the New Zealand Historic Places Trust as part of the Rotorua Government Gardens Historic Area.

The case study of the Polynesian Spa illustrates how the spa fantasy has changed over time. The nearby Rotorua Museum of Art and History was originally a bathhouse built in Tudor style by the New Zealand government for tourist purposes in 1908 (Erfurt-Cooper and Cooper 2009). It was known as the Great South Seas Spa with mud baths in the basement and pools in an Edwardian garden (Barrick 2007). The adjacent Blue Baths were built in the 1930s in Spanish mission style, a style reminiscent of and incorporating elements of Art Deco, when their mixed bathing was considered the height of modernity. At the time, New Zealand sought to position itself as 'the premier spa of the British Empire' (Eyewitness Guide 2008: 134) or the southern hemisphere (Pike 2008), using geothermally heated fresh water, rather than mineral springs. These days, the Blue Baths still incorporate bathing pools, but also house a museum and stage dinner shows, such as the nostalgic *1931: The Show*, complete with a jazz band. They are also a popular venue for weddings, corporate functions and conferences, with their glamorous architecture, potted palms and lido lounge. Like the Polynesian Spa, the Rotorua Museum of Art and History and the Blue Baths have been registered by the New Zealand Historic Places Trust.

In contrast to these two facilities, the Polynesian Spa combines an indigenous with a European theme, and local ingredients are incorporated into the spa offerings. Treatments include a body polish with Rotorua thermal mud or manuka honey, or scrubs using mango or coconut; which conjures up an image of tropical Polynesia and perhaps engenders bodily forms of authenticity linked to smell and touch. The treatments are carried out with care and attention on the part of the staff and may evoke corporeal or intra-personal existential authenticity when added to the indigenous ingredients and ambience within the treatment rooms. The visitor is made to feel special and nurtured. Alongside these experiences linked to New Zealand and its regional roots, one can partake in a Swedish massage or have a facial with US Priori products, famed for their use of the latest scientific research into anti-ageing. These fusion treatments jar with the indigenous theme of the Polynesian Spa facility. The natural environment is emphasised more in the modern spa, which features local trees and rocks and a scenic background of Lake Rotorua and the surrounding hills. These elements might evoke intra-personal existential or corporeal forms of authenticity with the

Figure 14.3 The Rotorua Museum of Art and History, formerly the Great South Seas Spa (photo by Jennifer Laing).

Figure 14.4 The Blue Baths in Rotorua, built in Spanish mission style (photo by Jennifer Laing).

connection to the visual and auditory senses and the sense of being immersed in an unspoilt landscape.

This miscellany of local and international influences has been highly success-ful for the Polynesian Spa, which has been awarded one of Condé Nast Traveller magazine's top ten thermal, medical and natural spas in recent years (Smith and Puczkó 2009); ranking number seven in 2011. Its blend of island fantasy and authenticity linked to its indigenous heritage and use of multisensory bodily treatments appears to play a large part in this success.

Conclusion

The growing popularity of spa tourism around the globe makes it imperative that we understand what is attracting tourists to these experiences and the nature and meaning of what is being experienced. This multicase study highlights three key findings, which advance our understanding of the spa tourism experience. First, it suggests that fantasy and authenticity are crucial ingredients and coexist or are facets of the same experience in many cases. They are linked to heritage in these case studies. For the Gellért and Thermae spas, fantasy is created by their royal and/or celebrity connections, grand or imposing architecture and/or air of luxury. In contrast, fantasy elements of the Polynesian Spa are more about finding a con-nection with Māori traditions of wellbeing and the image of a natural paradise that is associated with both New Zealand and Polynesia. Authenticity in all its guises is also evoked at these three spas through the existence and use of her-itage across elements as diverse as architecture, the natural environment, cultural rituals, and traditions and philosophies.

Second, this study demonstrates that spa tourism can be a useful context in which to explore the nature and effect of different forms of authenticity, some of which, like corporeal authenticity, have not been recognised in the tourism liter-ature to date. The application of Wang's (1999, 2000) concept of intra-personal existential authenticity to this context, particularly vis-a-vis bodily feelings, is another contribution of this study to the growing literature on spa tourism. The finding that spa tourism experiences can evoke authenticity on a number of dif-ferent levels suggests that these experiences are less shallow than they are popu-larly portrayed in the media or by some commentators. This research could be extended by interviewing spa tourists about the different types of authenticity evoked by undergoing treatments and therapies, as well as exploring how these intersect with fantasy elements.

Third, it is acknowledged that the three spas use language in their promotional material that is evocative of both fantasy and authenticity. Most have some element of fusion in their offerings to visitors, rather than relying on what is local or tradi-tional to their city or region. This perhaps acknowledges the globalisation of the spa industry with an increasingly homogenised offering. However, jumping on this fusion bandwagon might negatively affect tourist perceptions of the authenticity of these experiences. Understanding the interplay of authenticity and fantasy as moti-vations behind spa tourism appears to have implications for the way spa products and experiences are designed and marketed and also influences the development of these resorts, including architecture, ambience and facilities. Further research is needed to explore these issues on a broader scale.

References

Arfin, F. and Lee, B. (2008) *England Chic*, Godalming: The World's Best Hotels Ltd.

Barrick, K. (2007) 'Geyser decline and extinction in New Zealand: energy development impacts and implications for environmental management', *Environmental Management*, 39: 783–805.

Belk, R.W. and Costa, J.A. (1998) 'The mountain man myth: a contemporary consuming fantasy', *Journal of Consumer Research*, 25: 218–40.

Bodeker, G. and Burford, G. (2008) 'Traditional knowledge and spas', in M. Cohen and G. Bodeker (eds) *Understanding the Global Spa Industry*, Oxford: Elsevier.

Boorstin, D. (1964) *The Image: A Guide to Pseudo-Events in America*, New York: Harper and Row.

Bruner, E.M. (1994) 'Abraham Lincoln as authentic reproduction: a critique of postmodernism', *American Anthropologist*, 96: 397–415.

Burt, B. and Price, P. (2003) *100 Best Spas in the World*, Guilford, CT: The Globe Pequot Press.

Cohen, E. (1988) 'Authenticity and commoditization in tourism', *Annals of Tourism Research*, 15: 371–86.

Cook, P.S. (2010) 'Constructions and experiences of authenticity in medical tourism: the performances of places, spaces, practices, objects and bodies', *Tourist Studies*, 10: 135–53.

Corak, S. and Ateljevic, I. (2008) 'Colonisation and "taking the waters" in the 19th century: the patronage of royalty in health resorts of Opatija, Hapsburg Empire and Rotorua, New Zealand', in P. Long and N.J. Palmer (eds) *Royal Tourism: Excursions Around Monarchy*, Clevedon: Channel View, pp. 128–41.

Dann, G. (1976) 'The holiday was simply fantastic', *Tourist Review*, 31: 19–23.

Denzin, N.K. (1989) *Interpretive Interactionism*, Newbury Park, CA: Sage.

Erfurt-Cooper, P. and Cooper, M. (2009) *Health and Wellness Tourism: Spas and Hot Springs*, Bristol: Channel View.

Eyewitness Guide (2008) *New Zealand*, London: Dorling Kindersley.

Gyimóthy, S. and Mykletun, R.J. (2004) 'Play in adventure tourism: the case of Arctic trekking', *Annals of Tourism Research*, 31: 855–78.

Hogg, A.G., Higham, T.F.G., Lowe, D.J., Palmer, J.G., Reimer, P.J. and Newnham, R.M. (2002) 'A wriggle-match date for Polynesian settlement of New Zealand', *Antiquity*, 77: 116–25.

Jennings, G. (2010) *Tourism Research*, 2nd edition, Milton QLD: Wiley.

Laing, J. (2009) 'Peninsula Hot Springs – a new spa tourism experience "Down Under"', in M. Smith and L. Puczkó (eds) *Health and Wellness Tourism*, Oxford: Elsevier.

Laing, J. and Weiler, B. (2008) 'Mind, body and spirit: health and wellness tourism in Asia', in J. Cochrane (ed.) *Asian Tourism: Growth and Change*, Oxford: Elsevier.

Light, D. (2009) 'Performing Transylvania: tourism, fantasy and play in a liminal place', *Tourist Studies*, 9: 240–58.

Pearce, P., Filep, S. and Ross, G. (2010) *Tourists, Tourism and the Good Life*, Abingdon: Routledge.

Pike, S. (2008) 'A cautionary tale of a resort destination's self-inflicted crisis', *Journal of Travel and Tourism Marketing*, 23: 73–82.

Pohatu, P., Warmenhoven, T., Rae, A. and Bradshaw, D. (2010) 'Low enthalpy geothermal energy resources for rural Maori communities – Te Puia Springs, East Coast, North Island New Zealand', paper presented at the World Geothermal Congress, Bali, April 2010.

Reisinger, Y. and Steiner, C.J. (2006) 'Reconceptualizing object authenticity', *Annals of Tourism Research*, 33: 65–86.

Ryan, C. (2010) 'Ways of conceptualising the tourist experience: a review of literature', in R. Sharpley and P.R. Stone (eds) *Tourist Experience: Contemporary Perspectives*, Abingdon: Routledge, pp. 9–20.

Ryan, C. and Crotts, J. (1997) 'Carving and tourism: a Maori perspective', *Annals of Tourism Research*, 24: 898–918.

Smith, M. and Puczkó, L. (2009) *Health and Wellness Tourism*, Oxford: Butterworth-Heinemann.

Twigg, J. (2000) 'Carework as a form of bodywork', *Ageing and Society*, 20: 389–411.

Urry, J. (1990) *The Tourist Gaze*, 1st edition, London: Sage.

Urry, J. (2002) *The Tourist Gaze*, 2nd edition, London: Sage.

Voigt, C. (2010) 'Understanding wellness tourism: an analysis of benefits sought, health-promoting behaviours and positive psychological well-being', unpublished thesis, University of South Australia.

Voigt, C. and Laing, J. (2010) 'The structure of Australian wellness tourism providers: definition, typology and current status', paper presented at the Travel and Tourism Research Association (TTRA) European Chapter Conference, Budapest, September 2010.

Voigt, C., Brown, G. and Howat, G. (2011) 'Wellness tourists: in search of transformation', *Tourism Review*, 66: 16–30.

Voigt, C., Laing, J., Wray, M., Brown, G., Howat, G., Weiler, B. and Trembath, R. (eds) (2010) *Wellness and Medical Tourism in Australia: Supply, Demand and Opportunities*, Gold Coast: CRC for Sustainable Tourism.

Wang, N. (1999) 'Rethinking authenticity in tourism experience', *Annals of Tourism Research*, 26: 349–70.

Wang, N. (2000) *Tourism and Modernity: A Sociological Approach*, Oxford: Pergamon.

15 Wellness tourism

A perspective from Japan

Patricia Erfurt-Cooper

Introduction

Wellness tourism in Japan is largely based on the use of the abundant natural volcanic hot springs throughout the country. Natural hot spring spas and resorts, known as *Onsen*, are arguably Japan's most important destinations for healthy recreation. The residents of any Japanese locality are therefore generally very conscious of the health benefits of their communal hot springs, which are used by the majority on a regular basis for bathing. It is noticeable though, that other wellness therapies such as alternative medicine, the various forms of massage available in other parts of the world and traditional forms of medicine (Erfurt-Cooper and Cooper 2009) are not usually associated with wellness tourism or the daily use of *Onsen* in this country. There is also little demand for *Onsen* from foreign tourists other than those from China and Korea, partly because of the unfamiliar forms of the bathing rituals associated with their use (Kojima and Kawamura 2006; Erfurt-Cooper and Cooper 2009).

This chapter discusses the major traditions of wellness tourism in Japan through case studies, and is based on research for an unpublished thesis (Erfurt-Cooper 2012). The close relationship between wellness tourism and natural hot springs will be demonstrated with the magnitude of hot spring use in Japan, giving an indication of the actual size of the wellness tourism industry in that country. Although the Japanese commonly refer to their desire to travel to various domestic locations for *Onsen* bathing experiences rather than to 'wellness tourism', the English word 'wellness' is used in the Japanese language and is generally associated with *Onsen* travel even if it is not directly marketed as wellness tourism. The chapter further outlines the patterns of wellness tourism in Japan by revealing the historical, cultural and religious background of *Onsen* use and by clarifying the role of natural hot and mineral springs in the treatment of various health conditions in this country. Together this information contributes to an understanding of how important natural hot springs are to health tourism in Japan, where annual visitor numbers reach on average 150 million people utilising these resources for wellness purposes.

The historic background and current status of hot spring use in Japan

The island nation of Japan is situated in the northern Pacific and covers an area of approximately 377,944 km². Japan is made up of 6,852 islands with Honshu, Kyushu, Hokkaido and Shikoku the four largest, and has an estimated population of nearly 128 million people. The climate is predominantly temperate, but varies greatly from north to south. As of 2012 Japan enjoys the third largest national economy in the world after the USA and China and a highly regulated universal public health-care insurance system. This health system is provided by national and local governments and private sources, and covers a comprehensive range of services. It is subsidised for Japanese citizens and for foreigners residing in Japan and paying taxes (Castro 2009; Jeong and Hurst 2001).

Natural hot springs are among Japan's most important tourist attractions and are accepted as a resource that contributes actively to health and wellness (Chartrungruang and Mitsutake 2007; Ratz 2011). In Japan, as elsewhere, the popularity of wellness tourism is based on the main objectives of relaxation, the maintenance of good health and the prevention of illness. Visitor expectations, apart from relaxation and the therapeutic benefits of bathing in authentic hot spring water, include relaxing in natural surroundings, together with ease of access, reasonable pricing and the opportunity to experience regional cuisines (Koyabashi 2004; Erfurt-Cooper 2012).

It is important to understand though that *Onsen* bathing is practised as part of Japanese sociocultural traditions which also emphasise hygiene and purification in a religious and personal sense. The particular rituals and traditions associated with the use of this resource go back many centuries; Japanese hot spring or *Onsen* bathing for health and wellness is first recorded in the book *The History of the Kingdom of Wei* written in China in AD 297 (Clark 1999). *Onsen* bathing was popular in the Heian Period more than 1,000 years ago with remains of early baths apparent in the settlements found near natural hot springs (Clark 1999; Talmadge 2006). Mineral-rich natural hot springs have been accepted as an alternative health resource for centuries and still contribute actively to the maintenance of good health and wellness of many Japanese people. Anthropological studies show that everyday acts like Japanese *Onsen* bathing are embedded in historically grounded, culturally specific complexity (Clark 1999) as well as being deeply entrenched in *Onsen* therapy (spa medicine, balneology).

It is suggested by some scholars that the culture of hot spring use may have found its way from China through Korea to Japan. The promotion of *Onsen* bathing in Japan was recorded only after the Chinese and Koreans had established migratory ties with the country prior to AD 297, when the first documented use of natural hot springs in Japan was mentioned (Clark 1999). The custom of bathing in hot springs (*toji*) is recorded as having been adopted by farmers and city dwellers alike, as it was the only economical way to relax and recover from the rigours of their lives (Clark 1999; Ito 2003).

The oldest and most important *Onsen* destinations are mentioned in a text from AD 712 (*Kojiki*) due to their association with the Imperial family, wars or religious events. One of these, *Dōgo Onsen* in Ehime Prefecture on the island of Shikoku may have been used since approximately 3,000 years ago or even as early as during the Jomon (10,000 BC–300 BC or earlier) and Yayoi (300 BC or earlier–AD 300) settlement periods (Clark 1999; Erfurt-Cooper 2012). Much later, during the Edo feudal period (from 1603), even though travel strictly for pleasure was restricted, permission was given for special purposes, including visits to *Onsen* (Cooper *et al.* 2008) associated with pilgrimage to the important shrines. Attendance at shrines, temples and their associated *Onsen* became commonplace as the Edo Period progressed (Ashkenazi 1993; Plutschow 1996), indicating that *Onsen* tourism in the form of its association with religious pilgrimage has flourished in Japan for centuries (Cooper *et al.* 2008).

Even to this day many public bathhouses have little shrines at their entrance and larger facilities often provide prayer areas or small temples; both can be observed to be in use by at least some *Onsen* users, implying that the association of a shrine with the hot spring resource remains significant to the more tradition-bound visitor (Creighton 1997). There is however, little direct evidence in the present for anything more than a passing acknowledgement of the religious aspect by visitors in this secular (but culturally conservative and defensive) society (Kojima and Kawamura 2006).

While historical records indicate that the Shoguns and Emperors of different periods regularly visited hot springs for health, wellness and recreational purposes and even had water from special hot springs delivered to their residences, the use of specific hot springs, such as those in Beppu (Kyushu), quickly spread to the warlords and their armies during the Warring States Period (1477–1568), when it was discovered how effective hot springs were in healing battle wounds. With the peace and stability of the Edo Period (1603–1867), the custom of bathing in hot springs for therapeutical purposes was rapidly adopted by the developing urban working class (Ito 2003).

To this day bathing in natural hot springs is one of the greatest pleasures of the Japanese people. Part of the reason for this is of course the vast amount of geothermal water resources based on volcanic activity available in most parts of the country. Nearly all regions of Japan are able to cater for the demand for hot spring-based health resorts and spas, and the facilities range from five-star *Onsen* resorts to rock-lined river pools and mountain-top hot tubs. As a result of many centuries of use, many of the traditional *Onsen* in Japan offer a special natural ambience and bear little resemblance to the often sterile, clinic-like spas of the United States or Europe, or to the concrete blocks of Japan's better known *Onsen* towns like Beppu (Hotta and Ishiguro 1986; Neff 1995). The other reason is that the mineral content of the springs is as important for wellness as the hygiene standards promoted by bathing frequently in hot water.

The current pattern of Onsen *use*

In 2006 the Ministry of Environment recorded 3,157 *Onsen* resorts and approximately 6,400 public bathhouses, frequented by over 150 million visitors per year in Japan, mainly domestic tourists (Beppu International Tourist Office, pers. comm. 2007; Erfurt-Cooper and Cooper 2009). The Japanese domestic travel pattern relating to *Onsen* now includes the experience or collection of as many different hot springs as possible, emphasising the nation's passion for this activity. Major factors in the ongoing popularity of Japanese *Onsen* spas and resorts are:

- the promotion of collective wellbeing to Japanese people through social acceptance of the importance of the activity;
- the abundance of natural hot and mineral springs;
- a well-structured service industry including accommodation, retail opportunities, transport and restaurants in close proximity to the hot springs; and
- the easy accessibility of these destinations in a developed and prosperous country.

Today, *Onsen* attract a large percentage of all domestic tourists in Japan, who come on short weekend packages to soak in the hot spring baths and enjoy the local cuisine. Nevertheless, central and local governments and organisations like the *Japan Health and Research Institute* are working towards the further growth and spread of *Onsen* facilities, for example by linking *Onsen* to physical examination centres based on the concept of improvement and maintenance of good health in the future (Japan Health and Research Institute 2010). This is partly because *Onsen* are different from hot springs in other countries in several respects. First, the water is usually quite hot with average temperatures around 37–42°C. Second, each hot spring has its own unique mineral qualities, for which it has become known, and for which there are a corresponding set of physical and other ailments that benefit from these particular mineral compositions. And third, as noted above, the range of ancillary services is usually extensive. All this makes them attractive as locations for the development of wellness and medical tourism (Hall 2012).

The combination of *Onsen* facilities with the natural environment through traditional architecture in historical and cultural settings is also given special attention by destination managers and *Onsen* operators wherever possible (Kojima and Kawamura 2006; Altman 2000). Hot spring-based health and wellness resorts and spas combined with sports clubs and day spas, as well as venues for weddings or corporate events draw visitors from a wide range of sociocultural backgrounds. Many *Onsen* facilities combine their unique features with traditional Japanese garden settings and other local cultural aspects in response to a demand for traditional environments.

Types of Japanese health and wellness destinations – *Onsen* used as treatment facilities

Japanese *Onsen* come in a range of sizes, with some set up like a hospital or sanatorium, where treatment for various health conditions is available under medical supervision, while others are more like spas, where a range of wellness activities is provided in addition to healing waters (Altman 2000). Yet others, the majority, can be simple, no-frills bathing establishments catering to locals who stop by after work, but nevertheless rely on the benefits of hot spring bathing for their personal health and wellness. Some hot spring-based health resorts in Japan offer package tours for domestic visitors which include a general medical check-up with the option for further tests. In these, visitors are advised by qualified medical staff on the therapeutic benefits of hot spring water as part of a project to promote the medical use of natural hot springs. These projects are backed up by local hospitals whose officials hail them as a significant approach towards linking medical treatments with a natural and curative environment (Trends in Japan 2005).

Japan's hot spring resorts and spas are therefore among the most important destinations for wellness tourism in the country and offer a variety of options based on the occurrence of these natural resources. The Japanese way of using natural hot springs for *Onsen* tourism has found followers elsewhere in other countries such as New Zealand (Maruia Springs Thermal Resort, North Canterbury) and Australia (Peninsula Hot Springs, Melbourne). Within the country, *Onsen* can range from highly developed health and wellness resorts to modest rock pools in the wilderness with no facilities; however, it is a matter of personal preference which type of *Onsen* people choose to visit. Generally *Onsen* facilities offer a range of options to their visitors by using combinations of different *Onsen* settings and a variety of alternative treatments for health and wellness. A number of these are summarised in Table 15.1.

In the context of national culture the use of *Onsen* is an important part of Japanese life, and the close bond of the Japanese people with this national treasure has made them very critical when it comes to the quality of what is supposed to be a natural hot spring. Many such destinations promote particular types of hot spring water beneficial for specific health conditions, and the true connoisseur expects the genuine product and frowns upon artificially heated or recycled water, which requires the addition of chemicals to satisfy hygienic requirements. Even the addition of tap water for cooling purposes can result in the blacklisting for disreputable conduct of those facilities whose managers falsely advertise genuine hot spring water (Erfurt-Cooper and Cooper 2009). Cases of dishonest *Onsen* operators are rare, but when discovered they dominate the Japanese media for a considerable time, with public apologies one of the more minor sanctions applied in such cases. When it comes to health and wellness it is a matter of honour to cater for the expectations of the customer by supplying genuine hot spring water from a local source. Many *Onsen* have been owned and managed by the same family for centuries. This explains why the Japanese are particularly

Table 15.1 Wellness environments based on natural hot springs

Type of Onsen	Key characteristics	Purpose and advantage
Onsen Bathhouse (*Furo, Sento*)	• Traditional bathing environment for public use • Common throughout residential neighbourhoods with access to natural hot spring water • Can also be supplied with heated tap water in areas without access to natural hot springs • Still used widely, although most households have bathrooms	• Important element of Japanese bathing culture • Association with others (*tsukiai*) • Socialising, communicating with family, friends and neighbours • Hygiene, wellness
Private *Onsen*	• Residential connection to local hot spring water supply • Available in areas with clusters of hot spring sources • Pipelines provided by local municipalities as part of local infrastructure against a monthly user fee	• Ease of access • Relaxation on demand • Heat source in winter • Privacy • Wellness, health benefits
Onsen Theme Park (e.g. Spa Resort Hawaiians, Ooedo *Onsen* Monogatari, Nagashima Spaland, Spa World Osaka)	• Period scenery for authentic historic *Onsen* experience • Traditional style *Onsen* baths supplied with natural hot spring water • Variety of indoor and outdoor *Onsen* baths with different coloured hot spring water • Sports facilities • Restaurants and retail opportunities.	• Physical and mental relaxation • Enhanced health and energy (Ooedo Onsen Monogatari 2011) • Socialising with friends, family and colleagues • Corporate getaways • Wellness facilities
Aquatic Entertainment Centre (e.g. Suginoi Hotel, Beppu; Spa Hawaiians, Iwaki)	• Aquatic entertainment centres based on access to large volumes of natural hot spring water • Large hot spring-fed swimming pools • Spa baths/*Onsen* for all age groups • Combined with large hotel/resort complexes	• Fun activities for younger generations • Water sport • Socialising • Relaxation • Wellness facilities

Type	Features	Benefits
Kuahausu or Health Centre Special type of therapeutic resort (Clark, 1999)	• Aquatic entertainment centres based on the German 'Kurhaus' model • Offers activities to all age groups • *Onsen* complex which can include sports facilities • Variety of *Onsen* baths and saunas • Restaurants, shops, reading rooms, games rooms	• Socialising • Relaxation • Wellness, health improvement • Curative properties of hot spring water • Promotion of health
Onsen Resort, *Onsen* Ryokan, *Onsen* Hotel, *Onsen* Health Resort or Therapeutic Resort (*Tōjiba*)	• Traditional indoor and outdoor *Onsen* baths • Traditional resort setting • Themed spa baths • Restaurants, shops, cultural entertainment • Therapeutic resorts offer long-term spa therapy in combination with tourist facilities (Clark 1999)	• Healing and relaxation • Wellness, prevention of illness • Maintenance of good health • Company trips, corporate bonding • Fun attractions, entertainment
Onsen Hospital Rehabilitation Centre Medical *Onsen* (e.g. Beppu, Kyushu; Kusatsu, Honshu)	• Rehabilitation and convalescence based on natural therapy and CAM (complementary and alternative medicine) • Hot spring treatment for therapeutic use • Mineral mud baths • Steam pressure baths (Clark 1999)	• Rehabilitation after illness, accident, injury or surgery • Hot spring medical treatment (balneology, spa medicine) • Medicinal baths to treat health conditions
Outdoor *Onsen* or Rotenburo (e.g. Riverside *Onsen*, Lakeside *Onsen*, Cave *Onsen*)	• Natural settings are a preferred option • Outdoor *Onsen* are surrounded by nature • Tastefully designed and blended into the environment • Outdoor *Onsen* are often in addition to indoor facilities • They can be either public or private • Can be attached to hotel or ryokan (e.g. rooftop *Onsen* at Suginoi Hotel, Beppu)	• Important element of Japanese bathing culture • Relaxation, wellness • Be close to nature • Maintenance of good health • Association with family and friends
Sand Bath (*Onsen*)	• Unique setting using volcanic sand which is soaked with natural hot spring water and drained again before use (e.g. Kitahama Beach, Beppu)	• Relaxation, wellness • Treatment for some health conditions such as rheumatism or arthritis

sensitive about their hot springs and do not take kindly to the addition of chemicals, colouring agents, or recycled and artificially heated water, and expect absolute honesty when it comes to water quality (Erfurt-Cooper 2012).

Health benefits: spa medicine (balneology)

Hot spring use in Japan has a long tradition for improving health conditions. It is widely believed and expected that natural hot and mineral springs have curative value based on their mineral content. Medical procedures including *Onsen* therapy for rehabilitation are also an important component of the national health system in Japan and medical professionals continuously investigate the potential effects of spa medicine on a wide range of health conditions (Table 15.2).

The Japanese health-care system is said to be one of the best in the developed world and provides health care for every citizen, covering a comprehensive range of services (Castro 2009; Jeong and Hurst 2001), while being regulated by the government. Despite a revision of the Health Insurance Law in 1997, which resulted in cost-sharing by the insured as well as a charge for pharmaceutical items (Fukawa 2002), medical procedures with rehabilitation therapies based on natural hot and mineral springs have remained an important component of the national health-care system, mainly due to the widely held belief that the mineral content of hot springs has curative effects.

The position of spa medicine in Japan is strong because the use of natural hot spring water is recommended by doctors as beneficial for rehabilitation after illness or injury, and for the maintenance of good health as well as the prevention of illness (Agishi and Ohtsuka 1998). This view of the medical profession

Table 15.2 List of illnesses treated at hot spring hospitals in Japan

Health conditions treated at hot and mineral spring facilities

Aches and pains	Digestive disorders	Obesity
Allergies	Eye problems	Palsy, paralysis and
Anaemia	Fatigue	poliomyelitis recovery
Artherosclerosis	Female disorders	and rehabilitation
Arthritis	Gout	Relaxation and rejuvenation
Athlete's foot	Haemorrhoids	Respiratory system
Beautification	Heart problems	Rheumatism
Beriberi	Hypertension	Rest and recuperation
Blood circulation	Insect bites	Sciatica
Brain haemorrhage	Insomnia	Skin problems
Burns	Internal disorders	Sprains and breaks
Chilblains	Longevity	Joint problems
Common cold	Muscular problems	Stomach disorders
Detoxification	Nervous disorders, stress	Surface wounds
Diabetes	Neuralgia	Venereal diseases
		Whiplash

Source: compiled by author from Japanese literature.

partly dates back to the Meiji Restoration era (1868–1912), when hot spring spa medicine in Japan was widely promoted and further developed by the German Doctor Erwin Bälz, who arrived in Japan in 1878 and promoted *Onsen* bathing and its health benefits worldwide (Kusatsu Onsen Tourism Association 2013; Mönch 2005). During this period high-ranking Japanese politicians went on study tours to Europe and America to investigate modern forms of government, medical institutions and educational systems as well as military organisations (Kanamori 1998) while in return foreign lecturers, doctors and engineers were invited to work in Japan. Dr Bälz quickly came to appreciate the tradition of *Onsen* bathing and its health benefits. He was instrumental in the development of the *Onsen* town Kusatsu and spread the word of the Japanese hot springs' excellence for balneology worldwide (Kusatsu Onsen Tourism Association 2013; Mönch 2005).

Balneotherapy or *Onsen* therapy may be covered by health insurance if pre-scribed by a doctor, who verifies that the patient will benefit from this type of alternative treatment (Ito 2003). Subsequently, the position of health resorts and spas based on natural hot springs is supported by a wide range of stakeholders (Figure 15.1) with an interest to sustain and further develop *Onsen* tourism in Japan.

The health conditions listed in Table 15.2 can be treated by either immersing in natural hot spring water, inhaling the steam from hot springs or by drinking the mineral waters. Because of the different mineral and trace element composi-tions of hot springs some less common health conditions are treated in certain areas only, whereas others may be treated successfully at most locations. After the Second World War the country started to develop national hot spring hospi-tals to make the medical benefits of mineral-rich hot springs available to patients

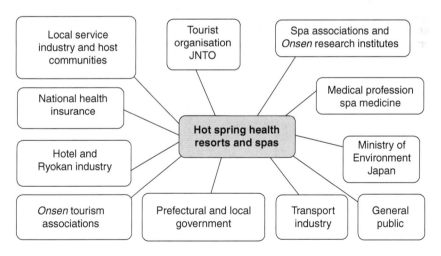

Figure 15.1 Stakeholders supporting the use of hot springs in Japan's health system.

Note: JNTO = Japan National Tourism Organization.

who were suffering not only from a number of illnesses, but also from external injuries, or for those who were in need of post-operative treatment and rehabilitation only. The Medical Treatment Centre for Atomic Bomb Victims in Beppu is one of the hot spring research institutes and a prime example of the coverage of all three types in one location.

National hot spring hospitals are now available in the majority of the 47 prefectures of Japan and their presence demonstrates how seriously *Onsen* medicine is taken in Japan. In addition to the large number of hot spring hospitals in Japan the government has established rehabilitation centres and research institutes throughout the country to advance knowledge about balneological treatments for medical purposes. These institutes are generally located in hot spring centres and carry out clinical trials using balneotherapy based on natural hot springs for external and internal use.

Protected by law – government policies and hot spring laws in Japan

The popularity of hot springs over the centuries has made them economically valuable and important tourist attractions. The Japanese government therefore decided that it had a paramount duty to protect natural hot springs by governing the use of subterranean water as part of water rights (Ramseyer 1989). National legislation regulates the use of natural hot springs, which have been protected for over 60 years by the Hot Spring Law of 1948. This law was revised in 1979 and further updated in 2005 and 2007 by the Japanese Ministry of the Environment (Ito 2003; Ministry of the Environment 2005, 2007). The recent amendments also recognise the problem that several facilities have interfered with the purity of hot spring water in order to enhance their business by adding chemicals or colouring agents, or simply just augmenting the hot water supply by heating it artificially (Ministry of the Environment 2005). This is a dilemma that perhaps goes back to the inadequate definitions of the original hot spring law, where the minimum temperature was set at 25°C (Otake 2004), but little was said about the admissible methods to ensure water quality or temperature. Under the Hot Spring Law as amended, the Japanese government recognises as *Onsen* only those hot springs that reach certain standards regarding temperature and mineral composition. On the basis of this law, the Minister of the Environment gives the designation of Hot Spring Health Resort to hot springs of good quality. As of March 2006, 91 such sites had been designated by the Ministry. Eventually, nine types of *Onsen* water were officially recognised in the revised 1997 Hot Spring Law as having proven medical benefits (Ito 2003).

Wellness environments: the sociocultural settings of Japanese hot spring destinations

As noted earlier, the use of Japan's volcanic hot springs has deep roots in cultural traditions, with *Onsen* bathing as one of the favourite pastimes for the majority of

Japanese people (Clark 1999; Hotta and Ishiguro 1986; Seki and Brooke 2005; Smith and Yamamoto 2001; Talmadge 2006). However, the common elements on which health tourism in Japan is based are not only the natural hot springs, but also include a generally well-established associated infrastructure and service industry, natural settings surrounding many of the *Onsen* facilities, the persistence of cultural and religious traditions, and the associated historical ambience of many such facilities. Many hot spring destinations are located within or nearby areas of outstanding natural beauty such as national parks, geoparks, quasi national parks and prefectural parks. One of the most enjoyable experiences in Japan and well catered for by *Onsen* operators is the combination of the changing colours of the natural surroundings throughout the four seasons with hot spring pools for relaxation either inside or outdoors (*rotenburo*).

Onsen *and the international tourist*

Onsen facilities, which are surrounded by lush forests and unspoilt views of rivers and valleys, are highly sought after and constitute an important foundation for destination development and management. In addition to the desire for health, wellness and recreation the combination of these elements has resulted in a large, but predominantly domestic (98 per cent) tourism industry (Beppu City Council, pers. comm. 2009). International visitors do not make hot spring visits their priority, unless they are from Korea, China or Taiwan, where a similar style of *Onsen* bathing is also part of their cultural heritage. Consequently, despite the important role that *Onsen*-based health resorts and spas in Japan play in the country's wellness tourism industry today, with more than 26,000 hot springs (26,796 officially registered in 2001) in over 5,500 hot spring areas (Erfurt-Cooper and Cooper 2009), virtually all of them attract domestic tourists.

Of course, the hot springs should be just as attractive to most foreign tourists as well as to the Japanese; so what is the reason for the low numbers of foreign visitors utilising the *Onsen*? While countries such as China and Korea have a common interest with the Japanese in hot spring bathing for health and wellness purposes, visitors from Europe or the United States are unfamiliar with the Japanese way of using hot springs. As touched upon earlier, the reasons for this have a lot to do with differing perceptions of appropriate bathing styles, where visitors do not normally bathe naked with strangers or perform a complicated cleansing ritual before stepping into the bath. Where private *Onsen* pools are made available (or family pools for one family) this cultural challenge problem can perhaps be overcome. However, at this point in time the difference between the marketing message from the Japan Tourism Agency and other promoters of the benefits of *Onsen* and wellness tourism for foreign visitors and the reality of the experience in a particular *Onsen* facility is affecting its take-up as a preferred form of tourism activity for many visitors. In fact the current promotional approaches that stress how important the bathing-related traditions of the use of this resource in Japan are as a subtext to the marketing imagery actually serve to blunt foreign visitor enthusiasm for *Onsen* bathing.

Case study one: Beppu City – Oita Prefecture

To further illustrate the patterns of domestic wellness tourism based on natural hot springs the next sections detail two popular, although contrasting, Japanese *Onsen* destinations. Beppu City (with a population of 125,664 as of January 2011), also known throughout Japan as the '*Onsen* Capital' and a national treasure, is located on the east coast of the southern island of Kyushu in the Oita Prefecture, and attracts an annual average of between 11 and 12 million tourists (Figure 15.2).

These are mainly domestic, with only around 200,000 being foreign visitors (249,000 in 2011), mostly of Korean and Chinese origin (Beppu City Council, pers. comm. 2012). That is approximately 2 per cent of the total number of visitors, which is a figure that is probably close to being the average for international tourists to hot spring destinations throughout Japan. The core attraction is the large number of volcanic hot springs (more than 2,600) in and around Beppu, which deliver a volume of hot spring water second only to Yellowstone National Park in the United States (Kudo 1996; Lund 2002), and the associated *jigoku* or hells.

Long-established bathhouses such as the Takegawara *Onsen* (Figure 15.3) offer traditional *Onsen* bathing and sand bathing with nostalgic ambience.

Facilities like this are a tourist attraction due to their time honoured Japanese architecture inside as well as outside. On the other end of the scale Beppu's mountainsides hide a number of rural *Onsen*, which attract many nature lovers who seek relaxation in a quiet setting (Figure 15.4). Natural hot springs like the Hebinyu *Onsen* in the forested hills of Beppu are only accessible via a narrow, rough, unpaved road which leads to the hot spring pools. Despite the remote location these hot springs are popular and they are frequented by people at all seasons.

A different, but nevertheless very popular attraction for wellness tourists are the sand baths (*Sunamushi buro*) at Kitahama Beach and Takegawara *Onsen* in Beppu. These are a unique form of *Onsen* where bathers wear a light cotton robe (*yukata*) and are covered by attendants in volcanic sand heated by hot spring

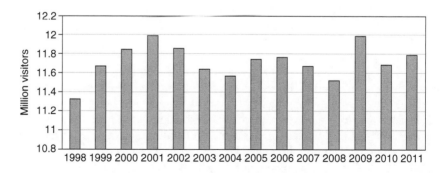

Figure 15.2 Annual visitor numbers to the '*Onsen* Capital' Beppu, Japan (source: compiled by author over several years from Beppu City Council data).

Figure 15.3 The *Takegawara Onsen* in Beppu (photo by author).

Figure 15.4 A natural hot spring in Kyushu, Japan (photo by author).

Note
This *Onsen* (*rotenburo*) is located in a rural setting with some facilities in the form of shelter, storage room, cleaning equipment and paved areas. The *Onsen* bathers in the picture were aware of being photographed and gave a friendly wave.

water and steam (Erfurt-Cooper 2012). The sand baths have been used by local residents for centuries and are a common and effective way to treat aches and pains while relaxing buried up to the neck in hot volcanic sand. Health and wellness benefits are sought especially by people suffering from rheumatic diseases, arthritis and gout.

The greater part of Beppu's geothermal resources however are utilised for *Onsen* facilities within the hotel industry and in precinct-based public baths. The Suginoi Hotel complex (Figure 15.5), for example, includes water slides, a Jacuzzi dream bath (*Ume-no Onsen*), flower bath (*Hana-no Onsen*), outdoor hot spring baths, a wave pool and a geothermally heated bowling alley (Kudo 1996). The abundance of hot spring water not only supplies the large variety of themed baths in the hotel and the aquatic entertainment centre, but also allows the Suginoi Hotel to operate their own geothermal power plant. This source of energy is sufficient to power the 2,100 guest-capacity hotel during normal periods of operation. Excess hot water from the Suginoi plant is also utilised for several public *Onsen* in Beppu (Kudo 1996).

Beppu's geothermal resources are largely located in eight distinctive *Onsen* districts or *Beppu Hatto* (Cooper and Erfurt 2009), but in addition there are many modern health and wellness resorts and spas, which also draw their supplies from the rich local geothermal resources (Japanese National Tourist Organization 2010a). Each of the eight main areas, though, previously flourished as an individual hot spring resort district, and some of them have a history going back to the beginning of the eighth century. During the Kamakura era (AD 1192–1333), sanatoria were built in the Kanawa area of the city to treat wounded soldiers from the battles against the Mongolians (Yoneie 2005) and from that time Beppu's healing hot springs have been referenced throughout history as a national resource. Various types of water with a diverse quality range can be experienced in the eight areas of Hamawaki, Beppu, Kankaiji, Kannawa,

Figure 15.5 The Suginoi Hotel complex in Beppu (photo by author).

Kamegawa, Myōban, Horita and Shibaseki, each in a different part of the city (Beppu City Oita 2010).

Although the main use of hot spring water in the city is for recreational bathing, medical treatments (balneology or spa medicine) are also available in Beppu. Virtually all of the main *Onsen* recognise the medical benefits of natural hot and mineral springs and focus on treatments for rheumatism and neuralgia, diabetes, female health disorders and various skin diseases (Erfurt-Cooper 2012; Hotta and Ishiguro 1986). It is likely that the potential for health (medical therapies) and wellness (relaxation) will be even more fully realised in the future as the city council has asked and encouraged *Onsen* owners and private hospitals to explore this avenue (Beppu International Tourist Office, pers. comm. 2007). The popularity of geothermal spas for both bathing and balneotherapy has made Beppu City one of the most established *Onsen*-based wellness destinations of Japan for domestic visitors (Cooper and Erfurt 2009; Erfurt-Cooper 2012).

Case study two: Spa Resort Hawaiians – Fukushima prefecture

The hot spring facilities at Spa Resort Hawaiians are in strong contrast to destinations such as Beppu. Spa Resort Hawaiians is a themed entertainment centre based on the rich geothermal resources of the Iwaki Yumoto hot spring area (regarded as one of the three most famous hot springs in Japan) in the Fukushima Prefecture, less than 200 kilometres north of Tokyo (Spa Resort Hawaiians 2011). The name indicates a theme revolving around Hawaiian and Polynesian culture, which has very little to do with hot springs or Japan, but more with daily Hawaiian dance performances in an artificially created tropical indoor water-based environment designed to attract visitors to a family-based recreation centre. In other words, Spa Resort Hawaiians caters for mass tourism at a single destination, in large percentage made up of young families, couples and groups of friends and colleagues, who do not mind noise and large crowds.

The history of the Spa Resort Hawaiians complex goes back to its opening in 1965 as the first resort facility and theme park in Japan, using the image of Hawaii as a dream island. By utilising the vast supply of local hot spring water, the former Joban coalmining area was able to create an undercover paradise of 'everlasting summer' as the promotional material states (Japanese National Tourist Organization 2010a). The all-weather dome of the water park has been a major feature of Spa Resort Hawaiians since its opening more than 45 years ago (Spa Resort Hawaiians 2011). The abundant geothermal resources allow for a large-scale tropical environment, including the cultivation of banana trees and orchids all year round. Visitor numbers during the first year reached nearly 1.2 million people (approximately 1 per cent of Japan's entire population). At this time the complex was still known as the Joban Hawaiian Center, which was only changed to the current name in 1998, at the same time when a new Spring Park was opened (Spa Resort Hawaiians 2011). Hotels were progressively built to provide accommodation for increasing visitor numbers, especially since a 27-hole golf course was added to the resort complex.

This *Onsen* theme park attracts visitors with tropical temperatures of constant 28°C combined with numerous entertaining water features. In 1998 large-scale open air baths, all fed by geothermal spring water, were built to offer more diverse attractions while at the same time the original theme-park facilities underwent renovation and modernisation to counteract the wear and tear imposed by millions of visitors. By 2002 the cumulative visitor numbers had reached 45 million people (Spa Resort Hawaiians 2011), an average of over 3,200 people per day (up to 10,000 on weekends). The natural hot springs not only supply the pools of the theme park with water, but also the guest rooms of the surrounding hotels. The combination of different themed environments (e.g. Spa Garden, Spring Park, Edo Period *rotenburo*) for all types of visitors and age groups include a number of restaurants and fast food outlets, retail opportunities, gaming areas and banquet halls. On the more serious wellness side beauty salons and wellness spas in the American tradition (Erfurt-Cooper and Cooper 2009) offer facials and massages along with aquatic exercise to enhance wellbeing and relieve stress through relaxation and exercise. The developers of the resort complex have taken care to draw large crowds and make the hot spring business economically viable in the long term by continually enhancing the facilities to cover every possible customer demand.

On-site hotels offer accommodation for all visitor budgets; however, the majority of *Onsen* tourists are day visitors who either live within travelling distance or stay in the surrounding towns such as Yumoto or Iwaki. At the time of visiting for research purposes in 2008–2009 and up until the Tōhoku earthquake in March 2011 the spa resort had an impressive internet presence including over 30 pages of information in English designed to promote the theme park to international visitors. These had numerous links to more in-depth information about the individually themed areas, opening times, entry requirements, online booking websites, voucher access websites and shopping related websites.

In summary, Spa Resort Hawaiians is a unique water-based theme park based on geothermal hot spring resources, which supply the water for all bathing pools, spa treatment facilities for health and wellness and create a tropical indoor environment all year round. Spa Resort Hawaiians is in direct contrast to the earlier example of Beppu City and illustrates the diversity of health, wellness and recreation based on hot springs in Japan. This theme park is evidently catering for demand based on a concept of deliberately including all popular aspects of hot spring bathing and wellness treatments in one complex, and became even more popular after featuring in the Japanese hit movie *Hula Girl* (2006). The Spa Resort Hawaiians attracts people looking for health and wellness benefits combined with large-scale aquatic entertainment (Japanese National Tourist Organization 2010b) and has done so successfully for nearly five decades.

Governance and marketing in the industry

Within the overarching framework of the Hot Springs Law from 1948 (as amended) the promotion of the hot springs resource for wellness tourism in

Japan is largely controlled by local tourism organisations and associations, which are in turn linked to the Japan Spa Association (Nihon Onsen Kyokai). These associations deal with all *Onsen*-related tourism issues including adherence to the requirements of legislation, service standards and community and private marketing strategies. A backup organisation, the Nippon Onsen Research Institute is a private company that provides research data to associations and private operators and also offers consultancy resources on the establishment and management of *Onsen* (Nippon Onsen Research Institute 2008). Thus, the promotional effort is very much local and domestic in scope, with the messages finetuned to the Japanese consumer and their well-known likes and dislikes.

All hot spring destinations provide promotional literature on their spring resources, associated services and the range of environments that they can offer to the visitor within which the hot springs experience may be gained. This is a very competitive domestic market in Japan, as might be expected, but in recent years the market has begun to see promotional literature increasingly being translated into several additional languages to cater for a slowly increasing number of foreign visitors. The number of *Onsen*-related internet sites now offering Chinese, Korean and English translations has also risen rapidly over recent years.

The main aim of this promotional effort is to promote the healing (wellness) effects of specific *Onsen* destinations (Tottori Sightseeing Association 2010; Erfurt-Cooper 2012) through the bathing experience and its associated food and drink experiences. Brochures and *Onsen* guides are used to promote individual health resorts and spa destinations and generally describe the most important aspects of the water source as understood by the Japanese client: (1) uncontaminated water; (2) the message that water is beneficial for health; (3) a favourable temperature range; and (4) the specific mineral content with its benefit of relieving physical ailments. Regional *Onsen* guides are designed like catalogues and feature every hot spring destination in a specific area of the country. Illustration of the facilities generally includes views of the indoor or outdoor baths or with people 'enjoying' their *Onsen* experience, photos of the types of accommodation and descriptions of how to access particular locations, and as a special attraction, illustrations of the regional cuisine to further entice visitors.

Frequently, illustrations of the bathing experience in *Onsen* baths also use the ambience of traditional buildings and the surrounding natural features to attract visitors. Some destinations use pictures with small groups of people enjoying an outdoor pool to demonstrate relaxation and contentment in a quiet natural atmosphere. In line with this general theme, steam emitting from a hot spring is also a very important feature in *Onsen* marketing and is used as a trademark or logo to represent natural hot water fresh from the spring.

Of course, these images are just as attractive to most foreign tourists. Therefore this facet of marketing and promotion is not the reason for the low numbers of such visitors utilising the *Onsen* that is a feature of the Japanese wellness industry. While countries such as China and Korea have a common interest with the Japanese in hot spring bathing for health and wellness purposes, visitors from Europe or the United States are unfamiliar with the Japanese way of using hot springs. Therefore the current marketing approaches that emphasise the importance of traditional *Onsen* use in Japan do not inspire foreign visitors to use *Onsen* facilities unless they are already familiar with the concept.

Conclusion

Wellness in Japan is recognised as the maintenance of good health and prevention of illness, with natural hot springs having been considered as a significant resource for both healing and recreation since ancient times. Traditional hot spring destinations enjoy an unabated popularity today due to the beneficial effects of the mineral-rich waters, which are widely accepted as an important health resource. The main expectations of the majority of the (domestic) clients though are relaxation and therapeutic benefits together with socialising in authentic hot springs, ease of access, reasonable pricing and the sampling of regional cuisine. As a result, value-adding attractions and activities are vital aspects for a hot spring resort or spa to consider when it is marketing to tourists. This has long been recognised by destination managers and independent *Onsen* operators, with nearly all regions of Japan offering broadly based wellness facilities with little resemblance to some of the traditional clinic-like spas of the West.

The majority of Japanese hot spring destinations are designed for the domestic tourism market (98 per cent), with many people travelling to *Onsen* resorts whenever they have the opportunity. Each year tour buses and other modes of transport carry approximately 150 million visitors to popular *Onsen* towns throughout the country, where the preferred accommodation is in the traditional style of Japanese inns (*ryokan*) with direct access to a natural hot spring. Most hot spring-based health and wellness resorts are well attended all year round by visitors of every age group, including children. Some health resorts are also combined with golf clubs, day spas and are used as venues for weddings and corporate events. Traditional Japanese garden settings and other cultural aspects of significance like temples and shrines are part of the special ambience of many hot spring resorts. The overall aim is to carry out this unique blend to perfection and draw visitors from a wide range of sociocultural backgrounds and, in recent years with the backing of the government, extend these benefits to international visitors and medical tourists.

References

Agishi, Y. and Ohtsuka, Y. (1998) 'Present features of balneotherapy in Japan', in *Global Environment Research*, 2: 177–185.

Altman, N. (2000) *Healing Springs: The Ultimate Guide to Taking the Waters – From Hidden Springs to the World's Greatest Spas*, Rochester, VT: Healing Arts Press.

Ashkenazi, M. (1993) *Matsuri: Festivals of a Japanese Town*, Honolulu, HI: University of Hawaii Press.

Beppu City Oita (2010) *Beppu Hatto Information*, online, available at: www.city.beppu.oita.jp/01onsen/english/01guide/guide.html (accessed 18 July 2013).

Castro, J.M. (2009) *Health Care in Japan*, online, available at: www.expatforum.com/articles/health/health-care-in-japan.html (accessed 29 September 2012).

Chartrungruang, B-on. and Mitsutake, M. (2007) 'A study on the promotion of tourism between Japan and Thailand: before-and after-travel images of Sapporo and its hot springs in the viewpoints of Thai tourists', *Sapporo Gakuin University Review of Economics and Business*, 23: 35–59.

Clark, S. (1999) *Japan, A View from the Bath*, Honolulu, HI: University of Hawaii Press.

Cooper, M. and Erfurt, P. (2009) 'Beppu reconstruction: a Japanese domestic hot spring destination in search of a 21st century global role', *Geographical Sciences*, 64: 127–39.

Cooper, M., Ogata, M. and Eades, J.S. (2008) 'Heritage tourism in Japan – a synthesis and comment', in B. Prideaux, D. Timothy and K. Chon (eds) *Culture and Heritage Tourism in the Asia Pacific*, Abingdon: Routledge.

Creighton, M.R. (1997) 'Consuming rural Japan: the marketing of tradition and nostalgia in the Japanese travel industry' *Ethnology*, 36: 239–254.

Erfurt-Cooper, P. (2012) 'An assessment of the role of natural hot and mineral springs in health, wellness and recreational tourism', unpublished thesis, James Cook University, Australia.

Erfurt-Cooper, P. and Cooper, M. (2009) *Health and Wellness Tourism: Spas and Hot Springs*, Bristol: Channel View Publications.

Fukawa, T. (2002) *Public Health Insurance in Japan*, Washington, DC: World Bank Institute.

Hall, C.M. (ed.) (2012) *Medical Tourism: The Ethics, Regulation, and Marketing of Health Mobility*, Abingdon: Routledge.

Hotta, A. and Ishiguro, Y. (1986) *A Guide to Japanese Hot Springs*, Tokyo: Kodansha International.

Ito, M. (2003) 'Getting into hot water for health', *The Japan Times*, 25 May 2003, online, available at: http://search.japantimes.co.jp/cgi-bin/fl20030525a3.html (accessed 30 September 2012).

Japan Health and Research Institute (2010) *Improve and Maintain Health with Onsen*, online, available at: www.jph-ri.or.jp/kenko_f/onsen_english/index.html (accessed 29 September 2012).

Japan National Tourism Organization (2010a) *The Largest Hot Water 'Gusher' in Japan: Various Strange Sites can be Viewed on a Tour of 'Hell'*, online, available at: www.jnto.go.jp/eng/location/regional/oita/beppu.html (accessed 3 September 2012).

Japan National Tourism Organization (2010b) *Iwaki Yumoto-Onsen Hot Spring*, online, available at: www.jnto.go.jp/eng/location/regional/fukushima/ iwakiiwakiyumoto.html (accessed 4 September 2012).

Jeong, H.-S. and Hurst, J. (2001) *An Assessment of the Performance of the Japanese Health Care System*, OECD Labour Market and Social Policy Occasional Papers 56, OECD, Directorate for Employment, Labour and Social Affairs.

Kanamori, S. (1998) 'German influences on Japanese pre-war constitution and civil code', *European Journal of Law and Economics*, 7: 93–5.

Kojima, J. and Kawamura, K. (2006) 'The delights of Japanese hot springs: 19 relaxing onsen retreats', *Kateigaho International Edition, Japan Arts and Culture Magazine*, 10: 135–51.

Koyabashi, M. (2004) 'Onsen in Tokyo: value-added relaxation for urbanites', *Japan Spotlight, Economy, Culture and History*, 3: 8–13.

Kudo, K. (1996) '3,000 kW Suginoi Hotel geothermal power plant', *Geo-heat Center Quarterly Bulletin*, 17: 7–8.

254   *P. Erfurt-Cooper*

Kusatsu Onsen Tourism Association (2013) 'Bathing facilities', online, available at: http://kusatsuonsen-international.jp/en/facilitie/ (accessed 18 July 2013).

Lund, J.W. (2002) 'Balneological use of geothermal waters', *GHC Bulletin*, Oregon: Geo-Heat Center.

Ministry of the Environment, Japan (2005) *Press Release: Ministerial Ordinance Partially Amending the Enforcement Regulation of the Hot Springs Law*, online, available at: www.env.go.jp/en/press/2005/0224a.html (accessed 7 September 2012).

Ministry of the Environment, Japan (2007) *Current Issues in Environmental Conservation and Formation of a Sound Material-Cycle Society, and Government Measures there on. 6. Conservation of the Natural Environment and Promoting Contact with Nature*, online, available at: www.env.go.jp/en/wpaper/2007/02.pdf (accessed 4 September 2012).

Mönch, M. (2005) *Freundschaftsreise des Verbandes der Deutsch-Japanischen Gesellschaften 20. März–03. April 2005*, online, available at: www.djg-saarbruecken.de/PDF-Dateien/Reisetext.pdf (accessed 10 September 2012).

Neff, R. (1995) *Japan's Hidden Hot Springs*, Tokyo: Tuttle Publishing.

Nippon *Onsen* Research Institute (2008) *Japanese Hot Springs Guide – Onsen in Japan*, online, available at: www.onsen-japan.info (accessed 18 July 2013).

Old Photos of Japan (2011) *Beppu 1926 – Hot Sand Bath*, online, available at: www.old-photosjapan.com/en/photos/227/hot-sand-bath (accessed 30 September 2012).

Ooedo Onsen Monogatari (2011) *Welcome to Ooedo-Onsen-Monogatari*, online, available at: www.ooedoonsen.jp/higaeri/english/index.html (accessed 30 September 2012).

Otake, T. (2004) '"Onsen": know what you are getting into. Most hot springs said to recycle water; some over-chlorinate, carry disease', *The Japan Times*, 14 August 2004, online, available at: http://search.japantimes.co.jp/cgi-bin/ nn20040814a5.html (accessed 7 September 2012).

Plutschow, H. (1996) *Matsuri: The Festivals of Japan*, Richmond: Japan Library.

Ramseyer, J.M. (1989) 'Water law in imperial Japan: public goods, private claims and legal convergence', *The Journal of Legal Studies*, 18: 51–77.

Ratz, T. (2011) 'SPA tourism in Japan and Hungary: a comparative analysis of perceptions and potential', *International Journal of Agricultural Travel and Tourism*, 2: 94–105.

Seki, A. and Brooke, E.H. (2005) *The Japanese Spa: A Guide to Japan's Finest Ryokan and Onsen*, Tokyo: Tuttle Publishing.

Smith, B. and Yamamoto, Y. (2001) *The Japanese Bath*, Salt Lake City, UT: Gibbs-Smith Publisher.

Spa Resort Hawaiians (2011) *Welcome to Spa Resort Hawaiians*, online, available at: www.hawaiians.co.jp/ (in Japanese only as at the date accessed: 18 July 2013).

Talmadge, E. (2006) *Getting Wet: Adventures in the Japanese Bath*, Tokyo: Kodansha International.

Tottori Sightseeing Association (2010) *Onsen Paradise*, online, available at: http://yokoso.pref.tottori.jp/dd.aspx?menuid=2864 (accessed 18 July 2013).

Trends in Japan (2005) *Healthy Holidays: Combining Leisure Travel with Medical Treatment*, online, available at: http://web-japan.org/trends/business/ bus050518.html (accessed 21 September 2012).

Yoneie, T. (2005) 'Rekishi to Basho: history and place', *Shigaku Kenkyu Kai*, 88.

16 Health tourism in the context of demographic and psychographic change

A German perspective

Christof Pforr and Cornelia Locher

Introduction

Since the 1990s Germany's health-care system has undergone dramatic changes as a response to spiralling health-care expenditure associated with significant demographic change, advancements in costly medical technologies and rising costs for health-care services. How immense the pressure is that has been building up on Germany's health-care system is well illustrated by the dramatic increase in public spending on health (Figure 16.1), which has risen from 9.6 per cent of GDP (approximately €159 billion) in 1992 to 11.6 per cent (€287 billion) in 2010. Calculated as total health expenditure *per capita*, this translates into a nearly twofold increase from €1,970 in 1992 to €3,510 (Statistisches Bundesamt 2012). These developments are, however, not a recent phenomenon but have been building up for the past decades. In fact, the percentage of GDP for total health expenditure has increased by 78 per cent over the past 40 years and is predicted to increase to about 15.5 per cent (€453 billion) by 2020 (Treugast 2010).

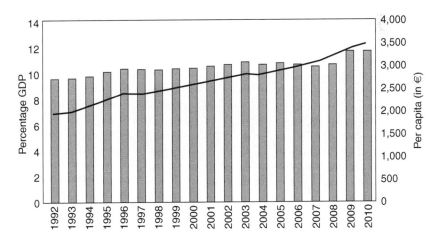

Figure 16.1 Annual health expenditure in Germany (1992–2010) (source: Statistisches Bundesamt 2012).

These challenges have prompted a number of reform measures, in particular of the health care system's financing and care structures. Promoted by health-care system reforms were, for example, the introduction and further expansion of economic and market-based elements, modernised and rationalised medical care alongside a liberalisation of many health-care services and the privatisation of treatments and services which traditionally had partially or fully been covered by the public health insurance system (Deutsche Bank 2012).

These changes have led to a significant increase in privately financed health expenditure and a growth in goods and services that are conducive to the preservation and restoration of health. Collectively, these expenses are referred to as Germany's Second Health Care Market. Over the past three decades growth in this sector has driven a paradigm shift from a cost factor health insurance system to a growth sector health economy (Klinkmann 2005). The privatisation of aspects of the health-care system was claimed to be not only a cost-cutting measure to alleviate the increasing financial strain on Germany's health-care system, but to promote greater personal responsibility for and ultimately commitment to health and well-being. It was argued that 'it would increase citizens' own sense of responsibility for their health, because greater participation in the costs would give them more incentive to lead a healthier life' (Gerlinger 2010: 119). Interestingly, although it is difficult to draw a direct correlation to health-care system reforms, greater health awareness across all age groups of German society alongside these developments has indeed been noted. This trend, which is commonly referred to as psychographic change, is particularly strong amongst the country's senior citizens, aged 65 years or older (Figure 16.2) (de Sombre 2008).

In this chapter the challenges of demographic change as an important driver for reforms in the German health-care system are first highlighted. The ensuing reform agenda, which ultimately transformed Germany's traditional public

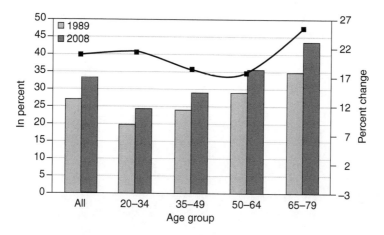

Figure 16.2 Health awareness amongst Germany's population (adapted from de Sombre 2008).

health insurance system into a competitive health economy, is reflected in the increase in privately financed health expenditure. In the context of this Second Health Care Market the chapter then focuses on health tourism, and here in particular on the wellness sector, which has experienced a boom in recent years, driven in the main by strong demand in the senior market segment.

Demographic change in Germany

On a global scale the world's population is predicted to continue to grow steadily from seven billion in 2011 to more than nine billion by mid-century. It is currently estimated that by 2100 more than ten billion people will live on this planet (United Nations 2011). Whilst this development is in the main concentrated on developing nations, which are predicted to see a population increase from currently about 5.7 billion to 8.8 billion in 2100, population numbers in highly developed countries are expected to decline (to 1.11 billion from 1.24 billion) although this trend might be cushioned by net migration from developing countries (United Nations 2011).

Some of these foreshadowed developments are already seen in Germany's population figures, which have been on a steady downward trend since the early 2000s. Over the next 50 years, it is forecast that the country's population will shrink by about 15 to 20 per cent from its current (2011) population of 81.8 million to between 65 and 70 million. Exact figures are hard to predict since they hinge on a number of factors, including actual birth rates, life expectancy and migration patterns. The complexity of demographic change is illustrated by the fact that actual birth rates per woman, for example, decreased from 2.6 births since the mid-1960s to plateau at 1.4 births over the past two decades, whilst at the same time a steady increase in life expectancy has been noted. The ageing of Germany's population has been evident for a number of decades and is predicted to continue well into the future. For 2010, for instance, 5 per cent of the country's population (4.3 million) were calculated to be in the 80+ age bracket, but this segment is projected to increase to 14 per cent (9.1 million) over the next 50 years (Statistisches Bundesamt 2009). Approximately one-third of the German population will then fall into the 65+ age segment and it is expected that there will be about twice as many 70-year-olds than the number children born in that year (Statistisches Bundesamt 2009). It is anticipated that the widening gap between birth and death numbers per year, predicted to be about half a million in 2060 (Statistisches Bundesamt 2009), will not be fully compensated by net migration to the country and that Germany's population will thus age and shrink quite dramatically in the years to come (Figure 16.3).

How significant these demographic developments are is aptly illustrated in an analysis of Germany's old-age dependency ratio, which expresses the number of people in the 65+ age bracket for every 100 persons aged 20 to 64 (i.e. working age). Whilst the number of those 20 years or younger, which have to be supported by Germany's working-age population, is predicted to remain relatively constant over the next 50 years, the old-age dependency ratio has climbed from

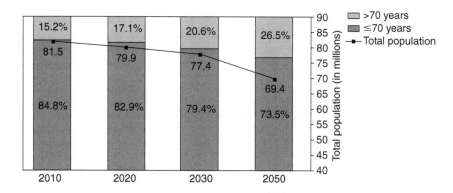

Figure 16.3 Germany's ageing population (2010–2050) (source: Statistisches Bundesamt 2009).

27 in 2000 to 34 in 2008 and is forecast to reach 67 in 2060 (Statistisches Bundesamt 2009). In other words, 100 Germans of working age will then need to support up to 67 people who are 65 years or older, plus 31 who have not yet reached the statistical working age of 20. A recent (2012) change to Germany's retirement age from 65 to 67 for men and women, which will be fully implemented in 2029, will obviously have some impact on these figures, but with a revised old-age dependency ratio of between 56 and 59, a significant burden on the country's working population can nonetheless be anticipated (Statistisches Bundesamt 2009).

Impacts of demographic change on Germany's health-care system

These demographic developments impact on all aspects of Germany's society and economy but resonate particularly strongly in the country's social insurance system. It is composed of schemes for health, retirement, accidents and unemployment which have been key constituents of the German welfare state since the late nineteenth century. For example, a characteristic feature of the public health insurance system, which covered in 2010 87 per cent of the population (70 million people) and 57.6 per cent of all health-related expenditure (Deutsche Bank 2012), is its financing by joint employer and employee contributions that are based on an employee's taxable income. Under this system, approximately 15 per cent of the employee's gross salary is jointly paid into the public health insurance system. Considering Germany's rather unique system of financing public health care, which is known as the Bismarck Model, it is obvious that a shrinking work force poses a significant threat to the financial viability of the country's traditional approach to health care. It is strongly dependant on high employment rates propelled by a booming economy and significantly impacted by broader socio-economic factors like an increasingly ageing society. In turn, it also has the potential to hinder Germany's international competitiveness by increasing labour costs (Gerlinger 2010; Pforr and Locher 2012).

However, the ageing German society challenges the system not only from a labour market perspective. Almost half of all health expenditure in Germany is linked to the 65+ age bracket (Nöthen 2011), thus to only about 20 per cent of the population (Statistisches Bundesamt 2009). Data from 2008 (Figure 16.4) illustrate that whilst the average per capita health expenditure for the age segment 30–44 was €1,700, it increased to €3,010 for those aged 45 to 64 and was nearly four times as high (€6,520) for those in the 65–84 years segment and more than eight times higher (€14,800) for seniors 85 years or older (Nöthen 2011). The annual health-related expenditure of the 85+ age segment has also risen significantly more (30 per cent) compared to those 65 years or younger (6 per cent) (Deutsche Bank 2012). These figures are not surprising, though, considering that the likelihood of suffering from cardiovascular disease, diabetes, cancer or dementia, for example, increases significantly with age.

A combination of advancements in medical technology and rising costs for health-care services coupled with the above outlined demographic developments undermine the traditional German health insurance system. In the light of these developments the need for reform of Germany's health-care system, its operations and funding, has been a focus of political and public debate.

In an attempt to create a fair but at the same time sustainable financing model, to contain spiralling costs but nonetheless maintain standards and quality, a string of reforms were introduced over the past three decades. Initially, the obvious need for change was addressed by rising premiums but it soon became clear that in the long term this measure was not sufficient to resolve the system's inherent problems. More radical change ultimately saw the German health-care

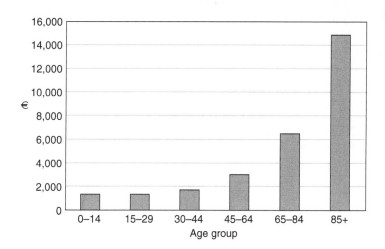

Figure 16.4 Annual health expenditure in Germany, by age (2008) (source: Statistisches Bundesamt, 2012).

system depart from being an important column of the German welfare state and develop into a significant and dynamic factor for new economic and social growth (Fretschner *et al.* 2002).

Although Germany is internationally probably best known for its automotive industry, it is the health sector that has developed over the past decades into the country's most important economic sector. Over the past two decades it has grown by more than 80 per cent, in the last ten years for example an average annual growth of 3 per cent was noted, which was significantly higher than that of the country's overall economy (1.9 per cent) (Deutsche Bank 2012). In 2009, the sector's total market volume amounted to €78.3 billion, on the back of a 5.2 per cent increase from the previous year (Dostal and Dostal 2011). The health sector also takes a significant share of the country's labour market (Hilbert and Kluska 2010). In 2010 it employed, for example, 4.83 million people (one out of nine employees). This equates to a 1.9 per cent increase over the previous year and a significant growth from the 4.1 million people employed in the sector in 2000. This trend is predicted to continue in the future with a 20 per cent employment forecast for the sector in 2030 (Statistisches Bundesamt 2012). When adopting a broader perspective by including data from outside the primary health-care sector (e.g. employment in wellness, fitness, health tourism), the figures are even more impressive with one out of seven employees (5.7 million) working in the broader health sector in 2009 (Bundesministerium für Gesundheit 2012; Deutsche Bank 2012).

These developments underline that whilst in past economic and labour market discourse Germany's health economy was considered mainly a burden on the country and its financing by joint employer and employee contributions seen as a significant impediment on the country's international competitiveness, these negative perceptions have started to change over the past two decades (Fretschner *et al.* 2002). As a labour-intensive sector, the health economy's positive contributions to Germany's employment figures and also its future growth potential are acknowledged in public debate and have helped to highlight the sector's increasing significance in the country's economic development (Fretschner *et al.* 2002; Henke *et al.* 2011).

Germany's Second Health Care Market

Interestingly, the fundamental reforms in Germany's health-care system that have placed much greater emphasis on higher individual co-contributions and preventive health measures have gone hand in hand with a stronger preparedness amongst Germany's population to take greater personal responsibility for their own health and wellbeing. Coupled with health-care system reform this psychographic change has seen good health and wellbeing develop into core values across all age groups (Forschungsgemeinschaft Urlaub und Reisen 2008; de Sombre 2008; Dörpinghaus 2009; Bundesministerium für Wirtschaft und Technology 2011). Whilst not comprehensive, a simple look at gym membership in Germany, which has grown annually by 8 per cent over the past six years (Deutsche Bank 2012), aptly illustrates this new health focus. It has helped to fuel a massive expansion of the country's Second Health Care Market. This sector of the country's health economy covers a very broad range of health-care products and services that are not subsidised or paid for by public or private health insurance, but fully funded by consumers. It consists of products and services that are conducive to the preservation or restoration of health (Henke *et al.* 2011). Whilst it is difficult to obtain accurate data due to difficulties in defining what goods and services should or should not be incorporated, it is nonetheless clear that the sheer size of this constantly expanding Second Health Care Market is a main contributor to the growth in Germany's health economy (Henke 2009). In 2008 it was worth approximately €64 billion, a more than 20 per cent increase over five years (Kartte and Neumann 2008). It has been estimated that on average Germans spend about €900 annually on health-related products and services in addition to their health insurance premiums. In 1998, for example, health expenditure amounted to 3.6 per cent of total household expenditure, in 2010 this figure had risen to 4.2 per cent (Deutsche Bank 2012). These numbers are predicted to grow even further in the years to come (Focus 2007). It therefore comes as no surprise that the Second Health Care Market in Germany is projected to grow by 6 per cent per annum over the next decade (Statistisches Bundesamt 2012). It is particularly this growth that has ensured that the German health economy, despite the various reform agendas over the past 30 years and their declared objective to cap or even cut costs and decrease health-related expenditure, remains a significant growth industry (Kliegel 2007).

Health tourism in Germany

As outlined above, two factors in particular have led to continued growth in Germany's Second Health Care Market; on the one hand an increased demand for health-related goods and services, which has been fuelled by broader shifts in health policy and the subsequent privatisation of many treatment and product costs, and on the other hand psychographic change towards health (RKW Kompetenzzentrum 2011). The latter refers to a growing health awareness, which is evident in all industrial societies and leads, for example, to more emphasis on prevention and health promotion, but also greater interest in complementary and alternative medicine and a broad range of wellness offerings. It is estimated, for example, that in 2007 the areas fitness and wellness alone injected about €17.3 billion into Germany's health economy (Henke 2009).

The desire for a healthy lifestyle has also created ample opportunities for new health services in a leisure setting as well as new products and services specifically geared towards the tourism market (Hall 2003; Bundesministerium für Wirtschaft und Technology 2011; Treugast 2010). This tourism segment contributed in 2007, for example, €3 billion to Germany's Second Health Care Market, up by 43 per cent from five years earlier (Henke 2009). On the back of these developments Germany's medical and wellness tourism industry has developed into an increasingly important player in the country's health economy.

In 2009, health was, for instance, an important aspect during their holidays for 36 per cent of the German population. This translated into four million health-related holiday trips in that year, a figure which is estimated to almost double by 2020 (Forschungsgemeinschaft Urlaub und Reisen 2010). Similarly, according to another study from 2010/2011 58 per cent of German travellers considered it as important or very important to look after their health during their holidays (Treugast 2010). This increasing importance of the aspect health for the travel sector is also reflected in a survey which found 19 per cent of the population considering taking a wellness holiday within the next three years and 9 per cent planning holidays with a particular focus on fitness (Forschungsgemeinschaft Urlaub und Reisen 2010). A recent study conducted by the German Wellness Association (Deutscher Wellness Verband) estimated the total expenditure for wellness offerings alone whilst holidaying to be about €2.5 billion annually and highlighted the enormous future growth potential for the wellness tourism sector (Treugast 2010). Similarly, the BAT Freizeitforschungsinstitut unveiled in 2010 that wellness holidays were very much sought after (35 per cent) second only to all-inclusive holiday packages which attracted the highest interest (37 per cent) (Treugast 2010). Focusing on the broader concept of health tourism in Germany, it was found that between 2002 and 2007 the interest in this market segment rose by 31 per cent with a further increase of 78 per cent being forecast until 2020 (Treugast 2010). Although estimates into the future need to be treated with caution, it is nonetheless obvious that the above data paint a rather positive outlook for Germany's health tourism market.

It needs to be acknowledged though that health is a very broad concept which means different things to different people. Whilst the above-cited figures are undoubtedly impressive, they cover a very wide field of health-motivated travel ranging from medical tourism undertaken by a sick person seeking a treatment or cure to activities with a more preventive or wellness dimension (Bundesministerium für Wirtschaft und Technology 2011). It is not possible in this chapter to discuss these different forms of health-motivated travel in detail, but Chapter 2 in this volume presents a very comprehensive discussion of the various nuances of health tourism. In brief, fuelled by a great range of different needs and expectations, health tourism serves as an umbrella concept integrating a broad range of different traditions. According to Rulle *et al.* (2010) these range from leisure activities that are geared towards mental and physical wellness and indulgence to preventive treatments and medical tourism for the purpose of essential or elective hospital treatments or surgery. Consequently, the health tourism market is commonly considered a continuum ranging from medical tourism to wellness tourism spanning across spa treatments, spiritual retreats, sport holidays and medical wellness. The latter is understood as a blend of medical aspects (e.g. prevention and health promotion, rehabilitation) with more passive wellness offerings (e.g. relaxation, lifestyle coaching). It entails a medically supervised program of health promotion as part of a wellness tourism experience (Dörpinghaus 2009). Within the very broad field of health tourism, medical wellness is generally seen as having the biggest growth potential in

Germany (Dörpinghaus 2009). For the next decade or so a 111 per cent growth in demand for this particular form of health tourism is predicted (Treugast 2010). This is not surprising considering the previously discussed developments in Germany's health-care system, in particular a greater focus on prevention and health promotion, liberalisation and modernisation of health-care services as well as more market-based elements which go hand in hand with a greater health awareness and also an increased preparedness to privately fund health-related activities, also when on holiday.

The blending of health with tourism is, however, not a new phenomenon but can, for instance in the context of coastal tourism, be linked back to the eighteenth century. As Wesley and Pforr (2009: 17) highlight, 'at first, the seaside attracted visitors for the perceived medicinal properties of sea water and sea air'. Lohmann (2010) goes even further in stating that health tourism constitutes the roots of modern tourism. Today, the sector's popularity is thus only a recurrent trend but, as outlined above, likely to experience continued growth well into the future.

The senior market

What is common to all these nuances of health tourism is that, in Germany, the importance assigned to the aspect health grows with the age of the traveller (RKW Kompetenzzentrum 2011). With this in mind it is no surprise that in 2008, for instance, the 60+ age bracket constituted 35 per cent of the wellness tourism market, a remarkable 75 per cent increase since 1999 (Figure 16.5) (Forschungsgemeinschaft Urlaub und Reisen 2008).

In 2010, 75 per cent of Germany's wellness tourists were 40 years or older and 62 per cent of those participating in health tourism activities were in the 60+ age segment (Lohmann 2010). Taking into account the earlier-discussed

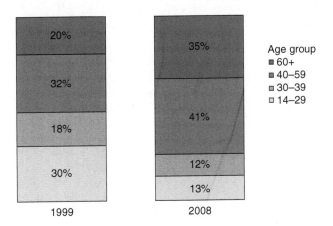

Figure 16.5 Germany's wellness tourists (1999–2008) (source: Forschungsgemeinschaft Urlaub und Reisen 2008).

demographic change and the significant shifts it creates in Germany's age pyramid, Opaschowski's (2007) assessment that health tourism will develop into a future 'mega market' does not seem to be too far-fetched.

Over the past three decades, not just in the health tourism segment, but overall Germany's seniors have been a main driver of tourism demand. A 29 per cent market share in 2007 illustrates this trend (Forschungsgemeinschaft Urlaub und Reisen 2008). A direct comparison of these seniors' travel propensity over the past four decades, which demonstrates for example an increase of 42 per cent for those in their sixties between 1990 and 2010 and a more than twofold increase for those in their seventies between 1970 and 1990, also highlights the remarkable role they play as drivers of tourism demand (Figure 16.6).

The senior market is, however, not a homogenous group but a diverse mix of people with rather different economic, social and health characteristics (Henke *et al.* 2011). This heterogeneity is also reflected in the wide range of age groups often covered by the term 'senior', ranging from 50+ to the 80+ age bracket. Most commonly, however, the term appears to be reserved for those 60 years or older (Petermann *et al.* 2006). Due to substantial gains in post-working life leisure time, coupled with more disposable income and higher levels of education as well as improved and prolonged levels of physical and mental mobility, long-term growth prospects in Germany's senior travellers market segment can be expected (Henke *et al.* 2011; Petermann *et al.* 2006). Already between 1993 and 2007 a 40 per cent increase in the number of tourists within this market segment and an even higher percentage increase in the number of holiday trips undertaken by this age group were noted. For 2020 it is predicted that these numbers are going to increase by a further 15 per cent and 18 per cent respectively (Grimm *et al.* 2009). Demographic change certainly contributes to these

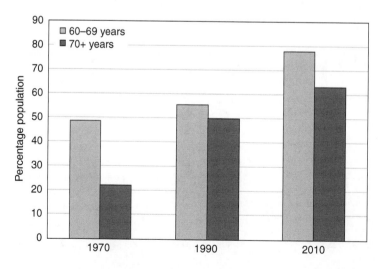

Figure 16.6 Travel propensity within Germany's senior market between 1970 and 2010 (source: Mundt 2013).

growth figures since statistically an increasing number of people join the 60+ age category every year. However, they also reflect continued tourism habits as these seniors have been enjoying travel and related leisure activities for many years (Grimm *et al.* 2009).

The implications of demographic change for tourism have been frequently highlighted in academic debate (e.g. Arnaschus 1996; Danielsson and Lohmann 2003; Dann 2001; Haehling von Lanzenauer and Klemm 2007; Hensel 1988; Javalgi *et al.* 1992; Lohmann and Danielsson 2001). It appears that high expectations of the quality of tourism products and services, price consciousness, experience and well-informed decisions characterise the senior tourism market (Grimm *et al.* 2009). This is certainly also true for the health tourism sector, where the demand for health- and wellness-related goods and services by the 60+ consumer generation is seen as an important driver for the sector's impressive growth over the past 20 to 30 years (Opaschowski 2007; Fontanari and Partale 2004). These seniors tend to value health and wellness particularly highly. Often referred to as 'Best Agers' they bring to their statistically increased life expectancy the desire to age well and, as much as possible, healthily.

Attracting a wide range of health-conscious consumers, medical wellness products and services, spas, health resorts and hotels with a range of fitness and sport offerings, beauty care services, relaxation and meditation activities, healthy lifestyle and weight-loss programs as well as other health- and wellness-related products will therefore constitute important columns of Germany's tourism sector in the years to come (Bundesministerium für Wirtschaft und Technology 2011).

Conclusion and future outlook

As outlined in this chapter, after decades of stringent reforms the German health sector is no longer necessarily perceived by many as a burden on the national economy but rather as an opportunity for future economic growth. The shift to a modern health economy is propelled by the country's growing Second Health Care Market complemented by greater health awareness across all sectors of society. These developments have led to growth opportunities for a range of health-related products and services including those in the tourism sector. The industry has benefited from a more holistic understanding of health with a shift in focus away from the treatment of a patient towards accommodating the health-related needs and expectations of a paying guest. These include, for instance, privately funded wellness and fitness offerings, spa treatments, healthy lifestyle programs and preventive health measures as part of a health tourism experience. One of the drivers of this extraordinary development is demographic change in the form of an increasingly ageing society. As was highlighted in the chapter, it Germany it is particularly the senior market that offers the greatest growth potentials for the health tourism sector. The needs and expectations of health tourists are, however, rather diverse and expressed in a range of different health-orientated tourism segments. These span from a strong emphasis on relaxation, wellness and pampering to curative or preventive medical services. At the same time excellent quality at a reasonable price is highly sought after so that in the future suppliers of health tourism-related products and services not only need to be able to respond to increasing demand for highly individualised and specialised packages. Rather, they will have to pay particular attention to the quality of their offerings to maintain a competitive edge in an expanding market. This could be done, for instance, with the introduction of particular quality labels, accreditation programs and associated quality control. In this context, and as discussed in more detail in Chapter 6 in this volume, a stronger local and regional collaboration amongst various health tourism providers will become a crucial prerequisite for the future development of health tourism destinations.

References

Arnaschus, A. (1996) 'Reiseverhalten von Senioren – heute und morgen. Die neuen Alten haben sich noch viel vorgenommen', *Fremdenverkehrswirtschaft International*, 20: 40–1.

Bundesministerium für Gesundheit (2012) *Gesundheitswirtschaft als Jobmotor*, Berlin: Bundesministerium für Gesundheit, online, available at: www.bmg.bund.de/ gesund-heitssystem/gesundheitswirtschaft/gesundheitswirtschaft-als-jobmotor.html (accessed 28 January 2013).

Bundesministerium für Wirtschaft und Technologie (BMWi) (2011) *Innovativer Gesund-heitstourismus in Deutschland*, Berlin: BMWi.

Danielsson, J. and Lohmann, M. (2003) *Urlaubsreisen der Senioren*, Kiel: Forschungsge-meinschaft Urlaub und Reisen.

Dann, G.M.S. (2001) 'Senior Tourism', *Annals of Tourism Research*, 28: 235–8.

de Sombre, S. (2008) *Der gesellschaftliche Wandel generiert neue Zielgruppen*, Allensbach: Institut für Demoskopie Allensbach, online, available at: www.ifd-allensbach.de/fileadmin/AWA/AWA_Praesentationen/2008/AWA2008_DeSombre_Zielgruppen.pdf (accessed 13 January 2012).

Deutsche Bank (2012) *Gesundheitswirtschaft: Weiteres Aufwärtspotenzial*, Frankfurt: Deutsche Bank Research.

Dörpinghaus, S. (2009) 'Medical Wellness: Zukunftsmarkt mit Hindernissen', *Forschung Aktuell*, 6, online, available at: www.econstor.eu/dspace/ bitstream/10419/57238/1/690101554.pdf (accessed 20 January 2013).

Dostal, A.W.T. and Dostal, G. (2011) *Potentiale im Zweiten Gesundheitsmarkt: Wellness, Gesundheitsvorsorge und Gesundheitsreisen*, Vilsbiburg: Dostal-Beratung.

Focus (2007) *Der Markt der Gesundheit*, München: Focus Magazin Verlag.

Fontanari, M. and Partale, A. (2004) 'Kurorte im gesundheitstouristischen Wettbewerb', in A. Brittner-Widmann, H.-D. Quack and H. Wachowiak (eds) *Von Erholungsräumen zu Tourismusdestinationen: Facetten der Fremdenverkehrsgeographie*, Trier: Geogra-phische Gesellschaft Trier.

Forschungsgemeinschaft Urlaub und Reisen (2008) *Reiseanalyse 2008*, Kiel: FUR.

Forschungsgemeinschaft Urlaub und Reisen (2010) *Reiseanalyse 2010*, Kiel: FUR.

Fretschner, R., Grönemeyer, D. and Hilbert, J. (2002) 'Die Gesundheitswirtschaft: ein Perspektivenwechsel in Theorie und Empirie', in Institut Arbeit und Technik (ed.) *Jahrbuch 2001/2002*, Gelsenkirchen: Institut Arbeit und Technik.

Gerlinger, T. (2010) 'Health care reform in Germany', *German Policy Studies*, 6: 107–42.

Grimm, B., Lohmann, M., Heinsohn, K., Richter, C. and Metzler, D. (2009) *Auswirkungen des demographischen Wandels auf den Tourismus und Schlussfolgerungen für die Tourismuspolitik*, Berlin: Bundesministerium für Wirtschaft und Technologie.

Haehling von Lanzenauer, C. and Klemm, K. (eds) (2007) *Demographischer Wandel und Tourismus*, Berlin: Erich Schmidt Verlag.

Hall, C.M. (2003) 'Spa and health tourism', in S. Hudson (ed.) *Sport and Adventure Tourism*, New York: Haworth Hospitality Press.

Henke, K.-D. (2009) 'Der zweite Gesundheitsmarkt', *Public Health Forum*, 17, online, available at: http://dx.doi.org/10.1016/j.phf.2009.06.009 (accessed 8 March 2013).

Henke, K.-D., Troppens, S., Braeseke, G., Dreher, B. and Merda, M. (2011) *Innovationsimpulse der Gesundheitswirtschaft: Auswirkungen auf Krankheitskosten, Wettbewerbsfähigkeit und Beschäftigung*, Berlin: Bundesministerium für Wirtschaft und Technologie.

Hensel, R. (1988) 'Der Markt der Alten', *Marketing Journal*, 21: 614–26.

Hilbert, J. and Kluska, D. (2010) 'Boombranche Gesundheitswirtschaft: "frische Rückenwinde" für die Zukunft der Sozialen Arbeit', *Diakonieunternehmen*, 7: 21–4.

Javalgi, R.G., Thomas, E.G. and Rao, S.R. (1992) 'Consumer behavior in the U.S. travel marketplace: an analysis of senior and nonsenior travelers', *Journal of Travel Research*, 31: 14–19.

Kartte, J. and Neumann, K. (2008) *Der Gesundheitsmarkt*, Berlin: Roland Berger Strategy Consultants.

Kliegel, I. (2007) 'Der Markt der Gesundheit. Daten, Fakten, Trends', *Focus Markt Analysen*, 12: 1–43.

Klinkmann, H. (2005) *'Mecklenburg-Vorpommern auf dem Weg zum Gesundheitsland Nr.1: Perspektiven und Probleme'*, paper presented at the 1st National Conference for the Health Economy Sector, Rostock-Hohe Düne.

Lohmann, M. (2010) 'Nachfragepotenziale im Gesundheitstourismus – Chancen und Herausforderungen im Quellmarkt Deutschland', *ÖGAF/ITF – Expertengespräch*, Vienna, 25 November.

Lohmann, M. and Danielsson, J. (2001) 'Predicting travel patterns of senior citizens: how the past may provide a key to the future', *Journal of Vacation Marketing*, 7: 357–66.

Mundt, J.W. (2013) *Tourismus*, München: Oldenbourg Verlag.

Nöthen, M. (2011) *Hohe Kosten im Gesundheitswesens: Eine Frage des Alters?*, Wiesbaden: Statistisches Bundesamt, online, available at: www.destatis.de/ DE/Publikationen/WirtschaftStatistik/Gesundheitswesen/FrageAlter.pdf?__blob=publicationFile (accessed 20 January 2013).

Opaschowski, H.W. (2007) *23. Deutsche Tourismusanalyse TA 2007*, Hamburg: BAT Freizeitforschungsinstitut.

Petermann, T., Revermann, C. and Scherz, C. (2006) *Zukunftstrends im Tourismus*, Berlin: Edition Sigma.

Pforr, C. and Locher. C. (2012) 'Impacts of health policy on medical tourism in Germany', in C.M. Hall (ed.) *Medical Tourism: The Ethics, Regulation, and Marketing of Health Mobility*, Abingdon: Routledge.

RKW Kompetenzzentrum (2011) *Tourismus 50plus: Anforderungen erkennen – Wünsche erfüllen*, Eschborn: RKW Kompetenzzentrum, online, available at: www.rkw-kompetenzzentrum.de/fileadmin/media/Dokumente/Publikationen/ 2011_WifA_Tourismus.pdf (accessed 3 January 2013).

Rulle, M., Hoffmann, W. and Kraft, K. (2010) *Erfolgsstrategien im Gesundheitstouris- mus*, Berlin: Erich Schmidt Verlag.

Statistisches Bundesamt (2009) *Bevölkerung Deutschlands bis 2060. 12. Koordinierte Bevölkerungsvorausberechnung*, Wiesbaden: Statistisches Bundesamt, online, avail- able at: https://www.destatis.de/bevoelkerungspyramide (accessed 26 January 2013).

Statistisches Bundesamt (2012) *Gesundheitsberichterstattung des Bundes*, online, avail- able at: www.gbe-bund.de/gbe10/pkg_isgbe5.prc_isgbe (accessed 4 January 2013).

Treugast (2010) *Gesundheitsmarkt Deutschland*, München: Treugast, online, available at: www.treugast.com/fileadmin/user_upload/PDF/Newsletter/09_10/20100920_   News- letter_Branchenticker_Gesundheit.pdf (accessed 22 September 2010).

United Nations (2011) *World Population Prospects: The 2010 Revision. Volume I: Com- prehensive Tables*, New York: UN, online, available at: http://esa.un.org/ unpd/wpp/ Documentation/pdf/WPP2010_Volume-I_Comprehensive-Tables.pdf   (accessed   20 January 2013).

Wesley, A. and Pforr, C. (2009) 'Historical dimensions of coastal tourism', in R. Dowling and C. Pforr (eds) *Coastal Tourism Development*, New York: Cognizant Communica- tion Corporation.

17 Australia's approach to health care and its implications for health tourism

Cornelia Locher, Christof Pforr and Cornelia Voigt

Introduction

Across all Western industrialised nations health care is nowadays established as a social right (Willis 2009), although the way it is organised and financed differs significantly from country to country. As Jakubowski (1998: 5) highlights, 'health care systems stem from specific political, historical, cultural and socio-economic traditions. As a result, the organisational arrangements for health care differ considerably (...) – as does the allocation of capital and human resources'. Hybrid models seem to increase in popularity (Rothgang 2009), but in principle three fundamentally different approaches can be noted (Wehkamp 2006; Jakubowski 1998). On the one hand there is a strongly market-driven system, which is shaped by demand and supply, where the level of medical care that can be accessed is dictated by individual financial means. Until recently, with the introduction of the Affordable Care Act (2010), the USA had been a prime example for such a market-based health care model. However, health care can also be organised as policy field which is fully financed through taxes. This system, which is known as the Beveridge Model, can be assumed to deliver more equitable health care compared to the market-driven approach, nonetheless it is not without significant shortcomings. In this system health is in competition to every other policy domain and hence the level of financial support it receives is a matter of negotiation and political priorities. Countries which have adopted this approach to varying degrees, like the United Kingdom, Denmark, Sweden, Italy, Greece and Spain, have just one national health insurance fund. Whilst access to this system does normally not incur any cost for the patient, the down side of the single national health service is that it needs to deal with an enormous demand, which translates into excessive waiting lists for some health services and also a substantial amount of bureaucracy. The United Kingdom, for instance, where the Beveridge system is implemented in its purest form, has for many years been plagued by one of the longest waiting lists in Europe for certain medical procedures (Siciliani *et al.* 2013). Consequently, this has fuelled the private health insurance market and also the phenomenon of medical tourism for those who are willing to and can afford to take up this option (Wehkamp 2006; Jakubowski 1998). In Germany and France, for example, yet another approach has been adopted, which is commonly referred to as the Bismarck Model. Here, health care is financed jointly by employers and employees as a percentage of taxable income. Whilst this approach liberates health care from competition with other tax-funded policy domains and provides equitable access to a high level of health care, critics of the system lament the impact this approach has on labour costs and ultimately international competitiveness. They also point to the lack of incentive for cost containment, which might contribute to the Bismarck Model being arguably the most expensive of the various approaches to health care (Wehkamp 2006).

This chapter explores if the specific health-care system adopted in Australia has had an influence on recent trends in health tourism in the country. It first describes Australia's approach to health care and discusses pressure points, and here in particular demographic developments, that have influenced Australia's health-care policy in past decades. Against this backdrop Australia's health tourism industry is then examined from a medical tourism and also a wellness tourism perspective and it is discussed to what degree health-care policy has shaped the development of these sectors.

The Australian health-care system

In Australia a mixed approach to health care, based on a combination of private and public elements, has developed over time. Its public component is aligned with the Beveridge Model and thus features the adoption of a single national health insurance fund known as Medicare which is open to all Australian citizens and permanent residents (Smith *et al.* 2012). Medicare funding is mainly drawn from taxes, an additional payment based on progressive taxation, the so-called Medicare Levy, covers approximately 16 per cent of publicly funded health care costs (Willis 2009). The raised Medicare funds are used to run public hospitals and to reimburse medical practitioners. For the public this translates into free access to public-hospital care and cover of the scheduled fee for consultations by a medical practitioner. Australians also have access to subsidised prescription medicines under the Pharmaceutical Benefits Scheme, which is funded by the federal government and leaves consumers with only a small co-contribution of approximately 17 per cent (Healy *et al.* 2006; Australian Bureau of Statistics 2012). According to the Australian Bureau of Statistics (2012), Medicare expenses in 2010/2011 amounted to AU$16.4 billion for, on average, just over 14 paid services (AU$723) per person annually. After the introduction of Medicare in 1984 as the country's public health insurance, many Australians dropped out of private health insurance schemes leaving only about a third of the population with private health care at the end of the twentieth century. Depending on the chosen individual package, this private system covers, for example, access to private hospitals, which often have considerably shorter waiting lists for elective surgery compared to the public system, permits free doctor choice, provides ambulance cover and payment of some allied health services as well as cover of certain co-payments arising from the public system (Australian Bureau of Statistics 2012).

Obviously, the drop in the number of privately insured Australians towards the end of the 1990s was of increasing political concern as it caused additional strain on the public system. In 1999, under the Howard Liberal–National Coalition government (1996–2007), Australians were enticed into private health insurance schemes with the offer of a government-funded 30 per cent rebate on their insurance premiums as well as an increase of the Medicare Levy from 1.5 per cent to 2.5 per cent for individuals and families without private health insurance (Willis 2009; Healy *et al.* 2006). Since July 2012 this private health insurance rebate has been income tested with reimbursement figures ranging from 40 to 0 per cent depending on age and income. As a result of these measures, the number of privately health insured Australians increased again within a year from 31 per cent (1999) to 43 per cent (2000) and currently sits on 45 per cent, which translates into 10.3 million Australians with private health insurance (Australian Bureau of Statistics 2012).

A health-care system under pressure

Australia's health-care system faces many pressures that are similar to those experienced by other developed nations. These include a growing demand fuelled by expectations of a health system of the highest standards; advancements in medical technology, in particular costly high-tech medicine; and an ageing population (Australian Bureau of Statistics 2011a; Healy *et al.* 2006; National Health and Hospitals Reform Commission 2009). Consequently Medicare expenditure has risen significantly over the past years (Figure 17.1).

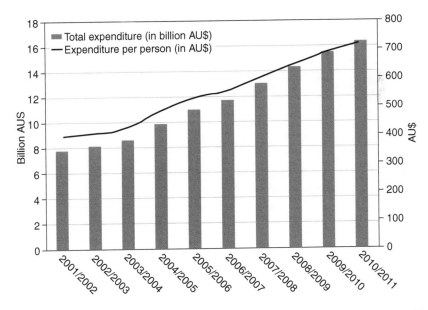

Figure 17.1 Annual Medicare expenditure in Australia (source: Australian Bureau of Statistics 2012).

Similarly, total public health expenditure in absolute figures and also expressed as percentage of GDP has also been in a steady upward trend (Figure 17.2). This trend can be expected to continue into the future with a predicted increase of public health expenditure to 12.4 per cent of GDP over the next two decades (National Health and Hospitals Reform Commission 2009).

Alongside these developments private expenditure for health care has risen, for example for medication not covered by the Pharmaceutical Benefit Scheme, for allied health professional services, for dental care and co-payments. Whilst in 1995/1996 out-of-pocket health expenditure covered 16 per cent of all health expenditure, in 2003/2004 this figure had risen to 20.3 per cent (Healy *et al.* 2006). According to the Australian Bureau of Statistics (2012), in 2009/2010 on average approximately 5 per cent of household expenditure for goods and services were related to health and medical care, up from 3.9 per cent in the mid-1980s (Australian Bureau of Statistics 2008). It is predicted that this trend of increasing private health expenditure will continue into the future, as will public spending on health (Healy *et al.* 2006).

Next to a general growth in income and national wealth, increasing health expenditure will be driven strongly by Australia's ageing population and also the absolute increase in its population numbers (National Health and Hospitals Reform Commission 2009). This trend is of such concern that 'many consider current spending growth unsustainable' (National Health and Hospitals Reform Commission 2009: 59). These developments are, however, not unique to Australia. A steady increase of health expenditure measured as a percentage of GDP

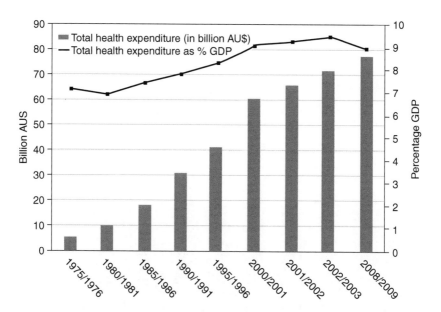

Figure 17.2 Public health expenditure in Australia (source: Healy *et al.* 2006; Australian Bureau of Statistics 2011b).

has been noted across all Organisation for Economic Co-operation and Develop-ment (OECD) countries over the past four decades (National Health and Hospi-tals Reform Commission 2009; Jakubowski 1998; Rothgang 2009), a trend that has also been discussed in Chapter 16 using Germany as a case example.

Pressure point demographic developments

An increasingly ageing society that has been highlighted as a main factor for the growing pressure on Germany's health care system (see Chapter 16 in this volume), also plays an important role in the Australian context. It is, for example, predicted that in 35 years' time the number of Australians 85 years or older (1.7 million), which constitutes at present the fastest growing age group, will be about five times as high as in 2007 (Australian Bureau of Statistics 2009a). Similarly, the proportion of the country's seniors (65+) has tripled during the twentieth century from 4 per cent to 12 per cent and is forecast to rise to approximately 30 per cent over the next century (Healy *et al.* 2006).

As has been discussed in Chapter 16, the social and economic impacts of an ageing population can be foreshadowed using the old-age dependency ratio, which expresses the number of people 65 years or older that have to be sup-ported by 100 people of working age. Statistically, in 2007 five people of working age (15–64 years old) supported one senior Australian (65+), which translates into an old-age dependency ratio of 20, whereas by mid-century this figure is expected to increase to more than 33 (National Health and Hospitals Reform Commission 2009). As the Australian Bureau of Statistics (2009a) emphasises, 'these [demographic] changes are important factors weighing on the future provision of income support, health and aged-care services as well as having implications for economic growth'. However, it also needs to be high-lighted that the trend towards an ageing society is not as pronounced in Australia as it is in some other developed countries. In Germany, for example, the old-age dependency ratio is predicted to increase from 34 (in 2008) to between 56 and 67 by 2060 (see Chapter 16).

An overall ageing society has two major drivers – on the one hand increasing longevity and on the other a decline in birth rates. Both trends can be observed, albeit to varying degrees, in Australia. Life expectancy at birth, for example, has increased significantly over the past century from 47.2 to 79.3 years for boys and from 50.8 to 83.9 years for girls (2009) and with this is ranked amongst the highest in the world. Unfortunately, however, there are significant differences within the Australian population with Aboriginal and Torres Strait Islander life expectancy trailing behind the rest of the population by nearly 20 years (Austral-ian Bureau of Statistics 2011a). Commonly referred to as 'closing the gap', addressing this inequality is one of the declared major aims of health policy in Australia (National Health and Hospitals Reform Commission 2009).

Similar to other OECD countries, birth rates in Australia have been on a steep downward trend in the latter half of the last century. In the mid-1970s the coun-try's total fertility rate eventually fell below the replacement level of 2.1 babies per woman. Since then birth rates have somewhat recovered and are currently on a slight upward trend with an average of 1.88 babies per woman registered for 2011, a figure which is nonetheless below replacement level (Australian Bureau of Statistics 2011d, 2007).

Combined, the two trends of significantly increased life expectancy and birth rates below recovery level, should lead to a rapidly ageing and shrinking society. However, in Australia these effects are cushioned by net overseas migration. Immigration to Australia has been estimated to have driven nearly two-thirds of its population growth over the past decade. This is a development which sets Australia apart from most other OECD countries. With recent annual growth rates of between 1.5 and 2 per cent, Australia's population is projected to increase from 22.3 million to up to 40 million over the next 40 years (Australian Bureau of Statistics 2010, 2012). As Australia turned into one of the most ethnically diverse countries in the world, multiculturalism and equality have become increasingly relevant issues in the delivery of health care. Unfortunately, not only Indigenous Australians are disadvantaged, there also tends to be a disparity in access to health care between the Australian-born non-indigenous population and migrants, especially those with limited English language skills (Bottomley and de Lepervanche 1990; Murray and Skull 2005).

Health-care system expenditure and reform in Australia

As briefly outlined earlier, the above-discussed demographic developments impact strongly on Australia's health-care system. Similar to what has been experienced in many other OECD countries, it has been under increasing pressure over the past decades, which is evident in growing government expenditure on health (see Figure 17.2) and a significant rise in private out-of-pocket health expenditure.

A large number of health-care system reforms over the past three decades have tried to address rising health-care costs, inequalities and deficiencies in effectiveness and focused on evidence-based practice, quality control and prevention. Overall, since the introduction of Medicare as a major reform initiative in 1984, the ensuing reforms have, however, been mainly incremental. With a combination of incentive and penalty measures, the public was, for example, enticed into taking up private health cover in 1999 to alleviate pressure building up on public hospitals. A range of health services has since been offered by the private sector. In 1998/1999 the average weekly household expenditure for medical care and health expenses was AU$32.74. This private weekly health expenditure had nearly doubled a decade later (2009/2010) to AU$65.60 per household and was mainly spent on accident and health insurance premiums, and health practitioner fees not covered by Medicare, as well as medicines, pharmaceutical products and therapeutic appliances (Australian Bureau of Statistics 2011c, 2000). This increase was, however, not a new phenomenon but a continuation of a trend which had already been noted since the mid-1980s (Figure 17.3).

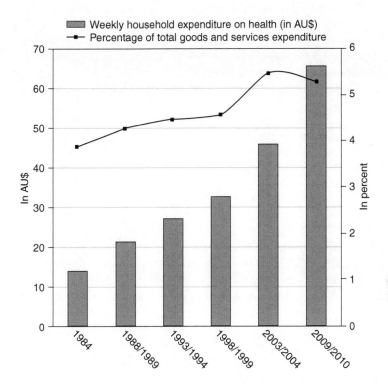

Figure 17.3 Increasing private health expenditure in Australia (source: Australian Bureau of Statistics 2006, 2011c).

As is the case in many other Western countries, in Australia the use of complementary and alternative medicine (CAM) therapies has strongly increased over the past years (Xue *et al.* 2007). Since there is no general agreement on what constitutes a CAM therapy, representative surveys including narrower and broader ranges of CAM modalities revealed that between 52 and 69 per cent of Australians are using CAM (MacLennan *et al.* 2002; Xue *et al.* 2007). Like in many developed countries, CAM is excluded from government support, however Australian private health insurers have increasingly started to subsidise CAM therapies. It is estimated that AU$4.13 billion are spent on CAM annually and that the estimated yearly number of visits to CAM health professionals (69.2 million) is almost as high as the number of visits to subsidised medical practitioners (69.3 million) (Xue *et al.* 2007).

Impacts on health tourism

As outlined in the previous sections, over the past decades Australia's healthcare system has been faced with similar challenges and developments as they have been experienced by other developed nations. In particular, demographic change and with it an increasingly ageing society have been identified as significant pressure points that have and will continue to impact on the country's health-care system and also translate into increased private health expenditure. In the German context, these developments have, as discussed in Chapter 16, led to strong growth in health tourism, in particular (medical) wellness tourism. In the light of similar prerequisites it is therefore interesting to see if the same trend can be noted in Australia although its approach to health care (i.e. Beveridge system) is fundamentally different.

Adopting the conceptual approach to health tourism as outlined in detail in Chapter 2 in this volume, in the following recent developments in Australia's health tourism sector will be discussed using a medical tourism and also a wellness tourism lens.

Medical tourism in Australia

With a predicted annual growth of about 35 per cent, medical tourism has been on the increase globally (Deloitte Access Economics 2011; Pogson 2011) as it is claimed to provide a number of benefits on an individual but also economically on a national level. Some even argue that health care is no different from other tradable goods and services and that medical tourism should thus be encouraged (e.g. Mattoo and Rathindran 2006). This view is, however, not without its critiques who cite issues like the responsibility for continuity of care and the social and financial burden as well as the legal complications of failed procedures overseas (Cheung and Wilson 2007; Pogson 2011).

Although accurate data are very hard to get by, in Australia, medical tourism appears to be a very small but nonetheless growing tourism niche market. It has a very strong outbound focus, in particular to Thailand, India, the Philippines, South Korea and Singapore for medical and surgical procedures (Pogson 2011). Whilst in the past medical tourism was often focused on aesthetic procedures, the spectrum of offerings has widened significantly in the past years to included advanced and specialised treatments with procedures ranging from orthopaedic and cardiac surgery over dental procedures to stem cell and IVF treatments (Marius 2011; Pogson 2011). A whole industry, including specialist medical tourist agencies that take care of travel arrangements, hospital liaison, pre-departure medical assessments and visa requirements, now deals with this global phenomenon of blending travel and health. It is reported that the Thai Bumrungrad International Hospital alone listed nearly 10,000 non-expatriate Australians as clients in 2010 (Pogson 2011). It can be assumed that the majority of these would have travelled specifically to this destination to receive what is sometimes referred to as 'sea, sun, sand and surgery' holidays (Connell 2006).

What are the reasons for this increase in demand for outbound medical tourism in Australia? It appears that two issues in particular drive Australians abroad for medical treatment, namely long waiting lists in the country's public hospitals and significantly lower costs (Cheung and Wilson 2007). For a total joint replacement it was found, for example, that actual waiting times on surgery lists of public hospitals, without even accounting for preceding assessment and consultation times, often exceeded what patients consider a maximum acceptable waiting period (Cheung and Wilson 2007). A comprehensive analysis of waiting times in Australian hospitals found that 'waiting times for elective surgery in public hospitals can be very long for some procedures. (...) Procedure that are assigned lower urgency tend to involve longer waits. Knee and hip replacement have the longest waiting times, followed by cataract extraction' (Johar *et al.* 2013: 79). Waiting lists have also not changed significantly over the past decade despite a number of costly initiatives (Johar *et al.* 2013).

Similarly, in popular private hospitals in India and Thailand costs of surgical and medical procedures by mostly Western-trained and English-speaking specialists are, for example, about one-tenth to one-third of the price incurred in most OECD countries (Marius 2011). Illustrating this with specific figures, a hip replacement in Australia for instance, will incur costs of approximately AU$23,000 whereas the same procedure when carried out in Thailand will cost half and in India less than a third (Pogson 2011). In some cases, luxurious features like high-quality accommodation and supplementary packaged holiday products and services are an added bonus (Marius 2011).

The above factors also help explain why inbound medical tourism in Australia, albeit annual growth rates of 14 per cent since 2005 (Deloitte Access Economics 2011), is insignificant although Australia's health-care system enjoys the reputation of being of a very high standard. In 2010 the market accounted for only 0.23 per cent of total visitors to the country (Deloitte Access Economics 2011). It is estimated that only about 7,000 international visitors per annum travel to Australia for the specific purpose of obtaining medical care (Voigt *et al.* 2010). Currently only patients from Papua New Guinea and New Caledonia travel to Australia in notable numbers for treatments as private patients in private hospitals, although patients from the UK, the USA and also New Zealand have also been identified as potential future source markets (Deloitte Access Economics 2011). High costs compared to competing medical tourism destinations in the region such as Singapore, Thailand, India, the Philippines and South Korea (Pogson 2011), are a major obstacle for growth in this particular medical tourism segment.

Wellness tourism in Australia

Wellness tourism on the other hand is an important and growing niche in Australia. Developing and employing a typology of three different wellness tourism providers, namely beauty spa hotel/resorts, lifestyle resorts and spiritual retreats (see also Chapter 2), a recent national audit of wellness tourism operators produced a database of 590 operators in 2009 (Voigt *et al.* 2010). Together, these wellness operators cater to over 2.2 million mainly domestic visitors every year and represent a tourism sector which generates a turnover of AU$277 million per annum (ibid.).

The three types of wellness tourism providers differ with respect to the services they offer and the level of facilities and amenities they include. However, in a wider sense one could argue that all wellness tourism operators are CAM providers, as most offer some forms of CAM modalities and therapies, especially when employing a broad definition of CAM.

The majority of Australian wellness operators consists of beauty spa hotel/ resorts (201) as well as day spas (282) which are basically identical to beauty spa hotel/resorts in their service offering, but do not include accommodation. Beauty spa hotel/resorts are more likely to provide beauty and body treatments as well as manicure and pedicure than the other two types of wellness tourism operators. They are also most likely to offer water-based therapies which are often considered as CAM, such as water massages (e.g. Vichy showers), saunas or aromatherapy (Voigt *et al.* 2010; Voigt and Laing 2010). Out of all wellness tourism operator categories, lifestyle resorts are the most capital- and labour-intensive category as they offer a broad range of facilities, CAM therapies and classes and education in a range of health behaviour areas such as nutrition, exercise and stress management. According to the audit in 2009, there were 28 lifestyle resorts in Australia (Voigt *et al.* 2010). Unlike beauty spa hotel/resorts which tourists often leave to engage in other tourist activities (e.g. sightseeing, shopping) lifestyle resorts represent 'gated properties' which are designed in a way that guests should only concentrate on getting healthier without distractions from outside. Similarly, guests rarely leave spiritual retreats of which 83 were located in Australia (ibid.). Spiritual retreats are most likely to offer mind/body CAM therapies such as guided meditation, yoga, as well as spiritual or religious studies. Their facilities tend to be much simpler and less luxurious in comparison with the other two types of wellness tourism providers. Some spiritual retreats also pursuit religious/spiritual or philanthropic rather than business objectives and therefore tend to be a lot less costly than the other two wellness provider categories or even offer their services on the basis of voluntary donations (9 per cent of Australian spiritual retreats operate on this basis according to Voigt *et al.* 2010).

The supply of Australian wellness operators is distributed differently across states and regions. The largest proportion of businesses is located in New South Wales (29 per cent), followed by Victoria (24 per cent) and Queensland (22 per cent); representing the more heavily populated Australians states and thus larger source markets. New South Wales also contains the majority of lifestyle resorts and spiritual retreats, whereas Queensland hosts the highest proportion of beauty spa hotel/resorts. Moreover, the majority of all wellness providers in Australia are located in regional areas (72 per cent) rather than in metropolitan areas (28 per cent), making wellness tourism especially important in regard to regional development strategies. The National Visitor Survey (Tourism Research Australia 2009a) designates the most visited Australian regions by domestic tourists engaging in wellness activities. The top three Australian wellness tourism regions are Daylesford/Hepburn Springs in Victoria (see Chapter 5 for a case study on this region), the Gold Coast in Queensland and the Mid North Coast in

New South Wales. The self-proclaimed 'Spa Country' Daylesford/Hepburn Springs mostly attracts intrastate travellers, as do most other regions in Victoria and New South Wales. In contrast, the Gold Coast and other regions in Queensland such as the Sunshine Coast and the Tropical North (see Chapter 3 for a case study on Palm Cove) tend to be visited by interstate visitors.

The aforementioned influx of migrants, particularly from Asian origin, brought with them various health practices which have been used for centuries in their home countries. The service offering, branding and decoration of many Australian beauty spas and lifestyle resorts are heavily influenced by Asian philosophies or healing techniques (Voigt and Laing 2010). Similarly, while spiritual retreats in Europe are regularly organised in Christian monasteries and nunneries, spiritual retreats in Australia tend to be closer connected to Asian spiritual influences or religious orders (e.g. from Buddhism and Hinduism) rather than the Christian faith. Some wellness operators also draw on the uniquely Australian Indigenous healing techniques or Aboriginal knowledge of the therapeutic value of Australia's flora (Voigt and Laing 2010). Ethical issues might arise here as those businesses are generally not owned by Indigenous people and employment of Indigenous staff is also very rare (Voigt *et al.* 2010).

From a demand point of view, Australian wellness tourists are not a homogenous group but visitors to the three categories of wellness operators differ significantly regarding their socio-demographic profile, travel behaviour and the benefits they seek from their wellness experiences (Voigt *et al.* 2011). For instance, in a study with 509 Australian wellness tourists, beauty spa visitors tended to be younger, active in the workforce and most likely to travel with a partner or friend. In contrast, spiritual retreat visitors tended to be older, more likely to be male in comparison to the other two groups of wellness tourists, most likely to hold a postgraduate university degree and most likely to travel alone. Lifestyle resort visitors tended to have the highest household income which is not surprising as lifestyle resorts are often the most expensive wellness business category out of all three categories. Nevertheless, the overall sample of wellness tourists was more likely to be female, middle-aged, highly educated, full-time employed with moderate to high household incomes. Interestingly, this socio-demographic profile coincides with that of a most typical Australian CAM user (MacLennan *et al.* 2002). While ethnic background was not a variable included in this study, stakeholders in interviews held for the nationwide survey of wellness tourism operators disclosed anecdotally that wellness tourists in Australia tend to be of Anglo-Celtic origin rather than from an Asian or Indigenous background.

Discussion and conclusion

With our analysis of recent developments in the health tourism sector in Australia and also Germany (see Chapter 16), which have adopted very different approaches to health care, we have been able to reveal a number of interesting trends. It seems that health tourism has taken two very different development paths in the two countries which can be, at least in part, linked to their respective health-care system and the reforms that have taken place. Over the past years both countries have been faced with very similar pressures, notably an ageing society which puts significant additional strain on a health-care system that struggles to remain financially sustainable. As a consequence, Australia and Germany have responded, amongst other measures, by passing on some of these cost pressures to consumers who have since been faced with increasing out-of-pocket health expenditure.

So how is it then possible that in Germany these developments have led to a strong growth in (medical) wellness, in particular in the senior market segment (see Chapter 16) whilst Australia, on the other hand, which is recognised as an emerging wellness destination, has a very different customer profile? Here, it is in the main the young, female, affluent and well-educated consumer that drives wellness tourism (Voigt *et al.* 2010). At the same time, medical tourism, though small in numbers, is also on the rise, but mainly as an outbound phenomenon. Reasons for some of these contrasting developments might indeed be found in the two countries' different approach to health care.

Based on the Beveridge Model, Australia's single national health service faces enormous demands. As there is no cap on health-care benefits the way of dealing with this increasing strain on public hospitals is to prioritise patients in terms of immediate needs and to create elective surgery lists. Consequently, waiting lists for procedures that are not considered a medical emergency can be excessive and amongst the longest in comparison to other OECD countries. Based on OECD data, in 2010 for example, 18 per cent of Australian patients waited four months or longer for elective surgery, in Germany (which adopted the Bismarck Model) the figure was 0 per cent. The UK and Sweden, which also follow the Beveridge Model even exceed the Australian benchmark with 21 and 22 per cent of patients respectively waiting for excessive periods of time for elective surgery (Siciliani *et al.* 2013). As a consequence Australians who are willing or able to afford it, take out private health insurance or pay outright to be treated as a private patient either in a public or private hospital. In this case Medicare only covers part of the specialist's fees, accommodation and any gap payment must be fully met by the patient (Healy *et al.* 2006). Consequently, most of an average household's weekly spending on medical care and health (AU$65.60) is used to cover private health insurance, practitioner fees, medicines and other pharmaceutical products (Figure 17.4). The remaining 3 per cent (AU$2.19) might be, amongst many other items, spent on wellness tourism or other forms of health-related travel. It is obvious that this small amount is unable to drive strong demand in this tourism niche market. However, as discussed earlier there is an increasing demand for CAM products and services in Australia, which are more and more covered or subsidised by private health insurance. Those CAMs which intersect with wellness tourism thus have the potential to support future growth in this market segment, in particular since the typical profiles of an Australian wellness tourist and a CAM user, being young, female, highly educated and affluent, correlate.

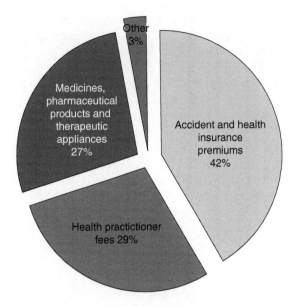

Figure 17.4 Average weekly household expenditure on medical care and health in Australia (2009/2010) (source: Australian Bureau of Statistics 2011c).

This is an interesting finding, in particular in the context of an increased health awareness and with it a generally greater preparedness to take responsibility for one's own health and wellbeing that is noted across most developed countries, including Australia. As Michaelidou and Hassan (2008: 164) highlight, '[h]ealth conscious consumers are aware and concerned about their wellness and are motivated to improve and/or maintain their health, and quality of life to prevent ill health by engaging in healthy behaviours and being self-conscious regarding health'. This increased health awareness tends to be high amongst the elderly, but in Australia it is obvious that this psychographic change has not markedly affected the travel behaviour of the senior (65+) market.

With a 21 per cent share of total domestic tourism expenditure in 2002, the Australian Bureau of Tourism Research identified older Australians (55+) as an important part of the country's travel sector and highlighted their importance for the future growth of the industry, also in light of Australia's demographic developments (Hossain *et al.* 2003). Since 2000 annual growth rates of about 3 per cent have been noted in this market segment (Tourism Research Australia 2009b). As has been discussed in detail in Chapter 16, the senior traveller market is a significant engine for tourism demand and also an important driver for growth in health tourism in Germany. The question needs to be raised, why health tourism, or more specifically wellness tourism, does not seem then to be a particularly appealing form of tourism for Australia's seniors although they strongly underpin growth in Australia's tourism industry and also despite their particular interest in ageing healthily. It was found, for example that Australia's seniors tend to prefer low-cost accommodation options (e.g. caravan parks and campgrounds) and spend less during their inbound travels (Hossain *et al.* 2003). In 2009 the expenditure per night of those aged 65 years or older, for instance, was just over half (58 per cent) the amount recorded for the average visitor aged 15 years or older (Tourism Research Australia 2010). Obviously travel behaviour changes not only with entry into retirement and family life-cycle changes, but also with the amount of disposable income and hence discretionary spending available.

In a broader context, the National Health and Hospitals Reform Commission (2009: 51) highlighted that

> It is difficult for many Australians to make healthy choices in the way they live their lives because of their socioeconomic circumstances or their living environment. In 2006–07, Australians spent about AU$94 billion on health. However, the proportion of this spent on preventing illness was estimated to be less than two per cent of this total.

Health tourism, and here in particular wellness tourism, can be considered one of these healthy choices, but an obvious reason for the lack of demand for this tourism niche market, in particular amongst the older segments of Australia's population, is the relatively low amount of disposable income available to these seniors. The Australian Bureau of Statistics (2009b) revealed that

> [i]n 2007, 10% of retired women aged 45 years and over had no, or negative, personal income (and therefore were relying on savings, assets or their partner's income) compared with 4% of men. Almost one in five women who had retired in the last four years had no (or negative) personal income.

These findings are reflected in the 2009/2010 Australian household expenditure study (Australian Bureau of Statistics 2011c) which found that with a weekly amount of AU$726 Australians aged 65 or older spent less than 60 per cent of the amount of an average Australian household (AU$1,236) on goods and services. For medical care and health, however, Australia's seniors spend with AU$68.84 more than the average Australian household (AU$65.60) and also a much higher percentage of their total weekly expenditure (9.5 per cent compared to an average of 5.3 per cent). These figures are a reflection of the increasing costs for medical care and other health services with age which also translate into higher private spending needs. Interestingly though, the percentage of expenditure on *other* health-related goods and services (see Figure 17.4) was with 6 per cent slightly higher amongst the older segments of the population. It can, however, be assumed that this is at least in parts caused by hospital and nursing home charges the Australian Bureau of Statistics includes in this category (Australian Bureau of Statistics 2011c).

Wellness tourism supply in Australia can be classified into beauty spas, lifestyle resorts and spiritual retreats with the two first categories specifically associated with the notion of being luxurious and pampering. It is, thus, no surprise that in a recent study Voigt *et al.* (2010) found household income to be an important driver of wellness tourism, a fact that the authors related to the high costs of typical beauty spa and health resort offerings. In short, they concluded that 'only wealthy people can afford to stay with wellness tourism providers' (Voigt *et al.* 2010: 49). With an income below the national average, senior Australians obviously do not fall into this category and are thus not a very important component of the wellness tourism demand-side.

In conclusion, with this Australian case study (and also with our account on the German situation as described in Chapter 16) we have been able to demonstrate that health policy can facilitate or hinder the development of health tourism (i.e. medical tourism and wellness tourism). It appears that in Australia the adopted health-care system (i.e. Beveridge Model) increasingly fuels outbound medical tourism. On the other hand, the lack of disposable income in some age cohorts, in particular Australia's seniors, as well as in ethnic minority and Indigenous population cohorts, can be an obstacle to broaden the wellness tourism market in Australia beyond its current younger and middle-aged, more affluent and Anglo-Celtic clientele. The disparity between Anglo-Celtic and ethnic minority groups, including Indigenous Australians, is troubling as Australian wellness operators tend to draw heavily on Asian healing philosophies and sometimes also on Indigenous knowledge to make their services and products more attractive to wellness tourists.

As commented by Rodrigues (2007: 2), 'health is generally considered to be a "luxury" good', despite an increase in health awareness in recent years. However, since our findings are based on only a single case example further research is warranted to investigate if in general a causal relationship exists between the adopted approach to health care and developments a country's medical and wellness tourism sectors.

References

Australian Bureau of Statistics (2000) 'Household expenditure survey, Australia: summary of results, 1998–99', online, available at: www.abs.gov.au/AUSSTATS/ abs@.nsf/ Lookup/6530.0Main+Features11998-99?OpenDocument (accessed 17 February 2013).

Australian Bureau of Statistics (2006) 'Household expenditure survey, Australia: summary of results, 2003–04 (reissue)', online, available at: www.abs.gov.au/AUS-STATS/abs@.nsf/Previousproducts/6530.0Main%20Features32003-04%20(Reissue) ?opendocument&tabname=Summary&prodno=6530.0 &issue=2003-04%20(Reissue) &num=&view= (accessed 17 February 2013).

Australian Bureau of Statistics (2007) 'Australian social trends, 2007: international fertility comparison', online, available at: www.abs.gov.au/AUSSTATS/ abs@.nsf/Latestproducts/7E874EFF832BAB79CA25732C002072CF (accessed 12 February 2013).

Australian Bureau of Statistics (2008) 'Household expenditure on health: a snapshot, 2004–05', online, available at: www.abs.gov.au/ausstats/abs@.nsf/mf/ 4836.0.55.001 (accessed 7 February 2013).

Australian Bureau of Statistics (2009a) 'Future population growth and ageing', online, available at: www.abs.gov.au/AUSSTATS/abs@.nsf/Lookup/4102.0Main+ Features-10March%202009 (accessed 7 February 2013).

Australian Bureau of Statistics (2009b) 'Retirement and retirement intentions', online, available at: www.abs.gov.au/AUSSTATS/abs@.nsf/Lookup/4102.0Main+ Features-50March%202009 (accessed 7 February 2013).

Australian Bureau of Statistics (2010) 'Australian social trends, June 2010. Population growth: past, present and future', online, available at: www.abs.gov.au/ AUSSTATS/abs@.nsf/Lookup/4102.0Main+Features10Jun+2010 (accessed 7 February 2013).

Australian Bureau of Statistics (2011a) 'Life expectancy trends – Australia', online, available at: www.abs.gov.au/AUSSTATS/abs@.nsf/Lookup/4102.0Main+ Features-10Mar+2011 (accessed 7 February 2013).

Australian Bureau of Statistics (2011b) 'Health services: use and patient experience', online, available at: www.abs.gov.au/AUSSTATS/abs@.nsf/Lookup/ 4102.0Main+Features 20Mar+2011 (accessed 7 February 2013).

Australian Bureau of Statistics (2011c) 'Household Expenditure Survey, Australia: summary of results, 2009–10', online, available at: www.abs.gov.au/ausstats/ abs@.nsf/Latestproducts/6530.0Main%20Features22009-10?opendocument& tabname=Summary&prodno=6530.0&issue=2009-10&num=&view= (accessed 7 February 2013).

Australian Bureau of Statistics (2011d) 'Birth Australia, 2011', online, available at: www.abs.gov.au/ausstats/abs@.nsf/mf/3301.0 (accessed 12 February 2013).

Australian Bureau of Statistics (2012) *Year Book Australia 2012*, online, available at: www.abs.gov.au/ausstats/abs@.nsf/Lookup/by%20Subject/1301.0~2012~Main%20 Features~Home%20page~1 (accessed 5 February 2013).

Bottomley, G. and de Lepervanche, M. (1990) 'The social context of immigrant health and illness', in J. Reid and P. Trompf (eds) *The Health of Immigrant Australia: A Social Perspective*, Sydney: Harcourt Brace Jovanovich.

Cheung, I.K. and Wilson, A. (2007) 'Athroplasty tourism', *Medical Journal of Australia*, 187: 666–7.

Connell, J. (2006) 'Medical tourism: sea, sun, sand and … surgery', *Tourism Management*, 27: 1093–100.

Deloitte Access Economics (2011) *Medical Tourism in Australia: A Scoping Study*, Kingston: Deloitte Access Economics.

Healy, J., Sharman, E. and Lokuge, B. (2006) 'Australia: health system review', *Health Systems in Transition*, Copenhagen: European Observatory on Health Systems and Policies.

Hossain, A., Lubulwa, M. and Bailey, G.N. (2003) 'Characteristics and travel patterns of older Australians: impact of population ageing on tourism', paper presented at International Conference on Population Ageing and Health: Modelling our Future. Canberra, 8–12 December 2003.

Jakubowski, E. (1998) 'Health care systems in the EU: a comparative study', *Public Health and Consumer Protection Series*, SACO 101 EN, online, available at: www.europarl.europa.eu/workingpapers/saco/pdf/101_en.pdf (accessed 2 February 2013).

Johar, M., Jones, G., Savage, E., Sharma, A. and Harris, A. (2013) 'Australia', in L. Siciliani, M. Borowitz and V. Moran (eds) *Waiting Time Policies in the Health Sector: What Works?* OECD Health Policy Studies, OECD Publishing, online, available at: http://dx.doi.org/10.1787/9789264179080-en (accessed 12 February 2013).

MacLennan, A.H., Wilson, D.H. and Taylor, A.W. (2002) 'The escalating cost and prevalence of alternative medicine', *Preventive Medicine*, 35: 166–73.

Marius (2011) *Australian Interest in Medical Tourism Increases, as Does Disease Risk*, online, available at: www.globalsurance.com/blog/australian-interest-in-medical-tourism-increases-as-does-disease-risk-361220.html, posted 31 May 2011 (accessed 2 February 2013).

Mattoo, A. and Rathindran, R. (2006) 'How health insurance inhibits trade in health care', *Health Affairs*, 25: 358–68.

Michaelidou, N. and Hassan, L.M. (2008) 'The role of health consciousness, food safety concern and ethical identity on attitudes and intentions towards organic food', *International Journal of Consumer Studies*, 32: 163–70.

Murray, S.B. and Skull, S.A. (2005) 'Hurdles to health: immigrant and refugee health care in Australia', *Australian Health Review*, 29: 25–9.

National Health and Hospitals Reform Commission (2009) *A Healthier Future for All Australians*, Canberra: Australian Government.

Pogson, J. (2011) 'Medical tourism: buyer beware', *ABC Health & Wellbeing*, online, available at: www.abc.net.au/health/features/stories/2011/07/28/3277842.htm (accessed 2 February 2013).

Rodrigues, M. (2007) *Consumer Trends: Household Spending on Health Products and Services*, Melbourne: ANZ Research.

Rothgang, H. (2009) 'Bismarck, Beveridge oder was sonst? Linzer Gesundheitspolitisches Gespräch', Gesundheitssysteme im internationalen Vergleich, Linz, January 2009.

Siciliani, L., Borowitz, M. and Moran, V. (2013) *Waiting Time Policies in the Health Sector: What Works?* OECD Health Policy Studies, OECD Publishing, online, available at: http://dx.doi.org/10.1787/9789264179080-en (accessed 19 February 2013).

Smith, P.C., Anell, A., Busse, R., Crivelli, L., Healy, J., Lindahl, A.K., Westert, G. and Kene, T. (2012) 'Leadership and governance in seven developed health systems', *Health Policy*, 106: 37–49.

Tourism Research Australia (2009a) *National Visitor Survey and International Visitor Survey January to December 2008*, Sydney: Tourism Research Australia.

Tourism Research Australia (2009b) *Mature Age Visitors in Australia 2008*, Canberra: Department of Resources, Energy and Tourism.

Tourism Research Australia (2010) *Generation Fact Sheet 2009*, Canberra: Department of Resources, Energy and Tourism.

Voigt, C. and Laing, J. (2010) 'The structure of Australian wellness tourism providers: definition, typology and current status', paper presented at the Travel and Tourism Research Association (TTRA) European Chapter Conference, Budapest, Hungary, 1–3 September.

Voigt, C., Brown, G. and Howat, G. (2011) 'Wellness tourists: in search for transformation', *Tourism Review*, 66: 16–30.

Voigt, C., Laing, J., Wray, M., Brown, G., Howat, G., Weiler, B. and Trembath, R. (2010) *Health Tourism in Australia: Supply, Demand and Opportunities*. Gold Coast: CRC for Sustainable Tourism.

Wehkamp, K.-H. (2006) 'Balanceakt zwischen Bismarck und Beveridge', *Das Parlament*, 50, formerly available online at: www.bundestag.de/dasparlament/ 2006/50/ Thema/026.html (accessed 18 March 2011).

Willis, E. (2009) 'The Australian health care system', in E. Willis (ed.) *Understanding the Australian Health Care System*, Sydney: Churchill Livingstone Elsevier.

Xue, C.C.L., Zhang, A.L., Lin, V., da Costa, C. and Story, D.F. (2007) 'Complementary and alternative medicine use in Australia: a national population-based survey', *The Journal of Complementary and Alternative Medicine*, 13: 643–50.

Part V

Conclusion

18 Concluding discussion

Implications for destination development and management

Cornelia Voigt and Christof Pforr

Introduction

This book has adopted a destination perspective on wellness tourism which is a novel contribution to the still limited scholarly activity on the supply-side of wellness tourism. In the light of wellness tourism being often referred to as one of the fastest growing tourism niches globally, it is important to better understand the way in which wellness tourism destinations develop and the specific drivers of that growth in a particular destination context. By adopting a range of perspectives and discussing many different case examples from around the world, the contributors to this volume have aimed to shed some more light on these emergent issues.

This final chapter will synthesise the theoretical and practical contributions and conclusions drawn from experiences around the world. Based on a review of emerging themes, an array of new insights into the development of wellness tourism destinations is brought together and discussed. These issues are summarised and depicted in a new framework of wellness tourism destination competitiveness. This is followed by posing a number of research propositions that could guide future research into the development, management and success of wellness tourism destinations and businesses.

Emerging areas of agreement regarding the conceptualisation of wellness tourism

Numerous authors in this book have highlighted the complexity of conceptualising wellness tourism and recognised it as a socially constructed phenomenon which varies across times and places. It can be concluded that it will be probably impossible to generate a universally accepted wellness tourism definition. This is in line with Bushell and Sheldon (2009: 230) who warn the academic community not to waste too much time on producing wellness tourism definitions 'for the sake of attempting to be precise with something that is complex, dynamic and blurry'.

While acknowledging that definitions are problematic and contested, some conceptual aspects emerged throughout the chapters where there appears to be a consensus among the authors. In particular, wellness and medical tourism were seen as essentially separate entities, although an overlap between these two forms of tourism was generally acknowledged. Consequently, throughout the book the term 'health tourism' has been used to refer to wellness *and* medical suppliers, or to hybrid business models, and wellness and medical tourism have been understood as two different sub-sectors of health tourism.

Nevertheless, the delineation und boundaries between wellness tourism and other forms of tourism – not only medical tourism – is not always easy to make. In Chapter 8, Baum and Lockstone-Binney highlight a range of allied and partially overlapping tourism sub-sectors of wellness tourism and in Chapter 5 Wray and Weiler argue that destinations will actually benefit from developing wellness tourism with similar and complementary tourism activities. In particular, several chapters (9, 10 and 11) emphasise the close affinity and match between wellness tourism, outdoor recreational activities and nature-based services. Concurrently, the authors of Chapters 2 and 13 predict an increasing hybridisation and crossover of wellness tourism provisions in the future.

Another salient area of agreement among many of the authors is that wellness tourism cannot be solely equated with the spa sector and with exclusively pleasurable and pampering luxury offerings, but that it also incorporates more alternative, holistic and spiritual products and services. Also, several contributors pointed out that wellness tourism has its forerunners since ancient times in many cultures all over the world. Weisz (2011) proposes that throughout history wellness tourism has revolved around the ever-changing interplay of two main functions, namely the pleasure and the therapeutic dimensions. Voigt (Chapter 2) suggests to add the function of spirituality as a third dimension, since themes of spirituality and religion have been interwoven with health tourism since ancient times and because secularised spirituality has been identified as a major trend impacting the growth of wellness tourism (see Chapters 1 and 13). Wellness tourism thus allows very different experiences, ranging from the typical image of a tourist seeking relaxation by luxuriously bathing in hot water, to tourists who want to find themselves through meditating for hours a day in a barely furnished ashram. Nevertheless, one can argue that the term contains and unites several tendencies and trends in the travel sector which otherwise would be difficult to assign to a certain tourism sector. To summarise, the term 'wellness tourism' is a vague concept, interpretable in different, also subjective, ways based on the expectations of wellness customers that have become increasingly individualistic on the one hand and on the product offerings that have grown to be increasingly pluralistic on the other.

Despite the difficulties in defining wellness tourism some theoretical markers have been specified to distinguish it from other forms of tourism. In all case studies of wellness tourism destinations in this book, the contributors describe certain wellness-specific superstructure (e.g. in form of health resorts, ashrams, baths, *Onsen*s, retreats) which is different from generic tourism superstructure (e.g. conventional hotels, guest houses, restaurants). It appears that generally a cluster of such a wellness-specific superstructure must exist before a destination is described as a wellness or health tourism destination – although a few opera-tors exist that are so well-known that the property is perceived as destination in its own right (e.g. so-called destination spas). Such wellness-specific superstruc-tures then offer certain wellness-specific services and while lists and descriptions of those are not completely congruent across the chapters (see Chapters 2, 12, 13, 14 and 15) they encompass beauty therapies, massages, hydrotherapy, com-plementary and alternative medicine, meditation, counselling, creative therapies and New Age services as well as activities or seminars on health-promoting life-style areas such as nutrition, exercise, stress relief, emotion and relationship management. It follows that the existence of wellness-specific superstructure offering wellness-specific services represent a crucial prerequisite to distinguish wellness tourism from other tourism experiences and wellness tourism destina-tions from other tourism destinations.

Importantly, this understanding excludes forms of tourism that do not rely on wellness-specific superstructure, but that have been previously referred to as wellness tourism, such as volunteer tourism or outdoor and adventure tourism (Devereux and Carnegie 2006; Lean 2009; Kulczycki and Lück 2009; Sheldon and Bushell 2009). Additionally, in Chapter 2 Voigt proposes that wellness tourism superstructures are – knowingly or unknowingly – health-care providers operating on the theoretical basis of the wellness health paradigm (as character-ised by the principles of holism, balance, self-healing, positive functioning, focus on health prevention, individualised care and subjective experiences) and cater to tourists with the need to maintain or improve their health. This distin-guishes them from medical tourism superstructures that operate on the basis of the biomedical health paradigm (as characterised by separation of mind and body, a focus on curing or alleviating symptoms, high-tech diagnostic, standard-ised care and objectively observable phenomena) and cater to tourists with the need to cure or treat a disease or medical condition.

From a practical viewpoint, the fuzziness of the concept of wellness tourism does not exempt destinations from communicating what wellness tourism means at a particular destination, especially when international tourists are targeted. The case study on Japan by Erfurt-Cooper (Chapter 15) shows that the unfamili-arity with Japanese bathing traditions and rituals as well as the lack of effective promotional messages have so far prevented many Western tourists from enjoy-ing *Onsen* bathing. In this case there is a very specific and unique product, but one that is mainly enjoyed by domestic tourists because language barriers, inef-fective communication and unfamiliarity with the product hinder many inter-national tourist markets from experiencing it. However, Smith and Puczkó (Chapter 13) state that the increasing provision of decontextualised and stand-ardised wellness products and services is not a solution. Standardised provisions are a risky business strategy in the long term because a growing number of well-ness tourists demands unique and localised experiences. Clearly, in wellness tourism multiple options, ambiguity and disorientation are closely linked. With such a range of experience possibilities and heterogeneous wellness tourism markets, wellness tourism destinations and businesses cannot be everything for everyone. Once marketers have decided which markets they want to target they have to find ways to increase market transparency and decrease uncertainty for the particular market. Mass photographs uniformly depicting young and beautiful women sprawling in steaming water may often not help to attract customers and also does not foster a diversified picture of wellness tourism and the concept of wellness (see Chapter 4).

Emerging implications for wellness tourism destination development and management

The development of any region, including those with a wellness tourism focus, into a successful tourism destination is a challenging undertaking; particularly in the light of an ever-more globalised world which offers consumers a wealth of often interchangeable experiences (see Chapters 1 and 3). Successful destination management therefore needs to identify ways of developing a unique and authentic destination profile which will provide the region with comparative advantages (Wray *et al.* 2010; Ritchie and Crouch 2000, 2003; see also Chapter 3). These challenges at the Destination Management Organisation (DMO) and also the individual business level have been discussed throughout the book (e.g. Chapters 3, 5, 6, 11 and 12).

As was highlighted in Chapter 3 by Prideaux, Berbigier and Thompson, competitiveness can be defined as 'the ability of a destination to successfully attract tourists over time in a marketplace where numerous other destinations are competing for the same or similar target markets'. Various aspects of destination competitiveness and different strategies to develop competitive tourism offerings were discussed in this chapter with reference to the wellness tourism sector. Adopting a global perspective, Smith and Puczkó (Chapter 13) highlight that a competitive wellness destination needs to adopt a multilayered approach to development and promotion, which reflects an awareness of unique resources and assets, as well as an understanding of its history, culture and traditions. This view was confirmed in Chapter 14 by Laing, Voigt and Frost using case examples from Hungary, the United Kingdom and New Zealand. All these examples had some elements of fusion in their offerings rather than relying on what was local or traditional, which underlines the globalisation of the spa industry and its increasingly homogenised offerings.

Core resources and competencies

In the context of destination competitiveness, the advantages of a resource-based approach for destination management was emphasised throughout the book. Such an approach gives appropriate consideration to a destination's capabilities, in other words to its endogenous resources and competencies which equip a destination with a unique and hard to imitate profile and thus, ultimately, with comparative advantages (Barney 1991, 1996; Foss 1997; Wernerfelt 1984; Pechlaner and Fischer 2006; Haugland *et al.* 2011). In the context of wellness tourism resources have also been referred to as 'assets' (Smith and Puczkó 2009; see also Chapter 13) or 'substance' (Hjalager 2011). Throughout the chapters in this book eight different types of wellness tourism resources have been identified:

1   **Natural resources**
    Typical natural resources that are utilised in the wellness tourism context consist of geothermal or mineral waters, and sometimes sea water (i.e. thalassotherapy) which was specifically exemplified in the cases of Daylesford/ Hepburn Springs in Australia (Chapter 5) and Japan (Chapter 15). The case study on the Kneipp therapy (Chapter 12) also revealed that normal tap water can be effectively employed for healing purposes. Sometimes, water and water bodies (e.g. rivers, wells) are not necessarily recognised because of their physical healing powers, but for their spiritual significance. However, as noted by Voigt in Chapter 2, water does not always play a defining role in wellness tourism destinations. Other natural resources that are used in form of traditional healing modalities and/or cosmetic products include muds, clays and plants. The climate itself can be known for its therapeutic value as exemplified by the certified German climatic health resorts. The aesthetic or perceived spiritual power of certain geographical features and landscapes may also contribute to the wellbeing of wellness tourists. Moreover, many wellness providers are located in regional areas, where tourists are not only surrounded by beautiful scenery, but where nature also offers ample opportunities to be physically active (see Chapter 11).

2   **Cultural, historical and spiritual resources**
    As explained in Chapters 2 and 13, wellness tourism has a rich historic background in many cultures around the world and therefore place-specific architecture and heritage exists (e.g. hammam, sauna, banyas, Roman baths) as well as non-material cultural and spiritual customs and rituals that are utilised in wellness tourism (e.g. incantations, mantras, cleansing and purification ceremonies). These might to some extent also influence or even prescribe the behaviour of visitors in wellness tourism facilities.

3   **Complementary and alternative medicine (CAM)**
    Closely connected to the previous type of resources are the CAM resources at a destination. CAM encompasses entire alternative medical systems from non-Western cultures (e.g. Ayurveda) and Western cultures (e.g. homeopathy, naturopathy, the Kneipp approach explained in Chapter 12) and an immense variety of modalities (e.g. Hawaiian Lomi Lomi massage, Chinese cupping, transcendental meditation) that are typically closely tied to certain regions. CAM incorporates the term 'complementary' because there is generally a lack of official recognition as well as a lack of regulatory and legal mechanisms. Balneology or spa medicine signifies an interesting special case. While it is generally considered to be part of CAM, balneology is still acknowledged as a form of effective rehabilitation (but not prevention) and thus officially subsidised in countries such as Germany and Japan (see Chapters 6, 7, 12, 15 and 16).

4   **Community mindset and wellness-related lifestyle**

According to Hjalager (2011: 56) the 'spirit and mindset' of the host population is essential to sustain a competitive wellness tourism destination. Concurrently, the case studies on Byron Bay and Daylesford/ Hepburn Springs in Australia (Chapter 5) written by Wray and Weiler demonstrate that communities with wellness-related values such environmental activism and an alternative, health-conscious lifestyle (see also the concept of LOHAS explained in Chapter 1) contribute to sustainable wellness tourism destinations by supporting wellness tourism development and attracting wellness tourists with congruent values, while protecting and safeguarding natural resources essential for the wellness tourism product at the same time.

5   **Human resources and competencies**

Cohen and Russell (2008: 383) emphasise that the spa, but also the entire wellness industry, is a highly personalised industry where 'people are the product'. They indicate that a qualified staff is one of the most important factors determining the success of a wellness provider. In the wellness industry, human resource requirements are as multifaceted as its varying products and services. In the spa sector, staff are often viewed as subordinated service providers who are there to serve all needs and desires of the clients, whereas visitors to spiritual retreats tend to look up to staff and view them as leaders, gurus or teachers (Voigt 2010). In Chapter 8, Baum and Lockstone-Binney have convincingly outlined that in wellness tourism human resource management issues are severely under-researched and developed an conclusive research agenda. Among other issues they point to the complexity and tensions between high versus low skilled, local versus imported, professionalised versus informal, and medical versus paramedical staff that all can be found within wellness tourism. Consequently, destinations are endowed with different labour-force bases managers of wellness tourism facilities can draw upon, a key competitive advantage in an industry where labour shortage and high turnover rates are one of the most pressing issues (Smith and Puczkó 2009; Voigt *et al.* 2010). Hereby, educational institutions at destinations can contribute to a qualified labour force that understands and is able to deliver wellness, coupled with the necessary business and communication skills needed to operate successful businesses. Concurrently, Pechlaner, Reuter and Bachinger (Chapter 7) suggest the establishment of an Academy for the Health Care Industry as a major future factor of success to turn Garmisch-Partenkirchen into a health tourism destination and to integrate medical and wellness service providers that currently work in isolation.

6   **Wellness-specific superstructure**

In the previous section the requirement for wellness-specific superstructure at wellness tourism destinations was discussed. Throughout the chapters different classifications of such superstructures have been presented. In Chapter 2, Voigt suggests a typology of three core wellness tourism providers (i.e.

beauty spa resorts/hotels, lifestyle resorts and spiritual retreats) as well as five hybrid medical/wellness business models. In Chapter 12 Locher, Voigt and Pforr highlighted the German classification of six types of officially certified health and spa resorts and in Chapter 15 Erfurt-Cooper describes ten different types of Japanese *Onsen*. Again, the key message here is not to waste too much time in finding a universally accepted typology of wellness tourism providers but to recognise that in all destinations wellness tourism is dependent on the provision of such superstructure in order to be classified as wellness tourism destination.

7 **Wellness-related events**

In the chapters of this book wellness-related events as a resource have only been mentioned in passing. Currently, there are probably only very few special wellness-related events through which a destination has achieved a unique and special reputation. However, events can be used to augment and strengthen the recognition of a destination as a wellness tourism destination. For instance, in Chapter 12 Locher, Voigt and Pforr report of the Unterallgäu Health Week, a very successful annual event that showcases the various health facets of the Unterallgäu health region in Bavaria, Germany. On the provider level, Thermae Spa in Bath, England, hosted a Malaysian Spa Festival to offer its customers new experiences (see Chapter 14). Other examples of the type of events that fit the wellness tourism context include fitness and beauty industry conventions, community health events and New Age festivals.

8 **Crossover of wellness with other activities/offerings**

In their model of destination competitiveness, Ritchie and Crouch (2003: 68) refer to the mix of activities offered at a destination as 'one of the most critical aspects of destination appeal' and point out that these types of resources can be developed most creatively and innovatively by destination managers. As already mentioned, Wray and Weiler (Chapter 5) have also highlighted the importance of crossover wellness products as well as cross-sectoral expansion. Existing examples concern the spa sector where spa-ing is complemented with other luxury tourism activities such as spa and skiing, spa and golfing, or spa and wineries (i.e. vinotherapy). In a similar vein, the authors of Chapter 11 highlighted the role of natural resources and the significance of the surrounding environment for the development of a wellness tourism destination. In the context of the Margaret River region in Western Australia, Pforr, Hughes, Dawkins and Gaunt demonstrated that wellness tourism can be closely aligned with nature-based tourism by using natural resources such as climate, forests and water to attract travellers in pursuit of wellbeing. Moreover, throughout this book the crossover and interlocking between medical and wellness (tourism) offerings have been emphasised. We predict that not only between different tourism sectors but diversification across different industry sectors (i.e. vertical networking) will increasingly play a role to develop innovative wellness tourism destinations and to achieve a unique selling point. Accordingly, and as will be explained in more detail in the following, issues of effective collaboration and network management will become ever-more decisive driving forces of wellness tourism destination development and innovation.

Collaborative destination governance

The challenge destinations face in context of wellness tourism is that wellness tourism experiences are delivered by a highly fragmented and diverse sector. Crouch (2011), for example, points out that in general the tourism experience is delivered by the cooperation of a number of stakeholders which include typical tourism enterprises and allied industries, a range of destination management organisations, government entities, and last but not least the host community. Their active participation and an effective coordination of activities becomes a crucial aspect of successful destination management. This assessment reflects the current view of destinations as 'loosely bounded networks of organisations that deliver the tourism experience' (Cooper 2012: 32).

Thus, wellness tourism destinations, as was for instance highlighted in Chapters 6, 7 and 12, not only need to adopt a resource-based approach but require a strategic approach to destination management, which sets out to identify the set of relevant stakeholders and their relational constellation and aims to coordinate the disparate supply elements in the destination (Haugland *et al.* 2011; Scott *et al.* 2008; Dredge and Pforr 2008; Denicolai *et al.* 2010). This strategy, which is often referred to as 'relational strategic destination management' (Fischer 2009), not only identifies but also enhances the core competencies of a particular regional setting (Bachinger *et al.* 2011; Pechlaner and Fischer 2006; Acedo *et al.* 2006) since it is 'the destination actors' collective ability to integrate, reconfigure, gain, and release distributed resources and competencies, and effectuate change' (Haugland *et al.* 2011: 273). In this vein, Pechlaner, Reuter and Bachinger (Chapter 7) discuss the concept of 'cooperative core competencies' (i.e. the ability of coordinating resources and capabilities among independent stakeholders) and highlight that the existence of collaborating networks is a decisive factor of destinations to stay competitive in the long run.

The implementation of such a collaborative approach is, however, often a difficult undertaking as Voigt and Laing, for instance, demonstrate in Chapter 4. Their literature review of case studies on collaborative wellness tourism development projects exposed that most of these fail due to collaboration problems, including lack of time, lack of managerial capabilities, lack of leadership, unequal financial contribution, disagreement among stakeholders about goals and commitments, language barriers and mistrust. Using Australia as a case example, the authors furthermore revealed that this destination is characterised by little collaboration between major groups of stakeholders, suggesting a list of strategies that might assist in creating a more integrated, unique Australian wellness tourism product. On the other hand, two case studies presented in Chapter 7 by Pechlaner, Reuter and Bachinger illustrate that a lack of interorganisational cooperation can sometimes also act as the seed for uncovering future cooperative core competencies in health.

In this context, destination governance was identified as a crucial aspect by a number of authors in this volume, not only because tourism destinations are complex networks that involve a large number of individual stakeholders but also because they increasingly compete in a globalised marketplace. Destination governance requires a stronger focus on a strategic organisational dimension of destination management, which needs to be equipped with appropriate tools to steer the stakeholders in a destination. Based on partnerships and collaboration aimed at using the resources of a destination jointly and more efficiently, these stakeholders then have the ability to create competitive advantages of the destination.

Engaging and harmonising the interests of a diverse range of stakeholders was, for example, identified in Chapter 5 by Wray and Weiler as an important element in the sustainable development of two particular Australian wellness tourism destinations. As outlined by Pforr, Pechlaner, Locher and Jochmann in Chapter 6 in more detail, a prerequisite for successful regional (health tourism) development is the identification and integration as well as the nurturing and utilisation of partnerships in form of regional network structures. These requirements were discussed in the context of the Health Region Kneippland Unterallgäu, which has developed into a health-focused region mainly due to its health tourism competences.

Thus, in the light of a very promising future outlook, health tourism has already been embraced as a strategy for regional development with the aim to diversify regional economic activities by offering new business opportunities, creating employment and income growth and facilitating investment in new infrastructure developments. As discussed, for instance in Chapter 12 by Locher, Voigt and Pforr using the case example of the Kneippland Unterallgäu region, a more holistic understanding of health (based on the teachings of Sebastian Kneipp) was translated into a broader regional development towards health-conscious, sustainable communities.

Case studies such as these also show that the governance of tourism is dynamic, constantly changing and highly complex. Destination management organisations (DMOs) can play a fundamental role in the governance of destinations and they often assume a leadership function. Their main purpose is to coordinate and facilitate the interaction and collaboration between all stakeholders concerned and promote a common cause (Dwyer and Kim 2003; Pechlaner *et al.* 2011). Accordingly, like the Unterallgäu GmbH introduced in Chapter 6 or Tourism Victoria in Chapter 5, DMOs establish links between different stakeholders and act as an intermediary between them, also across different sectors with diverse interests and they also function as an information broker.

The DMO in the Unterallgäu case study additionally introduced and monitored quality control measures. Similarly, the DMO responsible for Kerala in India (see Chapter 3) has developed an accreditation system for wellness operators providing Ayurveda services. Besides voluntary accreditation schemes, some destinations undergo an extensive accreditation process to fulfil strict quality criteria in order to be officially recognised as a health tourism destination, as in the example of state-authorised German health resorts (see Chapter 12). In this case, the German Spa Association is the certification authority, indicating that DMOs do not necessarily have to be the accreditation body and that industry associations can also play a critical role. In the eyes of some, the rapid growth of the wellness industry has resulted in the need for comprehensive and robust standards of accreditation. Accreditation standards ideally reassure customers, operators and destinations of the quality of products and services offered. However, wellness certification is not based as yet upon any agreed international standards and particularly in some European countries, many different wellness seals of approval have been created, thus even eroding market transparency and extending customer confusion.

Nevertheless, national and/or state tourism bodies may underpin the quality of service delivery in wellness tourism through the specification and monitoring of industry standards. Although this has not been discussed at length in this volume, DMOs may also contribute to the growth in demand through destination branding and communication. Another important element of a DMO's strategic planning and management is the responsibility to continuously review its key selling propositions and where appropriate identify new markets and develop new products (see Chapter 3). Thus, DMO managers are also responsible for the continual innovation and redevelopment of the tourism product at the destination in order to stay competitive in the long term. This represents a major challenge and does not only require cross-linking with other industry sectors as discussed before, but also a continuous monitoring of changing trends and external forces.

Monitoring changes, as Prideaux, Berbigier and Thompson remind us in Chapter 3, is an element of destination competitiveness that has thus far received too little attention in the literature. Many chapters in this book have referred to major socio-demographic and psychographic changes (or megatrends as referred to in Chapter 1) that have affected the worldwide growth of wellness tourism. Here, DMO managers must be vigilant that while similar trends can be noticed across many destinations, they do not need to have similar consequences for wellness tourism. For instance, Pforr and Locher (Chapter 16) and Locher, Pforr and Voigt (Chapter 17) listed statistical evidence for Germany and Australia that point to a similar growing health consciousness as well as the ageing of the population in both countries. However, while an ageing society in Germany has led to seniors constituting the major target market for health tourism, the same result cannot be assumed in Australia, because there, for example, lack of disposable income hinders seniors from participating in wellness tourism. This example shows that DMO managers have to carefully assess a wide range of factors before selecting the appropriate target markets for destinations, or before endeavouring new destination developments.

Finally, DMOs may be directly involved in policy advice and implementation as in the case of Daylesford/Hepburn Springs where the regional DMO (Tourism Victoria), supported by the state government and the local council assumed an indispensable role by directly contributing to the provision of significant infrastructure – in this case the core resource in form of a specific wellness tourism superstructure, namely a public bathhouse (see Chapter 5). Here, legislation was put in place to establish a Spa Levy that has significantly contributed funds to redevelop this bathhouse and upgrade mineral springs feeding it (Voigt *et al.* 2010). While local governments have specific knowledge and control over a particular destination (or several destinations), in order to implement policies effectively there should ideally be an overarching policy framework in place at national or even international level to provide necessary guidance (Dodds and Butler 2010). In tourism, collaborative governance ideally requires coordination between various public agencies that have jurisdiction affecting tourism developments and management. For instance, the case study on Japan (Chapter 15) showed that the Japanese Ministry of Environment established legislation to protect natural hot springs and ensure water quality at *Onsen*s. Policy areas such as environment protection, agriculture, regional development and labour generally affect tourism, although Dodds and Butler (2010) assert that there is often a lack of recognition of tourism in non-tourism government sectors. The health policy domain which hitherto only played a minor role in tourism, however, is put on the frontline in wellness tourism. This is particularly obvious in destinations such as Germany or Japan (see Chapters 12, 15 and 16) where specific wellness tourism services (mainly hydrotherapy) are an accepted form of rehabilitation and subsidised by national health insurance. In Chapter 17 Locher, Pforr and Voigt have demonstrated that even in destinations where no such legislation exists national health policy has a strong influence on the demand and consequently supply of health tourism (i.e. medical and wellness tourism) within a country. However, even in destinations where wellness tourism is somewhat medicalised and subsidised for sick people, there seems to be a lack of mutual recognition and a lack of collaboration between the public health domain and orthodox medical professionals on one side and wellness tourism businesses on the other (see Chapters 4, 12 and 13).

One strategy for the wellness tourism industry to gain more acceptance with mainstream medicine and the public health domain might be to focus on evidence-based wellness tourism services (see Chapter 13). In fact, there is mounting scientific evidence that lifestyle and certain CAM therapies and modalities (e.g. yoga, meditation), which are commonly offered as part of wellness tourism, are beneficial for people's physical and/or psychological well-being. However, medical professionals and health policymakers may still remain sceptical of their legitimacy as the gold standard of randomised controlled trials in clinical research cannot be easily applied to CAM and integrative medicine approaches (Bell *et al.* 2002; Carter 2003). While the scientific–reductionist approach might be the most suitable way of testing the effectiveness of a single component such as a specific medication, it does not easily lend itself to cope with the complexity of holistic CAM interventions (Carter 2003).

In this context, it is important to refer to more general discussions on the relationship between tourism and wellness. Jafari (2005: 5) emphasises that the tourism industry 'has not stepped forward to support research that would upgrade beyond their traditional break mould, to help establish the relationship between tourism and wellness.' Here, we suggest that wellness tourism offers the opportunity to stimulate the examination of the relationship between tourism and wellness as a positive conceptualisation of health (i.e. wellness). In this volume, Chapters 9 and 10 specifically focused on the relationship between recreation in parklands and wellbeing, and discussed the issue of branding parklands as wellness tourism destinations. Ascertaining whether there are clear causal links between access to parklands and improved health could, as Hughes in Chapter 9 argues, guide future support for investment in establishing and maintaining parklands as an important component of wellness tourism destinations. Thereby, Hughes outlines the complexity of measuring the concept of health and its varying facets (e.g. different health dimensions, objective vs. subjective measures, positive vs. negative measures) as well as the difficulty in establishing causal relationships. In Chapter 10, Deery, Filep and Hughes (Chapter 10) offer an exploratory evaluation of individual wellbeing derived from visitor experiences in Australian (Victorian) parks and nature reserves. They stress that understanding hedonic and eudaimonic wellbeing of visitors is relevant for all managers of wellness tourism destinations, including those managing parks and nature reserves as they might be in a position to influence visitors' wellbeing levels by providing opportunities for reflection and for the development of place attachments. Despite the difficulties involved in measuring wellbeing and establishing evidence that wellness tourism or other tourism activities lead to wellbeing it should go without saying that unsubstantiated claims and assertions of effectiveness of wellness tourism services are dangerous and put the tourists at risk. Wellness tourism managers are health-care providers and accordingly must assume certain responsibilities.

This assertion leads to the as yet under-researched facet of ethics in wellness tourism. Medical tourism has been portrayed as the epitome of a globalised, capitalist and commodified health care. Serious ethical issues involving medical tourism have been outlined including a lack of safety for patients, the use of public funds to promote private medical tourism providers that would be better used to invest in the already eroded public-health system, and a 'brain drain' of health professionals leaving the public system in order to earn better salaries in the private sector (Burkett 2007; Connell 2011; Turner 2007). In contrast, it has been suggested that tourism destinations should rather 'focus on the "wellness" niche of the medical sector' because its emphases on healthy living and incorporation of indigenous herbal remedies are perceived to be more culturally authentic and ethical (Chambers and McIntosh 2008: 932). However, it is especially the incorporation of indigenous knowledge that may be ethically problematic in cases where indigenous healing methods are exploited without benefitting the traditional custodians of that knowledge (Bodeker and Burford 2008; Voigt 2010). In addition, ethical dilemmas surrounding human resource management issues have been outlined in this book, pointing to the vulnerability of staff in regard to sexual, emotional and aesthetic labour (Chapter 9).

Interwoven with the topic of ethics is the theme of sustainability. Next to the importance of a resource-based view and the necessity to strategically manage and govern destination stakeholders and networks effectively in order for a wellness tourism destination to remain competitive, a further theme emerging from the various contributions to this book is the need to embrace sustainability (Ritchie and Crouch 2003). As was highlighted by Voigt in Chapter 2, due consideration of environmental and social aspects should be a *sine qua non* for all wellness tourism destinations considering their common reliance on natural and cultural resources and a broad understanding of health which includes environmental and social dimensions. Ideally, wellness offerings should, as was also argued in Chapter 6, not only benefit visitors but also contribute to the general wellbeing of the host community. Unfortunately, however, as Voigt (Chapter 2) concluded, 'the reconciliation between an economically focused business philosophy and a holistic, sustainable wellness approach to health still remains one of the greatest challenges of the wellness tourism industry'.

A framework of wellness tourism destination competitiveness

This section synthesises the previously discussed emerging themes concerning wellness tourism destination development and management in the form of a framework of wellness tourism destination competitiveness (Figure 18.1). Ritchie and Crouch's (2003) model of destination competitiveness is arguably

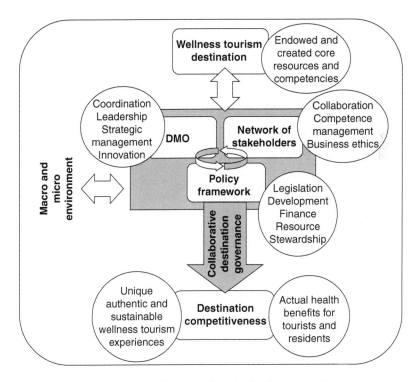

Figure 18.1 Framework of wellness tourism destination competitiveness.

the best-known approach to destination competitiveness. The framework presented here builds on their conceptualisation and also compares it with Sheldon and Park's (2009) model of wellness destinations, which in turn is also based on Ritchie and Crouch's model.

As we have argued that wellness and sustainability need to be intrinsically meshed at destinations, Ritchie and Crouch's (2003) understanding of destination competitiveness is particularly relevant because they understand a competitive destination as one that is sustainable in the long run, considering social and environmental dimensions, not only an economic one. Accordingly, the most competitive wellness tourism destination is one that creates wellbeing not only for the tourists, but also for its residents while safeguarding a healthy environment. Thus, one intended outcome of wellness tourism destination competitiveness is unique, authentic and sustainable tourism experiences, but also actual (and measurable) health benefits for tourists and residents alike (see Figure 18.1). To our knowledge, the focus on health outcomes as part of wellness tourism destination competitiveness has not yet been introduced in the literature.

In the present framework the basis of a wellness tourism destination consists of core resources and competencies. All eight types of core resources and competencies that were highlighted in the previous section represent the comparative advantage of a wellness tourism destination; the essential pull factors that make a destination attractive for potential tourists. The types of core resources listed in this chapter are similar to Ritchie and Crouch's (2003) conceptualisation of core resources, with the exception of complementary and alternative medicine (CAM) and wellness-related superstructure, which are unique in the wellness tourism context. Discussing destination competitiveness Dwyer and Kim (2003) differentiate endowed and created resources, a distinction which is useful here too. The first four of the eight suggested core wellness tourism resources and competencies (i.e. natural resources; cultural, historical and spiritual resources; complementary and alternative medicine; and community mindset and wellness-related lifestyle) are encompassing endowed resources, whereas created resources consist of the latter four types (i.e. human resources and competencies; wellness-specific superstructure; wellness-related events; and crossover with other activities). Importantly, while destination managers can only exert little to no control over endowed resources they are able to innovatively develop created resources in order to add value to the attractiveness of a destination.

Nevertheless, as pointed out by Prideaux, Berbigier and Thompson in Chapter 3 as well as by Wray and Weiler in Chapter 5, core resources and competencies are not sufficient for a destination's success because to achieve competitive advantage, destination management organisations must plan and manage the resources effectively and enhance their appeal. A strategic approach to planning and management is hereby essential and covers typical management areas such as destination branding, visitor management or human resource management. In their conceptualisation of wellness destination competitiveness Sheldon and Bushell (2009: 111) contest that a 'specific manifestation of collaboration is missing in Ritchie and Crouch's model'. Concurrently, the preceding discussion identified collaboration as a key competitive factor for wellness tourism development. We have propagated viewing a destination as a collaborative network that integrates multiple stakeholders, including the DMO, the community and the private and public sectors. Stakeholders in a destination need to collaboratively share resources and competencies in a way that enables them to supply tourism experiences that outperform alternative destination experiences. In Figure 18.1 the integration between various stakeholders from the private and public sector is symbolised by the circling arrows in the middle. As discussed before, the DMO often assumes leadership and coordinates the collaboration between stakeholders. Ideally, this network of collaborating stakeholders will steer the wellness tourism destination towards the dual goals of unique, authentic and sustainable tourism experiences and actual health benefits for tourists and residents – thus demonstrating collaborative destination governance (Figure 18.1).

Besides the emphasis on collaborative governance which distinguishes the present framework from previous conceptualisations of (wellness) destination competitiveness, this model also draws attention to the importance of an appropriate policy framework which includes the provision of a legal framework, perhaps an accreditation system, and regulates access to resources essential for the wellness tourism experiences. Clearly, local, regional and national government bodies can play a significant role in facilitating the development and professionalisation of wellness tourism. Collaborative governance requires horizontal and vertical networking across industry sectors as well as across policy domains. The specific role of the health policy domain within wellness tourism has been highlighted in the previous section. Another theme which has not been contained in destination competitive models before concerns the role of business ethics, which often regulate areas that are beyond government control. As wellness tourism providers should ideally take into account sustainable principles, ethical considerations are an essential prerequisite.

Finally, similar to Ritchie and Crouch's approach, this framework acknowledges the influence of the macro environment (e.g. demographic or sociocultural forces) and the micro environment (e.g. crises, competing tourism destinations) on the success of a particular wellness tourism destination. Here, however, the relationship is represented with a double arrow, indicating that DMOs, policymakers as well as individual wellness businesses must proactively monitor and evaluate these forces in order to continuously adapt or refine the destination product and/or image. This element of destination competitiveness was especially emphasised by Prideaux, Berbigier and Thompson in Chapter 3.

It is important to note that not all the factors and elements of the model must be fulfilled in order to secure destination competitiveness. There is no single effective way of creating a competitive wellness tourism destination, but several. For instance, as noted in Chapters 4 and 5, there are wellness tourism destinations with strong core wellness resources that are well known without a deliberate 'destination push' – the so-called organically emerged wellness tourism destinations

(Smith and Puczkó 2009). The case studies on Byron Bay (Chapter 5) and on Margaret River (Chapter 11) also highlight that in destinations with limited support by a DMO or other government bodies, horizontal networks between wellness providers may emerge to take on typical DMO functions such as destination branding or promotion. Future research needs to show which success factors are more essential than others. The following section discusses this and other items that could be part of a future research agenda on wellness tourism.

Recommendations for future research directions

The study of wellness tourism is still in its infancy, but based on the preceding discussion some directions for future research can be put forward. Similar to other models of destination competitiveness the framework of wellness tourism destination competitiveness presented here is abstract and conceptual, but not predictive or causal (cf. Ritchie and Crouch 2003: 60–1). Future research directions either concern the framework in its entirety, some particular competitive factors and elements, or the relationships between the different elements. Accordingly, the subsequent major research areas can be identified.

Advancing and testing the framework

The framework has been synthesised based on case studies of wellness tourism destinations around the world. Moreover, the case studies in this book represented different sizes (i.e. regional and national destinations) and different stages of development (i.e. emerging wellness tourism destinations such as Kerala or Margaret River and mature wellness tourism destinations such as Germany). It nevertheless seems that inside and outside this book, case studies on destinations in the Western world (i.e. Europe, North America and Australasia) dominate. More case studies from non-Western contexts are needed as well as comparative research, applying and analysing the same set of competitive success factors. Another obvious research step concerning the entire model would be to operationalise the model and evaluate the factors empirically. A particular challenge thereby would be, however, to select existing or even create new appropriate measures to assess some of the factors. For example, decisions must be made how to assess successful collaboration, or what facets of health should be examined. As already noted, as well as by Dwyer and Kim (2003), in regard to general destination competitiveness, more research is also needed to examine the relative importance of the various success factors and to examine whether there are some that are more essential than others. For instance, are there successful wellness tourism destinations that only rely on created core resources, or is it necessary to base the offering on natural, cultural, historical and/or spiritual sources? Finally, as noted before, there are also some single wellness tourism providers that have become so well known that they have become destinations in their own right. While this also applies to generic tourism superstructure (consider, for example, the Burj Al Arab in Dubai), this phenomenon seems to be particularly prevalent in the wellness tourism context. Further investigations could explore the factors that are a prerequisite for the tourists' perception of a single wellness business as a destination.

Extending research on wellness-specific superstructure and its staff

In this chapter wellness-specific superstructure has been recognised as a key component of wellness tourism destinations. The majority of existing literature deals with the spa sector and with only few exceptions (cf. Kelly and Smith 2009; Kelly 2010) the holistic and spiritual end of the spectrum has been largely ignored. Future research could explore the characteristics, management and promotional strategies of the spiritual/holistic side of wellness tourism. The people owning and working in wellness superstructures is another topic which has received little attention. To what extent are wellness operators guided by business, philanthropic, religious or lifestyle motives when starting a business? What is the typical competence profile and formal education of wellness tourism staff and the ratio of business/conventional medicine/complementary medicine and other skills? How do they define the concept of wellness? Are they living a wellness lifestyle (e.g. LOHAS)?

Identifying factors and processes that drive successful collaboration and effective coordination of stakeholders

Both horizontal and vertical collaborative relationships among and between public and private stakeholders have been identified as essential success factors of wellness tourism destination competitiveness. However, there seem to be more unsuccessful examples than successful cases of collaborative efforts within wellness tourism. While there is at least some evidence of horizontal networking in the spa sector in the form of collaborative promotional networks and industry associations, the spiritual sector seems to be largely consisting of isolated organisations which might even not consider themselves to be part of the tourism industry (Kelly 2010). There are also few detailed examples of vertical networking across industry sectors, which, as has been argued, is specifically important for innovation at the destination level. Consequently, future studies could identify positive examples and best practice models of collaboration in wellness tourism and extract the underlying factors and processes responsible for its success. In this context, also considering the highly fragmented wellness tourism sector, effective coordination of destination stakeholders appears to be crucial. Future research should therefore investigate the role of DMOs or other relevant organisations that demonstrate leadership in facilitating a common language (e.g. mutual goals and objectives); foster the development of, or enhance existing, network structures; initiate the collaborative development of projects and products; and provide emotional leadership to steer the ever-changing dynamics of these networks. It is also important to explore to what extent public policy influences the development of the health tourism sector and to analyse the underlying planning and policy processes.

Analysing the role of ethics and sustainability within wellness tourism

As emphasised in the preceding discussion ethical considerations should be paramount in the wellness tourism context, not only because wellness tourism is conceptually linked to sustainability, but also because wellness tourism operators are health providers in the broader sense and health services are the epitome of a public good. In contrast to the literature on medical tourism, ethics have been only a marginalised issue in the wellness tourism context. Future research could analyse the extent to which ethics and sustainability are accounted for in wellness business practices, industry organisations or as part of strategic planning on the destination level. Often, quality control mechanisms are employed in the implementation of sustainability principles into business operations. Considering the dramatic growth in the number of wellness tourism products and services that have been on offer in recent years, particular attention needs to be directed to the effectiveness of emerging quality control mechanisms such as accreditation and certification programs. To what extent and in what form do codes of ethics exist in wellness tourism and what ethical topics do they encompass? Is there a particular propensity among wellness business managers to consider it a moral obligation to operate a sustainable business and assume corporate responsibility, or do they merely engage in marketing rhetoric? Is there a genuine concern for the wellbeing beyond typical health and safety considerations of tourists and staff? Are business owners and destination managers aware of potentially violating intellectual property rights when utilising indigenous or local health knowledge?

Understanding the elements of wellness tourism experiences

Fundamentally there is a need to understand wellness tourism experiences and what wellness tourists actually consume as part of their experience. Within wellness tourism, there have been conceptual considerations specifically in relation to the meaning of authenticity in shaping tourists' interpretation of their experiences. It has been argued that authenticity in wellness tourism can take on different forms and fantasy was suggested as a further element of wellness tourism experiences which can actually coexist with authenticity (see Chapter 14). In the future, empirical studies are needed that explore the importance of authenticity. In addition, there is the question if all forms of authenticity and fantasy are equally important and if not, whether this depends on the individual and/or the different experience contexts (e.g. spa, lifestyle resort or spiritual retreat visitation).

Analysing health outcomes/benefits of wellness tourism

There is only limited evidence that wellness tourism actually contributes to the wellbeing of tourists or residents. As outlined in this book, the medical effectiveness especially of spa and hydrotherapy has played an important role in destinations where the spa cure has a longstanding tradition and thus has been subsidised as a form of rehabilitation. Consequently, a small body of research studies outside the tourism literature focuses on the effect of spa therapy on physical health in the form of assessing its effectiveness on curing diseases and bodily disorders such as psoriasis or back pain. However, in this book it was established that wellness should be understood as a positive conceptualisation of health with a focus on health promotion rather than cure. Accordingly, health outcomes in the wellness tourism context need to be investigated beyond utilising measures of ill health. Future research should be concentrated on positive health indicators assessing concepts such as eudaimonic and hedonic wellbeing or quality of life. Again, future studies must also move beyond the spa sector as the only branch of wellness tourism. It needs to be acknowledged that causality will be very difficult to establish because wellbeing can be dependent on so many factors, including individual and situational variables that are independent of the relationship between tourism and beneficial health outcomes. Longitudinal research designs may be particularly relevant for future studies because health status can be assessed before, during and after the wellness tourism intervention. In addition, future research should contribute to understanding the processes and mechanisms that may link wellness tourism to positive health outcomes. One such factor that has been frequently cited also in this volume is being in or viewing nature. Perhaps the natural environment in some destinations is intrinsically healthy and contributes to the wellbeing of people.

Concluding remarks

Wellness tourism has become increasingly prominent both as an academic area of study and a steadily growing tourism product all over the world. However, achieving a better understanding of the wellness tourism phenomenon and its development and management at the destination level is not straightforward. This chapter has presented areas of consensus with regard to the definition of wellness tourism as well as some key factors of wellness tourism destination management which were synthesised based on the contributions of this volume. On this basis a framework of wellness tourism destination competitiveness has been developed. Similarities to generic and wellness destination competitiveness models by Ritchie and Crouch (2003), Dwyer and Kim (2003) and Sheldon and Park (2009) have been acknowledged. However, several components in the present framework are unique, including the emphases on collaborative governance and business ethics, complementary and alternative medicine and a wellness-specific superstructure as vital wellness core resources.

Furthermore, the model accommodates the dual outcomes of unique, sustainable and authentic tourism experiences and actual health benefits for tourists and residents alike. In this chapter we also discussed major areas of future research directions in wellness tourism. It is obvious that future research needs to be multidisciplinary, but in particular research must build upon existing knowledge in tourism and health sciences in the broader sense. Health science domains that may be especially relevant in this context include positive psychology, health promotion, mind/body medicine and health geography. We hope that this book will contribute to a better understanding of wellness tourism particularly from a destination perspective and that we are able to stimulate further debate and research in this emerging field.

References

Acedo, F.J., Barroso, C. and Galan, J.L. (2006) 'The resource-based theory: dissemination and main trends', *Strategic Management Journal*, 27: 621–36.

Bachinger, M., Pechlaner, H. and Widuckel, W. (2011) *Regionen und Netzwerke*, Berlin: Springer Verlag.

Barney, J.B. (1991) 'Firm resources and sustained competitive advantage', *Journal of Management*, 17: 99–120.

Barney, J.B. (1996) 'Strategic factor markets: expectations, luck and business strategy', *Management Science*, 42: 1231–41.

Bell, I.R., Caspi, O., Schwartz, G.E.R., Grant, K.L., Gaudet, T.W., Rychener, D., Maizes, V. and Weil, A. (2002) 'Integrative medicine and systemic outcomes research: issues in the emergence of a new model for primary health care', *Archives of Internal Medicine*, 162: 133–40.

Bodeker, G. and Burford, G. (2008) 'Traditional knowledge and spas', in M. Cohen and G. Bodeker (eds) *Understanding the Global Spa Industry: Spa Management*, Oxford: Butterworth-Heinemann.

Burkett, L. (2007) 'Medical tourism', *Journal of Legal Medicine*, 28: 223–45.

Bushell, R. and Sheldon, P.J. (2009) 'Wellness tourism and the future', in R. Bushell and P.J. Sheldon (eds) *Wellness and Tourism: Mind, Body, Spirit, Place*, New York: Cognizant Communication Corporation.

Carter, B. (2003) 'Methodological issues and complementary therapies: researching intangibles?' *Complementary Therapies in Nursing and Midwifery*, 9: 133–9.

Chambers, D. and McIntosh, B. (2008) 'Using authenticity to achieve competitive advantage in medical tourism in the English-speaking Caribbean', *Third World Quarterly*, 29: 919–37.

Cohen, M. and Russell, D. (2008) 'Human resource management in spas: staff recruitment, retention and remuneration', in M. Cohen and G. Bodeker (eds) *Understanding the Global Spa Industry: Spa Management*, Oxford: Butterworth-Heinemann.

Connell, J. (2011) *Medical Tourism*, Oxfordshire: CABI.

Cooper, C. (2012) *Essentials of Tourism*, Harlow: Prentice Hall – Pearson Education.

Crouch, G.I. (2011) 'Destination competitiveness: an analysis of determinant attributes', *Journal of Travel Research*, 50: 27–45.

Denicolai, S., Cioccarelli, G. and Zucchella, A. (2010) 'Resource-based local development and networked core-competencies for tourism excellence', *Tourism Management*, 31: 260–6.

Devereux, C. and Carnegie, E. (2006) 'Pilgrimage: journeying beyond self', *Tourism Recreation Research*, 31: 47–56.

Dodds, R. and Butler, R. (2010) 'Barriers to implementing sustainable tourism policy in mass tourism destinations', *Tourismos: An International Multidisciplinary Journal of Tourism*, 5: 35–53.

Dredge, D. and Pforr, C. (2008) 'Policy networks and tourism governance', in N. Scott, R. Baggio and C. Cooper (eds) *Network Analysis and Tourism: From Theory to Practice*, Clevedon: Channel View Publications.

Dwyer, L. and Kim, C. (2003) 'Destination competitiveness: determinants and indicators', *Current Issues in Tourism*, 6: 369–414.

Fischer, E. (2009) *Das kompetenzorientierte Management der touristischen Destination*, Wiesbaden: Gabler.

Foss, N.J. (1997) *Resources, Firms, and Strategies: A Reader in the Resource-Based View*, Oxford: Oxford University Press.

Haugland, S.A., Ness, H., Gronseth, B.-O. and Aarsradt, J. (2011) 'Development of tourism destinations: an integrated multilevel perspective', *Annals of Tourism Research*, 38: 268–90.

Hjalager, A.-M. (2011) 'The invention of a Danish well-being tourism region: strategy, substance, structure, and symbolic action', *Tourism Planning and Development*, 8: 51–67.

Jafari, J. (2005) 'Bridging out, nesting afield: powering a new platform', *Journal of Tourism Studies*, 16: 1–5.

Kelly, C. (2010) 'Analysing wellness tourism provision: a retreat operators' study', *Journal of Hospitality and Tourism Management*, 17: 108–16.

Kelly, C. and Smith, M. (2009) 'Holistic tourism: integrating body, mind, spirit', in R. Bushell and P.J. Sheldon (eds) *Wellness and Tourism: Mind, Body, Spirit, Place*, New York: Cognizant Communication Corporation.

Kulczycki, C. and Lück, M. (2009) 'Outdoor adventure tourism, wellness, place attachment', in R. Bushell and P.J. Sheldon (eds) *Wellness and Tourism: Mind, Body, Spirit, Place*, New York: Cognizant Communication Corporation.

Lean, G.L. (2009) 'Transformative travel: inspiring sustainability', in R. Bushell and P.J. Sheldon (eds) *Wellness and Tourism: Mind, Body, Spirit, Place*, New York: Cognizant Communication Corporation.

Pechlaner, H. and Fischer, E. (2006) 'Alpine Wellness: a resource-based view', *Tourism Recreation Research*, 31: 67–77.

Pechlaner, H., Raich, F. and Kofink, L. (2011) 'Elements of corporate governance in tourism organizations', *Tourismos: An International Multidisciplinary Journal of Tourism*, 6: 57–76.

Ritchie, J.R.B. and Crouch, G.I. (2000) 'The competitive destination: a sustainable perspective', *Tourism Management* 21: 1–7.

Ritchie, J.R.B. and Crouch, G.I. (2003) *The Competitive Destination: A Sustainable Tourism Perspective*, Wallingford: CABI.

Scott, N., Baggio, R. and Cooper, C. (eds) (2008) *Network Analysis and Tourism: From Theory to Practice*, Clevedon: Channel View.

Sheldon, P.J. and Bushell, R. (2009) 'Introduction to wellness and tourism', in R. Bushell and P.J. Sheldon (eds) *Wellness and Tourism: Mind, Body, Spirit, Place*, New York: Cognizant Communication Corporation.

Sheldon, P.J. and Park, S.-Y. (2009) 'Development of a sustainable wellness tourism destination', in R. Bushell and P.J. Sheldon (eds) *Wellness and Tourism: Mind, Body, Spirit, Place*, New York: Cognizant Communication Corporation.

Smith, M. and Puczkó, L. (2009) *Health and Wellness Tourism*, Oxford: Butterworth-Heinemann.

Turner, L. (2007) ' "First world health care at third world prices": globalization, bioethics and medical tourism', *BioSocieties*, 2, 303–25.

Voigt, C. (2010) 'Understanding wellness tourism: an analysis of benefits sought, health-promoting behaviours and positive psychological well-being', unpublished thesis, University of South Australia.

Voigt, C., Laing, J., Wray, M., Brown, G., Howat, G., Weiler, B. and Trembath, R. (2010) *Wellness and Medical Tourism in Australia: Supply, Demand and Opportunities*, Gold Coast: CRC for Sustainable Tourism.

Weisz, G. (2011) 'Historical reflections on medical travel', *Anthropology and Medicine*, 18: 137–44.

Wernerfelt, B. (1984) 'A resource-based view of the firm', *Strategic Management Journal*, 5: 171–80.

Wray, M., Laing, J. and Voigt, C. (2010) 'Byron Bay: an alternate health and wellness destination', *Journal of Hospitality and Tourism Management*, 17: 158–66.

Index

Page numbers in *italics* denote tables, those in **bold** denote figures.